INDIA

FODOR'S TRAVEL PUBLICATIONS

NEW YORK • TORONTO • LONDON • SYDNEY • AUCKLAND

WWW.FODORS.COM

Copyright © Automobile Association Developments Limited
1998, 2001
Maps copyright © Automobile Association Developments
Limited 1998, 2001
Maps pages 54, 65, 93, 108 © Government of India.
Copyright 1998. Based upon Survey of India maps with the
permission of the Surveyor General of India.

Published in the United States by Fodor's Travel
Publications.
Published in the United Kingdom by AA Publishing.

ISBN 0-679-00707-5
ISSN 1531-5732

Fodor's Exploring India

Author: **Fiona Dunlop**
Revision verifier: **Carol Sykes**
Revision editor: **Felicity Jackson**
Original photography: **Frederik Arvidsson**
Cartography: **The Automobile Association**
Cover design: **Tigist Getachew, Fabrizio La Rocca**
Front cover silhouette: **David Sanger Photography**

Printed and bound in Italy by Printer Trento srl

10 9 8 7 6 5 4 3 2 1

How to use this book

ORGANISATION

India Is, India Was
Discusses aspects of life in modern India and places the country in its historical context, exploring past events whose influences are still felt.

A–Z
Breaks down the country into regional chapters, and covers places to visit. Within this section fall the Focus On articles, which consider a variety of topics in greater detail.

Travel Facts
Contains the strictly practical information that is vital for a successful trip.

Accommodations and Restaurants
Lists recommended establishments in India, giving a brief summary of their attractions.

ADMISSION CHARGES
Expensive: over 100 rupees
Moderate: 21–100 rupees
Inexpensive: up to 20 rupees

ABOUT THE RATINGS
Most places described in this book have been given a separate rating. These are as follows:

▶▶▶ Do not miss

▶▶   Highly recommended

▶   Worth seeing

MAP REFERENCES
To make the location of a particular place easier to find, every main entry in this book is given a map reference, such as 53C2. The first number (53) indicates the page on which the map can be found; the letter (C) and the second number (2) pinpoint the square in which the main entry is located. The maps on the inside front and inside back covers are referred to as IFC and IBC respectively.

Contents

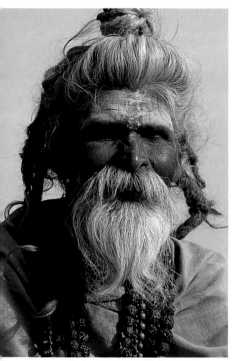

A–Z

Fiona Dunlop has written Fodor's Exploring books on Paris, Singapore and Malaysia, Vietnam, Costa Rica, and India. In researching this guide, she has spent countless hours in trains, buses, cars, boats and rickshaws, traveling and above all talking with locals.

My India

"Are you roaming?" one man enquires politely as I whirl through the great Indian subcontinent researching this book. Time there is circular, or perhaps elliptical, and the very air, the meandering sacred cows and the roadside *chai*-stands (tea-stands) hardly stimulate decisive action. It is a country that invites meditative visiting, and one whose soul takes time to absorb. So woe to this guide-researcher, propelled ever onward by the demands of encompassing the entire sweep.

Luckily, humanity here is great, not just in size but in quality. Communication is constant, drawing any traveler into the complex embrace of a nation riddled with history, with foreign legacies, with gaping inequalities, with on-going eruptions of unexpected and deadly violence, but above all with philosophy. For in no other country in the world have I had such deeply abstract conversations. It was the Indians, after all, who invented the concept of zero over 2,000 years ago. Aeons of Hindu rumination have permeated Muslims, Buddhists and Christians alike, creating an analytical predisposition that easily flips over into ironic humor. Yet dynamism is there too, in India's infinite intensity and in the will to survive seen in the ragged boy sweeping the railroad-car, in the ploys of hardened booth-holders in the bazaars and in the equanimity of a woman transporting her worldly possessions on the crowded night-train to war-torn Kashmir.

Sugar-sweet movie *ghazals* (songs) are sung from street-corners, heady perfumes drift from mounds of floral garlands, unidentifiable *thali* flavours subtly assault the palate, Mughal palace-forts loom on the horizon, Rajasthani women-laborers in brilliantly colored saris flash dazzling smiles, incense envelops worshippers in staggeringly crafted temples, and exhaust fumes envelop the passengers of auto-rickshaws roaring through Delhi. All-encompassing and all-mesmerising, India is a drug in itself. I shall be back again, next time to truly roam.
Fiona Dunlop

Generous of spirit, land, culture and people, India is in a state of flux. Freedom, democracy and tolerance are its treasures, but are under pressure: India's population will soon overtake China's. From mountains to plains, coasts to deserts, the subcontinent presents a staggering density of humanity, and an extraordinary variety of forms, color and history.

❏ Caste distinctions are deeply embedded in Indian society. In the past, relative social backwardness led the *dalits* (lower castes) to suffer discrimination in silence. Today, with a marked absence of central ideological leadership, India is experiencing the rise of the *dalits* both in government and in militant ethnic groups. ❏

Fifty million years ago the giant island that became India was rammed into the Asian mainland, heaving the Himalayas up to their icy heights and unfurling fertile, river-threaded plains at their base. This was the birth of the subcontinent. With the world's highest mountains to the north and the Indian Ocean

Hindu pilgrims bathe in the holy River Ganga (Ganges) at Varanasi

washing its coasts, it undergoes the extreme weather cycles of the monsoon winds. For three months of the year they bring essential rains that sometimes swell into devastating floods. If they fail, there is drought, although the tragic famines of only a few decades ago are being avoided because the infrastructure is better.

Within this immense territory of over 1 million square miles (a third of the size of the U.S.A., 13 times larger than the U.K.), live around a billion souls, fatalistic and fervent, Hindu and Muslim, peasant and industrialist, rich and poor. No other nation incoporates such a dazzling kaleidoscope of humanity.

CULTURAL TAPESTRY Dust, poetry, sweat, human misery, splendor, belief: these are just some of the threads that have combined to make India over the last 5,000 years or so. Deeply woven into the tapestry are the shadows of past invaders: Greeks, Turks, Persians, Afghanis, Portuguese and British—all left their mark on the social fabric and psyche. In the background rise minarets, domes, impregnable forts, churches, palaces, and extravagant train stations, each pointing to a cultural priority that may or may not have endured. What has remained, despite the horrors of partition that saw the world's greatest migrations, is a mesmerizing multiculturalism. Veiled Muslim women flit past Hindus weaving perfumed garlands of flowers outside a Siva shrine; pork is eschewed by the one and beef by

the other; turbanned, bearded, sword-bearing Sikhs chant from their sacred scriptures, the Granth, while pacifistic Buddhists and Jains meditate and pray. Religious belief is omnipresent, and occasionally omnidivisive.

LIE OF THE LAND In the north are the mighty Himalayas, with their colonial hill stations, Buddhist monasteries and lakes (notably in turbulent Kashmir). Skirting the mountains is the Gangetic plain, India's most highly populated and industrialized region. Stretching between the contrasting cities of Delhi and Kolkata (Calcutta), it includes Hinduism's holiest cities, the Mughals' greatest monument—the Taj Mahal—and the place where Buddhism began. To the west unfolds the Thar Desert, home of the Rajputs, and Gujarat, a Jain stronghold.

South of the plains, the forested Aravalli and Vindhya hills shelter

Ancient Buddhist structures high in the Himalayas at Ladakh

wildlife sanctuaries and majestic forts.

Halfway down the subcontinent starts the vast, boulder-strewn Deccan plateau, which embraces the cultural highlights of Ajanta, Hyderabad, Hampi and Mysore, as well as the burgeoning city of Bangalore. Along the coastline to the east is culturally rich Orissa; to the west lie Mumbai (Bombay) and Goa.

Finally comes the magical deep south, home to India's ancient Dravidian people. Here Hindus built astounding temples, early Christians erected churches, the British created Madras (Chennai) and the Keralans revel in their lush garden of Eden.

The subcontinent eventually ends at Kanniyakumari, where each April the moon can be seen rising at the same time as the sun sets.

India is the world's largest democracy and its fifth largest economy. In the decades following Independence, its development was successively steered by Jawaharlal Nehru and his daughter, Indira Gandhi. Today the Congress party they dominated has been weakened, and the country is governed by unstable coalitions.

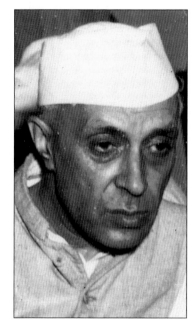

Jawaharlal Nehru, independence campaigner then Prime Minister

When Nehru became independent India's first Prime Minister in 1947, he headed a Constituent Assembly representing 275 million Hindus, 50 million Muslims, 7 million Christians, 6 million Sikhs, 100,000 Parsis and 24,000 Jews. The only common tongue among the 15 official languages and 845 dialects was English, soon replaced by Hindi, although even today much of the south understands little of this northerners' tongue. In 1950 the constitution (the world's longest) became law, embodying the principles of democracy, secularism and equality. India's parliament has a lower house (Lok Sabha) and an upper house (Rajya Sabha), and there are also state governments.

NEHRU'S INDIA Intent on creating an egalitarian socialist nation, Nehru embarked on abolishing prejudice against low caste Hindus or "untouchables" (one of Gandhi's pet aims), improving women's status and, above all, building up industry and agriculture through a series of Five Year Plans. By his death in 1964, India's food production was booming. For 17 years, Nehru had been a popular figurehead, whose honesty and dedication to his country were undisputed, but he was dogged by external problems that continued under the premiership of his daughter, Indira Gandhi. The still unresolved Kashmir issue has led to three wars with Pakistan; in 1948 (resulting in Kashmir's "temporary" division), 1965 and 1971 (which led to the creation of Bangladesh). Despite the repeated negotiations, the situation remains potentially explosive. Relations with China, complicated by the occupation of Tibet, resulted in a Chinese invasion in 1962. Nehru's greatest achievement in foreign policy was the promotion of non-alignment with world powers, and the principle that the developing countries should choose their own destinies.

INDIRA'S EMERGENCY The euphoria that met Indira Gandhi's election victory in 1967 gradually evaporated. With a divided Congress party losing votes to the right wing, a Marxist coalition ruling Bengal, and Naxalite terrorist activities, India was nearing crisis. Social unrest was fuelled by nationalizations, drought, the cost of

12

the 1971 war against Pakistan, the oil crisis and Indira Gandhi's high-handedness. In 1975 she imposed a dictatorial state of emergency. The press was censored and over 10,000 people were arrested, including opposition leaders. Indira's youngest son, Sanjay Gandhi, assumed increasing powers, implementing a controversial sterilization program. Although the 1977 elections gave the Janata party a majority and even saw a humiliated Indira arrested for corruption, the phoenix rose again to carry off the 1980 elections. However her political astuteness had faded, and an assault on Amritsar's Golden Temple, leading to the massacre of 700 Sikhs, resulted in her assassination in 1984.

DESTINY Sanjay having died in a plane crash, Indira's successor was her eldest son, Rajiv, whose charisma and sincerity did not succeed in solving Hindu–Muslim confrontations, trouble in the northeastern states and the Punjab, or the Tamil issue in Sri Lanka. He was assassinated by a Tamil fanatic in 1991 and the baton of the Nehru dynasty has now passed to Rajiv's widow, Italian-born Sonia Gandhi, who is gaining increasing popularity as the head of the Congress party.

BOOM Since 1991, India has been governed by coalitions that include the Bharatiya Janata Party (BJP), Congress and the Communists (a tradition that the 1998 election result —which led to the formation of a multi-party coalition government under the leadership of Ata Behari Vajpayee (BJP)—has ensured will continue, at least for the foreseeable future). An economic about face came

in the early 1990s during the premiership of Narashima Rao, whose reforms attracted a flood of foreign capital. The newly buoyant economy fuelled new enterprises and resulted in the expansion of a prosperous educated middle class. However this economic dynamism exists alongside widespread use of child labor, poverty, illiteracy, corruption and religious conflicts (such as the bloody 1992–1993 Ayodhya riots, when deep-rooted tensions between Hindus and Muslims surfaced). Nehru's dream state has yet to be realized, although democracy endures.

Above: Indira Gandhi and her son, Rajiv. Below: modern India; still to realize Nehru's dream

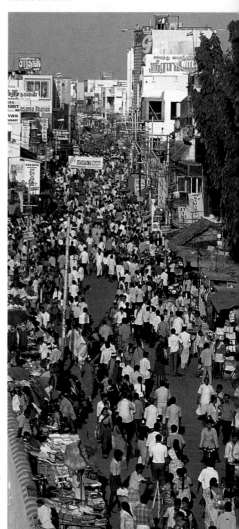

From birth to death, the lives of devout Hindus are punctuated by ceremony. Food, hygiene, marriage and worship all fall into a prescribed pattern that has existed for some 3,000 years, although this is being increasingly eroded by Western lifestyles in the cities. Muslim ritual, keeps a far lower profile.

At Hindu marriages the bridegroom traditionally rides a white horse

The prescribed rituals of ancient Vedic texts steer the daily lives of hundreds of millions of Hindus today. Faith runs deep, and evidence of it can be seen everywhere. *Sadhus* (Hindu ascetics) travel the highways, and wayside shrines are filled with offerings of flowers. Cows are sacred, as are certain plants. Meditation and cremation are important ritual practices, and numerous rites are performed to promote fertility. Muslim ritual is far less visible. Prayer is the most obvious practice, with the faithful called five times a day by the distinctive wail of the *muezzin* (crier) from the minaret. The principal event in the Muslim religious calendar is the month-long festival of Ramadan, when eating or drinking between dawn and dusk is forbidden.

MARRIAGE Central to traditional Hindu society is the family, welded together by arranged marriages in which adolescent girls bring negotiated dowries to the selected husband. Such marriages join not simply two individuals but also two families, clans or even communities. Money, land, tradition, and social convenience all play a part. Times are changing though. With education and birth control more widely available, women now have far greater control over their own lives, and love marriages are increasingly accepted by the middle classes.

BIRTH Rituals surrounding fertility range from making offerings at *naga* shrines (dedicated to the snake god, symbol of fertility) to donating black stones to an ancient cactus at Calcutta's Kali temple. When a desert woman in Rajasthan dons a *pido*, a yellow veil with a large red spot, it announces her pregnancy and acceptance by the community. Simply being fertile, however, is not enough. Vedic verses honor sons followed by more sons, but never daughters. When a boy is born, conch shells are blown in Bengal and Assam, and drums are beaten in Maharashtra. When a girl is born, the women of Rajasthan retreat behind their veils and wail. In traditional Hindu households throughout India, an ancient rite to produce a male child is still performed over pregnant women.

❑ In the 1980s, a survey revealed that of 8,000 abortions carried out in India after prenatal sex determination, only one was a male fetus. ❑

❏ The cows that meander through every Indian street are identified with Mother Earth: both are sources of food, fuel and fertilizer. The cow is said to be an embodiment of the benevolence of the gods, and its five products (*pancagavya*)—milk, curd, *ghee*, urine, and dung—are believed to have purifying properties. Hindus will touch the forehead of a passing cow and utter a prayer in a gesture of devotion and respect. ❏

Some groups in Indian society perform ritual body piercing

DEATH In the philosophical Vedic text the *Bhagavad Gita*, Krishna explains that at death, the soul passes into another body. Hindus traditionally cremate their dead on funeral pyres, preferably on the banks of sacred rivers such as the Ganga (Ganges), where the ashes are later scattered so that the cycle of reincarnation can be broken. Seemingly indifferent to the emotions of the bereaved families, priests bargain over the price of each verse of the *Vedas* (sacred texts) to be recited while the body burns. The first son performs the last rite at his parents' cremations, thereby guaranteeing their release from this world. *Sati*, the rite of a widow throwing herself on her husband's pyre, was banned by the British in 1829; this left widows who were shunned by society, unable to remarry whatever their age. Though illegal, *sati* is performed on rare occasions and in rural communities widows are still stigmatized.

Muslims, unlike Hindus, believe in resurrection after death, and in the existence of heaven and hell. It is customary for Muslims to bury, rather than cremate, their dead.

15

A woman prepares a ritual offering or puja

Brahma, Siva, and Vishnu head the Hindu pantheon of millions of gods, reflecting the basic cycle of life, death, and rebirth. Their multiple incarnations and consorts play out the eternal and divine ordering of the cosmos as revealed in the Vedas, or sacred texts, and have inspired a stream of completely fantastic and often paradoxical myths.

16

The notion of a divine triad is rooted in early Indian belief, perhaps in a cult of the sun, which creates with its warmth, preserves with light and destroys with scorching rays. Over the centuries the members of the triad evolved, and during the Brahmanic period (see page 33) they finally assumed their present identities, Brahma (standing for creation), Vishnu (standing for preservation), and Siva (standing for destruction and reproduction); in other words, a trinity symbolizing life, death, and rebirth.

Below: Hindu holy man or sadhu in a yogic meditative trance
Right: a statue of Brahma, the creator

BRAHMA As creator and progenitor of the human race, Brahma is often perceived as the first of the gods, framer of the universe and guardian of the world. When recognized as an equal to Vishnu and Siva, he was represented as the god of wisdom,

❏ While Brahma and Vishnu were quarrelling, a fiery pillar appeared. They set off to find its origins, an investigation that took 1,000 years. Vishnu followed the column downwards in the guise of a mighty boar, while Brahma traveled upwards as a swan. When neither reached the end, they wearily returned to their starting point. Then Siva stepped in to reveal that the column was his *lingam* (phallus), proving himself the greatest of the trinity. ❏

with the four *Vedas* springing from his head. His powers were later interpreted as those of merely creator and therefore inferior to those of other members of the trinity. This inferiority is illustrated in a myth in which Brahma is the victim of a demon, a situation in which Vishnu or Siva must intervene. Born with one head, Brahma acquired four more in order not to lose sight of the female partner he had created, but Siva reduced this by one. Brahma is usually depicted astride a goose, with four arms.

VISHNU As the preserver of the universe and cosmic order (*dharma*), Vishnu embodies mercy and goodness. He is the cosmic ocean, Nara, which existed before the creation of the universe. As Narayana ("moving in the waters") he is represented in human form asleep on the coiled serpent, Ananta, floating on the ocean, a posture he resumes after every destruction of the universe. Vishnuite worshippers claim that his mild self-assurance proves that he is the greatest of gods. Vishnu, a handsome young man with blue skin, dressed in regal attire, is often depicted with his much revered wife, Lakshmi, goddess of fortune, reclining on the serpent, seated on a lotus or riding his bird-man steed, Garuda. As preserver, Vishnu periodically descends to earth in human form to re-establish the balance of good and evil. His *avatars* (incarnations) so far total nine. The eighth, Krishna, inspired a huge body of mythology related in the lengthy

Mahabharata and is a popular god in his own right. The ninth *avatar* was Buddha, an astute attempt to subordinate Buddhism to Hinduism. The tenth and last has yet to come.

SIVA The trinity's most popular god is Siva the destroyer, a development of the terrifying Vedic god of fire, Rudra, and the pre-Aryan Lord of Beasts, the bull. Siva's activity as destroyer is essential to his role as reproducer: Siva is Supreme Lord, and the *lingam* is the phallic symbol of his creative power. He repeatedly demonstrated the mastery of austerities, gained through yoga, as the source of power, and is described wandering for thousands of years as an ascetic. Demon slayer, giver of long life, distributor of India's seven holy rivers, creator of *amrita* (ambrosia) to strengthen the gods against the demons, god of storms, dancer of death: Siva is the most complex deity. With his vehicle Nandi, the bull, and his wife Parvati (depicted in numerous forms), he embodies omnipotent force.

Granite statue of Siva's bull, Nandi, on Chamundi Hill in Mysore

17

Much of the majestic architecture of India is closely linked with its numerous religions, and it can be viewed as three-dimensional odes to gods and beliefs. Centuries of outside influences, from Turks, Mughals, the British, and others, have also contributed to a unique and idiosyncratic architectural legacy.

From delicate chalk paintings on tribal mud-huts to sprawling palaces bristling with turrets, Indian domestic architecture is incredibly varied. There are the elaborately carved and painted merchants' *havelis* (courtyard houses) of northwest India, beautiful Keralan Nayar houses in tropical hardwoods, Portuguese-inspired Goanese dwellings, and British colonial bungalows. Whether Rajput forts, Mughal palaces, or thatched tribal huts, buildings display a love of decoration. In the domain of temple architecture, wonders of the world may be seen, each period inspiring the next.

BEGGING-BOWL STYLE For the Buddhists, the *stupa* (dome) was the ultimate symbol, its generous shape a reflection of the holy Mount Meru or, alternatively, an overturned begging-bowl. The earliest of the Buddhists' soaring rock-cut *chaityas* (worship halls) date from the 2nd century BC, and some 1,200 examples were to be carved by Jains and Brahmans in the following centuries, as were *viharas* (literally shelters, but used to mean very simple, austere monasteries). The best examples are the *stupas* at

18

Above: the 5th-century Dhamekh stupa at Sarnath
Below left: decorative wall painting, Great Rann of Kachchh

Sanchi and Sarnath, and the *chaityas* and *viharas* of Ajanta and Ellora. Hundreds of years later, Buddhism also produced the staggering monasteries of the Himalayas.

WRITHING FACADES Hindu temple architecture developed from the forms evolved by the Chalukya people (6th–8th centuries) around Badami. These inspired the great southern dynasty, the Pallavas, whose influence spread well beyond India. Mamallapuram and Kanchipuram are the places to see their work. Their techniques and vision were further refined by the neighboring Cholas in

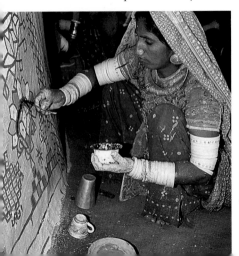

Above: the exquisitely carved interior of a Jain temple, Ranakpur
Left: erotic sculpture, a hallmark of Hindu temple architecture

Chittaurgarh. It is often said that Jain temples reflect a more serene metaphysical approach, but in fact the interiors show bold combinations of features, in a kind of Indian baroque. The prosperous Jain community ensures that the temples are well maintained. Another major circuit of Jain temples exists in Karnataka, where Jain was once the state religion, its finest work the 10th-century colossus of Shravanabelgola.

ALLAH IS GREAT Turkish invaders in the 13th century brought Islamic architectural traditions to India. Mosques, *minars* (towers), and mausoleums rose from the rubble of Hindu and Jain shrines. Under the Mughals India's greatest imperial monuments were created. The Red Fort and tombs of Delhi, the Taj Mahal, Fatehpur Sikri, and Golconda Fort are just the cream of a decorative style that blanketed northern and central India, producing delightful pockets such as Mandu, and infusing Rajput palaces with Persian decorative detail. It also produced vast monuments such as Hyderabad's Jama Masjid. British architects of the Raj took inspiration from Islamic structures for their Indo-Saracenic style, which can be seen in a range of colonial structures.

Thanjavur and the Hoysalas around Mysore. For filigree carving, the temples here are unsurpassed, and the writhing sculptures that face their lofty *gopurams* (gatehouses) became a hallmark of all southern temples. Other major Hindu architectural schools were developing to the north, in Khajuraho and Orissa, both perfecting the design of gently curved, ribbed and carved towers. Erotic imagination and sculptural skills culminated in the breathtaking Surya temple at Konark, in the 13th century.

NOT SO PLAIN JAIN Contemporary with these were the Jain temples. Rajasthan and Gujarat's astounding examples include the exquisitely carved marble interiors of Ranakpur and Mount Abu, as well as important structures at Jaisalmer, Osiyan, and

Inventive, skillful, ingenious and immensely varied, whether produced in mud huts or urban factories, handmade crafts are among India's greatest attractions. Persuasively marketed throughout the country, they make compelling viewing on the great subcontinental trail.

The basis of India's crafts industry is an enormous and low-waged labor force, employed in cottage industries or mass-production to churn out the symbols of the nation's cultural diversity. When a Western visitor carries away a hard-bargained-for carpet, he or she should bear in mind that it may have been produced by underpaid children. Ethics aside, the wealth of handmade crafts becomes confusing. A choice is difficult; should it be a Kashmir shawl or a rosewood carving from Kerala, a bronze statue of dancing Siva, or an inlaid sandalwood box from Mysore?

❏ India's inexpensive, stylish clothing is perfectly adapted to the climate. Few female visitors don a sari, however beautiful its fabric, but many adopt the *salwar kameez*, a long-sleeved dress and matching pants originally worn only by Punjabi Muslims. This makes an acceptably modest outfit for less-visited areas and is also practical. Cotton *kurtas* (the long tunics worn by Indian men) are another practical item for male and female visitors, as are Nehru-style waistcoats. Indian tailors are everywhere and are adept at copying clothes to order. ❏

BIG-CITY BUYS The finest-quality goods usually find their way to the bazaars and emporia of Delhi, Mumbai (Bombay), Kolkata (Calcutta) and Chennai (Madras). Thousands of "craft-stores" are run for foreigners in tourist towns, but few crafts are actually designed as tourist souvenirs. This means that foreign visitors can also shop for craft items alongside locals, in expensive antique stores, state emporia or booths in small bazaars. The main centers of large-scale production are Rajasthan (producing fabrics, jewelry, glass, pottery, miniature paintings, rugs, brass and wood inlay, camel-hide products, and embroidered slippers), and Kashmir, which despite its turbulent political situation still manages to produce carpets, shawls, embroidery, and decorative papier-mâché objects. Kashmiri merchants

A selection of typical Indian handmade crafts

20

have spread throughout India and are often the toughest businessmen, but they generally have quality stock.

Camels are frequently the subject of folk art in Rajasthan

MINORITY ARTS Some of India's most intriguing crafts are produced by its many tribal communities. They include the fine wire animal *tarakashi* of Orissa, and Nagaland's larger bronze sculptures. Specialties abound: one-of-a-kind tribal weavings in Assam, Mizoram's bamboo hats, and the Khachchhs's mirror embroideries and copper-bells. In the Himalayas, a vast amount of Tibetan and Ladakhi silver, turquoise, and coral jewelry is available, some of it, sadly, once the property of Tibetan refugees. This mountainous area is also the source of woolen shawls of wildly varying quality.

GLITTER Indian jewelry stores specialize in the very bright 22-carat gold that is popular throughout Asia. Tribespeople often trade in their traditional silver jewelry for this seemingly more attractive investment, and jewelers may have sacks full of chunky silver bracelets and anklets under the counter. They are usually sold by weight. Less expensive brass and copperware is superbly worked as trays, cups, or plates. The

best was made in Varanasi a few decades ago and is still available. Bidriwork, a Deccan specialty of Aurangabad and Hyderabad, is a matte gun-metal alloy finely inlaid with silver and gold, that is used to make boxes, vases, and *huqqas* (water pipes). Stainless steel kitchenware, a great bargain that has the added advantage of being extremely light, is sold throughout India.

Traditional silver jewelry worn by a tribeswoman in Rajasthan

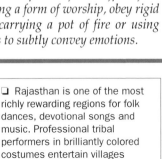

Music, the mirror of India's soul, encompasses classical Hindustani ragas, melodramatic movie soundtracks and the sound of a solo flautist on the ramparts of a Rajput fort. Dancers, enacting a form of worship, obey rigid rules, whether carrying a pot of fire or using minute gestures to subtly convey emotions.

❏ Rajasthan is one of the most richly rewarding regions for folk dances, devotional songs and music. Professional tribal performers in brilliantly colored costumes entertain villages throughout the state, with mesmerizing fire dances, dramas on mock horses and cymbal and drum-dances, to the accompaniment of haunting ballads and simple handcrafted instruments. ❏

Above: the colorful Bharat Natyam Dance of Orissa
Right: traditionally, playing musical instruments was a male preserve

In spellbinding solos or group displays of swirling color, glittering ornaments and fluid movements, Indian dance forms can be enjoyed purely for their visual appeal. At the other extreme are the intent, almost motionless groups of cross-legged musicians who pluck the spirit and emotions as they create a melodic build-up of rhythms, that although improvised, conforms to predetermined movements. Behind both forms lies India's diverse regional cultures and historic fusion of Vedic, Turkish and Persian musical traditions.

DEVOTIONAL DANCE Originating from the chanted hymns of the sacred *Vedas*, music evolved to express the seasonal cycle and the rhythm of agricultural work, becoming interlinked with dance forms to celebrate the harvest, greet a particular season, or worship a specific god. Classical dance rules were set down in the 2nd century BC, categorizing three aspects: *nritta* (pure dance); *nrittya* (emotional expression), and *natya* (drama). Young dancers became a part of worship, performing on purpose-built platforms in Hindu and Jain temples and inspiring countless sculptural renderings (*apsaras*) of their ritualized dance positions. Orthodox Hinduism later came to frown on what bordered on seduction, even prostitution, and temple dancing was eventually banned. One of the few events to show Hindu dance in its original home, the temple precinct, is the Khajuraho Dance Festival held in March.

STAR TURNS Of the many dance forms of worship, each with its own vocabulary of emotions, poses, and steps, the best known is the dramatic and colorful Kathakali of Kerala. This is a male-only dance form, with larger-than-life characters symbolically made up. Equally captivating is Odissi, Orissa's ancient dance form.

Odissi performances of Hindu myths in extravagant costumes and jewelry, accompanied by musicians and singers, are sometimes staged in Puri's Jagannath temple and may be seen every November during the Konark Dance Festival.

MUSLIM MOODS The courts of the Turks and Mughals gave rise to the tradition of the *ragas*, melodic structures of between five and twelve notes within which musicians improvise. *Ragas* are defined and played according to the time of day and season and their suitability for a masculine or feminine audience, and players try to match the ambient mood. Within each *raga* are several movements, each of which would once have lasted for hours but is now reduced to suit shorter concentration spans. The final movement, sub-divided into three sections, introduces percussion, in complex patterns of sound and rhythm. Although instruments were traditionally a hereditary male domain, women contributed as vocalists and are now becoming musicians in their own right. Southern India's Carnatic music developed in the 18th century in Thanjavur, and, although following the *raga* structure, is livelier and uses modified versions of the traditional instruments. Major music festivals are held in New Delhi, Mumbai (Bombay) and Chennai (Madras), with Gwalior's Tansen Festival a highlight every December.

❏ String instruments include the sitar, invented in the 13th century, its smaller version the sarod, the sarangi (said to be one of the most difficult instruments in the world as its 40-odd strings are held by the fingernails), and the santoor, a zither of Persian origin. The shahnai is the main wind instrument, similar to an oboe, and bamboo flutes are widely played. Percussion is dominated by the versatile tabla, whose invention is attributed to the creator of the sitar. ❏

23

Countless festivals pepper the Indian calendar. They may be devoted to gods, seasonal agricultural celebrations, politics, culture, camels, or the anniversary of a philosopher, but all are excuses for reenacting customs that may date back hundreds, if not thousands, of years, and offer mesmerizing images drawn from India's deep-rooted beliefs.

India's festival calendar is enviable. Whether the occasion is a desert camel festival in Rajasthan, the Onam festival snake-boat races in Kerala,

events, and hundreds of thousands will turn out to cheer for their cricket heroes. For visitors, some festivals make pleasant chance interludes, but others should be firmly fixed on the itinerary.

HINDU FANFARES Each religious group in India has its own calendar of major festivals. For Hindus, the beginning of winter (late October through November) is marked by Diwali (Deepavali), the festival of lights, inspiring the lighting of millions of oil lamps in the home and firecrackers outside. These celebrate the homecoming of the hero Rama and his wife Sita (the subjects of the epic poem, the *Ramayana*), while prayers are made to Lakshmi, goddess of wealth, and boxes of sweets are exchanged between friends, families, and business associates. This five-day festival is the Hindu equivalent of Christmas, also widely celebrated. Spring brings Holi, a riotous festival in which colored water and

The paint-splattered face of a Hindu during the riotous festival of Holi

kite-flying in Ahmadabad, dragging Lord Jagannath's chariot in Puri or a monastery ceremony in Ladakh, the size and enthusiasm of the crowd will probably be enormous. Traditional festivals are now rivaled by sports

paint are liberally scattered, leaving most people who venture into the street streaked with pink, blue and silver (which happens to be toxic). Northern India in particular revels in the social leveling that occurs during Holi. Specific gods have their festivals: Siva has Shivatri, Ganesh has Ganesh Chaturthi, celebrated in

Maharashtra, and Durga, Durga Puja, celebrated in Bengal for nine days.

PROPHETS AND SAINTS The Muslim community holds major celebrations for Id-E-Milad, the birthday of Mohammed, as well as for Muharram, the Islamic New Year and Idul Fitr, the feast that ends the 28-day Ramadan fast. Saints' shrines, for example at Ajmer, give rise to particularly fervent anniversary celebrations. Sikhs pay annual homage to each of their ten gurus, with processions to *gurudwaras* (places of worship), readings of the holy Granth and feasting. The biggest Jain festival celebrates the birth of the religion's founder, Mahavir in April, and Buddha's birthday at full moon in May is marked by major processions in Sarnath and Bodh Gaya. The Parsis celebrate Jamsedi Navoroj, their new year, in March–April.

CAMELS AND ELEPHANTS Pushkar's camel fair is one of the most popular regional festivals; others take place at Tarnetar in Gujarat and at Bikaner. These are social focal points for local tribal people and present unparalleled images of India at its most exotic. The south has its own

Above: the Great Elephant March at Thrissur, Kerala
Above left: Sikhs celebrating outside a gurudwara, in the Punjab

fabulous celebrations; Onam is the August and September harvest festival, marked by races of snake boats from the Keralan backwaters. In January the Great Elephant March at Thrissur is a three-day extravaganza led by 101 caparisoned elephants. Tamils go wild at the same time for Pongal, also celebrated in Karnataka and Andhra Pradesh, with processions of cows whose horns and bodies have been brilliantly painted. *Ragolis* (chalk floor drawings) are renewed, and a sweet porridge is consumed by all—cows and people.

❏ The festival of Kumbh Mela is held every three years in one of four holy towns: Nasik, Ujjain, Allahabad or Haridwar. According to Hindu mythology, drops of pure ocean water fell on them *en route* to the Himalayas. The number of pilgrims is estimated at about 12 million each time. ❏

Habitats ranging from the snowy Himalayas in the north to the rainforests of the south give India a unique selection of wildlife. This rich world is threatened by poaching and the growing population. If conservation measures are not strictly enforced, much of it will soon be relegated to history.

❏ Squawking vultures and crows monopolize urban birdlife—head for the hills to watch bulbuls, flycatchers, wagtails, and pheasants. In the mountains, eagles and other birds of prey circle through the skies. Elsewhere, India's national bird, the peacock, is ubiquitous, while grasslands nurture storks, minas, drongos, hoopoes, and weavers, and the marshes have cormorants, cranes, and storks. Flocks of brilliant green parakeets are a sure sign that you have reached subtropical climes. ❏

India plays host to an astonishing 350 mammal species, 2,100 bird species, and thousands of different amphibians, reptiles, and fish. Concern over animals and their habitat is ages old,

An increasingly rare sight, the one-horned rhinoceros

as much of Indian mythology and ritual is inextricably linked to the deification of creatures and plants. Emperor Ashoka (3rd century BC) called upon his subjects to conserve forests, which were reserved for meditating ascetics and saints, and to refrain from slaughtering wildlife. Hindu gods are depicted riding their faithful mounts—Siva's bull, Vishnu's Garuda bird-man and Brahma's goose. Today, India boasts over 400 reserves, including 29 major wildlife sanctuaries, 80 national parks, 16 bird reserves, and 22 UNESCO biosphere reserves. Yet the magnificent tiger is an endangered species (see page 100).

GOING, GOING... As forests diminish by an estimated 932 square miles each year to make way for farms, mines, hydroelectric projects, human occupation, or just for fuel, wildlife is directly jeopardized. Only an estimated 13 percent of the subcontinent remains under forest cover and even

this is subject to fires which propel tigers and elephants into nearby villages to create havoc, if not to kill. Respect for wildlife is greatest amongst the traditional inhabitants of the forest, usually tribal people who have an intuitive understanding of animal habits. During the days of the Raj, they were favored as trackers and *mahouts* (elephant handlers).

At the other extreme are gangs of poachers working with smugglers. Elephants are massacred for their ivory tusks, and tigers for their skins and numerous other parts prized in China and elsewhere as aphrodisiacs. Poorly equipped forest rangers are unable to stop the slaughter.

SURVIVING GLORIES What remains is still a fabulous array. The Himalayas are home to the legendary snow leopard, yak, musk deer, ibex, and a variety of pheasants. There are chinkara stag, black buck, barking deer, and bear on the higher slopes, and musk deer, red pandas, and blue sheep lower down. The varied vegetation of the vast Gangetic plain harbors herbivores such as elephants, sambar deer, wild boar, and chital (spotted) deer, as well as leopards and tigers, and, in the rivers, even freshwater dolphins. The rare one-horned rhinoceros is found only in Assam, while Gujarat, to the west, has the last Asiatic lions. The barren wastes of the Thar Desert are home to the Indian bustard, wild asses, black buck, and nilgai (blue bull), as well as domesticated camels, commonly seen chewing leaves off roadside shrubs. In the distinctly wetter, subtropical south, rainforests are home to numerous monkeys, civet cats, elephants, sloth bears, tigers, and leopards.

Monkeys such as Hanuman langur live in both towns and forest

NATIONAL PARKS You are never very far from one of India's national parks. They offer the best chance of seeing wildlife; start in the cool of dawn if you can. The isolation of many parks makes access tricky, phones do not always function and reservation schedules constantly change: the best bet for independent travelers is often simply to turn up and hope for a cancellation. Bird sanctuaries are richest from November through February when they fill with migratory species. Most parks close down during the monsoon months.

Who said curry? In India, this dish does not exist. Instead, there are countless aromatic regional dishes reflecting historical influences. With rich meat dishes in the north and subtle vegetarian mixtures in the south, gastronomic experiences are high on the list of Indian pleasures, and few visitors are disappointed.

Beans, nutritious and inexpensive, feature in many Indian dishes

Other countries may have Indian restaurants, but these usually offer only a pale and partial imitation of the real thing. In India itself you can sample succulent roadside *pakora* (vegetable pasties), have a feast of *thali* (small servings of several dishes) served by attentive waiters, slurp a Tibetan noodle soup, or crack open a lobster straight from the Indian Ocean. As varied as everything else in the subcontinent, Indian cuisine can be subtly spiced or chili-hot, succulent meat or purely vegetarian, savory or sweet, simply baked or simmered in rich sauces of yogurt and coconut. The much misused word "curry" may come from the Tamil *kari*, one of the plants that contributes to the spicy masala sauce favored in the south. Another misused word is chutney: the

real Indian thing is a divinely fresh, herbal concoction that has little to do with the sweet bottled variety.

SPICES At the heart of Indian cooking are spices: black pepper, cardamom, cinnamon, cloves, cumin, ginger, turmeric, nutmeg, and others, all of which grow on the fertile slopes of the Western Ghats. In the 16th and 17th centuries, western countries fought wars over the spice trade, fortunes were made and lost, empires were created and spices far exceeded gold in value. Many were first used for medicinal purposes, as they act as both appetite stimulators and digestives. They also help the body cope with long periods of heat, a property shared by numerous varieties of chili.

SOUTHERN APPETITE South India, more strongly Hindu than the north, has a predominantly vegetarian cuisine, accompanied by rice flavored with coconut or lime. *Thalis* were once served on banana leaves, but now come on a tray packed with steel bowls and are generally eaten with fingers and *chapatis* (unleavened bread) to mop up more liquid sections. *Masala dosa*, a puffy rice pancake filled with spiced potato and vegetables, is the south's favorite snack and is eaten for breakfast. Other fillers that start the southern day are *iddli*

Above: rich and creamy buffalo milk, purified by boiling
Left: spicy snacks, eaten for breakfast

sambar (steamed rice cake with a spicy lentil and vegetable sauce), *oopma*, a spicy semolina, and its sweeter cousin *kesari* (syrupy semolina with raisins). India's equivalent to pizza is *uttapam*, a filling rice pancake topped with onions. Fish is widely consumed, including pomfret, shark, kingfish, prawns, crab, and lobster.

MUGHAL FLAVORS Hyderabad, with its long Muslim traditions, is a gastronomic highlight. Mumbai (Bombay), too, offers a wide range, including the pungent Bombay Duck, which is actually dried bummalo fish. The north has a tradition of very rich cooking, much influenced by Mughal cuisine and characterized by the use of yogurt (*dahi*), cream, fried onion, nuts, and saffron in meat dishes. Mildest of all is *biryani* (rice cooked with saffron or turmeric, lamb or chicken and dried fruits). *Tandoors*

(clay ovens) are used for baking chicken, lamb, or fish marinated in yogurt, herbs, and spices. Other outstanding dishes include *gushtaba*, spicy meatballs, *paneer*, cubes of cottage cheese, fried and served in a butter-based sauce or with vegetables, and the omnipresent *dal* (lentils), consumed with rice and *roti* (unleavened bread). *Dal* is the staple diet of India's poorer inhabitants.

❑ Typical sweets are *kulfi*, ice cream flavored with cardamom, pistachio nuts, and saffron, *rasgulla*, cream-cheese balls in syrup, *gulab jamun*, ground almond balls with honey, and *firnee*, a richly flavored rice pudding. Ancient Ayurvedic culinary principles stressed the importance of all six *rasas* (flavors): sweet, salty, bitter, astringent, sour, and pungent. ❑

India's version of Silicon Valley has propelled it to the forefront of world computer technology. This is the most obvious reason not to consider India as a backward agricultural country. Abstract thought, when it is applied to something other than the complexities of Hindu metaphysics, is a potentially profitable national talent.

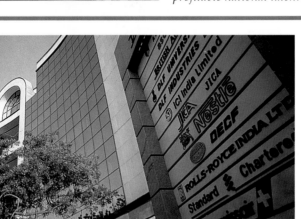

Information technology attracts multinational investment

firms. Savings can be substantial as salaries paid to Indian accounting staff are about one-fifth of those paid in the West, while improved communications systems and computer networks mean that advantage can be taken of time differences across the world. India's fast-growing computer industry has increased software exports by over 70 percent in the last decade and seems set to expand, although traditional products such as textiles and jewelry still dominate the export table.

Bangalore is the undisputed capital of information technology in India, flourishing in the middle of Karnataka's cotton and millet fields. The city is the proof of India's technological progress, and is the world's third-largest assembly of scientific and technological manpower. Television-assembly plants, satellites, millions of new telephone lines, nuclear submarines, combat aircraft, and rockets are among the many items produced and/or designed as a result of the consistent technological research and development spearheaded by India's first nuclear test in 1974.

BANGALORE BRAINS Large foreign companies are now flooding to Bangalore to make use of low-cost data-processing. Clients include British Airways and numerous international banks and accountancy

❏ One of the offshoots of the Indian proclivity for computers is a widespread trade in illegal unbranded products. Homemade computers are assembled by engineer whizzkids from circuits, hard disks, floppy drives, and other peripherals purchased at markets in Mumbai (Bombay) and elsewhere. The machines cost about 25 percent less than brand-name computers and, according to purchasers, their performance is equally satisfactory. However, this activity is being targeted by the authorities and there are signs that it is now being curbed. Such entrepreneurial ventures are not perceived benignly by India's tentacular bureaucracy. ❏

India Was

Around 4,500 years ago, a sophisticated urban civilization emerged in the Indus Valley. It eventually succumbed to Aryan invaders and their rulers, priests, rituals, and Sanskrit language. Aryan literature, especially the Vedas, *formed the religious and social foundations of the Hindu system that still endures today.*

India's earliest traces of human activity date back to 400,000– 100,000 BC but it was only around 7000–5500 BC that crudely made brick houses, agriculture, pottery, and jewelry appeared. Excavations in Baluchistan, the western province of Pakistan, have revealed more sophisticated craftwork and workshops dating from 4000–3000 BC. These represent the genesis of a cultural unity that encompassed Baluchistan, Afghanistan, southern Turkmenistan, and the fertile Indus Valley.

HARAPPAN CIVILISATION The mighty Indus River, flowing down from the mountains of Kashmir to the Arabian Sea, nurtured this sophisticated civilization that reached its zenith in 2500–2000 BC. Urban settlements emerged, at Mohenjodaro and Harappa (both now in Pakistan),

A copper vase, over 4,000 years old, dating from the Harappan period

Rajasthan's Kalibangan and Gujarat's trading-ports of Lothal and Maliya Miyana near Rajkot. Evidence survives of brick-built citadels, *tanks* (artificial lakes), drainage, irrigation, and two-storied houses. Finds have included steatite seals engraved with enigmatic animal designs, terra-cotta figures and bullock-carts, toys, bronze statues, and jewelry, made or inlaid with semiprecious stones, shell, ivory, gold, and copper. By no means isolated, the so-called Harappan civilization traded as far away as the Arabian Gulf, but its pictogram script, composed of over 400 signs, still remains undeciphered.

ARYAN ADVANCE The end came around 1700 BC, brought about by both environmental changes and Aryan invaders from the northwest. The latter brought a hierarchical system that was to form the basis of India's castes. They also brought Sanskrit and India's oldest literary source, the *Rig Veda*, probably composed over a long period starting in 1300 BC. It consists of 1,028 hymns guiding priestly activities, and is the origin of the influential Vedic culture that persists today. From their regional base between the Yamuna and Sutlaj rivers (roughly corresponding to the Punjab and Rajasthan), the Aryans gradually subjugated local Dravidian peoples, enslaving them, intermarrying or driving them south. Their

❑ Vedic rituals stemmed from the notion of *agnihotra*, the basic reciprocal relationship between man, the gods and the universe. They included drinking fresh milk before sunrise and after sunset, animal and even human sacrifice, and the consumption of the sacred liquid *soma*. This was probably a hallucinogenic obtained from mushrooms, which led to a state of heightened consciousness. ❑

political system was based on a *raja* (ruler) who shared sovereignty with two tribal consultants (of undefined roles), a military general and a priest, who performed sacrifices to ensure each tribe's prosperity and victories.

CASTE DIVISIONS It was during the Vedic era that the four divisions of society appeared: the *Brahmins* (priests); the *Kshatriyas* (warriors); the *Vaishyas* (merchants), and the *Sudras* (serfs). Each *varna* ("color") was sub-divided into a multitude of sub-groups (*jâtis*) that correspond to castes. At the basis of Aryan society was the family unit, patriarchal and monogamous, dependent on a mixed economy of cattle and agriculture,

with horses used for battle, and goats and sheep for wool. Their ritualistic religion was dominated by three divinities, Mitra, Varuna and Indra. Boys were initiated at seven years' old to receive religious instruction and learn the rites and oral formulas of the *veda* (knowledge) until, at the age of 17, they were ready to marry. Girls were not instructed.

POSTVEDIC As the centuries rolled by, another body of Vedic literature took shape, the *Brahmanas*, whose legends included the story of Janaka, king of Videha, father-in-law of Rama and protector of sages, propagated in the new mystic doctrines of the *Upanishads*. These Sanskrit sacred texts probably date from 600–400 BC and reflect an evolved post-Vedic society which had also produced the great epic poems, the *Mahabharata* (including the Bhagavad Gita, much consulted by Gandhi) and the *Ramayana*. Originally transmitted orally they were written down centuries later. Aryan society was thus poised for its first great dynasty, the Mauryas.

Right: limestone die
Below: Harappan bangles and ear studs

33

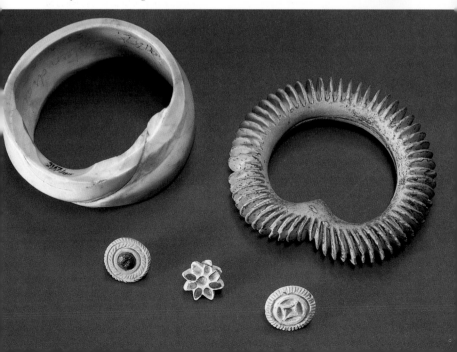

Within a key period of two centuries, India witnessed the birth of two religions, Buddhism and Jainism, saw influences brought by Alexander the Great from Persia and Greece, and produced its most influential dynastic emperor the Mauryan Ashoka.

A 15th-century illustration of Alexander taking his troops east

Valley in 326 BC from his vast Persian and Mediterranean empire. The last of Alexander's garrisons was forced to leave India in 317 BC but their impact was such that, even 70 years later, Greek was still widely spoken in northwest India. The relatively short-lived Mauryan dynasty filled the political vacuum left by relentless battles and alliances between Persians, Greeks, and Indians. Greeks were employed in Persia's administration and army and, according to one ancient text, became accepted as *Kshatriyas* (warriors), despite them being non-Brahmans and therefore impure.

The Mauryan dynasty ruled over most of the subcontinent from about 320 to 185 BC, and was much influenced by the statecraft of Alexander the Great, who invaded the Indus

❏ The first Persian incursions into India took place during a major crisis in Brahmanism in the 6th century BC. This was also when Buddhism and Jainism first appeared. Buddha and Mahavir (founder of Jainism) underwent their *nirvanas* (enlightenments) in around 527 BC and 498 BC respectively. Both taught in northeastern India, in what is now Bihar, which consequently became more important. ❏

RISE TO POWER Alexander the Great had been advised by Chandragupta Maurya to advance to the Ganga (Ganges) and attack the powerful but unpopular Nanda dynasty, whose rule stretched to Bengal. In the event it was Chandragupta himself who deposed the Nandas. From his capital at Pataliputra (in today's Bihar), the sovereign expanded his kingdom, built up a centralized bureaucracy supported by efficient judicial and espionage systems, and used Sanskrit as the official language. Buddhism and Jainism were meanwhile gaining ground and Chandragupta retired to a Jain monastery, leaving the state in the hands of his son. The empire spread into the Deccan, and in about 272 BC, Emperor Ashoka came to the throne. He was to leave a lasting legacy throughout India.

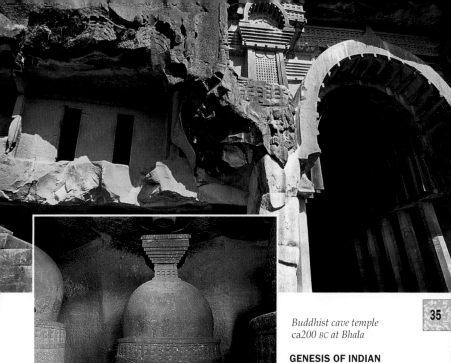

Buddhist cave temple ca200 BC at Bhala

THE FIRST EMPEROR Ashoka's momentous reign is well recorded by his inscriptions. These are a boon for historians as they clearly define his principles. Soon after his accession, Ashoka's declarations became infused with the Buddhist doctrine of *dharma*, and discouraged his citizens from killing (although insisting on the need to "reform" the people of the forest). Government methods became more flexible, assuming a paternalistic tone, animal sacrifices were forbidden and pilgrimages to Buddhist sites replaced hunting expeditions. Though Ashoka was tolerant of all religious beliefs, it was during his reign that Buddhist canons written in Pali were taken by missions throughout Asia.

❏ The Pali script, derived from Sanskrit, appeared in the 3rd century BC and became the language of ancient Buddhist texts. It is still used in Sri Lanka, Myanmar (Burma), Laos, Thailand, and Cambodia. ❏

GENESIS OF INDIAN ART At the same time, the foundations of Indian art were being laid. Magnificent stone capitals surmounted the enormous pillars inscribed with Ashoka's edicts. Proof of their lasting impact is that, in 1947, the lion capital at Sarnath was chosen to be the emblem of independent India. Not only pillars but thousands of *stupas*—reputedly 84,000—were erected. Each contained a relic commemorating events such as Buddha's *nirvana*, a miracle, or his death, or even marking one of his footprints. These masterpieces in stone, visible in all their glory at Sanchi, are the first substantial relics of Indian art. Indian architecture, too, developed during Ashoka's reign. Cave temples reminiscent of Persian tombs were carved into the Barabar Hills in Bihar, north of Bodh Gaya, as retreats for Buddhist monks. These temples initiated a tradition that was to produce the marvels of Ajanta and Ellora and last over 1,000 years.

Ashoka's death, in 232 BC, sparked off a war of succession among his sons, and the administrative strength of Mauryan rule was eroded. The empire fragmented and, in 185 BC, the last Mauryan emperor was killed.

The fall of the Mauryan empire marked the end of Indian unity, as rival powers fought over the different regions. Initially the strongest was the Kushan dynasty; later the Gupta Empire was predominant. The arts flourished as never before but could not stop India's next invaders, the Huns.

By the beginning of the Christian era, orthodox Hinduism using Vedic sacrifices was developing as a counter to Buddhism. Some time after the first century AD, a doctrine based on the *Upanishads* was codified into the *Vedanta* ("end of the Vedas"). This contained the Brahma Sutras, still revered in modern intellectual Hinduism today.

36

Another important element to emerge was yoga, a physical and mental discipline leading to self-knowledge. It represented the concept of self-denial and penance performed by Siva, at that time still perceived as the Vedic god Rudra.

KUSHANS North India was again beset by foreign invaders. Bactrian Greeks, Scythians, and Yueh-Chi (southern Mongols) fought over tiny kingdoms but were overcome by the Kushans from Afghanistan, whose greatest leader, the Buddhist Kanishka (1st century AD) controlled a

The Ajanta caves, near Aurangabad, were chiseled from layered granite rock

> ❑ Gandhara's Buddhists originated the changes that ultimately produced Mahayana Buddhism, a more humanistic faith that split from the old monastic Therevada Buddhism. ❑

vast empire from Central Asia to Varanasi. His immense power was celebrated in his three titles: the Indian "Maharaja" ("great king"), the Iranian "King of Kings", and the Chinese "Son of Heaven". From their capital in Peshawar (Pakistan), the Kushans promoted the art of statuary, notably in the Greek-influenced schools of Gandhara and Mathura. This was also the most important era of the Silk Road, the great trading route from China to Rome. Alternative routes taken by camel caravans connected the high plateaus of Central Asia with the ports of Gujarat.

SOUTHERN TURMOIL Meanwhile, the south saw endless bloody battles between the Cholas, the Ceras, and

the Pandiyas, despite the pacifist presence of numerous Buddhists and Jains. Under the Sungas and Andhras, who controlled much of the Deccan, Buddhist *stupas*, *viharas*, and *chaityas* multiplied, becoming increasingly sophisticated in structure, proportion, and sculpture. Sanchi's magnificent *toranas* (gateways) date from the Andhra period as does the Great Stupa at Amaravati, where the first image of the figure of Buddha was made, *ca*200. With the decline of Andhra power in the Deccan, Brahmanism again came to dominate the center and south.

GUPTA ART In about AD 320 Chandra Gupta founded a dynasty in northern India which for the next 150 years witnessed a new sophistication in Hindu art, literature, and science. During this crucial period the foundations of India's Classical Age were laid; concepts developed over the previous centuries ripened and took fresh life from the new spiritual outlook of Brahmanism. Buddhism was by no means eclipsed: the serene Buddha figures of Mathura were carved at this time, and at Sarnath a wealth of sculptures embodying an increasingly refined and perfected style was produced. Around AD 400, this artistry overflowed into Gupta Hindu art, and some of the first examples of Indian painting were made at Ajanta.

RISE AND FALL Chandra Gupta II (376–415) propelled the Guptas to their zenith, expanding his kingdom over most of northern India and the Deccan, and establishing his capital at Ujjain. During his reign, the works of the great poet and writer, Kalidasa, outlined the

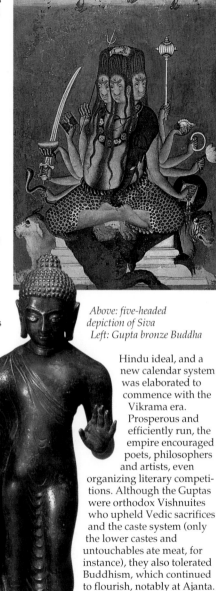

Above: five-headed depiction of Siva
Left: Gupta bronze Buddha

37

Hindu ideal, and a new calendar system was elaborated to commence with the Vikrama era. Prosperous and efficiently run, the empire encouraged poets, philosophers and artists, even organizing literary competitions. Although the Guptas were orthodox Vishnuites who upheld Vedic sacrifices and the caste system (only the lower castes and untouchables ate meat, for instance), they also tolerated Buddhism, which continued to flourish, notably at Ajanta. This harmonious era was not to last. Under Kamaragupta, successor to Chandra Gupta II, the Huns started attacking the north. Both victories and defeats followed, but Gupta power had been definitively eroded by 550.

As the Gupta Empire disintegrated, India became a patchwork of independent kingdoms that went on to produce some of central and southern India's greatest temples and finest sculpture. While their influential styles spread overseas, rival empires flourished and declined as they fought for internal power.

By the 7th century, Hinduism was firmly established in the south and in the Deccan, giving rise to the fabulous temples of the Chalukyas, Pallavas, Cholas, Hoysalas, and Pandiyas. Jainism flourished under the Chalukyas and Hoysalas, leaving a string of important shrines. The south was unaffected by the advance of Islam in the north, and was able to nurture an unrivaled and unhindered flowering of Hindu and Tamil culture.

Gatehouse at Kamakshi Aman temple, Kanchipuram

CHALUKYAN From successive capitals around Badami between the 6th and 8th centuries, the Chalukyan dynasty carried out India's first great experiments in temple building. Evolving from the earlier *chaitya* and *vihara* forms (see pages 18–19), the increasingly imaginative designs had a far-reaching influence. *Mandapas* (pillared halls) and *shikharas* (towers marking the location of the deity), both became dominant features in Hindu temples. Although confirmed Vishnuites, the Chalukyas encouraged Sivaite and Jain worship. At their most powerful they controlled a vast empire extending to Kanchipuram and Orissa. It included Ajanta and propelled their fame as far as Persia, but this affluence and power attracted enemies who eventually destroyed them. Their successors in the Deccan from around 750, the Rashtrakutas, were responsible for the wonders of Ellora's rock-cut Kailasa temple.

PALLAVAS One of Badami's attackers was the great Pallava dynasty. Since the 4th century, the dynasty—whose people were renowned as great traders and seamen—had held sway over southeast India from Kanchipuram. They were to spread their influence to much of Southeast Asia, and there is evidence of early links with Greece and Rome. Originally Buddhist, they converted to Brahmanism in the 5th century. Over the next three

38

Chola bronzes from the 10th century

centuries they developed a style of cave temples, carved granite mono-liths and astounding bas-reliefs that is still visible today at Mamallapuram (its name means "place of the wrestler", referring to the great Narasimha Varman I). The Pallavas disappeared in the 9th century when they were conquered by the neighboring Cholas.

CHOLAS This dynasty had already experienced periods of power from its base at Thanjavur, but enjoyed a renaissance around 850 that began 300 years of momentous expansion. Sweeping through Pandiya and Cera territory, the Chola kingdom eventu-ally encompassed today's Tamil Nadu, Kerala, Sri Lanka, the Lakshadweep and Maldive islands, southern Andhra Pradesh and Karnataka, Orissa, and part of Bengal. Their zenith was during the reigns of Rajaraja (985–1014) and Rajendra (1014–1044), when naval expeditions accomplished the partial occupation of Myanmar (Burma), Malaysia, and Sumatra, as well as control of the profitable trade routes of the Indian Ocean. This political stability, accom-panied by economic prosperity, encouraged a blossoming of the arts and Tamil culture.

❏ Cholan artistry survives in their extraordinary Sivaite temples at Thanjavur, incorporat-ing refined versions of Pallavan stone sculpture, and above all in their bronze sculpture. Cast with the lost-wax technique using clay molds, Cholan bronzes reached unsurpassed heights of grace, symbolism and detail. ❏

LAST GASPS By the mid-13th century the Cholas had been superseded by their old enemies, the Pandiyas of Madurai in the south and, to the west, the Hoysalas. The Pandiyas, too, had been a great trading power from the first centuries AD, establishing links with Greece, Rome, and China. They also fostered a flowering of Tamil literature. Their new supremacy lasted only until 1364, when they were absorbed by the spreading Vijayanagar empire of Hampi. The Hoysalas, originally a group of hill chieftains who had been feudal subjects of the Chalukyas, are known for their temples at Halebid, Belur and Somnathpur, whose ornate fili-gree carvings are totally different from the geometric style of early Pallavan structures.

Rajputs, Palas, Turks, and Arabs were the chief protagonists of northern India's turbulent "medieval" period. While Islamic invaders encroached on the north, Hindu and Buddhist temple architecture experienced a last period of flowering quite unaffected by Islamic styles.

Carved chariot wheel at the Surya (Sun) Temple at Konark—crowning glory of Orissan medieval art

Of the numerous rulers and short-lived dynasties that immediately followed the Guptas in northern India, there is little significant trace, except in the case of the philosophically inclined Harsa (606–647). Both the poet Bana and the Chinese pilgrim Hsuan Tsang made detailed accounts of his kingdom, which stretched from Gujarat to Bengal. Hsuan Tsang relates that Buddhism was noticeably declining and that new practices such as *sati* and Tantric cults had appeared in Hinduism. From the 8th through the 10th centuries, two dynasties shared the spoils of northern India: the Palas of Bihar and the Rajputs of Rajasthan. Obsessive power struggles eroded their power, and their domains fragmented into many vulnerable kingdoms.

PALA POWER The height of Pala power in Bihar was reached under King Dharmapala (770–810) who revived Buddhism and even exported it to Tibet. Surrounded by a sea of Brahmanism, only the Buddhist sites of Bodh Gaya, Nalanda, and Sarnath still functioned, supported by streams of Buddhist pilgrims from Southeast Asia in search of *darshan* (mystic ecstasy). The monastery of Nalanda reached heights of splendor, vividly described by Hsuan Tsang who stayed there in the 7th century. Pala sculptors expanded the Bodhisattva pantheon and created numerous symbolic icons, yet their style became increasingly lifeless and stylized. By the 12th century, Buddhism and Brahmanism started to overlap, and Buddha was even accepted by Hindus as the ninth incarnation of Vishnu.

TEMPLE TRYST Parallel to this decline in Buddhism, Hinduism was creating

> ❏ From the 7th century onwards, Tantric ideas permeated both Buddhist and Brahmanic philosophies. Tantra asserted that *shakti* (the female principle) was the dominant force in the universe through its power to energize the dormant male force, a belief that gave rise to the agitated consorts of the Hindu trinity. The notion of ecstatic bliss achieved through sexual union led to the formation of secret Tantric groups but was eventually suppressed by Hindu orthodoxy. Muslim invaders were particularly efficient at effacing its images. ❏

spectacular temples in Orissa, including the Kesari dynasty's countless structures at Bhubaneshwar and the Ganga dynasty's masterpieces at Puri and Konark (*ca*1240). The distinctive Orissan style was the climax of centuries of development and was the last great expression of Hinduism before the influences of Islam were felt. Erotic sculptures at Konark and at Khajuraho, a product of the Rajput dynasty of the Chandelas (10th–13th centuries), point to the rise of Tantric thought at this time.

RAJPUTS Thought to be descended from the Huns and their accompanying Central Asian tribes, the bellicose Rajputs (meaning "sons of kings") held sway over Rajasthan and part of Gujarat from the 7th century onwards, but were never able to maintain a united front. Despite being constantly embroiled in war, these warriors built stupendous forts that peppered the hills and desert of Rajputana. Individual princely states rose and fell but the Rajput clan (the warrior caste) went on, instilling fear even in the Mughals and the British.

ISLAM ARRIVES After gathering strength throughout Central Asia and conquering Sind in 712, the Arabs consolidated their power and that of Islam, but it was not until 988 that India was deeply affected. In that year Mahmud of Ghazhi, the son of a

Above: lavishly carved marble columns at Mount Abu, Rajasthan
Top: Hindu temple complex, Bhubaneshwar, Orissa

Turkish slave and self-promoted champion of Sunnite Islam, was employed by the Caliph to rid the Indus Valley of all Hindus. Increasingly motivated by the immense wealth he found, he made several raids, including attacks on Mathura in 1017, Delhi in 1018, and Somnath in 1026. Later Turkish invaders defeated the Rajputs in 1192, and then attacked Gwalior, Varanasi (Benares) and Lahore. In 1206 Delhi fell to the Turks, and by 1236 Turkish domination of north India was complete.

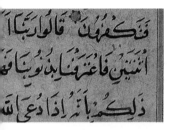

For some 300 years India endured the oscillating power of the Sultans of Delhi. Whether barbarous or enlightened, illiterate slaves or erudite nobles, these Turkish rulers maintained a firm hold on their conquests, suffering at the hands of the Mongols but only finally destroyed by internal rivalries. Meanwhile, Hinduism saw its last great dynasty at Vijayanagar.

Left: the Qutb Minar marks the triumph of Islam in Delhi
Below: Genghis Khan

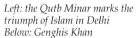

❏ Urdu, the Muslim language of India and Pakistan, evolved in the military camps of India's first Turkish invaders (the English word "horde" comes from "urdu"). It was later written down in the Arab-Persian alphabet and, although an Indo-Aryan language, incorporates numerous Arab and Persian terms. ❏

A slave soldier named Iltumish seized power in 1211 and consolidated Turkish rule. The Mongols, led by Genghis Khan, swept through central Asia, causing a stream of Turkish and Persian refugees to join the Turkish administration in Delhi. In 1221 the Mongols reached the Indus Valley, where they turned back. In 1296, another Mongol advance to the Indus led to the rise of a new Turkish dynasty, the Khaljis, whose Sultan Ala-ud-din extended the Sultanate across the Deccan and Gujarat. Although illiterate, Ala-ud-din nurtured architecture and the arts, and made Urdu the official language.

UPS AND DOWNS Rebellions, assassinations, and death in battle were common events of the Sultanate, which went into marked decline

The Jama Masjid in Old Delhi

under the Tughluqs (1320–1414). Under the threat of Mongol and Chinese invaders from the north, they set up a second capital at Daulatabad. Gradually the Sultanate fragmented as the Vijayanagar kingdom grew stronger and numerous independent sultanates appeared, such as those in Bengal, Kashmir and Madurai. From 1351 an interlude of peace and prosperity under Firuz saw the introduction of free hospitals and aid to the poor, and even the translation of 1,500 Sanskrit manuscripts into Persian. Indian Muslims governed and Hindus were employed in their administrations.

TURKISH FINAL Central power was definitively on the decline, however, and was helped on its way by the Mongol Timur, an adept at devastation, pillage, and butchery, who reached Delhi in 1398. An estimated five million people died in the ensuing genocide, and the resultant famines and plagues accelerated the end of the Sultanate. The Sayyids in 1414 were followed by the Lodis in 1451. Under the Lodis, Afghan nobles became an influential force of dissent, causing Ibrahim Lodi to turn to the Punjab governor for support. The latter's decision, in his turn, to call on Babur, the ruler of Kabul for help, opened the doors to India's next great conquerors, the Mughals.

VIJAYANAGAR Meanwhile southern India was witnessing the rule of one of its greatest Hindu dynasties, the Vijayanagar, who had emerged after a revolt against the Tughluq governor in 1336. Their adopted name came from a Vedic master, Vidyarana, who was the spiritual guru of two young local Hindu princes. Successive Vijayanagar rulers oversaw a new Hindu renaissance and expanded their territory, governing from a glorious and prosperous capital. It was financed by tribute from vassal states that by the early 15th century spread south to Madurai. Devaraya I (1406–1422) employed Muslim soldiers for whom he built a mosque.

DAZZLING Inexorably, internal ambitions frittered away Vijayanagar power. Nevertheless, Krishna Deva Raya (1509–1529) was described by early Portuguese accounts as a magnanimous king, wrathful yet inclined towards poetry, ruling from a fabulous city and head of a powerful army of elephants and javelin-throwers. Vijayanagar provinces were ruled by Nayaks who oversaw the rajahs of small territories; all were obliged to attend the grand festivities held in the capital and some were permanent courtiers. Public order was ceremoniously maintained with the help of mutilation, impalement, and hanging. Rice was exported to the Persian Gulf and sugar to Southeast Asia, while cotton, diamonds, pearls, and tropical hardwoods were also produced. Krishna Deva's successors saw Vijayanagar power crushed by the combined forces of the Deccani sultanates, and led by Akbar in 1565 they ransacked the majestic capital.

The Mughal Empire made monumental changes in Indian culture, religion, and government. Islam dominated, but enlightened rulers ensured religious tolerance, while artists, writers, and craftsmen received imperial patronage—until the religious fanatic Aurangzeb provoked the empire's downfall.

Babur, founder of the Mughal dynasty, was descended from the ferocious Mongol Timur and from Genghis Khan. "Mughal" derives from the Arab-Persian word for Mongol, but Babur's immediate origins lay in the hills of Turkestan, from where he conquered Kabul. In 1526 he defeated Ibrahim Lodi, the last of the Delhi Sultans. Although unimpressed by his Indian conquest, he laid the foundations of political and military power, and established courtly traditions of the arts that were adopted by all subsequent Mughal emperors.

AKBAR'S EXPANSION On Babur's death in 1530, he was succeeded by his son Humayun, who was equally well educated but less militarily astute, and was ousted by an Afghan chief, Sher Shah, within a decade. In 1556 Humayun recaptured Delhi but, plagued by bad luck, died accidentally a month later, leaving

Anup Talao pavilion, part of Akbar's ambitious capital at Fatehpur Sikri

a 13 year-old son as his heir. This was Akbar, who in the years to come was to prove himself as a great statesman, conqueror, and mystic. From 1561 onward he launched assaults that reduced the power of the Rajput (who later became allies), annexed the maritime states of Gujarat and Bengal, and swallowed up Bihar and Orissa. In 16 years he had constructed the Mughal Empire.

ECLECTIC TALENTS Under Akbar's rule (1556–1605), the empire was strengthened. Power was centralized, a reformed administration introduced fairer taxation and rents, the *durbar* (public audience hall) became a feature of court rituals, and religious tolerance prevailed. Philosophical debates led Akbar to found a new religion combining several beliefs and much influenced by *Sufism*. Among his other passions were elephant fighting, music, poetry, painting (nurtured during his childhood in Persia), and architecture (reflected in the ceremonial capital of Fatehpur Sikri and the fort palace of Agra).

ART AND OPIUM In 1605 Akbar was succeeded by his son, Jehangir, whose upbringing in his father's scintillating court inclined him towards the arts rather than warfare. Jehangir later wrote his memoirs and commissioned countless works of art and literature. His adored Persian wife, Nur Jahan, a highly intelligent, artistically inclined princess, assumed a significant hold on state affairs from 1622 onward,

44

as Jehangir succumbed increasingly to the pleasures of alcohol and opium.

URBAN PLANNER Jehangir's death brought his son, Shah Jahan (1628–1658), to the throne. Far from being a pronounced aesthete like his father, Shah Jahan set about renewing Mughal military conquests, west into Central Asia and south into the

Mughal miniatures: Shah Jahan with Qudsia Begum (left) and fort construction in Agra (above)

Deccan. Yet he also had his more refined traits: he built the Taj Mahal (whose romantic inspiration was the death of his favorite wife), and the new walled city of Shahjahanabad, better known as Old Delhi, as well as enriching the forts of Agra and Lahore.

THE ZEALOT Despite these marvels, the Mughal Empire was disintegrating, and its last ruler, Aurangzeb, did not have the moral qualities which had helped his predecessors to hold it together. This son of Shah Jahan, usurped his brother, the designated heir, in front of their dying father. He then used all his military and political skills to try and strengthen the unwieldy empire.

However, his religious enthusiasm led to the introduction of orthodox Islamic laws, destroying Hindu temples and withdrawing imperial patronage of the arts. On his death, in 1707, the Mughal Empire shrank to the environs of Delhi.

❏ The Mughal school of painting originated in a state workshop founded by Akbar. It employed about 100 artists, mainly Hindu, working under two Persian masters brought to India by Humayun. By the time of Akbar's death his library held about 24,000 illuminated manuscripts. The Akbari style blended Persian art with Indian elements, using extended space, lively action and even European realism, inspired by illustrated bibles brought by Portuguese Jesuits from Goa. ❏

While the Mughals were developing Islamic civilization inland, India's coastline was increasingly encroached upon by European powers. After the Portuguese came the English, establishing strong bases, that through astute manipulation, eventually led to the hegemony of the East India Company.

In 1498, Vasco da Gama laid anchor at Calicut, on India's Malabar Coast, inadvertently opening the gates of India to European powers. The arrival of Alfonso de Albuquerque as Portuguese viceroy in 1508 gave the impetus for the establishment of strategic west coast trading posts, and above all for the development of the capital at Goa, all of which remained under Portuguese control until 1961. Close on their heels, in 1605, came the Dutch East India Company (VOC), but its Javanese interests left little time for expansion in southern India.

over the Portuguese off Surat, in 1612, led to their being accorded trading rights at Surat by Emperor Jehangir. Within 40 or so years, the British had established effective control over southeast India (founding Madras, modern Chennai, in 1639) and Bengal. Control over the latter was confirmed by Robert Clive (known in British schoolbooks simply as Clive of India) in 1757 at the battle of Plassey. This was a crucial point in British involvement, which was centered on the burgeoning city of Calcutta (now Kolkata).

British king, William III's Grant of Arms to the New East India Company dated 1698

TURNING POINT The commercial appetite of the British had been awakened by tempting tales of spices, silks, and sandalwood. A landmark victory

CONFLICT AND EXPANSION Relations with the Mughals in north India were much aided by the East India Company's habit of paying for cloth in silver bullion. In the south, ongoing wars between minor kingdoms gave the British the perfect opportunity to practice "divide and rule" tactics, allying with one ruler against another in exchange for trading rights and taxes. In 1799, the British carved up the state of Mysore, ending more than a century of Franco-British rivalry in India, which had started when the French established a trading post at Pondicherry in 1674. War broke out in 1744, giving France temporary supremacy in Madras and expanding its influence in the Deccan and Orissa.

❏ A treaty signed with the Mughal emperor in 1765 gave Clive (representing the East India Company) control over taxation in Bengal, Orissa, and Bihar. Under Governor Warren Hastings, nominated in 1772, the Company gained monopolies over salt, opium, and saltpeter. In Britain, the 1784 India Act gave the government authority over Company governor-generals. ❏

Lord Clive, who turned the East India Company into a military power

In 1758 a new governor was given the task of seizing all British possessions. The taking of Madras by the the British in 1760 put an end to Gallic ambitions in the subcontinent outside existing French *comptoirs* (trading posts). It also ended the ambitions of Hyder Ali and his son, Mysore's hero, Tipu Sultan, who was previously allied with the French. He died in battle against Arthur Wellesley, later Duke of Wellington, in 1799.

MUGHAL VICTIMS Meanwhile, the Mughal emperors had been under threat from the Marathas to the south ever since the latter's Hindu leader, the ruthless Sivaji, had killed the Nawab of Bijapur and set up a powerful base at Pune. Sivaji's death, in 1680, put an end to Marathi aspirations for a while, but they resurfaced under the Maratha confederacy, which united under the banner of Maharashtra nationalism (still simmering today). Land to the south was unassailably dominated by the Nizam of Hyderabad, but to the north, the weak Mughal Empire offered better pickings (this weakness had already been exploited by a Persian invader in 1739, who massacred thousands and looted treasures from Delhi's palaces). By the 1750s, Delhi's gates were simultaneously threatened by the Marathas from the south and Afghans from the north. A battle between these two forces left the Afghans victorious, but they were forced by internal problems to retreat, while the Maratha confederacy fell apart. Seizing their opportunity, the British stepped in. By the early 19th century, British control over India was virtually absolute.

47

British power was strengthened through the East India Company, until the Uprising of 1857 precipitated momentous change. Queen Victoria was appointed Empress of India, and the subcontinent became the legendary "jewel in the crown" of the world's largest empire. Inevitably, though, colonialism nurtured a desire for independence.

After definitively quashing the Marathas (see page 47) in 1818, gaining Assam through war with Myanmar (Burma), and taking control of Sind, Punjab, and Lower Burma (Myanmar) in 1852, the British had complete supremacy over India. A network of princely states were supposedly independent allies, but a law introduced by Lord Dalhousie (Governor-General 1848–1856) stipulated that the state of any ruler who died without a male heir would automatically be annexed. Thus Oudh, the last major independent state of north India, passed into East India Company control in 1856.

REFORMS The East India Company had lost its commercial monopoly in 1813 but expanded its political and

military role. It controlled the taxation system, appointed British officers to lead the *sepoys* (Indian soldiers) of the army, and appointed governor-generals. After centuries of war, India's infrastructure was in ruins. The countryside was terrorized by *dacoits* (bandits) and *thuggee* (who ritually sacrificed their victims in the name of Kali, goddess of destruction). From the 1820s, governor-generals began to instigate reforms, some stimulated by humanist thinking at home. *Sati* was abolished and attempts were made to eradicate *thuggee*. Western-style schools and colleges were founded, English ousted Persian as the official language, and canals, roads, railways, and telegraph systems were developed.

THE UPRISING Known by the British as the Indian Mutiny, India's first war of independence was sparked off in

Storming of Delhi in 1857, by George McCulloch

❏ Some 3,000 people (mainly British families and their loyal Indian servants and soldiers) were besieged for three months at Lucknow in 1857. When finally freed by a battalion of Scots and Sikhs, only 1,000 were alive. ❏

1857. Hindu and Muslim sepoys were offended by having to bite gun cartridges which they believed to be greased with cow and pig fat (respectively counter to their religious beliefs). From Meerut, the mutineers marched on Delhi and gained the backing of the last Mughal emperor, Bahadur Shah, then in exile in Kanpur, and the royal family of the recently annexed Oudh, in Lucknow. The rebellion spread fast, igniting the latent fears of Indians who had been undergoing radical changes to their traditional lifestyle. There were atrocities on both sides. Within a year the British regained control and executed thousands of Indians. Bahadur Shah was exiled to Rangoon.

BRITISH RAJ The momentous result of the Uprising was the abolition of the East India Company and establishment of British government control through a viceroy. In the new organization, local maharajas and nawabs were cosseted as never before: their territorial sovereignty was assured, and their egos were polished by medals and cannon-salutes. The 1858 India Act also established the Indian Civil Service. The Indian Army played a major role not only in regional conflicts against Afghanistan and Myanmar (Burma), but also worldwide, anywhere British

Regal statue of Queen Victoria as Empress of India in Calcutta

interests were at stake. Queen Victoria's coronation as Empress of India in 1877 marked the zenith of the British Raj.

RUMBLING DISCONTENT A new, western-educated, Indian elite arose, including businessmen, civil servants and landlords, who saw the shortcomings of a political system that negated Indian identity, and of an economic system exploiting India's raw materials and its huge market for British manufactured goods. A British initiative produced India's first political party, the Indian National Congress, in 1885. Wary of Hindu dominance, the Muslim community formed its own associations, leading, in 1906, to the creation of the Muslim League. Then, in 1915, a certain Mohandas Gandhi returned to his country from South Africa.

Gandhi's return to India gave impetus to a struggle marked by civil unrest, riots, and repression, as well as the rational radicalism of Nehru's Congress party. The Quit India campaign and growing Hindu-Muslim violence resulted, in 1947, in Lord Mountbatten's hasty preparations for independence.

show of silent resistance. The protesters were not all silent, and in Amritsar, General Dyer's troops fired into the crowds, killing 379 and wounding another 1,200. This notorious event set the fuse of resistance alight. The writer and philosopher Rabindranath Tagore returned his knighthood to the Viceroy, riots erupted all over India, and martial law was imposed. Gandhi initiated non-cooperation, including the boycotting of schools and law courts, and the burning of British textiles. He soon found himself in prison, not for the last time. In 1921 he took to wearing the homespun *dhoti* (loincloth).

Mohandas Gandhi had spent 21 years in South Africa, masterminding the use of *satyagraha* ("strength of the truth"), or passive resistance to government, to oppose apartheid. Back in India, he found a country ripe for revolt. Britain, fully aware of the mounting threat, instigated more administrative autonomy but soon after, tightened repression through imprisonment without trial.

AMRITSAR MASSACRE In 1919, Gandhi's first overt act of opposition was to organize a *hartal* (day of mourning), in fact a general strike and

PROGRESS The 1930s began with the Congress party's declaration of Independence Day, inspired by a combative Nehru who had now assumed leadership, and by Gandhi's well-publicized salt march (see page 84). Demonstrations, strikes, and political imprisonments increased until finally Viceroy Irwin and Gandhi struck a truce, and the latter, clad in his *dhoti*, traveled to London for talks. The Government of India Act of 1935 gave increased power to Indian ministers within the context of a federation, yet kept finance and defence in the hands of the Viceroy. This advance helped Congress in the 1937 elections.

Left: Gandhi—known as Mahatma, meaning sage
Right: Nehru with Lord and Lady Mountbatten

CRACKS India's Muslim community was far from happy, however. The first riots between Hindus and Muslims took place in 1930, and the leader of the Muslim League postulated the formation of a Muslim state, Pakistan, to encompass Punjab, Afghania, Kashmir, and Sind. When Congress did not share power, after its 1937 electoral successes, in provinces with substantial Muslim minorities, the Muslim League leader, Mohammed Ali Jinnah, became the unyielding advocate of the creation of Pakistan.

ESCALATION In World War II, the Indian Army played a major role for the Allies, but British prime minister Winston Churchill remained hostile towards Indian independence. In 1942, Gandhi and Nehru encouraged Congress's adoption of the Quit India Resolution, which resulted in the imprisonment of most party leaders. Tension was exacerbated when countless people died in the 1943 famine in Bengal, and a further 10,000 were killed there in riots. There was also widespread violence in the Punjab.

FREEDOM AT A PRICE In 1947, when the new viceroy, Lord Mountbatten, was instructed to negotiate independence, India was on fire. Gandhi, Nehru, and Patel (Congress's other leader) agreed on the need for speed, but Jinnah's demand for Pakistan proved an obstacle. Consensus was finally reached: India was to be partitioned, with Bengal and the Punjab becoming East and West Pakistan. In the following months, over 10 million people were uprooted, as Hindus moved into India and Muslims into Pakistan. Between 500,000 and one million were brutally killed in circumstances described by Mountbatten as "sheer madness". However, on August 14, Nehru's words as India's first Prime Minister rang out to a delirious, free nation.

> ❏ "Long years ago we made a tryst with destiny… At the stroke of the midnight hour, while the world sleeps, India will awake to life and freedom. A moment comes, which comes but rarely in history, when we step out from the old to the new, when an age ends, and when the soul of a nation, long suppressed, finds utterance…"
> Jawaharlal Nehru, New Delhi, August 14, 1947. ❏

Delhi

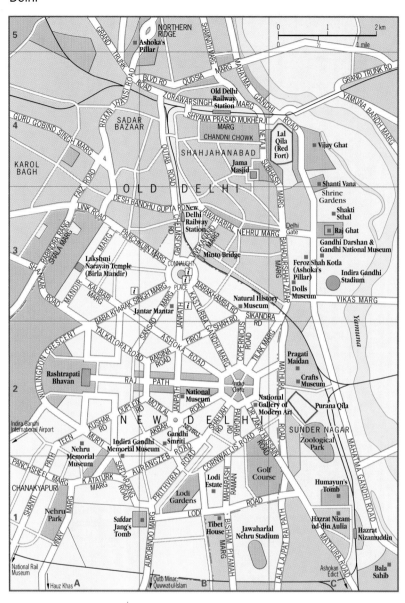

54

Previous pages: a panoramic view of the city from the Jama Masjid, India's largest mosque

DELHI Of all India's cities, the capital, Delhi, is the most accessible and rewarding for first-time visitors. Parks and gardens are plentiful, street life is colorful, the people outgoing, and amenities wide ranging. Above all, the immense sweep of the city's turbulent history has left magnificent monuments dating back to the 12th century and up to the 20th century (the elegant results of Lutyens's urban planning and colonial buildings that marked the transfer of the capital from Calcutta in 1931). Today, Delhi has 12 million inhabitants, and sprawls haphazardly over 300 square miles of verdant avenues, traffic-choked back streets and pungent markets packed with booths.

Although beggars still occasionally accost cars at traffic lights and plead with pedestrians, this is a prosperous city experiencing the benefits of India's recent growth. As such it provides a fascinating cultural introduction to this multifaceted country.

Above: Chandni Chowk, Old Delhi
Below: in the Red Fort

LAYOUT Traditionally said to be formed out of seven successive cities, Delhi is an agglomeration of numerous districts, each with its own history and character. At the center is a triangle formed by Connaught Place (the commercial hub), India Gate (the war memorial and symbol of freedom), and Rashtrapati Bhavan, the presidential residence and symbol of authority. To the north lies Old Delhi, site of the massive Red Fort, the Jama Masjid, and the narrow lanes of the bazaars. Here too is Old Delhi Train Station. New Delhi Train Station lies closer to Connaught Place. Southeast of India Gate is another cluster of sights, including Purana Qila, Sunder Nagar, the zoo, and several museums, ending at Humayun's Tomb in the district of Nizamuddin. West of here stretch leafy residential areas starting at the Lodi Gardens and ending with the Diplomatic Enclave and luxury hotels of Chanakyapuri. Farther south is trendy Hauz Khas and, farther still, Delhi's oldest monument, the Qutb Minar. Almost due west of here is the airport.

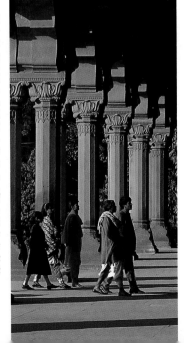

Delhi

HISTORY Although legend and archeological excavations point to the Purana Qila as the site of an early settlement dating from around 1000 BC, the first Delhi was founded by the Rajput Tomar kings in the 8th century AD (see page 41). Four centuries later came the first Muslim sultan and Delhi's longest surviving monument, the Qutb Minar. Under Humayun, the second Mughal emperor, the walls of the Purana Qila were built; later his widow built his domed tomb, an architectural landmark. Major transformations came when Shah Jahan (see page 45) constructed Old Delhi, an ambitiously planned walled city that still claims India's largest mosque, and includes a palace that evokes the grandeur of his reign and the zenith of Mughal arts. From the late 17th century until the early 20th century, Delhi slumbered while foreign powers were developing India's port cities. Then in 1911, George V announced that the capital of the British Raj would move from Calcutta to Delhi, and that a completely new city would be built to accommodate it. Sir Edwin Lutyens was appointed to plan the city (see page 64), and so appeared the leafy imperial avenues and whitewashed residences

Above: gateway to the 16th-century citadel of Purana Qila
Right: busy, narrow streets typical of Old Delhi

that still characterize New Delhi. The official inauguration took place in 1931. Just 16 years later Independence provided the first momentous occasion for the new capital to witness massive celebrations.

TODAY'S FACE Lutyens designed the city for some 70,000 inhabitants, and it now has a population of over 170 times that figure, which creates havoc with the overstretched infrastructure. Attempts are being made to cater to the poor, whether with public housing (usually inexpensively built concrete apartment blocks), or night dormitories for the homeless. Few tourists see the living conditions of an estimated 30 percent of the population, squeezed into shacks around the perimeter, although sleeping bodies on the sidewalks of the center are a common sight. Just as typical are shining new sports stadiums, the now ubiquitous cellphone, golf clubs, and an optimistic buzz in the streets. This is India's duality: prosperity and modern technology alongside low living, and it is visible to an even greater extent in other cities. Delhi is a city worth giving time to, as it effortlessly encapsulates so many stark contradictions.

INDEPENDENT DELHI
"Temples, mosques and Sikh gurudwaras were outlined in garlands of light bulbs. So, too, was the Red Fort of the Moghul emperors. New Delhi's newest temple, Birla Mandir, with its curlicue spires and domes hung with lights, looked to one passerby like a hallucination of Ludwig of Bavaria. In the Bangi Sweepers Colony, among whose Untouchables Gandhi had often dwelt, independence had brought a gift that many of those wretched people had never known—light."
Larry Collins and Dominique Lapierre, *Freedom at Midnight*, 1975

57

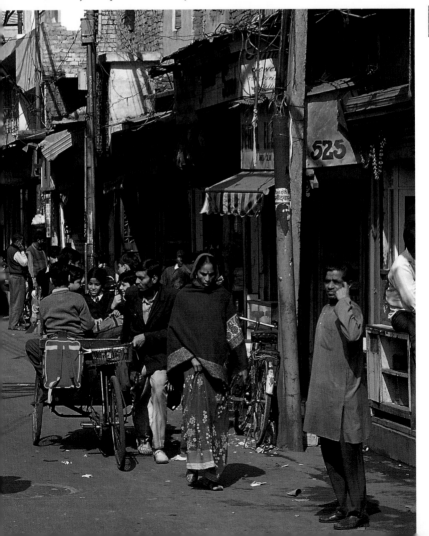

Delhi

VILLAGE IN THE CITY

The Crafts Museum has steered clear of locking objects in the past. Instead, it interweaves past and present, so following the timeless traditions of Indian crafts. Fragments are displayed in glass cases without captions, so that India's dense craft history is left open to interpretation. Charles Correa's architecture adds to the sense of spontaneity, while the presence of 50 artists and craftspeople (fewer during the monsoon when they must work indoors), who are invited on a monthly basis, gives a living dimension. The adjoining village complex, a remnant of an exhibition set up in 1972, has been decorated by visiting tribal and rural painters.

58

Statue of Gandhi, Gandhi Darshan and Gandhi National Museum

▶▶▶ Crafts Museum　　　54C2

Pragati Maidan, Bhairon Marg
Open: Museum Tue–Sun 10–5. Village and craft demonstrations daily 10–5:30.
Admission free

This exemplary complex, a relative newcomer on the Delhi cultural scene, offers a fabulous view of India's multifarious crafts. Innovatively designed by contemporary Indian architect Charles Correa, the museum is meant to resemble an Indian street, with tiled roofs, courtyards, shrines, passages, and carved doors. A large courtyard is set aside for invited craftspeople to demonstrate and sell their creations. Whatever your preference—the giant 18th-century *bhuta* figures from Karnataka, the fine tribal bronzes of Orissa, sacred Jain cloth paintings, or the entire carved courtyard house from Gujarat—it is an exceptional display. Leave plenty of time to explore the village dwellings, and don't miss the excellent, well-priced selection of handmade crafts in the store.

▶▶ Gandhi Darshan and Gandhi　54C3
National Museum

Raj Ghat
Open: Tue–Sun 9:30–5:30. Admission: inexpensive

This park on the banks of the Yamuna River is where Mahatma Gandhi, Indira Gandhi (who was Nehru's daughter), and her son Rajiv were all cremated. Memorials commemorate them. Immediately opposite stand pavilions with photographs, letters, and paintings illustrating the life of the Mahatma and his inestimable contribution to India's independence struggle, that tragically ended with his assassination by a Hindu militant in 1948.

▶▶▶ Indira Gandhi Memorial Museum　54A2

Safdarjang Road
Open: Tue–Sun 9:30–5. Admission free

The elegant whitewashed house where Indira Gandhi lived out her political career now houses a fascinating photographic display covering her life. Visitors flock here on weekends, ending the carefully defined tour at the spot in the garden where she was assassinated in 1984. Photos, excerpts from her speeches, letters, personal accounts (including the premonitory one made shortly before her death), and press coverage are presented beside selected memorabilia (including her spectacles and blood-stained sari). There are views into the family rooms from the exterior. Her close relationship with her father, Jawarharlal Nehru, and her sons, Sanjay and Rajiv, is apparent. The last room is devoted to the tragedy of Rajiv's own life and assassination in 1991. Altogether the

museum paints a captivating picture of the woman who did so much to shape contemporary India.

Sandstone frieze from Sultan Ghari's tomb in the National Museum

▶▶▶ National Museum 54B2

Janpath
Open: Tue–Sun 10–5. Admission: inexpensive

Over 200,000 exhibits of Indian and foreign origin covering 5,000 years of history are displayed in this airy modern museum inaugurated in 1960. Laid out on three floors, the collection is actually too rich and large to take in on one visit and it is worth picking up a plan to define where your interests lie. The first floor covers India's early civilizations, from the Indus Valley to Gandhara and Gupta pieces, Cholan bronzes, and Tantric art. An extensive Buddhist gallery includes the relics of Buddha unearthed in Piprahwa and over 80 superb *thangkas* (Buddhist scrolls), sculptures, and terra-cottas. The decorative arts section contains some outstanding exhibits, such as an intricately carved ivory screen, an elaborate silver *huqqa* (water pipe), and a room full of jewelry that no maharana would reject. Upstairs are miniatures (17th to 19th century), and manuscripts, while the more limited top floor covers pre-Columbian art. The displays are often reshuffled to accommodate temporary exhibitions, but there is always a wealth of treasures to admire.

▶▶ Nehru Memorial Museum 54A2

Teen Murti Bhavan, Teen Murti Marg
Open: Tue–Sun 10–4:45. Admission free

This imposing 1930s palace surrounded by lawns and rose gardens is devoted to the life of Jawarharlal Nehru, who lived here as India's first Prime Minister, from 1947 through 1964. Less dynamic in spirit than the museum devoted to his daughter Indira Gandhi (see opposite), it nevertheless offers fascinating insights, through the photographic display, into Nehru's British education at Harrow and Cambridge, his prodigious interests and the early years of the independence movement. Formal reception rooms, his study, and the bedroom where he died, all packed with hundreds of books and memorabilia, add to the portrait of this far-sighted statesman. His interest in astronomy is recalled in the neighboring planetarium, where English language shows are staged on Tuesday and Sunday at 11 AM and 3 PM.

RAILROAD BAZAAR
At the southern end of the Embassy quarter of Chanakyapuri and a short rickshaw ride from the Indira Gandhi Memorial Museum is a railroad enthusiast's paradise, the National Rail Museum (*Open* Tue–Sun 9:30–1, 2–5). Whether or not you have experienced the wonders of India's rail transportation, this is an excellent way to learn about its background. Outside stands a collection of vintage locomotives and cars that include gilded Maharaja specials and India's first train, an 1855 steam locomotive. Model trains are displayed in the indoor section.

Above: Humayun's Tomb, a Mughal masterpiece
Right: the beautifully colonnaded Quwwat-al-Islam mosque, dating back to the 12th century

HUMAYUN'S CONTRIBUTION
The history of Delhi from the late 12th century is one of a succession of conquerors, each leaving an important mark on the face of the city. With the advent of the first Mughal ruler, Babur (1526–1530), Indo-Islamic culture began to blossom, but it was thanks to his son, Humayun, that the art of miniature painting was adopted and developed in India. This was a result of Humayun's enforced exile by the Afghan rebel Sher Shah, which led him to spend 15 years at the Persian court. Here he became enamored of the art of miniatures. On recapturing Delhi in 1556 he was accompanied by two Persian masters who were to found the new Mughal school of Indian miniatures.

▶▶▶ Humayun's Tomb   54C1

Mathura Road, Nizamuddin
Open: daily dawn–dusk. Admission: inexpensive

This was the first example of a Mughal garden tomb in India and remains Delhi's best-preserved Mughal structure. It was built in the late 1560s (and completed in 1573), by Humayun's widow, who camped on site during construction, and was later buried beside her husband. The 125 foot-high double dome, arches, and symmetrical layout of the water channels and walled garden (*char-bagh* or quartered garden) were all later copied, notably at the Taj Mahal, but their origin lies in Central Asia. The tomb was also the final refuge of Delhi's last emperor, Bahadur Shah II, before he capitulated to the British in 1857. Humayun's white marble tomb itself lies inside the towering octagonal structure of red sandstone inlaid with white and black marble. Lattice screens of stone and marble and endless arches enhance the rhythmic geometry of the building. There are several other tombs at the site. The shady lawns are a pleasant place to retreat from Delhi traffic, and are far less visited than Old Delhi's equivalent, the Red Fort.

▶ Lodi Gardens and Tombs   54B1

Lodi Road
Open: daily dawn–dusk. Admission free

Another escape route from pollution lies in these delightful and historic gardens and tombs constructed by the Sayyid and Lodi dynasties (see page 43). Flowers, lawns and scurrying squirrels surround a cluster of 15th- and 16th-century tombs, with joggers and juvenile cricketers weaving their way in between. The largest, most central structure is the low-domed Bara Gumbad (1494) and its adjacent mosque. About 55 yards. north of this lies the Sheesh Gumbad. The tomb of Mohammed Shah (1450), the third Sayyid ruler, prefigures the Mughal style of Humayun's tomb.

▶▶ Purana Qila   54C2

Mathura Road
Open: daily dawn–dusk. Admission: inexpensive

This 16th-century walled citadel was built on the

legendary site of Indraprastha, the 1000 BC Aryan capital, by the rival emperors Humayun and Sher Shah. The picturesque stone ramparts, gateways, and *chhatris* (domed, open-sided pavilions) dominate Mathura Road, where the main entrance leads through the imposing Bara Darwaza. Inside stands Sher Shah's most outstanding monument, the well preserved Qila-i-Kuhna mosque (1541), built in typical Mughal style of sandstone inlaid with marble. Immediately south stands a two-story octagonal tower, probably used as a library and observatory. This is where Humayun accidentally met his death in 1556, reputedly rushing to the call of the *muezzin*. Overgrown paths and the occasional *sadhu* add to the fort's atmosphere of crumbling glory.

▶ ▶ ▶ Qutb Minar
Aurobindo Marg, Mahrauli
Open: daily dawn–dusk.
Admission: inexpensive

Delhi's oldest monument, dating from the 1190s, takes some getting to as it is now engulfed by an inglorious suburb served by potholed highways on the far southern outskirts. Yet it is a striking memorial to the triumphant arrival of Islam. The tapered

minar (main tower), 240 feet high with a base diameter of over 45 feet, still dominates the area, 800 years on. It was built as a victory monument by Qutb-ud-din-Aibak, the successor of the Afghan conqueror Muhammed Ghuri.

From the main entrance a path leads through the verdant complex to the tower. It is faced with Koranic inscriptions, above which it rises in sections to the summit. These are a result of its lengthy construction period and successive patrons. The 379 steps inside are now closed to the public following various fatal accidents.

Adjoining the tower are the beautiful colonnaded courtyards of the Quwwat-al-Islam mosque, built in the same period using stone from demolished Hindu and Jain temples and twice extended later. At the center stands a 4th-century relic of the Gupta period, a black iron pillar that was originally part of a Vishnu temple. Immediately to the north stands the rough beginnings of another tower, the Ala'i Minar, initially intended to rise above the Qutb Minar but stopped at just over 82 feet. Other structures of interest include the Ala'i Darwaza (south gate—AD 1311), several tombs and a *madhrasa* (Islamic college). Guides, drinks, and snacks are readily available.

THE IRON ENIGMA
The secret of the iron pillar in the Qutb Minar complex has yet to be unlocked. Sanskrit inscriptions on the pillar reveal that it honored Vishnu in memory of a 4th-century Gupta king, and it was once crowned by a *Garuda*, the mythical bird-man that Vishnu rides. However no one has fathomed how it came to this spot nor how the cast iron has remained so impeccably rust-free over a period of some 1,600 years. Legend has it that whoever manages to stretch his arms backward and embrace the pillar—as many have done—will have good fortune, but it is now fenced off.

Muslim girl at the Jama Masjid

OLD DELHI Despite its name, Old Delhi is far from being the oldest part of the capital, as it dates from the mid-17th century when Shah Jahan moved back to Delhi from Agra. A decade of frenetic building produced a walled city, Shahjahanabad, punctuated by 14 gates and crossed by the main shopping street, Chandni Chowk. India's largest mosque, the Jama Masjid, was built near by and the Lal Qila (Red Fort) erected on the banks of the Yamuna River. Only five of the gates still stand and the fortress palace is suffering from the effects of time and tourists, but Chandni Chowk and the Jama Masjid continue to function as if the centuries had never passed.

▶▶▶ Jama Masjid   54B4
Open: daily dawn–dusk. Admission free

The so-called "Friday Mosque", dating from 1656 and an integral part of Shah Jahan's plan, stands south of Chandni Chowk by Delhi Gate. A vast open courtyard is enclosed by a low arcade with three massive gates on the north, east, and south sides, each approached by exterior stairs where visitors should remove their shoes. To the west, the direction of Mecca, rise three generous domes and two towering minarets overshadowing the covered prayer hall and *mihrab* (prayer niche). It is possible to climb the southern tower (small admission charge) for a fabulous view over Delhi. At the center of the 2,953 square foot courtyard is a large pool where Muslims perform their ablutions before prayer. Beside it stands a platform designed so that a second prayer leader could copy the main *imam* inside, although today's loudspeakers have made this redundant.

▶▶▶ Lal Qila (Red Fort) 54C4
Netaji Subhash Marg
Open: daily dawn–dusk.
Admission: inexpensive

The main entrance to this huge palace of 1648 lies on the west side by a parking lot. Beyond the main gateway is a covered bazaar, Chatta Chowk, now lined with the usual predictable souvenir shops. From here an open space stretches to the pretty red sandstone Hathi Pol (Elephant Gate, also called Drum Gate), where visitors once dismounted from their traditional transportation before entering the royal palace, serenaded from the musicians' gallery above.

A path leads between lawns to the Diwan-i-Am, a raised, colonnaded hall dominated by a throne where the ruler gave public audiences. Today's somewhat bare aspect belies its original opulence when it was draped in fine cloths and silk carpets, and the polished plaster surfaces were painted with intricate floral designs. From here a path leads left (north) through the

gardens, which were originally landscaped as a *char-bagh*, with fountains and canals dividing the symmetrical layout. At the far northern end of the gardens stand pavilions, including the octagonal Shahi Burj in the northeast corner.

Walking south from here along the walls that once overlooked the Yamuna River (it has since shifted), you come to the tiny Moti Masjid, an ornate white mosque built by the last Mughal emperor, Aurangzeb *ca*1660. Next are the *hammam* (bath) rooms, with water channels laid into the floor and fountains that once spouted rose water. Beyond stands the finest structure of the fort, the white marble Diwan-i-Khas, where the emperor held private audiences. Although the inlaid precious stones and gold and silver ceiling have disappeared, the delicate structure has echoes of its early grandeur. The adjoining Khas Mahal served as the emperor's private palace and has some remarkable carved marble screens separating the different areas.

Next, to the south and fronting a garden, is the Rang Mahal (Palace of Color) where the extensive harem was housed. Again, sadly, most of its extravagant decoration (mirror mosaic, gold and silver inlay, fine paintwork) has long since gone, although the cooling "stream of paradise" remains, albeit now waterless.

Completing the circuit is the Mumtaz Mahal (Palace of Jewels), once an annex of the women's palace and now converted into a small, but very worthwhile museum with a wide variety of archeological and other exhibits (*Open* Sat–Thu 10–5. *Admission: inexpensive*, get ticket from the window in Hathi Pol before you enter the palace). From here, a path leads back past a drinks stand to Hathi Pol.

THE SUN AND THE MOON
The southernmost room of the Khas Mahal, known as the Tosh Khana (Robe Room), displays a superb filigree marble screen. Looking from the north (that is, facing the throne-room of the Diwan-i-Khas) you can see a bas-relief of the scales of justice surrounded by small suns. The sun was a symbol of royalty, much used by the Rajputs of Rajasthan and also by Shah Jahan's French near-contemporary, Louis XIV. When viewed from the south, the scales of justice are surrounded by moons.

63

Lal Qila, or Red Fort, is so named because of its red sandstone walls

For nearly 20 years Sir Edwin Lutyens struggled to produce a style of architecture in keeping with India's Imperial status and reflective of its context. Hampered by the demands of officialdom and obsessed with classicism, he nevertheless created a green capital long before the concept became fashionable elsewhere.

VICEROY'S HOUSE

Now renamed Rashtrapati Bhavan and occupied by the President of India, this vast palace suffers from one of Lutyens' mistakes, as he himself confessed. Miscalculating the gradient of Raisini Hill, he realized too late that the palace would not be entirely visible from the base of the processional route on Rajpath. Nor did his concerns include the number of servants needed to keep the 340 rooms shipshape and the 321 acres of gardens manicured. Under Mountbatten, over 400 gardeners were employed, including 50 bird chasers. More successful than Lutyens' perspective calculations, the central dome recalls that of the Buddhist *stupa* at Sanchi.

Rashtrapati Bhavan, formerly the Viceroy's House, in New Delhi was designed by Lutyens

Sir Edwin Lutyens (1869–1944) was an architect steeped in the imperial grandeur of the Edwardian years. This made him the ideal candidate for drawing up an urban plan for the new Delhi—an architect's dream project as it was to include monumental symbols of the empire. Working beside Lutyens was his friend Herbert Baker, who in 1912 became responsible for the design of the Secretariat and the Legislative Assembly, leaving the Viceroy's House to Lutyens.

Clash of wills Their task was far from simple, as opinions ranged from that of George V, demanding something resembling the style of the Mughal landmarks, to the Viceroy Hardinge, who wanted a western design with "oriental motifs". Add to these the liberal voice of Bernard Shaw advocating a totally Indian approach, and you have stylistic and conceptual conflict. Lutyens himself took an obstinate stand: "Personally, I do not believe there is any real Indian architecture or any great tradition. There are just spurts by various mushroom dynasties with as much intellect as there is in any other art nouveau."

Fancy dress Lutyens insisted that there were two ways of transferring Western ideas into an alien environment, either to produce "fancy dress" (meaning a hybrid design) or to create "an Englishman dressed for the climate". The latter he achieved in the elegant residential bungalows of the Lodi Estate where the English style is clad in Indian, Persian, Palladian, or Grecian clothing. For his government buildings, Lutyens bowed to pressure by adding the odd *chhatri* and other local features to what were essentially grandiose English buildings.

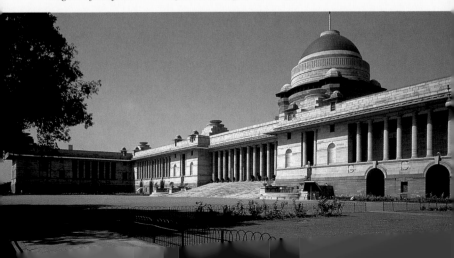

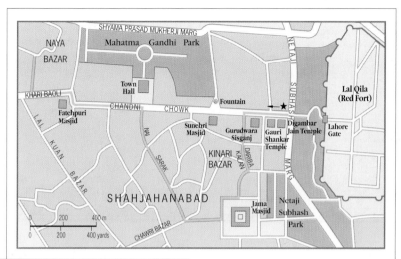

Walk

Old Delhi

Start at the southeastern corner of Chandni Chowk at the Digambar Jain temple. This red sandstone temple (1656) houses a bird hospital from which, in true Jain life-preserving style, the cured patients are released to liberty. There is also some impressive decoration surrounding the main shrine dedicated to Parshvanath, the 23rd manifestation of Mahavir. Immediately west, and announced by mounds of fragrant garlands, is the marble Gauri Shankar temple, Delhi's most sacred Siva temple, sheltering an ancient 12th-century *lingam*.

Following Chandni Chowk west through the mayhem of shoppers, vendors and traffic, the next spiritual landmark is the Gurudwara Sisganj, a Sikh temple. This stands just beyond the corner of Dariba Kalan, a turn to the left that runs through the heart of the Kinari Bazar. Here the lanes are crammed with numerous tiny stores—glittering jewelers' and suppliers of festival finery—foodbooths and

shoppers. Try to follow Dariba Kalan south, making a few detours, until it ends at the massive Jama Masjid. After visiting the mosque, go to its northwestern corner, Chawri Bazar, once famed for dancing girls but now specializing in papermaking and selling a huge amount of metalwork. Head north to Nai Sarak. This is another main artery, with stores dealing in books, stationery, blankets and woolen garments. These stores offer endless bargains.

Continue back to Chandni Chowk, turn left and head west to Naya Bazar on Khari Baoli. This pungent spice market is the main wholesale center for Delhi, so traffic in this area is dense. After glimpsing Fatehpuri Masjid, hail a rickshaw and head back to New Delhi.

Shoppers taking advantage of one of the many rickshaws in Old Delhi

Oberoi Maidens, Old Delhi, providing atmospheric, colonial-style luxury

Accommodations

Delhi, like Mumbai (Bombay), is far from being a budget-traveler's paradise. Accommodations follow the pattern of real estate and come at a price, about twice to three times that of the rest of India. There are four main areas: Old Delhi, Connaught Place, Sunder Nagar, and the expensive hotel district of the Lodi Estate and Chanakyapuri. Delhi's sights are scattered, but transportation remains reasonably inexpensive (after bargaining) and each quarter has its attractions, so ultimately your decision will depend on budget and room availability. Reservations for mid-range and luxury accommodations can be made on arrival at the airport and train station tourist offices, but for budget accommodations just hire a rickshaw and search.

CENTRAL Old Delhi has the atmospheric Oberoi Maidens at the top of the range, and peeling hovels with shared bathrooms at the bottom. There is not much choice in the middle except for the excellent Broadway, well placed between Old Delhi and Connaught Place. In busy Paharganj, near New Delhi's train station, there is a concentration of budget accommodations, mostly insalubrious and with shared facilities. Exceptions are the Metropolis and Star Palace Hotel, both of which benefit from the lively atmosphere of the Main Bazaar. Further south around Connaught Place, Delhi's commercial hub, lies a wide range of accommodation, for example the popular Nirula's and the large Hotel Marina and, farther south down Janpath, the plush refurbished Imperial, complete with pool and gardens. This area is particularly convenient for restaurants and shopping.

SOUTHWARD Farther south a handful of hotels surround the antique stores and gentrified residences of Sunder Nagar. This peaceful, convenient location is much favored by businessmen, and if there were more restaurants it would make an excellent tourist base. Southwest of India Gate lies a nucleus of luxury accommodations, including the traditional Claridges, the reliable Taj Mahal, Ashok and, farther afield in Chanakyapuri, the Maurya Sheraton and the Taj Palace.

Restaurants

Delhi's eating places are as varied as its history, ranging from roadside booths selling samosas to top-class restaurants in the luxury hotels. Although prices are high at the latter establishments, many serve excellent value lunchtime buffets. Most mid-range restaurants are gloomy, indoor affairs (though with air conditioning); if you want to eat outside, the best choices are hotels such as the Imperial with its pleasant garden bar and restaurant.

CENTRAL EATS Connaught Place has a concentration of restaurants, coffee shops, and fast-food outlets that are as popular with office workers as with tourists. Most offer Western-style cuisine beside the North Indian classics and also serve beer. The United Coffee House is particularly lively and has excellent service. Nonsmokers and vegetarians might enjoy the neighboring Kovil, a stylishly decorated South Indian restaurant.
The Rodeo offers a complete contrast: tequila slammers to wash down the tortillas, and waiters in cowboy gear. The ever popular Nirula's offers several different restaurants, while those with a yen for the familiar will be able to find branches of some western fast-food chains.

Beyond this area, heading towards Lal Qila (Red Fort), is the excellent Chor Bizarre in the Hotel Broadway where delicious Kashmiri and Tandoori dishes are served in gangster-style surroundings complete with a vintage getaway car. Farther south down Janpath, Le Méridien houses Delhi's best French restaurant, the classic Pierre, and also offers excellent multi-cuisine lunchtime buffets or Continental and Indian dinners at Le Belvédère.

SUBURBAN SAMPLING South of India Gate in the smarter residential areas there is a vast choice of restaurants, but they can be reached only by long taxi rides. Closest is the Ambassador Hotel's highly recommended South Indian restaurant, Dasaprakash. Its Chinese Room specializes in Szechuan and Cantonese cuisine. Make the effort to reach the gentrified area of Hauz Khas and you will have a wide choice at the popular restaurant complex of the village Bistro, near the Deer Park.

A cup of hot, sweet tea or chai is never far from hand in Delhi

EATING HOURS
The more expensive restaurants are usually open 12:30–3 and 7:30–11:30. Some hotel coffee shops have 24-hour service. Establishments around Connaught Place are open from breakfast until 11 PM or midnight and serve anything from a coffee or a Kingfisher beer to a full-blown meal.

Delhi

OPENING HOURS
Government emporia open
10–6; private stores operate 9:30–7:30, and often
close for a one-hour lunch.
All stores around
Connaught Place,
Janpath, Sunder Nagar,
Chandni Chowk and the
Santushti Arcade are
closed on Sundays. This
is the day to head south
for the market and stores
at Lajpat Nagar (closed
Monday) or Hauz Khas
(closed Tuesday).

Shopping

Delhi is full of places that tempt you to empty your wallet. Bargaining is part of any transaction except in fixed-price state emporia and the more expensive stores, places which for some visitors will be a relief. Avoid being whisked away to a "special address" by your rickshaw or taxi driver as drivers' commissions are built into the price you will pay, adding on 20–40 percent.

Visitors interested in handmade crafts should visit the Crafts Museum (see page 58) as its store and the resident craftspeople offer a selection of quality goods at reasonable prices. Near here, at Sunder Nagar, is Delhi's antique market, in reality a string of specialist stores where you can stock up on anything from carved chairs to bronze Buddhas—all at a price. A favorite for quality furnishings and contemporary Indian designs is the Santushti Shopping Arcade, NWC Race Course near Chanakyapuri, where individual stores are dotted around a pretty garden. Just south of Sarojini train station is Dilli Haat, a market for crafts (and cuisine) from many regions. Even farther south, and equally fashionable with the local clientele, are the excellent and varied stores of Hauz Khas Village. Back in the center, Connaught Place is always a useful area for a variety of goods, including a wide selection of books at Bookworm (B-29) and the New Book Depot (B-18). Don't miss exploring the Palika Bazaar, an underground shopping mall entered from the corner of Janpath, which offers a cornucopia of goods. Two blocks down Janpath opposite a string of so called "Tibetan" stores is the government-run Central Cottage Industries Emporium, with a wide selection of handmade crafts, carpets, household goods, and fabrics. More spread out but with an even greater choice are the various state emporia and the excellent stores selling *khadi* (handmade, hand-printed cloth) along Baba Kharak Singh Marg running southwest of Connaught Place. Best of all for everyday domestic goods, saris, and spices, there is the entire bazaar area of Old Delhi to check out.

Traders sell a wide range of merchandise, but be prepared to bargain

Practical details

One of Delhi's ubiquitous black-and-yellow taxis

WARNING At New Delhi train station deal *only* with the International Tourist Bureau on the second floor—staircase to the left of the main information board. Ignore anyone, however plausible, who tells you it is elsewhere.

MOBILITY For a quick overview of Delhi's scattered and numerous monuments, take a guided tour. The ITDC (tel: 332 0031), and Delhi Tourism (tel: 331 5322/4229), offer similar tours, lasting a half day or full day. Otherwise getting around the vast expanse of Delhi is best done by taxi or auto-rickshaw, as buses are confusing, overcrowded, and favorite haunts of pickpockets. Although taxis are metered, it is rare to find a driver who uses the meter for foreigners. If he does, an adjustment should be made to the meter fare—ask to see his fare chart. If your time is short, negotiate a half-day or full-day rate: this saves energy. Hotel staff will give advice on a reasonable current rate. Bicycle rickshaws are banned from the center.

GUIDES There is no shortage of English-speaking guides at each monument but ask to see their official identification as unofficial guides are legion, usually loitering around the ticket offices outside.

MONEY Delhi banks are open Mon–Fri 10–2 and Sat 10–noon. Outside these hours you can change money at Thomas Cook's at the Imperial Hotel, at the Ashok Hotel's 24-hour Central Bank, or at the airport. Otherwise there are plenty of authorized money changers at large hotels and certain stores but these are usually for customers only. Avoid street touts—an apparent gain is generally a loss.

CULTURE To get the most out of Delhi and to get a flavor of Indian cultural life, sample the art exhibitions, concerts, and dance and yoga courses. The best source of information is the weekly listings magazine, *Delhi Diary*, available at large hotels or from newsstands on Connaught Place.

TOURIST OFFICES
Government of India Tourist Office, 88 Janpath (*Open* Mon–Fri 9–6, Sat 9–4:30; tel: 011 332 0005/0008/0342, fax: 011 332 0109, www.tourismindia.com). Counters at airports.
ITDC, L-Block, Connaught Place (*Open* daily 7 AM–9 PM; tel/fax: 011 332 0331).
DTDC, N-36 Connaught Place (*Open* daily 7 AM–9 PM. tel: 011 331 4229/5322, tel/fax: 011 331 3637, email: info@delhitourism.com, www.delhitourism.com). State Emporia Complex, Baba Kharak Singh Road (*Open* daily 7 AM–9 PM).

SON ET LUMIÈRE
Soak up Delhi history in sound and light shows at Lal Qila (covering 326 years) or Purana Qila (from the *Mahabharata* to Independence). English performances, lasting an hour, begin between 7:30 PM and 9 PM depending on the season. Reserve through Government of India Tourist Office or ITDC for Lal Qila and DTDC for Purana Qila (*Admission: moderate*)

The Northwest

▶▶▶ **REGION HIGHLIGHTS**

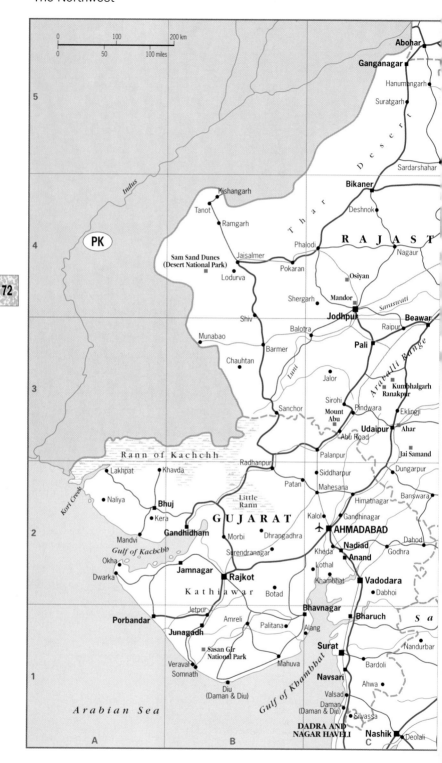

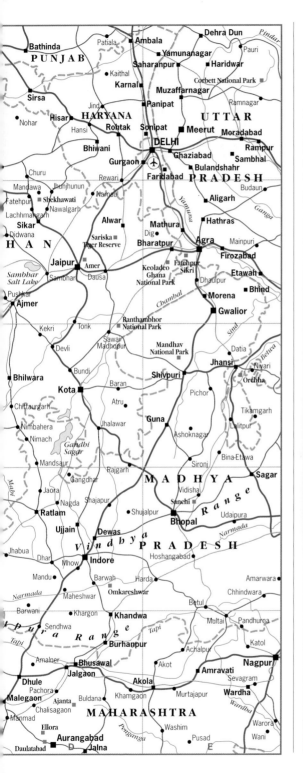

*Previous pages:
celebrating Rajput style,
Jaipur
Below: Rajasthani
woman dressed in
dazzling colors*

The Northwest

74

PALATIAL TRAINS

Rajasthan and Gujarat have two luxury train services, best described as first-class traveling hotels, that recall a glorious past.

The Palace-on-Wheels uses replicas of cars originally built for maharajas and the British viceroys, and operates week-long tours. Starting at Delhi, it rattles to Jaipur, Amer, Jaisalmer, Sam dunes, Jodhpur, Ranthambhor, Chittaurgarh, Udaipur, Bharatpur, Fatehpur Sikri, Agra, and back to Delhi. Travel is overnight with the day free for sightseeing and shopping. This is a marvelous way to cover the major sights of India's most popular tourist area.

The equally stylish Royal Orient, also takes a week Delhi to Delhi, visiting Chittaurgarh, Udaipur, Junagadh, Somnath, Sasan Gir, Diu, Palitana, Sarkhej, Ahmadabad, Jaipur, and Amer.

These top-price tours can be reserved through Palace-on-Wheels, RTDC, Bikaner House, Pandara Road, New Delhi (tel: 011 338 1884/6069, fax: 011 338 2823, email: jaipur.rtdc@jpl.dot.net.in), or Royal Orient, HK House, Ashram Road, Ahmadabad (tel: 079 658 9172/7217, fax: 079 658 2183, email: tcogl@edl.vsnl.net.in).

U.K. agents for both: Peregrine Holidays/Indian Experience, 41 South Parade, Summertown, Oxford, OX2 7JP (tel: 01865 559988, fax: 01865 512583, email: palace@peregrineholidays. co.uk) and SD Enterprises, Wembley (tel: 020 8903 3411, fax: 020 8903 0392, email: dandpani @dircon.co.uk).

U.S. agents: Sita World Travel Inc., Burbank, CA (tel: 818/990-9530, fax: 818/990-9762) and Travel Corp (India) Ltd, New York (tel: 212/935-4825, fax: 212/753-3956).

NORTHWEST Nudging India's border with Pakistan are two major states: Rajasthan and Gujarat. Desert, scrub, and forested hills are their terrain, and palaces, forts, and Jain temples are their landmarks. Rajasthan is the most visited Indian state and Gujarat one of the least visited, but both are now suffering from the effects of a long drought.

CONTRASTS The impressive expanse of Rajasthan's Thar Desert ends to the east at the Aravalli Range and to the south in Gujarat's Kathiawar peninsula. These clear geographical frontiers outline the desert provinces of Jaisalmer, Jodhpur, Bikaner, and Khachchh, where populated outposts are few and far between, but when they do appear, are breathtaking. Beyond the Aravallis is a dense concentration of former Rajput principalities, their hunting reserves converted into wildlife sanctuaries, their monkey-ridden forts into museums and their maharajas' palaces into luxury hotels. Here too are fabulously painted *havelis*, such as in the crumbling villages of Shekhawati, and the jewel-like lake city of Udaipur. Though less scenic, the Kathiawar peninsula has interesting spots, and some beaches.

CROSSROADS Both states have a strong history of trading that enabled wealthy rulers, nobles, and merchants to pour profits into fabulous mansions and palaces. In Gujarat, the Portuguese traded at the ports of Diu and Daman in the 16th century, and soon after the first British outpost was established at the port of Surat. For centuries earlier these ports were used by pilgrims to Mecca and traders from Arabia, Africa, and Central Asia. The harsh desert climate has inspired some monumental structures, such as the Aina Mahal in Bhuj, the golden sandstone ramparts of Jaisalmer, the exquisite fort palaces of Jodhpur and Bikaner, and the mirror-encrusted, white-washed mud huts of the Kachchh's Rabari tribe.

CITY LIFE The only large cities are Jaipur, capital of Rajasthan, and Ahmadabad, former (and still unofficial) capital of Gujarat. Both cities offer fascinating cultural introductions to their states. Ahmadabad in particular is a vibrant combination of old and new, though somewhat marred by industrialization and congestion. Jaipur is the crafts capital *par excellence*, where numerous specialist bazaars trade in jewelry, embroidery, fabrics, miniature painting, pottery, leather ware, or carpets made in the city. Jaipur's popularity has made traders particularly sharp, and some visitors find them aggressive. Retreat to Rajasthan's smaller towns, and this problem diminishes.

The Indus Valley, home of the 5,000-year-old Harappan civilization and India's earliest known settlements, has its source in Pakistan but includes part of Rajasthan and Gujarat. One of the most impressive sites is at Lothal, south of Ahmadabad near the Gulf of Khambhat. Mud-brick ruins clearly delineate this port and citadel, laid out in a grid pattern, where finds have included beads, gold, and copper jewelry, ivory work and board games using terra-cotta pieces. From its harbor, boats loaded with semiprecious stones and beads sailed to Iraq, Arabia and Egypt.

PILGRIMAGES Jains have a high profile in this region, with major temple complexes at Palitana, Osiyan, Mount Abu, and Ranakpur, and other important ones at Jaisalmer and Bikaner. Mount Abu and Ranakpur have 11th-century temples featuring spectacular carving. Palitana's 863 temples beckon from a summit reached by over 3,000 steps; steps also lead to the temples on Mount Girnar at Junagadh. Osiyan, remote and requiring effort to visit, has the region's oldest Jain structures.

BACK TO NATURE There are relaxing beaches on the little island of Diu in Gujarat. The northwest also has numerous wildlife sanctuaries, with Asiatic lions at Sasan Gir, tigers at Ranthambhor and Sariska, and prolific birds at Keoladeo (Bharatpur). The scrub and sand dunes of the Thar Desert itself offer plentiful sightings of desert foxes and cats, black buck, eagles, and the great Indian bustard.

BALANCE The dynamism of Rajasthan's tourist services, its rich and romantic heritage, the temptations of palace-hotels, and the added draw of riotous festivals mean that little can stop the inexorable advance of tourism. Its main towns feel increasingly artificial, and a trip into the more low-key Gujarat helps redress the balance.

Above: the golden city of Jaisalmer, perched above the Thar Desert
Below: a café in Pushkar, Rajasthan

Below: Ahmadabad, with a foreground of marigold—much used in Hindu worship
Right: the "shaking minarets" of Sidi Bashir

Gujarat

▶▶ Ahmadabad 72C2

The hot, dusty and chaotic city of Ahmadabad ("Ahmbad") was replaced as Gujarat's capital in 1970 by the new city of Gandhinagar, about 20 miles to the north. However it is Ahmadabad that reveals the spirit, dynamism, and history of Gujarat through a wealth of fine museums and an exceptional crafts tradition developed by the Mughals. At its heart, on the right bank of the wide Sabarmati River (often completely dry), is the old fortified city erected in the early 1400s by Ahmed Shah, ruler of Gujarat. Several original gates survive, as do traditional *havelis*, while veiled Muslim women, markets, mosques, camels, and fax offices coexist picturesquely. West of the river is the administrative new town, bristling with modern architecture. Many hotels lie just across Nehru bridge in Khanpur, a lively part of the old town. Ahmadabad's traffic is appalling and the scattered sights are not always known by auto-rickshaw drivers, so allow plenty of time for traveling.

Textile mania First priority for any visitor should be the fabulous **Calico Museum▶▶▶** (*Open* Thu–Tue. *Admission free*, only on guided tours; in English at 10:30 and 2:45, lasting about two hours); located at Shahibag in the northeast of the city. This exemplary private foundation is housed in a superb 17th-century *haveli* standing in lovely gardens. It displays a superlative collection of textiles, embroidery, carpets, and costumes alongside a gallery of miniatures and bronzes, and a research center. The highly informative tours explain the background to the priceless exhibits, many of which originated in the imperial workshops established by Akbar at Agra, Lahore, and Ahmadabad, while others demonstrate the richness of indigenous techniques.

Folk customs South of the city, across Sardar bridge, is the unusual **Kite Museum▶** (*Open* Tue–Sun 10–noon, 4–6. *Admission: inexpensive*), with hundreds of exhibits reflecting Ahmadabad's obsession with kites, which culminates in a kite-flying festival every January 14. Everyday items

are the focus of a quirky private collection in the **Utensils Museum▶** which is located in the Vishalla restaurant complex, Sarkatj Road (*Open* daily 10–8 PM. *Admission: inexpensive*). Among the exhibits in the **Institute of Indology Museum▶**, Gujarat University (*Open* Mon–Sat 11–5:30. *Admission: inexpensive*) is a fine collection of items connected with Jainism.

Folk traditions are explored in depth at the **Shreyas Folk Museum▶▶**, Shreyas Hill (*Open* Tue–Sun winter 10:30–5:30, summer 8:30–1. *Admission: moderate*), which contains a fabulous collection of toys, costumes, jewelry, furniture, utensils, and metalwork. The rich tribal traditions of the region are also explored at the **Tribal Museum▶**, Gujarat Vidyapith, Ashram Road (*Open* Mon–Fri 11:30–7:30, Sat 11:30–2:30. *Admission: inexpensive*). North along this road is **Gandhi's Sabarmati Ashram▶▶** (*Open* daily Apr–Sep 8:30–7, Oct–Mar 8:30–6:30. *Admission free*), where he lived from 1917–1930. It is now a monument to commemorate this remarkable son of Gujarat.

Within the walls The lively old city delineated by Delhi Gate in the north, Kalupur Gate in the east, Khanpur Gate in the west and Jamalpur Gate in the south, radiates from Ahmed Shah's Bhadra fort (1411). Now mostly administrative offices, it is surrounded by Ahmed Shah's mosque, the later, more attractive **Sidi Sayid mosque▶** (1570s), and the striking, but always crowded **Jami Masjid▶▶** (1423) that rises to the east. Beyond this is **Manek Chowk▶▶**, a maze of traditional fabric stores and jewelers and the site of the **Rani-ka-Hazira**, the tombs of Ahmed Shah and his wives. On the eastern periphery, near the train station, stand the last surviving "shaking minarets"—15th-century *minars* built by Sidi Bashir to withstand earthquakes. Their soft sandstone foundations allow them to sway, and this can be tested from an upper balcony of the nearby Bibi-ki-Masjid minaret (1454). Other sights of the old city include the equally ingenious **Dada Harini Vav▶▶** (*ca*1500), an elaborately conceived step well (see panel opposite), the large lavishly carved Hathi Singh (1848), one of Ahmadabad's many Jain temples, and the **Rani Rupmati mosque▶**, that combines Hindu and Islamic features of the early 1500s.

TOURIST OFFICES
Gujarat Tourism, (TCGL) HK House, Ashram Road (*Open* Mon–Fri 10:30–1:30, 2–6, also first and third Sat each month).
Large hotels have better information (tel: 079 658 9172/9683, fax: 079 658 2182, email: tcgl.ahd@rmt. sprintrpg.ems.vsnl.net.in).
Tourist Office, Ahmadabad Municipal Corporation, near Khamasa Gate (*open* Mon–Fri 11–6; tel: 079 365610).
Counters at the airport and train stations may also provide useful information.

Nomadic tribal people can still be seen in Gujarat, though many have settled in villages

SHOPPING
Kachchhi tribes produce some of India's most exuberant and intricately worked textiles (see pages 86–87), including bandhani tie-dye in earthy colors, heavily embroidered Ahir mirror-work, and simpler block printing. Shroff Bazar in Bhuj is the place to find them, and while there it is worth tracking down Kachchh Dharshan Handicrafts whose motto "Save time, time is more than money" reflects a wide selection and fair prices. At the eastern end, in Maher Ali Chowk, is Kala Sagar, a small textile store stuffed with a wide selection of Gujarati cottons and embroidered bandhani silks. Prices here are very reasonable, reflecting the low-key nature of Bhuj's tourist trade.

▶ **Bhavnagar**   72C1

Although of no historical interest, the port of Bhavnagar is sometimes a necessary stopover on the long Gujarat trail. It has a handful of decent hotels, from a ritzy palace to an extraordinarily decrepit one crowned by a clock tower in the heart of the bazaar. This atmospheric old part of town, south of the train station, continues its craft traditions and specialist trades, in sharp contrast to the region's greatest economic asset, **Alang▶**, 31 miles south. This is the ship cemetery of the world, its high tides used by captains from all over the world to beach obsolete ships and so create an immense scrapyard. After thoroughly picking over the soon-skeletal vessels, local dealers break them up and sell the metal.

▶▶ **Bhuj**   72A2

Bhuj has an indefinable magic and is pleasantly small in scale. Completely isolated in Rann of Kachchh (Kutch), a desert on the Pakistan border, it was ruled by the Khengarji family from 1548 until 1947, and has several palaces, *chhatris*, a hill fort and city walls. In the mid-18th century, the particularly enlightened Maharao Lakhpatji employed a Dutch-trained craftsman, Ramsingh, to design and decorate his palace as well as set up glass and tile factories. Ramsingh's wide-ranging influence is apparent in the unique character of Kachchhi architecture, enamelwork, jewelry, and interior decoration.

Street life Despite recent growth, the population is a modest 200,000, and a colorful mixture of Kachchh tribes-people and Muslim, Jain, and Hindu Gujaratis concentrated in a maze of narrow, brightly colored streets, dense with cows, bicycles, and glittering textiles. Shroff Bazar is the main shopping street; while the market square is near Bhid Gate and boasts a towering, richly carved dovecot. Slow paced, exceptionally friendly, little-visited though offering a good selection of hotels and vegetarian restaurants, Bhuj makes an excellent base from which to discover the Kachchh.

Golden reflections The first area to visit is the northwest of the old town, where two palaces stand within a walled precinct. Ramsingh's **Aina Mahal**▶▶▶ (*Open* Sun–Fri 9–noon, 3–6. *Admission: inexpensive*) contains royal apartments, a museum and the staggeringly decorated Hall of Mirrors. Here, white marble walls are faced with gilt-framed mirrors, and lit by elaborate Venetian chandeliers suspended over a tile-lined pool with a raised platform. Although this hall lies on the third floor, Ramsingh devised pumps and siphons to raise the water and furnish the fountains which sprayed water between flickering candles lining the water channels. The state apartments, blanketed in intricate Kachchhi embroidery, contain an eclectic display: Dutch clocks, clockwork toys, costumes, European glass, Chinese ceramics, drawings by Hogarth, stuffed tigers in the hunting room, and royal portraits studded with the occasional jewel. You can see Ramsingh's glass in colored panels set into lattice walls, and the beautiful Durbar Hall has doors inlaid with shell.

Gateway into Aina Mahal, famed for its elaborate interior decoration

Other sights The neighboring **Prag Mahal**▶ (1870s) is far less imaginative. Designed by a British engineer, it heavily combines Italianate, Victorian, and Kachchhi styles, and has an echoing Durbar Hall faced in false marble, where countless dead beasts stare forlornly from the walls. The best part is a tall clock tower (*Admission: inexpensive*) offering a sweeping 360-degree view. To the southwest, by the large Hamirsar *tank*, stands the gaudy Swaminarayan temple, always packed with devotees and *sadhus*. Across the *tank* is the **Sharad Bagh**▶ (*Open* Sat–Thu 9–noon, 3–6. *Admission: inexpensive*), the Maharao's 1900s winter palace in the former botanical gardens. Art nouveau furniture, family photos, and the largest tiger shot in India (measuring an awesome 10½ feet) can be examined to the sound of squawking peacocks in the gardens outside.

Museums Back on the east side of the *tank*, near Mahadev Gate, is the **Kachchh Museum**▶▶ (*Open* Thu–Tue 9–noon, 3–6. *Admission: moderate*), dating from 1877. It makes an excellent introduction to the region, displaying carved doors, statuary, bronzes, coins, finely embossed silver and gold, *rogani* (painted utensils), textiles, and, upstairs, an ethnographic section. More of the Kachchh's fabulous folk art and replica tribal huts are exhibited at the far-flung **Bharatiya Sanskriti Dharshan**▶ on Mandvi Road (*Open* Tue–Sun 9–noon, 3–6. *Admission: inexpensive*).

TOURIST OFFICE AND PERMITS
Maharao of Kachchh (Kutch) Tourist Office, Aina Mahal (*open* Sun–Fri 9–12, 3–6; tel: 02832 24910/20004). Efficiently and enthusiastically run, with maps and in-depth information on the Kachchh. Permits are required to visit villages north of Bhuj near the sensitive Pakistani border, but not for the southern half. Count on three hours and two offices to have a permit issued, and work out your precise itinerary beforehand.

Excursion

Rann of Kachchh▶▶ Bounded by sea to the south and west, and by sand to the north and east, this arid, inhospitable terrain is tormented by earthquakes and sandstorms. Despite this, formerly nomadic cattle breeders and shepherds have settled here in tiny villages. A visit to the Kachchh gives an interesting insight into their lives. Nascent tourism means that their handmade crafts are often ready for visitors, who may need to be diplomatic.

Bordering extensive salt flats to the east is the Little Rann, site of the Wild Ass Sanctuary, best visited from Adeser. The southern Kachchh is oddly affluent in places. Many of the large modern houses here belong to Gujaratis living in Britain, in particular the enormous Patel family, which has its opulent Swaminaryan temple in Kera. Near the coastal town of Mandvi is the **Vijay Vilas palace▶** of the Maharao of Kachchh, a regal legacy of the 1930s.

Thatched houses decorated with dried cow dung and mirrors are typical in the Kachchh

Tribal peoples The word "Banni" covers the groups living to the north of Bhuj, whose heavily encrusted embroidery and mirrorwork are among the region's finest. Among them are the Muslim Jats who migrated from Persia some 500 years ago, the dairy-farming Ahir who came from Pakistan, and the mysterious, seminomadic Rabaris. They are thought to have come from Afghanistan via Baluchistan and Rajasthan. The heavily bejeweled women make and wear brilliantly colored embroidery, while the turbaned men don beautifully pleated white shirts, baggy pants and *puttees* (cloths wound round the legs). Their immaculate thatched huts, as well as their clothes, are elaborately decorated with mirrors.

Temples You can see the crumbling 10th-century walls and Siva temple of the former Kachchh capital at **Kera▶**.

Here you will also find the remote **Kotai temple▶**, which is notable for its strikingly eroded sandstone statues and bell-shaped roof. The largest and most evocative structure in the area is the 18th-century **Than monastery▶▶**, whose Sivaite and Vishnuite shrines, cells and halls sprawl up a hillside.

▶▶ Diu 72B1

Alcohol is forbidden in Gujarat, except in the former Portuguese colony of Diu, a tiny, elongated island (barely 22 square miles) off the south coast of the Kathiawar peninsula. The branching palms along the access road from the fortified town of Goghla are unique, having been introduced from Africa centuries ago. Beyond a checkpoint and across the bridge lined with beer bars, an unmistakably Portuguese fort and white churches rise over tiled rooftops. Dating back to the 16th century, the pretty, winding streets are lined with whitewashed houses, palm-trees, banyans, and a few hotels. An old city wall ends between the southeastern beaches of **Jallandhar and Chakratirth▶**, an easy walk or bicycle ride from the center.

Short circuit To the west is the popular tourist beach of **Nagoa▶**, a tree-lined crescent offering camel rides and water sports. The north is mainly mud- and salt flats with good birdwatching. Diu is usually quiet, but has a high season from October through early January, with daily flights from Mumbai (Bombay).

Military might The impressive **fort▶▶** (*Open* daily 7–6. *Admission free*) was built 1535–1541 and covers a vast 44,252 square yards, washed by the sea on three sides. The solid walls and bastions, plus a few cannons and cannon-balls, are still intact but much of the interior is overgrown, with vegetation creeping through the cracks of the old chapel, and 16th-century tombstones lying in fragments. **Panikot fort▶** stands on a tiny island in mid-channel: this can be visited by boat from the main jetty, where there is a small information office.

The island of Diu, a relaxing break from the Gujarati interior

CATHOLIC CRISIS
Although many Diu inhabitants are distinctly Portuguese, Catholicism is fighting a losing battle. Of the three picturesque though peeling churches, only St. Paul's (1691) still functions. The Jesuit St. Francis of Assisi is now a hospital and St. Thomas's has become a museum. The latter is well worth visiting (*Open* daily 8–8. *Admission: free*) for its evocative collection of carved wooden statues, silver reliquaries, crucifixes, and a recumbent Jesus whose pierced hand gratefully accepts donations from visitors.

Mosque domes and minarets characterize the skyline of Junagadh

►► Junagadh 72B4

The small, ancient town of Junagadh lies at the base of the Girnar Hills, a rare undulation in the otherwise monotonous flatness of the Kathiawar peninsula. It had an illustrious early history as the capital of Gujarat under the Buddhist Mauryas (see page 34). After Ashoka's death, in the 3rd century BC, Junagadh was successively ruled by Hindu, Rajput and Muslim dynasties. Today it functions as a market center for the region. Its colorful history is reflected in Buddhist caves, the ruins of Uparkot citadel, and above all the sacred Mount Girnar, whose shrines and temples draw streams of Hindu and Jain pilgrims.

Main sights The town center is full of character, with lively bazaars, city gates, mosques, mausoleums, and attractive old buildings. Regal relics are exhibited in the **Durbar Hall Museum►** (*Open* Thu–Tue 9–12:15, 3–6. *Admission: inexpensive*) inside the old nawabs' palace. To the northwest stand the ornate, 19th-century **muqbara►** (mausoleums) of Junagadh's Muslim rulers. To the northeast, up a cobbled street curling around to the main triple gateway, is the **Uparkot citadel►►** (*Open* daily 7 AM–6:30 PM. *Admission: inexpensive*). Above are a huge *tank*, waterwheel and gardens with paths leading to the roofless but stunningly situated Jama Masjid and, farther north, the Adi Chai Vav, a 15th-century step well. Deeper still is the 11th-century Navghan Kuva. To the west are the remains of 3rd-century BC Buddhist caves, and earlier rock-cut temples and a *stupa* lie in the vicinity. As all these sites are scattered and overgrown, making them difficult to find, a local guide is particularly useful.

Mystical climb Junagadh's oldest monument is an Ashokan rock-edict (*ca*250 BC), 2.5 miles east at the base of **Mount Girnar►►**. This 3,280 foot high volcano is hewn with several thousand well-traveled steps, rising past booths offering *chai* and water to Jain and Hindu shrines and temples, and exceptional views. Allow about three hours for the ascent, and start early to avoid the heat. Below the summit is a large complex of 16 Jain temples, some beautifully carved, which were built of marble in the 12th and 13th centuries. The oldest is dedicated to Neminath, the 22nd Tirthankara (Jain prophet), who is said to have died here. Looming above and scattered over the ridge are Hindu shrines, including the Amba Mata temple and one dedicated to the goddess Kalika (Durga) that attracts fervent *sadhus* with an interest in the rites of death. There is also a Muslim shrine.

▶ ▶ ▶ Palitana   72B1

Open: daily 6:30–5. Admission free

Little can equal the architectural grandeur of the 863 Jain temples at Palitana, crowning a hilltop wreathed in Jain legends. The town below exists almost solely for pilgrims, and is monopolized by their guesthouses. Even the Edwardian-style palace, the Hawa Mahal, was built with the taxes levied on Jain visitors. Like Mount Girnar, Palitana entails a long, hot haul to the top. The fact that you cannot see the temple complex as you climb up is discouraging, as is being overtaken by energetic Jain nuns, but there are shady trees, sweeping views, and booths serving pure spring water on the way. The ascent up to 1,968 feet covers 2.5 miles and takes under two hours. At the gates of the complex, creamy buffalo curd in terracotta bowls restores energy. *Dhooli* chairs are available.

Victory Shetrunjay, the name of the hill, means "place of victory" and it does have the air of a citadel; a walled complex encloses multiple towers, domes and courtyards, with bells and flags marking the breezes. To the left of the shady main courtyard are the more recent, ostentatiously decorated temples favored by the pilgrims, while high up on the right is the more peaceful, older section. The oldest temple may date from the 11th century and is dedicated to Lord Adinath, the first Jain Tirthankara. The Chaumukha temple houses his four-faced image. Jain prosperity is evident in the conservation and ongoing restoration of these temples, and Jain regard for every form of life is reflected in the numerous resident birds and constant sweeping by the yellow-robed priests (see panel).

JAIN RULES
The strict tenets of Jainism make it an extremely puritanical religion, despite the gaudily decorated dance halls in some temples. The buffalo curd available at the entrance to Palitana is not for Jains, as they must not touch dairy products nor wear leather. Every living creature is considered sacred, a belief that results in the wearing of mouth masks (so as not to swallow an insect) and the sweeping of floors (so as not to tread on one). Meat, smoking, and alcohol are strictly prohibited, and fasting should be practiced four times a month. The Jains' complex metaphysics involve the rejection of objective truth, which allows for an infinite number of viewpoints on everything.

83

Shetrunjay at Palitana is a sacred place of pilgrimage for Jains

The Northwest

SALT MARCH
Gandhi's salt march was organized from Ahmadabad in March 1930 and was a turning-point in the independence movement. In protest against the British Raj's monopoly of the production and sale of salt, Gandhi and some 80 followers set off on foot towards Danti, a small coastal town 199 miles to the south near Surat. One month later, they arrived and set about boiling sea-water to produce salt in an overtly subversive act that was followed by a symbolic sale of their produce. Widespread protests and police aggression culminated in Gandhi's imprisonment without trial. His release, in January 1931, was followed by the Gandhi–Irwin pact and negotiations for India's independence.

Asiatic lion, Sasan Gir National Park

▶ **Porbandar**   *72A1*

Due west of Junagadh and about two hours away by road lies Porbandar, known above all as the birthplace of Gandhi in 1869. This is just one of his many close associations with Gujarat, as he attended school in Rajkot, university in Bhavnagar, began his mass civil disobedience movement in Bardoli (Surat), and began his salt march at Ahmadabad (see panel). His 200-year-old ancestral house is in the western promontory of Porbandar, but the main attraction is the neighboring **Kirti Mandir▶▶**, (*Open* dawn–1, 2–dusk. *Admission free*; but tip guide), where a museum illustrates Gandhi's life through photographs, memorabilia, and a prayer hall with a bookstore. This house was where his wife, Kasturba, was born. Southeast of here on the seafront is the Hazur palace, now a college. It was built by the ruler of Bhavnagar as part of his daughter's dowry when she married the Jethwa prince of Porbandar in 1902.

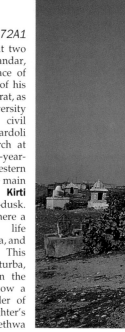

▶ **Rajkot**   *72B2*

Right in the center of the Kathiawar peninsula is Rajkot, founded by the Jadeja Rajputs in the 16th century and later the scene of numerous clashes between its ruling nawab and the British. Two relics of this period are the **Watson Museum;** Jubilee Gardens (*Open* Thu–Tue 9–12:30, 2:30–6. *Admission: inexpensive*) and the adjacent **Lang Library,** both grandiose Victorian edifices surrounded by lawns in the town center. The museum has a collection of rare exhibits relevant to this region, from Indus Valley artifacts to sculptures, bronzes, manuscripts, and Rajput miniatures. Also here is a portrait gallery with images of bejeweled local rulers and a portrait of Queen Victoria.

▶▶ **Sasan Gir National Park**   *72B1*

Open: mid-Oct to mid-Jun, usually 7–11, 3–5.
Admission: expensive

The national park, halfway between Junagadh and Somnath, is the last habitat of the Asiatic lion, a species that was almost extinct at the beginning of this century. The story goes that the Viceroy Lord Curzon was invited on a lion hunt by the local nawab but that, after public outcry, the trip was cancelled and Curzon, instead, advised the nawab to protect this rare animal. Spread over 540 square miles of undulating terrain, the park consists of savannah, dry deciduous thorn forest, and some evergreens. Apart from lions, estimated at close to 300 and usually found in prides of eight to ten, there are black buck, hyenas,

sambar, panthers, spotted deer, chinkara gazelles, langurs, and marsh crocodiles. There is a crocodile-rearing center by Sindh Sadan.

The temple at Somnath was once one of the richest in India

Lion tracking At the heart of the sanctuary is a core "interpretation zone" for which permits are required. These are issued at the park headquarters, where a wide selection of accommodations are located next to the lively hamlet of Sindh Sadan. Jeeps and guides set off at dawn or late afternoon to explore rather well-covered terrain, stopping at observation towers during the three-hour circuit. Longer trips can be made outside this zone, though rough road surfaces discourage the majority of visitors. Wildlife and termite mounds are abundant but the lions remain elusive, despite sporadic attacks on villagers.

▶ Somnath   72B1

Just outside the port town of Veraval, the temple of Somnath has an illustrious place in Hindu history, but the structure you see today dates from 1950 and reflects little of its original magnificence. It is said to have been built by the moon god, Somraj, in gold, silver, wood, and stone to redeem himself in the eyes of Siva, who had laid a curse on him. Its legendary wealth led to repeated plundering by Muslim invaders from the 11th century onward, but it always rose again. Veraval was for a long period the region's main port for Muslim pilgrims sailing to Mecca, and traditional *dhows* (ships) are still built here. Today's Sivaite temple faithfully reflects the original architectural style with a soaring central tower that shelters one of India's 12 highly sacred *jyotirlingas* (miraculously formed *lingams* surrounding which there are many myths). A museum (*Open* Thu–Tue 9–noon, 3–6. *Admission: inexpensive*) displays fragments and sculptures from Somnath's former incarnations.

AFRICAN FACES
Porbandar's historical trading links with East Africa may account for the entire villages of "Siddis"—people of African origin—that exist between Sasan Gir and Porbandar. It is thought that they were bought from Arab slave-traders by local rulers, the women to work as palace servants and the men as hunters. Another version is that the Siddis came as slaves of invading armies, while still another suggests that slaves were imported by the rulers of Bengal in the early 15th century but were eventually driven out and settled in the far west. Certainly Mahmud of Ghazni, the Turk who sacked Somnath in 1024, employed Siddis as drummers in his army.

For many people India quite simply means textiles. Fine muslin, calico, chintz, embroidery, ikat, block prints, silk brocades, and tie-dyed cottons are all specialties of the subcontinent, resulting in a dazzling, diaphanous array at every bazaar. Above all, Rajasthan and Gujarat produce a bewitching selection, painstakingly made by hand or more profitably by machine.

IKAT

The *ikat* technique has long existed from Persia to Indonesia and flourishes in Central America. The word itself comes from the Malay meaning to tie or bind, referring to the threads on a loom that are bound with dye-resistant fibers. Successive plunges into dye vats create different tones, with new ties being added each time to create the overall pattern. The cloth is subsequently woven by hand or machine. Apart from the silk saris made in Patan (Gujarat), ikat is most widely produced in Andhra Pradesh.

86

India's textile history is a lengthy one, with evidence of exports by land and sea to China, Mesopotamia and Rome as far back as the 1st century AD. Fragments of Gujarat cotton have been excavated in Egypt, while Java's royal courts had a particular penchant for *patola*, silk lengths woven using the complex double-ikat technique, also a Gujarati specialty. Desert people such as the Jats and Rabari have been using needles artistically to decorate textiles for centuries, producing embroidered and mirror-encrusted quilts, hangings, and tunics that enliven the monotonous sandy tones of their environment. Today, both Jaipur and Ahmadabad sell a fantastic variety of fabrics, still much sought after by the Western market.

Trading textiles Indian muslins have long been coveted, their different qualities leading to poetic names such as *abrawan* ("running water", which when immersed in a stream became invisible); *baft hava* ("woven air", as it floated like a cloud); and *shabnam* ("evening dew"). The Romans admired them, and handspun, handwoven Indian muslins continued to be prized in Europe even after the rise of machine-made imitations, as the former's yarn had

far greater strength. The astute East India Company also traded in fine embroideries from Bengal and Gujarat, the latter peaking in popularity during the 17th and 18th centuries. Marco Polo (1254–1324) referred to the exquisite Gujarati embroideries "depicting birds and beasts in gold and silver thread sown very subtly on leather". Leather covers were later replaced by heavy silk sewn with decorative chain stitch, first acquired from Cambay and subsequently from Surat.

Calico and chintz Further south, from Calicut, came a cotton fabric that became known by European traders as calico. This fabric was

block printed and hand painted by Persian craftsmen, and eventually evolved into chintz (from the Hindi *chintz* meaning "variegated"), which was often decorated with adapted European designs. This was an area exploited by British manufacturers and soon their imitations were indistinguishable from Indian originals. Chintzes were also produced by machine in the larger textile centers of Ahmadabad and Mumbai (Bombay). It was only Gandhi's *swadeshi* (home-produced goods) movement that revived the domestic market for handmade production in the 1920–1930s. Indian brocades (mainly from Ahmadabad and Varanasi) were also imitated, but were more prized than European look-alikes because of their enduring color and the luster of the fabric.

Bandanna The spotted bandanna worn (in pictures if not in real life) by pirates, gypsies, cowboys, and bandits from Britain to the Wild West actually originated in India, when it was exported from the 18th century onward. Bandanna derives from *bandhani* which means "tying" in Sanskrit, a succinct description of the laborious process originally involved in producing the dots. Some of India's most fabulous textiles, generally silk in Gujarat and cotton in Rajasthan, are made in this way.

Knotting The process used in tie-dyeing is basically the same today, except that chemical dyes are used. The most widely used motif in *bandhani* is the simple dot formed by pinching and knotting a small area of cloth; after dying, the thread is removed to reveal either a white circle or the previously dyed color. Jamagar in Gujarat is considered to be where the most elaborate and accomplished silk *bandhani* is produced, but this widely used technique is also applied to coarse wool, as among Kachchhi tribes. The finished product, which might be a *odhani* (head cloth), *layariya* (turban), or *duppatta* (scarf), is often sold still tied up in a coil, giving the customer the assurance that it is genuine and not a printed imitation.

MIRROR, MIRROR
Gujarat and Rajasthan tribes excel in creating brilliantly colored embroidery incorporating tiny mirrors, used for skirts, quilts or wall hangings. A tribal girl spends her formative years learning basic patterns and color combinations from older women, and the rest of her life embroidering the contents of her tiny home. The finest work is produced by the Banni community north of Bhuj, where minuscule mirrors are combined with dense embroidery on tunic yokes and covers.

The Rann of Kachchh has a long tradition of embroidery

PUSHKAR CAMEL FAIR

Some 200,000 people descend on Pushkar during its annual *mela* (fair), held at the full moon in October–November. Originally for local farmers and breeders—the men traded camel accessories while the women traded textiles and jewelry—it now encompasses horse- and camel races, parades, circus acts, music, dance, and food galore. Rajasthani visitors usually camp on the fairground in the desert just west of town, creating mesmerizing nocturnal scenes. Overlapping with the fair is Pushkar's annual pilgrimage, bringing hordes of devotees and *sadhus* to the Brahma Mandir and above all to bathe at the *ghats*. Reserve accommodations well in advance, or contact the RTDC in Jaipur for a room in their specially erected tents.

The annual camel fair brings thousands of camels to Pushkar

Rajasthan

▶ Ajmer   73D4

Ajmer's turbulent history since the defeat of the Chauhan Rajputs by Sultan Mohammed Ghauri in 1193 has left it with a rich mixture of Hindu and Islamic monuments. At the heart of the city and its bazaar is the **Dargah**▶▶, the much revered tomb complex of the Sufi saint Khwaja Muin-ud-din (who died in 1236), extended over the centuries by the Mughal emperors. Its many mosques include an elegant structure erected by Shah Jahan, and the tomb itself stands in a domed marble pavilion. The Dargah is considered a second Mecca by South Asia's Muslims. It is a place of intense religious fervor especially during the annual Urs celebrations, when people commemorate the saint's death with six days of non-stop music. If you sign the "visitor book" you are committing yourself to a hefty donation!

North of this stands the **Adhai-din-ka-Jhonpra**▶(*Open Sat–Thu 10–5. Admission free*) Its name refers to the two-and-a-half days allegedly taken by Ghauri, in 1193, to build the present mosque, transforming a Sanskrit college and temple that he had sacked. Pillars originating from at least 30 Hindu and Jain temples are incorporated into this early example of Indo-Islamic architecture. Ajmer's remarkable past is illustrated by sculpture and Mughal and Rajput miniatures at the museum (*Open Sat–Thu 10–4:30. Admission: inexpensive*), housed in Akbar's palace, the Daulet Khana, in the Daulat Bagh.

Excursion

Pushkar▶▶ A scenic drive through dry hills 7 miles northwest of Ajmer takes you to the site of the camel fair (see panel). Pushkar is a delightful lakeside town though no

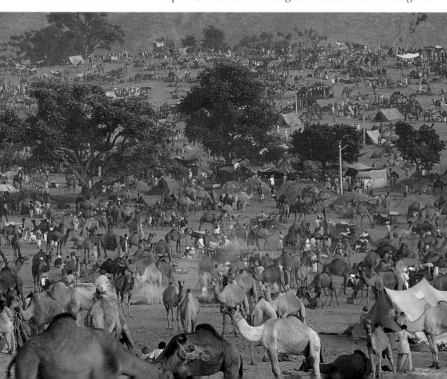

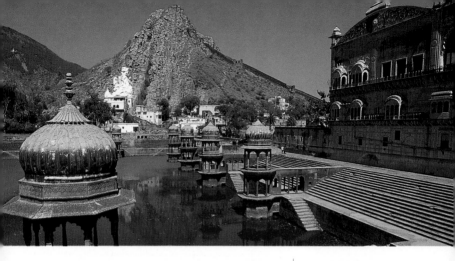

longer the peaceful haven of a few years back; commerce and tourists have taken their toll. However, its legendary creation by Brahma, who dropped a lotus flower into the desert to make a sin-purifying lake, gives it a poetic start. The Brahma Mandir is always thronged with pilgrims, but the priests make forceful demands for donations. In return they issue a "Pushkar passport", a red braid that you can flourish to ward off other demands. Both Saivitri Mandir and Gayitri Mandir crown a hilltop and respectively offer beautiful sunset and sunrise views.

Vinay Vilas Mahal, in Alwar, stands in splendor by a vast tank

▶ Alwar 73D4

Alwar's proximity to imperial Delhi inspired in its Mewar inhabitants a particularly rebellious and bellicose character until Sultan Baban (1267–1287) finally crushed their resistance. In 1770 a Kachhwaha Rajput won back Alwar and created his own principality. The town nestles picturesquely in a valley of the Aravalli hills where lakes and woods nurture rich wildlife, and is watched over by a forbidding fort high on a rocky ridge. Most of the fort's structures are dilapidated, and entry is restricted. Inside the walled city below stands the grandiose late 18th-century **Vinay Vilas Mahal▶▶**, an extravagantly decorated palace fronting a large *tank*. The museum upstairs (*Open Sat–Thu 10–4:30. Admission: inexpensive*) displays a fascinating regal hodgepodge including a silver dining-room table, rare Arabic, Persian, and Sanskrit manuscripts, and an exceptional collection of Rajput and Mughal miniatures. Behind the palace, several temples edge the lake, including the lovely **Moosi Maharani Ki Chhatri▶** and the **Purjan Vihar▶▶** (Company Garden) laid out in 1868.

Tiger country 23 miles southwest of Alwar lies **Sariska Tiger Reserve▶▶** (*Open* daily, Oct–Feb 7–4, otherwise 6:30–5, but minimal wildlife Jul–Aug. *Admission: expensive*), offering good opportunities for spotting nilgai (blue bull), sambar, chital, four-horned antelopes, wild boar, and abundant monkeys. The 309 square mile sanctuary of mainly dry deciduous forest was established in 1955 and in 1979 joined Project Tiger (see page 100). Jeep safaris around the sanctuary are organized by the Forest Reception Center, opposite the Lake Palace Hotel, Jaipur Road (tel: 0144 41333).

TOURIST OFFICES
Tourist Reception Center, Hotel Khadim, Savitri Girls College Road, Ajmer (*Open* Mon–Sat 8–noon, 3–6; tel: 0145 52426). Counter at train station.
Tourist Office, Nehru Bal Vihar, opposite Purjan Vihar garden, Alwar (*Open* Mon–Fri 10–1:30, 2–5; tel: 0144 21868).

The Northwest

Tourist Reception Centre, RTDC Hotel Dhola Maru, Bikaner (*Open* Mon–Sat 10–5; tel: 0151 544125). Very helpful. Good literature and paying guest information.
Tourist Office, Janata Avas Grih (near train station), Chittaurgarh (*Open* Mon–Sat 10–5; tel: 01472 41089).Tours and help with hiring auto-rickshaws, *tongas* or cars. Bicycles can be rented near the station.

Hand prints at Junagarh Fort, a lasting memorial to the widows who performed sati

SHIPS OF THE DESERT
India's only camel breeding and research center (*Open* Mon–Sat 3–5. *Admission free*) lies 5 miles south of Bikaner. Since it was set up in 1975 it has become the main source for the country's camels. In 1993 Bikaner inaugurated an annual January camel fair to encourage local camel craftsmen. The two-day event includes camel races and plenty of music and dance. Camel safaris are also plentiful in this area: contact Vinod Desert Safari (tel: 0151 204445, fax: 0151 525150).

▶▶ Bikaner   72C4

Bikaner, lost in the dry, flat scrub of the Thar Desert, is India's camel capital (see panel). Despite bleak surroundings, Bikaner's location on the caravan route into India from Central Asia made it a great trading center and since its founding by a prince from Jodhpur in 1486, the fortified town has become Rajasthan's fourth largest city. Overtly hardworking, with scattered sights, and a business community of astute Marwari traders (see page 106), it is little touched by tourism and makes a welcome change from Rajasthan's more commercialized destinations.

Fort of palaces Towering dramatically over the town is **Junagarh Fort▶▶▶** (*Open* daily 10–4:30. *Admission: moderate*, including guide). Inside this mammoth that was never conquered are 37 palaces, private temples, and pavilions built between 1588 and 1943, an architectural span that is also immaculately conserved. Projecting balconies, *jali* (latticed) screens, and oriel windows add grace to the facade rising above 29 foot thick walls, although Bikaner's pink sandstone is less delicately carved than that of Jaisalmer (see pages 96–97), because it is harder. The main entrance through Suraj Pol (Sun Gate) takes you past the handprints of 59 wives who performed *sati* on the death of their husbands, the last dating from 1837. Of the numerous interlocking palaces, the most lavish is the Anup Mahal (1788–1828), where marble columns painted by Persian artists, lacquerwork, and inlaid mirrors add to the opulence of the red and gold coronation room.

Maharaja Gaj Singh's Chandra Mahal (Moon Palace) and Phul Mahal (Flower Palace) offer interesting decorative contrasts. Phul Mahal has delicately lacquered floral paintings and marble, while gloom pervades the Chandra Mahal, which is used for prayer and meditation. The palace of the enlightened Maharaja Ganga Singh (1887–1943), with its vast Durbar Hall (accessible by Rolls-Royce), has been converted into a museum housing some extraordinary and varied exhibits, including a World War I fighter plane.

More luxury Visitors who have enough energy after touring the fort's amazing sights can also visit **Lalgarh Palace▶** (*Open* Thu–Tue 10–5. *Admission: moderate*), just over a mile north. This early 1900s design in sandstone by Sir Swinton Jacob became part hotel and part royal residence. A museum and the Anup Sanskrit Library are housed here; the latter displays old photographs, wildlife trophies, and manuscripts. Bikaner also has Jain merchants' *havelis*, concentrated in Rampuria Street in the ramshackle old city. On one facade reliefs depict the British King George V and Queen Mary. Surrounding Kote Gate is the huge old **bazaar▶**, where camel-hide products, rugs, and lacquerwork abound.

Southwest of here are the 16th-century **Bhandasar and Sandeshwar Jain temples▶▶**, built by two brothers with elaborate decoration using mirrorwork, frescoes, enamel, and gold leaf.

Rats 19 miles away is Deshnok, home to the 17th-century **Karni Mata temple**►► (*Open* daily 6 AM–9:30 PM. *Admission free*), dedicated to an incarnation of the goddess Durga (see page 252). It has become a sanctuary for thousands of plump rats, believed to hold the souls of Karni Mata's devotees. There are also two gigantic cauldrons, used during its biannual festival to feed 7,000 people.

►►► Chittaurgarh 73D3

Between 1303 and 1567, Rajasthan's oldest fort (*Open* daily dawn–dusk. *Admission: inexpensive*) three times witnessed the Rajput ritual of *jauhar* (the mass suicide of women by fire), before their men plunged into a battle they had no chance of winning. The fort dates from the 7th century, and was the capital of Mewar in the 15th and 16th centuries. High above the modern town, 3 miles of walls encircle the ruined citadel, its palaces, towers, and temples abandoned since Akbar's siege in 1567. Of outstanding interest are the richly carved, 121 foot high Vijay Stambh (victory tower) built to commemorate a 1440 victory, and the 72 foot Kirti Stambh (tower of fame). The latter was the work of a 12th-century Jain merchant, dedicated to Adinath and plastered with his images over six stories. At the southern end stands Padmini's Palace in its pool. Padmini was a Rajput beauty whose image, glimpsed in a mirror, seduced the Sultan of Delhi in 1303. He attacked the fort to win her, but only inspired Padmini and her women to perform the fort's first incidence of *jauhar*.

Above: sacred rats at Karni Mata temple
Below: Chittaurgarh

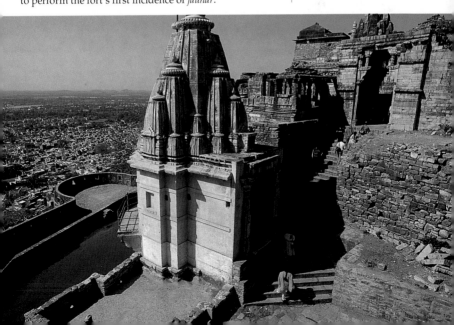

▶▶▶ Jaipur 73D4

The pink capital of Rajasthan, traffic choked, dynamic, highly commercialized and not to be missed, was founded by the Rajput Maharaja Jai Singh II in 1727. The grid layout, sandstone palaces, *havelis,* avenues, and bazaars of the old walled city offer an unrivaled harmony, although Jaipur now sprawls chaotically outward to encompass two and a half million inhabitants. To the north are the ruins of the hilltop Nahargarh Fort and to the south the Ram Niwas gardens, with various later monuments, institutions, and accommodations. Much of Jaipur's attraction lies in its wealth of atmospheric hotels converted from old *havelis* standing in spacious gardens.

Royal center Dominating the central grid is the **City Palace▶▶▶** (*Open* daily 9–4:30. *Admission: expensive*) composed of the Chandra Mahal (Moon Palace), still the residence of the former ruling family, and several other edifices converted into a museum. Picked out with delicate white patterns, the sandstone walls and arches, marble columns and guardian elephants offer a wonderful fusion of Hindu and Mughal styles. Exhibits throughout the pavilions are all of superlative quality, whether costumes, textiles, arms, manuscripts, miniatures, carpets, furniture, or astronomical instruments. In the beautiful courtyard of the Diwan-i-Khas (1730) stand the much photographed giant silver urns commissioned by Madho Singh II to carry holy water from the Ganga (Ganges) on a trip to England.

Royal fantasies Opposite the main entrance to the palace is the **Jantar Mantar▶▶▶** (*Open* daily 9–4:30. *Admission: inexpensive*), the biggest of Jai Singh's five remarkable observatories. Constructed of stone and marble between 1728–1734, these large, highly complex structures were designed by Jai Singh himself to prove to the Mughal emperor that Hindu astrology was based on precise scientific calculations. Their curiously modernistic appearance adds to the fascination. East of here, rising above the main north–south avenue and bazaar, is the fabulous facade of the **Hawa Mahal▶▶** (*Open* daily 9–4:30. *Admission: inexpensive*). This dates from around 1800, when it was built for the ladies of the harem by the poet king, Pratap Singh. The name means "palace of the winds", and the lavish five-story structure was designed to catch the breeze through the multiple *jali* screens, balconies, and arches. A popular **Govindji temple▶**, devoted to Lord Krishna, Jai Singh's family deity, stands in gardens north of the palace.

Open space The **Ram Niwas Gardens▶** lie south of the frenetic walled city. This park with zoo, aviary, herbarium, and sports grounds was built under Ram Singh II in 1868 as a famine relief project. Rising from the lawns is the impressive Indo-Saracenic "Albert Hall", designed by Sir Swinton Jacob and opened as a museum in 1887. This **Central Museum and Art Gallery▶▶** (*Open* Sat–Thu 10–4:30. *Admission: inexpensive*) displays sculptures, miniatures, metalware, decorative art, natural history, and Rajasthani folk art. It also runs the Ravindra Rangmanch, containing a modern art gallery (*Open* Sat–Thu 10–4:30. *Admission free*), auditorium and open-air theater.

TOURIST OFFICES
Government of India, State Hotel, Khasa Kothi (*Open* Mon–Fri 9–6, Sat 9–1; tel/fax: 0141 372200, www.goitojpr. satyam.net. in). Helpful and arranges tours including Amer. It is well worth hiring a guide to explain the intricacies of Jaipur's colorful history. Some guides are specialists in the City Palace.
Tourist Reception Centre, Paryatan Bhavan Tourist Hotel, MI Road (*Open* Mon–Sat 10–5, closed second Sat each month; tel: 0141 365256, fax: 0141 376362, www.rajasthantourism. com). Supplies brochures.

93

Top left: Hawa Mahal, where, from behind jali *screens, women could observe without being observed*
Bottom left: one of the many emporiums that make Jaipur a shoppers' paradise

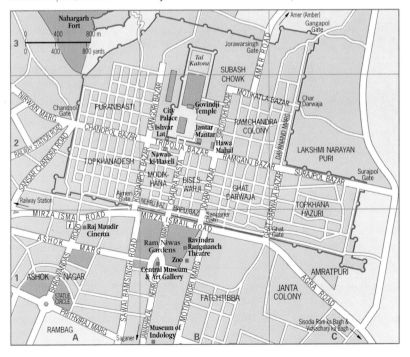

The Northwest

ELEPHANT FESTIVAL
Every March during the national festival of Holi, Jaipur's magnificent elephants are paraded through the city streets in dazzling finery. Decorative *howdahs*, bejeweled hangings and superbly clad drivers plunge the streets of the old city back into its colorful and illustrious past, to the rousing accompaniment of drums and trumpets. Less stately but fun are the polo games organized with these ungainly beasts.

Excursions

Amer, the former capital of the Kachhwaha rulers, lies 7 miles north of Jaipur, reached by a scenic rural road that passes the Man Sagar lake, and its elegant water palace, the Jal Mahal (1735). Now being restored, this is likely to become a major tourist attraction once visits are possible. Not far away is **Kanak Vrindavan**, a complex of renovated temples and gardens. Opposite lies **Gaitore▶**, the royal cremation ground where the cenotaphs of Jaipur's rulers are dominated by that of Jai Singh II. Near the Ramgarh crossroads stands the queens' memorial ground, the **Maharana-ki-Chhatri▶**.

Amer▶ ▶ ▶ (*Open* daily 9–4:30. *Admission: inexpensive*). The palace complex of Amer is stunningly situated, its sandy color blending into a backdrop of rocky hills overlooking the Maota lake at its feet. Monkeys are constant companions and the main sections are often filled with tour groups, but it remains exceptional. Building started in 1037; what remains today is the work of Raja Man Singh (which was begun in 1592) and subsequent rulers until Jai Singh II moved on to create Jaipur. Access to the hillside palaces, pavilions, gardens, temples, and walls is by a long steep path. Elephants and jeeps are available, but hard bargaining is needed to secure them.

Public domain The huge front courtyard, entered through the Suraj Pol (Sun Gate) is edged by steps leading up through the Singh Pol (Lion Gate). To the right is the green marble temple devoted to Shila Mata, Kali's incarnation as goddess of war, whose image was brought from East Bengal, and ahead is the spectacular pillared hall of the Diwan-i-Am (1639). Rising at the southern end of this courtyard is the massive, three-story painted gateway, the Ganesh Pol, that divides public from private areas. The rooftop and upper chambers offer fabulous views over the site.

Private domain Beyond the corridors and galleries on either side of a small *char-bagh* garden are, to the right, Sukh Niwas, a pleasure pavilion with water channels and inlaid doors, and, to the left, the Jai Mandir or Sheesh Mahal (mirror palace) conceived as the private audience hall. This and the upper floor, known as Jas Mandir (1630s), form the apex of Jai Singh I's palace, displaying dazzling fine glass mosaics, mirrorwork, stucco, stained glass, and exquisitely carved marble *jali* screens, all harmoniously blending Mughal decorative features with a Rajput setting. The older, simpler structures at the far end were built during the reign of Raja Man Singh in the late 16th century. A pretty arched pavilion at the center of this labyrinthine palace was used as a meeting-place for the palace ladies.

Village and fort North of the palace are the ruins of its prosperous settlement of nobles and craftsmen. There is little to recall the former inhabitants apart from the beautifully decorated **Jagat Shiromani temple►►**, which has an image of Lord Krishna, the old temple of Narsingh, and the impressive step well, Panna Mian-ki-Baoli. In contrast, the **Jaigarh fort►►** (*Open* daily 9–4:30. *Admission: inexpensive*), whose battlements loom high on the western ridge, is a remarkably well-preserved structure, its watch towers having witnessed hardly any military action. The huge complex commands breathtaking views as well as housing several temples, a cannon foundry, a small museum and one of India's largest cannons, the Jai Ban. It is a long, hot haul to reach the fort from Amer village but there is direct highway access from below. This same highway eventually leads to **Nahargarh Fort►**. This is mainly in ruins, apart from some 19th-century additions offering wonderful views south over Jaipur. A path leads down directly into the old city.

Agra Road Several sights lie northeast of Jaipur on the busy Agra road. Most notable are the landscaped gardens constructed by kings and nobles in the 18th and 19th centuries. The largest, the **Sisodia Rani ka Bagh►** was built by Jai Singh II for his Sisodia queen and contains terraced gardens with fountains, water channels, and painted pavilions. Equally well preserved is the Vidyadharji Ka Bagh, a garden laid out by Jaipur's brilliant 18th-century urban planner, Vidyadhar.

RAJASTHANI CRAFTS
Despite devoting so much energy to wars, Rajasthan developed a rich crafts tradition under the patronage of its numerous kings and nobles. The parched landscape may have stimulated the desire to decorate the walls of buildings, from simple mud huts to *havelis*, forts, and palaces. Hardworking Rajasthani women wear heavy jewelry, from nose rings to anklets, even while carrying hods of earth or tilling the fields. Courtly jewelry became more refined and was much influenced by skilled enamel workers brought by Man Singh from Lahore. The delicate art of enameling is known as *meenakari*. Jaipur's other glittering specialty is *lac* bangles, often inlaid with glass.

95

Tours of Amer Palace can be made on caparisoned elephants (below and left)

DESERT FESTIVAL

Full moon in late January or early February is the time of Jaisalmer's three-day desert festival, with a sound and light show, Gair dancers, fire dancers, puppet shows, turban-tying competitions, camel races, and the Mr Desert contest, with a grand finale of moonlight festivities at Sam sand dunes. Hotel rates rocket, and all accommodations must be reserved in advance.

SHOPPING

Jaisalmer is famed for its handmade crafts, including embroidery, superbly embroidered soft leather slippers, camelhide stools and silver jewelry. Good places to start are the Rajasthani Government Emporium and the Khadi Emporium, where fixed prices prevail. In Asani Road, Vijay Leatherworks has slippers, belts, and bags, and Geeta Jewelers stock antique tribal ornaments and Kundan jewelry. Dhanraj Sweets, in Bhatia Market, is a specialty sweetmaker.

▶▶▶ Jaisalmer 72B4

No other town in Rajasthan epitomizes the desert culture like Jaisalmer. Isolated in the far western wastelands characterized by the sand dunes of the Thar Desert, perched in spectacular fashion on a high outcrop, this golden city of winding lanes, exquisite *havelis* and burgeoning crafts is enchanting. Yet the days of caravans loaded with silks and spices that inspired its foundation in 1156 are long gone, and Jaisalmer, remote and untouched by outside influences for centuries, has now bowed to the demands of tourism. The magic remains but it is fast becoming a museum, a Rajput theme-park which now derives all its income from the omnipresent army of visitors. Touts abound.

The crown Dominating the walled city is the fort, entered through four successive gates from the east. Four thousand people, mainly Brahmins, live within its walls among temples, palaces, hotels, and stores. Parts of the towering **Maharaja's Palace▶▶** (*Open* daily Oct–Feb 8–5, Mar–Sep 9–5. *Admission: inexpensive*) date from the early 1500s, and other sections were added by successive rulers until the late 19th century. There are some exceptional details—Italian and Chinese tiles, stone doors carved to resemble wood, mirrorwork, intricate *jali* screens, and carved balconies—but renovation is limited and much has deteriorated. Far better maintained are the nearby **Jain temples▶▶▶** (*Open* daily 8–1. *Admission free*), their sandstone and marble imaginatively and profusely carved between the 12th and 15th centuries. The Parsvanath temple is outstanding, with lively images including Hindu gods. Palm-leaf manuscripts that are among India's oldest and other items of ancient Jain culture are preserved in a 1,000-year old library, called the Gyan Bhandar.

Havelis Outside the fort gate is the busy main marketplace, the Manak Chowk, from where a maze of atmospheric streets spreads northward. These lead to Jaisalmer's fabulous **havelis▶▶▶**, their oriel windows and columns rising three to five stories around central courtyards, and all minutely carved out of Jaisalmer's honey-colored sandstone. Most were built between the mid-18th and late 19th centuries by wealthy merchants and moneylenders. The Nathmal *haveli*, the work of two Muslim brothers in the 1880s, displays seven ornate balconies, each carved from a single stone, with stone elephants and an asymmetrical facade due to fraternal rivalry. Five adjoining houses, the Patwa *haveli* (*Open* daily 10:30–5. *Admission: inexpensive*), built by one family in 1800–1860, have a magnificent display of verandas, fountains, niches, pillars, gold-painted

ceilings, and frescoes. East of the fort gates is the extraordinary Salim Singh *haveli* (Moti Mahal) with six stories sprouting 38 balconies. It was built in the late 18th century by a prime minister who tyrannized Jaisalmer and even its royal family. (*Open* daily 8–6. *Admission: inexpensive*).

Outskirts Just over a mile to the southeast of the citadel, **Gadisar lake▶** was the town's only source of water before the completion of the 1987 canal. Edged by delicately carved pavilions and temples, some dating back to the 14th century, it makes a peaceful spot that attracts numerous waterbird species. Close by stands the **Jaisalmer Folk Museum▶▶** Gadi Sagar (*Open* daily Oct–Mar 9–7, Apr–Sep 9–noon, 3–6. *Admission: moderate*), the work of an inspired local teacher who has been collecting and documenting regional folk art since 1984. His Desert Cultural Center (*Open* daily 9–8. *Admission: inexpensive*), next to the Tourist Reception Center, stages music and dance performances in season.

Desert sights West of the town lie the **Sam sand dunes▶**, 26 miles away, where the rolling dunes of the Desert National Park unfold. An ideal spot for sunset camel-rides with drum and flute accompaniment, it also offers accommodations for those enamored of the desolate drifting sands. An afternoon circuit by car can take in **Bada Bagh▶** (ruined 16th-century gardens and royal cenotaphs), **Amar Sagar's▶** *tanks* and temples, and **Lodurva▶▶** (*Open* daily 8–noon. *Admission: free*), the capital before Jaisalmer replaced it in the 11th century, and site of a lovely Jain temple rebuilt in the 1600s.

Jaisalmer's merchants prospered from its position on a camel-caravan route and invested in their houses

TOURIST OFFICES
Tourist Reception Center, Gadisar Road, about 500 yards mile from the train station, on southern perimeter of citadel (*Open* Mon–Sat 10–5; tel: 02992 52406). Exchange post office, travel and ticket arrangements, rest rooms. Guides and cars available. Half-day tours. Also a travel counter at the train station (open to meet trains).
Bicycles are available for rent, and are a good way of touring the nearby sights.

►► Jodhpur 72C4

Nearly 6 miles of city walls and countless bastions give Rajasthan's second largest city an aura of invincibility, and the traditional trades of cattle, camels, wood, salt, and crops remain its mainstays. It is also distinctive for its "blue city", a sprawl of indigo-colored houses originally occupied by Brahmins but now also inhabited by other people. Painting a house indigo deflects heat from sandstone walls, keeping the interior relatively cool, and blue houses can now be found dotted throughout Jodhpur.

Fort In 1459, advised by a sage to establish an impregnable base, Rao Jodha, ruler of Marwar, moved his capital from Mandore to this towering outcrop and built one of Rajasthan's most impressive places, with walls rising up to 118 feet. **Fort Mehrangarh►►►** (*Open* daily Oct–Mar 9–1, 2–5; Sep–Apr 8:30–1, 2–5:30. *Admission: moderate*) dates mostly from the 17th century and consists of a rambling complex of palaces and courtyards, all impeccably conserved or restored. Fine filigree sandstone *jali* screens for the women's quarters, and silvered handprints of women who performed *sati* (at the Loha Gate) indicate the strong Rajput traditions.

Regalia Outstanding exhibits include arms, miniatures, *howdahs* (seats for riding on elephants), and *palanquins* (covered litters), jewelry, costumes, musical instruments, furniture, elaborate cradles, silverware, and model trains in ivory, all displayed in suitably regal settings. Among the numerous palaces, the mid-18th-century Phool Mahal (Flower Palace) has delicate gilded wall paintings and colored glass inlays; the Takhat Vilas has an outrageously decorated Maharaja's bedroom (mid-19th century) with suspended glass baubles; the Sheesh Mahal (early 18th century) has mirrorwork; and its contemporary, the vast Moti Mahal, boasts a Durbar Hall to beat them all, with mirrored and gold casement ceilings designed to reflect flickering oil lamps and candles in wall niches. Well-geared to visitors, the fort has a resident palmist, bookshop, restaurant, and turbaned guards who will give evocative flute recitals for a tip.

Art deco In contrast, the British-influenced **Umaid Bhawan palace▶** was designed in the 1920s and stands among lawns and bougainvillea. It was commissioned by the Maharaja to provide employment for famine relief, and building work continued for 14 years. Today it is partly inhabited by descendants of the royal family, partly a museum and partly a hotel. The museum (*Open* daily 9–5. *Admission: moderate*) offers an idiosyncratic collection of arms, clocks, glass, tableware, polo trophies, and model planes. The lofty domed atrium, throne room frescoes by Norblin, and modernist washrooms are particularly impressive.

Past and present Close to the fort at **Jaswant Thada▶** (*Open* daily 9–1, 2–5. *Admission: inexpensive*) is a cluster of elaborate white marble cenotaphs built in 1899. The **Government Museum▶** (*Open* Sat–Thu 10–4:30. *Admission: inexpensive*) in Umaid Park, has exhibits ranging from stuffed animals to textiles. Jodhpur's lively central market areas, the **Girdikot and Sardar bazars▶▶** sprawl north and south of the landmark clocktower, a British relic of 1912. Narrow dusty streets, lined with old houses and courtyards in terra-cotta and blue hues, offer a dazzling array of goods.

Excursion
Mandor▶▶ This ancient capital lies 5 miles north of Jodhpur and contains the grandiose cenotaphs of Marwar's rulers, beautifully sculpted in dark red sandstone. In a pillared compound is the Hall of Heroes, a shrine to Hinduism's 330 million gods. More enticing are the lush gardens surrounding the hall, much enjoyed by picnicking families.

Above: the Hall of Heroes at Mandor Top: the interior of Fort Mehrangarh Left: Jodhpur's clocktower

MARWAR FESTIVAL
Traditional Marwar music and dance are celebrated during Jodhpur's annual festival. It is held each October, but the dates vary considerably, so check before planning a trip around it.

India's tiger population is now estimated at under 2,500, a dramatic and worrying drop from that of a few decades ago. Project Tiger has, in some places, kept numbers steady, but poaching and the shrinkage of natural habitat are overwhelming problems. Is the roar of this magnificent wild animal destined to disappear?

FEROCIOUS, FELINE, IMPERIAL

"The ultimate wild things are incidentally dangerous—white sharks, harpy eagles, polar bears—and unpredictable. Even the most gorgeous tiger is less athletic, more complicated than a leopard, say, which may sometimes seem like a single, lengthy muscle. But the tiger's spirit, when ferocious, feline and imperial, can parallel ours... Tigers are less heartbreaking than the beleaguered elephant, because they are not social creatures, are reactive, not innovative. But they are an apex, a kind of hook the web of nature hangs from. To know them marked my life."
Edward Hoagland, *Wild Things*, 1996

100

The tiger (*Panthera tigris*) is incontestably the most splendid of India's beasts, and stalks through a wide range of the subcontinent's habitats: the Himalayas, the mangrove swamps of the Sunderbans, the Gangetic plain, the sandalwood forests of Karnataka, and Rajasthan's national parks. Tigers were the favored quarry of every self-respecting maharaja, nawab or Mughal emperor, and *shirkar* (tiger hunting) was adopted by the British as a true *pukka sahib's* (gentleman's) sport. At the beginning of the 20th century, there were an estimated 40,000 tigers, but by 1947 this number had already been halved.

Awakening Despite the example set by individuals such as Jim Corbett (see page 124) and certain enlightened maharajas, the post-Independence years saw the tiger population plummeting even further. This was mainly due to the widespread destruction of forests and to poaching. By the early 1970s fewer than 2,000 tigers survived, and Prime Minister Indira Gandhi stepped in to declare a total ban on tiger shooting. She also set up Project Tiger.

Project Tiger Initially nine areas of forest were declared reserves. Their human inhabitants were resettled with compensation, and armed rangers employed to keep poachers at bay. Today, despite the existence of 23 such sites, specialists are pessimistic. Poaching remains a huge problem as rangers in remote areas are ill equipped to combat the forces of the lucrative trade in much coveted tiger products. The tiger in the wild may soon be a thing of the past.

▶▶ Keoladeo Ghana National Park (Bharatpur)

73E4

Open: daily 6 AM–6 PM. Admission: expensive, including guide and transportation.

Declared a national park in 1983, this 11 square mile reserve is one of the world's best for waterbirds, with over 350 bird species. Before converting it into a sanctuary in 1956, the local Maharaja used it as his hunting reserve. The shallow marsh water, lakes and partly submerged thorny babul trees are favored by nesting birds in July and August, and breeding continues until October and November. The most common species are the open-billed stork, painted stork, egret, pelican, ibis, cormorant, darter or snake-bird, spoonbill, and grey heron. Exotic migrants also arrive from Afghanistan, Central Asia, and Tibet.

Easy viewing As well as birds, Keoladeo has sambar, black buck, chital, nilgai, feral cats, hyenas, otters, and mongoose. Pythons are easily visible at Python Point. Unusually for an Indian national park, Keoladeo can be visited independently by bicycle (easily rented in town) or even by rickshaw; knowledgeable rickshaw drivers and guides are available at the entrance and, a little farther on, a boat jetty is the departure point for lake tours. Dawn and dusk are the best viewing times.

In town The reserve is sometimes known as Bharatpur after the adjoining town—which is easily reached from Agra (34 miles)—and is much visited by tourists on whistlestop tours. Few visitors make it to the 18th-century **Lohagarh Fort▶** whose ingenious defence mechanisms consistently repelled attacks by the British. Little remains of the walls but there are three adjoining palaces in a sunken garden, blending Mughal and Rajput architecture. The central wing houses the **Government Museum▶** (*Open* Sat–Thu 10–4:30. *Admission: inexpensive*), displaying fine Jain sculptures, arms, and manuscripts. An excursion can be made 19 miles north to **Dig (Deeg)▶▶**, once the summer resort of Bharatpur's royal family, with superb palaces, gardens, and a fort.

Painted storks nesting at Keoladeo Ghana National Park

TOURIST OFFICE
Tourist Reception Center, Hotel Saras, Agra Road, Bharatpur (*Open* Mon–Sat 10–5, closed second Sat of month, tel: 05644 22542), paying guest list.

DESERT DWELLERS

The Bishnoi community are the desert dwellers of the Jodhpur–Jaisalmer–Bikaner triangle. They live according to 29 rules, of which the first is to protect flora and fauna. Their immaculate round mud huts crowned by conical thatched roofs are usually grouped in compounds with sheep and goats. They use camels for transportation. The notoriously arduous desert climate ranges in temperature from 32°F during winter nights to highs of 104–122°F in April and May when the *loo* (desert-wind) blows. Sandstorms and the scarcity of water-sources are other major challenges.

Chilis drying in the sun in the Osiyan region

►► Mount Abu

72C3

This holy mountain and Jain pilgrimage site lies at the southern extremity of the rugged Aravalli hills, overlooking the arid, rocky plains of the Gujarat border. The steep, 4,503-foot climb up the mountain twists through a wildlife sanctuary where dense vegetation interspersed with sculptural boulders is alive with langurs and birds. The town of Mount Abu itself, sprawling among palm trees, has something of the atmosphere of an oasis about it. For centuries it has served as a retreat for sages and seers, who have left a trail of legends in their wake. Its main sights are its beautiful Jain temples. Streams of honeymooners and weekending Gujaratis are drawn here also by the cool, fresh air, boating lake, and endless souvenir stands.

Jain prowess Half hidden by mango groves, the five **Dilwara temples►►►** (*Open* daily noon–dusk. *Admission free*) lie about 2.5 miles northeast of the town center on the road to Achalgarh. Their facades were purposely kept simple in order to deceive Muslim attackers. The fabulously worked interiors are in total contrast. The earliest, Vimal Vasahi, was started in 1031, allegedly employing 1,500 masons and 1,200 laborers for 14 years. They created a feast of sculpted white marble that illustrates the 24 stages of Mahavir (the founder of Jainism), with cusped arches, ornate capitals, dome rosettes carved with exquisite dancers and elephants, and a colonnaded transept and ambulatory lined by 52 small shrines, each housing a statue. In front stands an elephant hall (1147) in homage to the hard labor involved.

The other masterpiece is the Vastupal and Tejpal temple (1231), named after its two founding brothers and dedicated to Neminath, the 22nd Tirthankara. Doorcasings, friezes, architraves, pillars, and porticoes are all intricately carved, and rivalry between the brothers' wives is indicated in two tilting female heads sculpted above the lateral altars. At the back, the priests' prayer hall can be spied through a lattice wall. Less interesting are the unfinished Risah Deo temple, and the Chaumukhi temple at the entrance, where the stone quality is mixed and carvings distinctly inferior.

Views About 500 yards beyond the temples is **Trevor's Tank►**, a small wildlife reserve with slothful-seeming crocodiles, pheasants, partridges, and peacocks. The 7 miles road from here to the ruined 14th-century fort of **Achalgarh►** and its 15th- to 16th-century temples, traverses beautiful countryside, alternating between wild landscapes of rocks and cacti, and wheat fields and farms roamed by donkeys. A few miles farther looms the highest point in Rajasthan, Guru Shikhar, with a small Sivaite shrine at the top of 300 steps. The views from here are superb, and at sunset the open-air café below fills up with shy honeymooning couples. Their other favorite destinations are west of town at Sunset Point, Honeymoon Point and above all Nakki Lake, specializing in kitsch souvenirs, photo opportunities, and boating.

▶▶ Osiyan   72C4

Magical and remote, this ancient Brahmanical and Jain center lies 40 miles north of Jodhpur. Flat desert scrub dotted with camels, black buck, goats, and Bishnoi hamlets suddenly ends with dramatic hills. These announce the temple town of Osiyan. Of the couple of dozen temples, three are outstanding: the Surya (Sun) temple (early 8th century); the still functioning Sachiya Mata temple (11th–12th century) and the main Mahavir temple. This last is a riotous mixture of styles, with vaulted ceiling, gold leaf, pillars that are between three and 500 years old, and 7th-century Pali inscriptions. The interior of the Sachiya Mata temple, its *shikhara* rising out of a cluster of turrets, displays 19th-century mirrorwork, tiles, colored glass, and an altar to Durga (see page 252). A separate group of Harihara temples dating from the 8th and 9th centuries stands south of the town center by the bus-stand. Decorative features include carved spiraling serpents, goddesses, and extensive friezes.

TOURIST OFFICE
Tourist Reception Center, opposite bus-stand, Mount Abu (*Open* in peak season Mon–Sat 8–11, 4–8; otherwise 10–1:30, 2–5; tel: 02974 43151). Also at Abu Road train station. Helpful with guides, taxis, half-day tours. Paying guest list.

The Mahavir temple in Osiyan

A 16th-century illustration depicting Krishna, the eighth incarnation of the Hindu god Vishnu, and Radha, his wife

MEWAR SCHOOL OF PAINTING
The school of Mewar, based in Udaipur (see page 108) was at the forefront of art, architecture, music, and devotional literature, especially under the Maharanas Kumbha and Sanga. Illustrated manuscripts were produced from the 13th century onward and by the early 17th century sets of miniatures were being painted in a well-defined, bold and colorful style. These were followed by large court paintings showing the Maharana in processions, on hunting expeditions or attending religious festivities. Portraits, folk legends, and divinities extended the subject matter. A good selection is displayed at Udaipur's City Palace Museum, and copies are produced in the back streets.

▶▶▶ **Ranakpur**   72C3

Peacefully situated in a beautiful valley at the western end of the Aravalli hills, Ranakpur requires a special effort to visit. This is repaid fully by its remarkable temple complex, one of the five holiest Jain sites, dating from 1439. Entering the main **Chaumukha temple▶▶▶** (*Open daily 12–5. Admission free*) is like walking through three-dimensional lace: every conceivable surface of the white marble walls, pillars, and ceilings is carved with unbelievable intricacy and imagination. The only element not in marble is the stone floor that supports this symphony of domes, arches, towers, and 1,444 pillars, of which no two are alike. The central open-sided sanctuary, rising majestically on three stories, contains a quadruple image of Adinath, the first Tirthankara (Jain prophet), surrounded by four subsidiary shrines. Altogether 29 halls and 66 shrines crowned by spires, and five monumental *shikharas*, their flags and bells moved by the breeze, make up this staggering celebration of Jain beliefs.

Images include floral designs, animals, and superb human figures, including erotic figures on the facade of the 14th-century **Parsvanath temple▶▶**. Here, equally astounding carving surrounds a black marble image of Parsvanatha and, nearby, another beautiful temple honors **Surya▶** the sun god. Ranakpur monkeys are aggressive, so watch out.

Mighty fort A day trip to Ranakpur from Udaipur (56 miles) can also include the remote, impregnable and evocative fortress of **Kumbhalgarh▶▶**. Dominating 13 surrounding hills that now form a wildlife sanctuary, its 22 miles of ramparts enclose 365 ruined temples, shrines, and a palace. There are Hindu temples dating from the 14th century, but the majority are Jain structures, some going back to the 3rd century BC when it is thought a grandson of Emperor Ashoka ruled here. The Nilkanth Mahadev temple dedicated to Siva houses a black marble *lingam* surrounded by finely fluted, tapering pillars, and there are some royal *chhatris* nearby.

Looming above the temples and reached by a steep path through seven sturdy gateways is the Badal Mahal (Cloud Palace), founded in 1415 by Maharana Kumbha of Udaipur and rebuilt and extended in 1813. The palace is partially ruined but retains lovely colors, floral murals, and features such as the royal toilet, revealing a precipitous drop below. A roaring wind and rattling shutters promote a suitably desolate atmosphere, reinforced by sweeping views of the once powerful state of Mewar.

▶▶ Ranthambhor National Park   73D3

Open: daily Oct–Jun. Three hour safaris begin Oct–Feb at 7am and 2:30pm; Mar–Jun at 6:30 AM and 3:30 PM.
Admission: expensive, including guide
This popular wildlife reserve of 151 square miles lies 7.5 miles from the town of Sawai Madhopur on the main Delhi-Mumbai (Bombay) railroad, so is relatively easy to visit. Its focus is a 10th-century fort that had a turbulent history under Delhi sultans, Rajput and Mughal rulers before it was taken over by the Maharaja of Jaipur in the early 18th century. From then on, it was a royal hunting reserve used by such illustrious visitors as Queen Elizabeth II. The fort's unique style of construction means that it is barely visible from a distance: the walls follow the ridge lines winding up the forested, sheer precipice. Apart from a temple devoted to Ganesha, who receives bags of fan mail and wedding invitations daily, the interior structures are mostly in ruins but offer wonderful views. There is a selection of accommodations just outside the park, and all hotels organize jeep safaris, or minibuses, for visitors.

Fauna Since joining Project Tiger in 1979 (see page 100), Ranthambhor has supplied frequent sightings of tigers, now thought to number about 30. Poaching is by no means unknown. The undulating dry deciduous forest also shelters sambar, chital, nilgai, wild boar, chinkara, jackal, and langur, most of which are favored by tigers as prey. Over 120 bird species are attracted by the many lakes and *tanks*, including laggar falcon, several types of eagle, and migratory birds such as sandpipers, black storks, lapwings, and geese.

TOURIST INFORMATION
Tourist Reception Center, Project Tiger office, within RTDC's Vinayak Tourist Complex, Ranthambhor Road, Ranthambhor (*Open* Mon–Sat 10–1:30, 2–5; tel: 07462 20808/21333/ 21169, fax: 07462 21212). Park information, jeep and minibus rentals.

The battlements of Kumbhalgarh fort, stretching out over the Aravalli hills

GARDEN OF SHEKHA
In the early 15th century the childless Mokal Singh, ruler of a tiny principality called Barwara, was advised to consult a *fakir* (religious mendicant) named Sheikh Burman in order to produce a son. The consultation accomplished, Mokal Singh did finally produce an heir who in honor of the *fakir* was named Shekha. Shekha ascended the throne in 1433 at the tender age of 12 to begin a reign that was to last 43 years. His kingdom came to be known as Shekhawati ("garden of Shekha").

▶▶ Shekhawati 73D4

The 20 or so towns and villages of Shekhawati have a wealth of superbly painted *havelis* and forts that make this semi-arid region well worth exploring. They were the unintended result of heavy taxation by the East India Company, which drove the entrepreneurial Marwaris away from here to create trading houses and industries elsewhere in India (the Birlas being the most famous). They sent their profits back home, and the result is an astonishing abundance of traders' mansions handpainted with unique images that make a lavish visual record of social history between 1750 and 1930. Today, apart from pockets of nascent tourism, Shekhawati has returned to being a sleepy backwater with many *havelis* permanently shuttered up or crumbling gracefully.

Practicalities Rough roads impose an average speed of 25mph, all the better for observing neatly walled mud hut compounds of desert tribes, camel carts, brilliantly appliquéd saris, and the surrounding countryside, visibly more fertile than the neighboring desert. Some villages are

mere sandy streets where a few stores and derelict *havelis* front piles of rubble picked over by peacocks, but others have more majestic sights, with whimsical decoration that demands hours to decipher. The best way to enter Shekhawati is either from NH11 between Jaipur and Bikaner or directly from Delhi, about 93 miles to the northeast. Most accomodations are in superb but scattered forts, and public transportation is limited, so a car is essential if you want to make the most of the region.

Themes *Havelis* were built around courtyards that offered safety, privacy for women, and protection from the harsh climate. Several generations lived together under one roof. Early frescoes were made with crushed lime, marble, and natural pigments on wet plaster, as in Italy, but chemical dyes and PVA paints are widely used for restoration. The most prolific period for Shekhawati wall painting was 1830–1900, when mythological frescoes were interspersed with illustrations of local legends, daily life, animals, portraits, and hunting and wrestling scenes. These were gradually replaced by a broader range of images influenced by European lithographs and photographs. *Chiteras* (artists) would depict trains, gramophones, planes or cars without ever having seen them, and the gods became strolling *sahibs* and *memsahibs* with dogs on leashes.

Starters In the capital of Shekhawati, **Jhunjhunun▶▶** is the beautiful Khetri Mahal (Wind Palace) alongside the accessible *havelis* of Marugh Das Tibriwal, Mehau Das Modi and Khaitan, all displaying ornate wall paintings. There are more frescoes at the Bihariji temple, and the domed and turreted structures of the Birdi Chand well are also worth seeing. Southwest of here is **Dighal▶**, where a beautiful century-old *haveli* on the main square comes as a complete surprise. Typically, its owners now live in Mumbai (Bombay), returning only once a year to a modern house nearby. Centrally located **Fatehpur▶**, although not the most attractive town of Shekhawati, was founded by Muslim nawabs in the mid-15th century, and its prosperous merchants later funded some unrivaled frescoes. Indian and Western styles fuse in the Devra and Singhania *havelis*, with mirrorwork and Japanese tiles depicting Mount Fuji adding to the eclecticism.

Fort towns Far more dramatic are fort towns such as **Lachhmangarh▶**, **Mukundgarh▶**, a town built around a temple square and known for its *bandhani* fabrics and brassware, and **Nawalgarh▶▶**. This last boasts not only two forts, but also a palace hotel, decorative temples, countless crumbling *havelis* and, best for frescoes, the Senior Secondary School. This much restored masterpiece displays a wealth of striking, idiosyncratic images. Atmospheric **Mandawa▶▶** has a fort hotel with a magnificent interior, some notable *havelis* and a Siva temple with rock crystal *lingam*.

Shekhawati is like a huge open-air art gallery, with superbly painted havelis *as the works of art (above and left)*

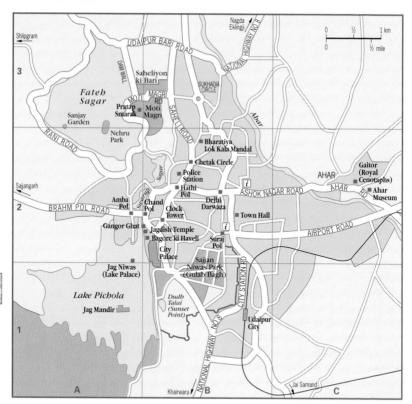

TOURIST OFFICES
Tourist Reception Center, Fateh Memorial, near Suraj Pol (*Open* Mon–Sat 10–1:30, 2–5. tel: 0294 411535).
Also counters at airport and at the train station. Well organized, with guide and car services. Half- and full-day tours include Chittaurgarh. Paying Guest program accommodations.

▶▶▶ **Udaipur**   *72C3*

Romance and magic fill the air of this city of lakes, palaces, gardens, *ghats*, temples, craftspeople, and painted houses. It was named after its founder, Maharana Udai Singh who, on being forced out of his citadel of Chittaurgarh by Akbar in 1567, consulted a *sadhu* and was advised to move to Lake Pichola. Nestling in a beautiful valley rimmed by verdant hills, Udaipur developed around three lakes, to become the last and greatest capital of Mewar. Still dominated by gregarious, meat-eating Rajputs, Udaipur now generates 60 percent of its income from tourism, but the influx of foreign visitors does little to change the aura of this enchanting town.

Palatial genesis Dominating the east bank of Lake Pichola is the majestic **City Palace**▶▶▶ (*Open* daily 9:30–4:30. *Admission: expensive*) that expanded from the late 16th century onward to become Rajasthan's largest palace. It is well worth hiring a guide to explain the intricacies and stories behind each structure. The approach is through Tripolia (triple gate), with its eight carved arches. This is the spot where rulers were weighed in gold or silver whose value was distributed as food to the poor. Behind the balconies and turrets of the towering facade is a succession of restored palaces: the Sheesh Mahal is characterized by beautiful mirrorwork, Krishna Vilas by superlative frescoes, Moti Mahal by mirrors, colored glass and inset paintings, Chini Chitrasala by blue-and-white

Chinese and Dutch tiles, Bhim Vilas by wall paintings of the Radha and Krishna stories, Mor Chowk by vivid mosaics of peacocks, and the Mosaic Gallery by stained glass portraits and panoramic city views. A museum near the entrance displays royal armor, arms, and toys. Through the courtyard of the Queen's Palace at the southern end is the residence of the royal descendants. A neglected government museum (*Open* Sat–Thu 9:30–4:30. *Admission: inexpensive*) in the northwestern corner displays miniatures and regional temple sculptures including a superb 8th-century head of Siva.

Mosaic glasswork in the City Palace (inset) and views of the City Palace and Shiv Niwas from Udaipur's Lake Pichola

The **Fateh Prakash Palace** has a **Crystal Gallery**▶▶ (*Open* daily 10–1, 3–8. *Admission: expensive*) displaying extraordinary 19th-century items made of crystal—including furniture! It overlooks the **Durbar Hall**▶, now a dining room with huge chandeliers, royal portraits, and weapons.

Heart of Udaipur Just to the north is a 1651 **Jagdish temple**▶▶ dedicated to Vishnu as Lord Jagannath and replete with carved marble columns and sculptures. Jagdish Temple Road, Udaipur's attractive main shopping street, runs northeast from here past the Clock Tower to end at Hathi Pol (Elephant Gate). Downhill and northwest from the crossroads is **Gangor Ghat**▶▶, a picturesque archway framing the lakeshore where women and children habitually bathe, swim and thwack laundry. Through a courtyard on the left is the

109

Colored glass characteristic of Moti Mahal, in Udaipur's City Palace

THE SUN KINGS
A golden sun with a moustached human face is a recurring image throughout Udaipur. This is the emblem of the Mewar rulers whose last capital was Udaipur. Former capitals were Ahar, Nagda and Chittaurgarh, established by the Sisodia Rajputs, head of the 36 royal clans. Claiming descent from Lord Rama, King of Ayodhya and hero of the Ramayana epic dating from around 500 BC, the Sisodia Rajputs trace an unbroken line of kings of Mewar from AD 144. Their dynasty became more firmly established in the 8th century when Bappa Rawal, a legend-inspiring king, defeated the prince of Chittaurgarh and founded an enlarged kingdom that was to blaze a trail of Rajput valor through Indian history.

Western Zone Cultural Center►, newly converted to exhibit crafts and stage music and dance performances. The most atmospheric streets of old Udaipur meander south of here parallel to the lake. Whitewashed houses with colorful murals, tiny shutters, and balconies rise to precipitous heights with shrines squeezed in between, while aromas of incense, food, fruit, and flowers waft through the air. Many are converted into budget accommodations and restaurants.

Lake Pichola In the lake are two island palaces, the 18th-century Jag Niwas, now a luxury hotel, and the 17th-century **Jag Mandir►►**, where Shah Jahan once took refuge from his father. The domed sandstone pavilion contains some beautiful rooms fronted by stone elephants and gardens. Boat trips round the lake (some solar powered) stop here, offering magical views of the shore at sunset.

Fateh Sagar lake Sights north of the center on the eastern shore of Fateh Sagar lake include the lush, peaceful **Saheliyon ki Bari►►** (*Open daily 9–7. Admission: inexpensive*), laid out in the early 18th century with pools, fountains, delicate pavilions, and marble elephants. These gardens were designed to amuse 48 young ladies-in-waiting sent as part of a royal dowry. Another promenading spot close by is the hilltop **Pratap-Smarak►** (*Open daily 9–6. Admission: inexpensive*). Here a statue of the heroic Maharana Pratap astride his beloved steed presides over fountains and a rock garden with views across the lake to distant hills. Fateh Sagar's island contains **Nehru Park** frequent boats leave from the eastern jetty 8–6:30. In the new town east of here the main sight is **Bharatiya Lok Kala Mandal►►** (*Open daily 9–6. Admission: inexpensive*), a museum of folk art displaying masks, *thapas* (finger paintings), folk deities, toys, a mobile temple, costumes, musical instruments, and photographs of India's tribal peoples and their art. Amusing puppet shows, an Udaipur speciality, are held daily at 6 PM with shorter versions during the day. (For information, tel: 0294 529296.)

East and west Another of Udaipur's delights is its wealth of sights scattered outside the town. These include the rather artificial though revealing **Shilpgram►►** (*Open daily 11–7. Admission: inexpensive*), about 2 miles west, an arts-and-crafts village of 26 traditional huts from Gujarat, Goa, Maharashtra, and Rajasthan where some mesmerizing performances are held. A few miles farther through idyllic rural landscapes looms the **Sajjangarh►** (Monsoon Palace). It is closed and derelict, and shares its strategic hilltop site with a telecommunications station, but the courtyard and ramparts offer fabulous views. East of Udaipur lies **Ahar►**, the ancient capital of the Sisodias who created Mewar. This forest of crumbling white marble *chhatris* includes the royal cenotaphs of Mewar and a museum (*Open Sat–Thu 10–4:30. Admission: inexpensive*) that houses a rare collection of 4,000-year-old artifacts.

North Twelve miles northeast of town, beyond a long stretch of marble workshops, lie the ruins of another former capital, **Nagda▶**, where three 11th-century temples survive in a peaceful lakeside spot. Intricate sandstone and marble carvings surround the main porch of the Saas-Bahu temple, the intricate carving continues inside the building while ribbed, carved towers curve gracefully behind. The facades are alive with countless gods, *apsaras* (dancers), floral designs and some erotic couples.

Two miles farther lies **Eklingji▶▶**, a tiny village that is centered on a huge temple complex dating from 734 but rebuilt in the 15th century. No fewer than 108 shrines and temples are discreetly enclosed behind high walls, all devoted to Eklingji, an aspect of Siva and the deity of the Maharanas of Mewar whose descendants still come here to worship. Pilgrim souvenirs, flowers, and garland-sellers line the entrance that leads to the white marble main temple, faced by a statue of Bappa Rawal, the 8th-century Mewar hero. Sculpted friezes depict musicians, a few erotic couples, elephants, and *apsaras*. Inside, engraved silver screens shield the altar faced by a solid silver *nandi*. Eklingji has plenty of bicycle-rentals offering the possibility of some very pleasant pedaling and sightseeing around its rural environs.

South Thirty miles to the southeast lies **Jai Samand Lake▶**, one of Asia's largest artificial lakes. It was created by Maharana Jai Singh in 1685. The scenic *ghats* are lined with graceful marble *chhatris* and on either side are the queens' summer palaces. The Bhils, a local tribe, still inhabit the islands in the lake, and a wildlife sanctuary shelters many species, including panther, wild boar, deer, antelope, mongoose, and flocks of migratory birds.

FESTIVAL TIME
Every March–April, Udaipur welcomes the spring with the riotously colorful Mewar festival of Rajasthani culture. Songs, dances, processions, devotional music and firework displays keep the city's 400,000 or so inhabitants and tourists entranced. In the evening the Gangor procession takes place: groups of women dressed in brilliant yellow, green, purple, and scarlet saris carry images to Gangor Ghat, while boat processions bring the horizon alive.

A family at work on an Udaipur street booth

Rajputana, land of the bellicose Rajputs, pos-sesses a legacy of palaces and forts which are among the greatest cultural riches of the subcontinent. With a history veering from courageous deeds to preposterous extravagance (a Maharaja once shot crane from his private plane), the Rajputs are people of intensity, vivid legends and larger-than-life characters.

According to legend, the Rajputs were born from the fire offering of the gods on Mount Abu. In reality they emerged in the 6th century from Scythian and Hun invaders to become the fearsome rulers of Rajputana. By appointing themselves *kshatriyas* within the ancient Vedic system, a move supported by the priestly caste of Brahmins, they gained a semi-divine status and claimed descent from the sun (in Udaipur) or the moon (in Jaisalmer). Reaping the rewards of their feudal system, the Rajput princes constructed daunting forts and developed a warriors' code of honor and fearlessness. Whether they were fighting neighboring kingdoms, Turks, Delhi Sultans or Mughals, they were unrivaled for their military prowess and heroism. Proof of their ferocity is the fact that the Mughals, and the British after them, sought conciliation rather than do battle with them, with some notable and bloody exceptions.

112

Rajput opulence in interior decoration

Chivalry and valor Honor came first for the Rajputs, and countless men and women sacrificed themselves rather than lose it. If a battle was turning definitively against them, the mass suicide by fire of the women would accompany the men's final and equally suicidal onslaught. The notions of retreat and surrender were unknown, and defeat was intol-erable to them. A classic Rajput legend describes Maharana Pratap being so traumatized by his family's loss of Chittaurgarh that he aban-doned the comfortable Udaipur palaces to haunt the forests of the Aravalli hills, relentlessly but unsuccessfully attempting to win back the capital city from the Mughal conquerors.

Extravagances After Britain's haphazard, piecemeal conquest of India, most Rajput rulers retained their autonomy in exchange for ceding control of foreign affairs and defence. They indulged in hunting, polo matches, bejeweled elephants, private train cars, Rolls Royces, marble palaces, harems, and glittering banquets, and jewels were an obsession. The fabulous treasure of the Maharaja of Jaipur was so precious that it was buried in a hillside and guarded by a particularly fearsome Rajput unit. Each maharaja would visit the hoard to select one item for his reign; the choice ranged from a three-tiered necklace of egg-sized rubies to three giant emeralds weighing 90 carats. A Maharaja of Jodhpur sported diamond eyebrows; the Maharaja of Bharatpur preferred ivory masterpieces, and his favorite automobile was a silver-plated Rolls Royce. More extraordinary still was the Maharaja of Alwar's self-styled, gold-plated Lanchester, with a steering wheel of carved ivory and a body designed as a replica of the British coronation coach.

Social sustenance Visiting the palaces of Rajasthan gives an idea of the anachronistic, often eccentric lifestyle that continued unabated until Independence, among silver cradles, inlaid ivory beds, Bohemian glass chandeliers, golden *howdahs*, and endless wildlife trophies. There was another, paternalistic side to these rulers, though, that sometimes gave their people benefits and privileges unknown elsewhere in India. Enlightened rulers invested in improving the state infrastructure and industrial technology, as with Ganga Singh of Bikaner who brought railroads, elevators, mining, and the world's longest concrete-lined canal to his parched state in 1925–1927. In addition, various famine relief projects were instigated—one example of these was the construction of Jodhpur's Umaid Bhawan palace.

ROYAL ARMIES
Despite handing over defence responsibilities to the British, each Rajput ruler trained, equipped and maintained his own private army. During the two World Wars these armies played significant roles. In 1917, the Maharaja of Jodhpur's Lancers led the charge that took Haifa from the Turks in the Palestine campaign; in 1943 the Maharaja of Jaipur led his First Jaipur Infantry up the slopes of Monte Cassino in Italy. Also in World War II, the Maharao of Bundi won the Military Cross for his battalion's action in Myanmar (Burma), while Bikaner's Camel Corps fought beside Britain in China, Palestine, Egypt, France, and Myanmar.

113

Hunting was considered essential proof of valor by the Rajputs

The North

▶▶▶ **REGION HIGHLIGHTS**

*Previous pages: Hindu
faithful bathing in the
sacred waters at Varanasi
Below: a Hindu sadhu,
in a yogic position*

116

A Sikh holy man, wearing the ritual dagger, bracelet, and turban

*Above: Buddhist prayer
flags at Leh
Below: Tibetan refugee in
Dharmsala*

NORTH Radiating northwards and eastwards from Delhi, the North reaches from the densely populated Gangetic plain to the towering Himalayas that feed it from their snows and glaciers. The fertile plain was the original heartland of India, where hunter gatherers became farmers along the Indus, Yamuna and Ganga (Ganges) rivers some 5,000 years ago. The original Dravidian people were driven to the deep south by fair-skinned Aryans who introduced Sanskrit and the fundamental texts of Hindu philosophy and religion. Persians, Greeks, and Mughals were successively seduced by this region, long before the British made Delhi their capital and chose the western Himalayas for their summer retreats.

HIGH CONTRAST It is a region of stark contrasts, that includes the desolate heights of Ladakh, the blossoming valleys of Himachal, the Mughal glories of Agra, the erotic temples of Khajuraho, the tigers of Corbett National Park ,and the tumultuous human hordes descending on the holy sites of the Ganges. Such a kaleidoscopic sweep puts demands on visitors, who need considerable mental and physical energy, respect for the climate, and, in the case of Kashmir, awareness of political developments. Places in northern Madhya Pradesh that are most easily combined with destinations in Uttar Pradesh are also included in this section. Amritsar, capital of the comparatively colorless Punjab, has not been included, as it offers only one major, albeit spectacular sight, the Golden Temple. Separatist activities have made this an insecure, unpredictable destination that hardly merits the organizational effort required.

PILGRIMS AND PYRES Uttar Pradesh, India's most heavily populated state, dominates national culture through its language (Hindi). It is also of immense importance to Hindus as site of India's holiest city—Varanasi (Benares). Here Mother Ganges is treated with infinite respect: it is believed that to be cremated by the river at Varanasi releases the body from the endless cycle of rebirths. Cremations account for just a fraction of the daily activity on the *ghats*, however, and Varanasi also maintains an illustrious cultural and crafts tradition. Closer to its source in the Himalayas, the Ganges has also fostered Haridwar and Rishikesh, two smaller but equally intense pilgrimage destinations.

ARCHITECTURAL HERITAGE Varanasi, Haridwar and Rishikesh are spiritual centers, with a heightened atmosphere of faith and mental discipline. Agra is much more worldly: you could give it a miss were it not the site of the Taj Mahal, built in the 17th century at the zenith of the Mughal artistic and architectural prowess. This had its genesis in the earlier Agra Fort and the architecturally imaginative, but abandoned, town of Fatehpur Sikri. Also deserted are the palaces and Hindu temples of Orchha, dating from the same period and now an increasingly popular and atmospheric destination. Between the two is the magnificent fort of Gwalior, started long before any of the above. To the east are the fabulous temples of Khajuraho, created as a Hindu celebration of erotic pleasures as a way to self deliverance.

UNADULTERATED NATURE The end (or the beginning) of the North lies in the Himalayas. In the foothills lies the popular national park, Corbett, and from there the terrain rises abruptly into Himachal Pradesh. This gentle state of rolling pine-clad hills, rivers, orchards, and shepherds, dotted with small hill-towns like Shimla, Dalhousie, Chamba, Manali, and Dharmsala, is bordered to the north by the violence-prone state of Jammu and Kashmir. Here the plateaux of the Western Himalayas hover around 11,483 feet and snowy peaks tower above to 19,685 feet The highest town is Leh, remote in the bleak and magnificent Ladakh. Buddhism rules between the Ladakhi and the Tibetan community of Dharmsala, but Islam is strong in neighboring Kashmir.

GETTING AROUND
Traveling in Uttar Pradesh is relatively easy, as a dense network of buses and trains serves its large population. The fast Shatabdi Express covers Delhi, Agra, Gwalior and Jhansi (for Orchha). The Delhi–Agra–Khajuraho–Varanasi air route is quick too, but is often full months in advance because of tour groups. Even if you have a confirmed ticket, you may not have a seat. Leh's inaccessibility and short season also create overbooking havoc. Himachal Pradesh has airports at Shimla and Kullu; from there, buses and jeep-taxis are the only way to go— slowly. An alternative is the night train to Pathankot, giving easy access to Dharmsala, Dalhousie and Jammu.

Temples at Khajuraho

▶▶▶ Agra   116B2

Agra's prominence on the tourist trail is due to one monument alone, the Taj Mahal. This is the glory of Mughal India, its white marble facade, domes and minarets glowing in a projection of grandeur that is far from the reality of India today. Built as an expression of love, it is now surrounded by a polluted, industrialized city whose heart beats to the commercial rhythms of tourism. The best advice is to see the monuments, and head to Fatehpur Sikri.

Capital Agra's history really started when Sultan Sikander Lodi moved his capital here from Delhi in 1504 to keep a closer eye on his extensive but war-prone kingdom to the south. His city rose on the eastern banks of the Yamuna River, but just 22 years later the Sultanate was crushingly defeated by Babur, the first of the Mughal emperors, and his son, Humayun (see pages 44–45). With the construction of the fort by Humayun's son, Akbar, Agra reassumed its role as capital, this time of the Mughal Empire. So it remained for a further century, except for the short, ill-fated interlude of Fatehpur Sikri. In the 17th century Shah Jahan built his labor of love, the Taj Mahal (see pages 122–123), at Agra, but his ambitions led him to redevelop Delhi and move to its expanded Red Fort. It was in Agra Fort that he ended his days, however, imprisoned by his merciless son, Aurangzeb. This last Mughal emperor definitively adopted Delhi as his capital and Agra was later successively taken by the Jats, the Marathas and, in 1803, by the British.

Above: marble inlay on Itmad-ud-daulah's tomb in Agra
Right: a back street in Agra

Practicalities This city of nearly two million inhabitants is relatively easy to get around. Its main monuments, the Taj and the fort, rise above the banks of the Yamuna. Hotels are mainly in the central cantonment area, south of the fort, with budget lodges huddled in the narrow streets just south of the Taj. Services on Taj Road link the two. On the eastern bank lies the peaceful, inlaid marble tomb of **Itmad-ud-daulah**▶▶ and, a few miles north, the **Ram Bagh**▶, (*Open* daily dawn–dusk. *Admission free*) Babur's ruined pleasure gardens, now being restored. Agra's tongas, bicycle- and auto-rickshaws need extra-hard bargaining, but bicycles can be rented in the Taj Ganj area. Delhi trains stop at Agra Cantonment station, trains to Rajasthan use both Cantonment and Agra Fort station.

The fort Surrounded by high red sandstone walls, **Agra Fort**▶▶▶ (see panel) is entered from the south through Amar Singh gate. From here a long elephant ramp leads through a garden to the main section open to the public. It was built by successive emperors from the 1570s throughout the 17th century, and combines Akbar's walls and tiled gates with Shah Jahan's delicate Moti Masjid (Pearl Mosque) and once-elegant palaces.

Start in the south, at the solid red sandstone Jahangiri Mahal, the women's palace, incorporating numerous Hindu features, with a more modest palace to the south. North lies the Anguri Bagh, a symmetrical garden edged to the east by two golden pavilions with curved roofs. These flank the central Khas Mahal, a partly restored marble pavilion that was probably a breezy retiring room. Beyond this is the Musamman Burj, an octagonal tower crowned by an exquisitely decorated open pavilion where, legend has it, Shah Jahan lay on his deathbed, gazing at the Taj Mahal. Next door are the *hammams* (bathing rooms), with complex water channels. From the tower a staircase leads to the Diwan-i-Khas, the private audience hall, with finely inlaid pillars opening onto a wide terrace dominated by a black marble throne. West of the ruined Macchi Bhawan is the beautiful Diwan-i-Am (public audience hall). Finally, stop at the pretty marble Nagina Masjid and Mina Bazar, both built for the women of the harem.

TO SHOP OR NOT?
Agra has a fine selection of locally made jewelry, carpets, inlaid marble, and soapstone objects, but it is also a hotbed for con-men who deal ably with naive tourists. Prices are high and include hidden commissions, and many salesmen are dishonest. Try to save your rupees for less touristy towns.

The North

LABOR OF LOVE
The Taj Mahal was built by Shah Jahan in memory of his favorite wife, Mumtaz Mahal, who died giving birth to her 14th child. The heartbroken emperor determined to construct an unsurpassable memorial tomb and 22 years later, in 1653, after tons of Jodhpur marble and semi-precious stones from all over Asia had been transported to the site by elephants, the masterpiece was complete. Some 20,000 craftsmen and laborers are said to have worked on it. Shah Jahan was imprisoned by his son and spent his last eight years languishing in Agra Fort, but he was able to gaze out at the tomb of his wife, beside whom he was buried when he himself died in 1666.

122

Taj Mahal However many images you may have seen of the **Taj Mahal**►►► (for entry information, see panel page 120), the reality is still breathtaking, its scale stupendous and its surface ever changing with the light. Favorite visiting times are sunrise and sunset, when the translucent white marble seems to float in a soft, often misty glow, its reflection shimmering in the long, rectangular water channel that leads through the gardens. At any time of day it is thronged with visitors, from foreign tour groups to picnicking families and young Indian couples.

Ultimate balance The gardens were designed in typical Mughal style to evoke an Islamic paradise of peace and tranquility. They are cut into quadrants by waterways and lined with flowering shrubs and shade-giving trees. Their symmetry is reflected in the two buildings flanking the tomb: to the west, a sandstone and marble mosque, and to the east, the *jawab* ("answer") which exists purely for visual balance. This symmetrical purity continues in the four slender minarets that rise at each corner of the enormous square platform, and the four domes surrounding the central "pearl".

Sumptuous handiwork Access to the vast platform is by a central staircase, where shoes must be removed. From here you enter the domain of superlative craftsmanship and design, embodied in beautifully engraved Koranic calligraphy and floral motifs, niches, carved balustrades, and

immaculate stone inlay. Views across the Yamuna are particularly atmospheric at sunset. Inside, the real tombs are housed in the crypt, while the lavishly inlaid "public" tombs stand beneath the lofty dome. Perfectly aligned with the main entrance gate, Mumtaz' tomb is joined to one side by the larger one of Shah Jahan. Surrounding them is another masterpiece, a magnificent lace-like marble *jali* screen studded with precious stones. A small **museum** (*Open* Sat–Thu 10–5. *Admission free*) displays portraits of Mughal emperors, architectural drawings and models of the Taj, porcelain and photographs.

Excursion

Fatehpur Sikri▶▶ (see panel page 120) Some 23 miles west of Agra lie the remains of the ambitious city built by Akbar *ca*1570–1585 but virtually abandoned within 20 years, for reasons of state, and not as legend has it, because of lack of water. The delicate, red sandstone palaces have been carefully restored and the city is an atmospheric destination, easily covered in half a day.

Palaces As you approach from Agra Gate past the Mint, the Diwan-i-Am (public audience hall) opens onto a courtyard with the emperor's throne room to the west. Behind this is one of Fatehpur's most intriguing structures, the Pachisi board, a gigantic stone board game for which Akbar is said to have used slave girls as pieces. Rising to the north is the Diwan-i-Khas (private audience hall) where decorative features combine Hindu, Muslim, Christian, and Buddhist symbols. At its center is the throne pillar topped by a circular platform from which radiate four bridges used for Akbar's theological discussions. In the southeast corner stands the intricately decorated Anup Talao pavilion, once the palace of Akbar's favorite wife.

South of this are the emperor's own quarters, the Daulat Khana, arranged on two stories. Beyond the *zenana* is Fatehpur's most arresting sight, the Panch Mahal. This five-storied palace tapering to a single *chhatri* and bordered by broad overhanging eaves is a feast of pillars, each one an individually decorated symbol. Other palaces include the lovely Hawa Mahal and the elaborate palace of Raja Birba.

Mosque The imposing Jami Masjid is fronted by a massive gateway opening onto a vast courtyard that seethes with hawkers. Inside are several royal tombs but it is the *dargah* (tomb) of the Sufi saint, Salim Chishti, that is the most elaborate. Gleaming white marble is carved with masterly delicacy beneath a canopy inlaid with mother-of-pearl, a fitting tribute to the man who inspired Fatehpur (see panel).

SHEIKH SALIM CHISTI
The Sufi saint buried in glory at Fatehpur Sikri was behind the misjudged selection of this site for a city. Akbar, finding himself childless, did the rounds of the holy men to gain spiritual support and encouragement for the production of an heir. Chisti, who lived in the village of Sikri, foretold that Akbar would have three sons. This prophecy was borne out, and when the saint died in 1571, the emperor decided to build a new city on the site of Chisti's village in his honor. Fatehpur ("town of victory") was added to the name of the village, but by the end of the 16th century the city lay deserted.

123

The Taj Mahal (above and left), is Shah Jahan's monument to love, and India's most enduring icon

Spotted deer, or chital, are a common sight at Corbett National Park

TIGER JIM
Jim Corbett, the instigator of the national park which bears his name, was a local man born in Naini Tal of Anglo-Irish parents in 1875. His upbringing brought him into close contact with nature and above all with the jungle. He became an excellent shot, and disposed of numerous man-eating tigers and leopards that had terrorized local villagers. When he became an army officer, his interest in wildlife took a more protective turn and he spent years photographing his former quarry and later writing several books. After Independence, he left India for Africa where he died in 1955.

TOURIST OFFICES
MP Tourism, Hotel Tansen, 6a Gandhi Marg, Gwalior (*Open* all day; tel: 0751 340370, fax: 0751 340371). Also at train station (*Open* 9–1, 5–9). Permits for Dhikala/ Corbett are obtainable from the Main Reception Center, Ramnagar, (*Open* daily 8–1, 3–5; tel: 05946 85489, fax: 05946 85376).

▶▶▶ **Corbett National Park**   116B3

Open: mid-Nov–mid-Jun dawn–dusk.
Admission: expensive

Often considered to be India's finest wildlife reserve, Corbett National Park lies in the Kumaun foothills of the Himalayas, 180 miles northeast of Delhi. Famed for its tigers (it was among the first participants of Project Tiger in 1973), it also offers contrasting landscapes and flora, as it rises from 1,312 feet to 3,937 feet within an area of 50 square miles. This is India's classic safari destination, with luxury hotels in beautifully isolated locations and rudimentary bungalows (no electricity or food) within the park. Park headquarters (with a library, wildlife film shows, and a restaurant) is in the scenic heart of the park, at Dhikala, and you need a permit (from Ramnagar—see panel) for this area. Access from Delhi to Ramnagar is by bus via Naini Tal or Ranikhet, or train via Moradabad: count on seven to eight hours. Winter nights can be very cold, so come prepared.

Natural gift India's first national park came into being in 1936 thanks to Jim Corbett (see panel), although it did not bear his name until later. Today it is a rare patch of true wilderness, incorporating dense jungle (dominated by sal trees), grasslands, and bamboo groves. The many streams and ravines become waterless during the dry season; exceptions are the Ramganga River and a large reservoir. Altogether the park has over 100 tree species and around 60 tigers. Leopards are rare here. Corbett is nevertheless rich in wild elephants, jackal, wild boar, chital (spotted deer), sambar, hog deer, langurs, and rhesus monkeys. The waterways have crocodiles as well as a wide range of waterbirds. These, together with birds of prey and woodland birds, make up Corbett's total bird count of over 600 different species.

▶▶ **Gwalior**   116B2

Madhya Pradesh's northernmost city inspired Emperor Babur's epithet, "the pearl among the fortresses of Sind". Rising abruptly on a rocky outcrop from the surrounding plains, the fort's bastions and delicately fretted domes were a majestic backdrop to a momentous history that saw successive Rajput, Afghan Muslim, Mughal, Maratha,

and British rulers. Down below, the city has developed into a typically characterless sprawl of concrete, relieved only by the Muslim quarter with its mosque and the elegant 16th-century **tombs of Ghaus Mohammed and Tansen▶**. Tansen was a singer, who was one of the "nine jewels" of Akbar's court. To the south lies the ostentatious, Italianate **Jai Vilas Palace and Museum▶▶** (*Open* Tue–Sun 9:30–5. *Admission: expensive*), containing a mindboggling collection of treasures belonging to Gwalior's last rulers, the Scindia family (see panel). Numerous **Jain sculptures▶** dating from the 7th to the 15th centuries are carved into the rock of the cliffs. The best are to the west, at Urwahi.

Past glory The imposing **fort▶▶▶** (*Open* daily 8–6. *Admission: moderate*) has a wealth of Indian architecture covering seven centuries. Much of the work was done under the Rajput Man Singh, who was killed by the Lodis in 1517. At the fort's heart is his four-storied Man Mandir, a masterpiece of ornate, palatial stonework faced with decorative mosaics. The more sober interior consists of vast chambers divided by *jali* screens, behind which court ladies would watch and listen to their music teachers. To the north stand the Vikram Mandir, the Karam Mandir and, in the northeastern corner, the Gujuri Mahal, built by Man Singh to win a soulful-eyed peasant girl. This now houses a museum (*Open* Tue–Sun 10–5. *Admission: expensive*). The southern end of the fort contains its oldest monuments. The 8th-century Teli Ka Mandir, towering over 98 feet, was a Vishnu temple that the British blithely used as a soda water factory. To the east, is the graceful Sas-Bahu Ka Mandir, two 11th-century Vishnu temples with beautifully carved interiors. West of this is a huge *tank*, the Suraj Kund.

Above: Jain sculptures at Gwalior depicting the incarnations of Mahavir Inset: mosaic detail, Gwalior fort

SCINDIA EXCESS
In 1875, Jayaji Rao Scindia installed some extra fixtures in his palace to prepare it for a visit by the Prince of Wales and his retinue of 1,000. Having learned the size of Buckingham Palace's largest chandeliers, he placed an order in Venice for two bigger ones for his Durbar Hall. They weighed over 3.5 tons each, so the Maharaja tested the ceiling strength with eight (or 10) elephants, using a 1,640-foot ramp (or a crane). He also had a silver toy train that chugged around the table dispensing post-prandial cigars and brandy.

The Ganga, or Ganges, is India's most revered river. It flows 1,555 miles, from the chilly heights of the Himalayas and across the scorching plains to its delta on the Bay of Bengal. Along this winding course lie India's most sacred pilgrimage spots, from Gangotri to Varanasi. However, the river's spiritual purity is far from matched by its increasingly polluted waters.

LIQUID ARMS
"...There the Ganga reached out and enfolded me in its enormous liquid arms, just as my mother had drawn me into her arms and painted for me a word picture of the Ganga flowing through the celestial world, the terrestrial world and the nether world."
Raghubir Singh, *The Ganges*, 1992

126

Below: crowds on Mir Ghat, Varanasi
Right: Hindu faithful in meditation and prayer by the Ganges

Central to Hindu and Buddhist cosmology is mythical Mount Meru, the cosmic mountain and axis connecting heaven and earth, from which flow four rivers. Meru has an earthly incarnation in Mount Kailas, rising 22,027 feet between two lakes. It was here, in the Trans-Himalaya of Tibet, that the source of the Ganges was long considered to lie. Kailas' majestic domed shape became the inspiration for ancient Hindu and Buddhist temples, and a divine enclosure around the mountain was said to be the abode of the gods, presided over by Brahma. Encircling this heavenly domain three times over was Ganga, the elder daughter of Himalaya, who was eventually persuaded to flow through the tangled hair of Siva to descend to earth (see panel page 235).

The source In reality the Ganges emerges at the Gangotri glacier, due west of Kailas. Here, a swift crystalline stream flows through a desolate landscape of snow and rocks, its freezing waters already crowded with thousands

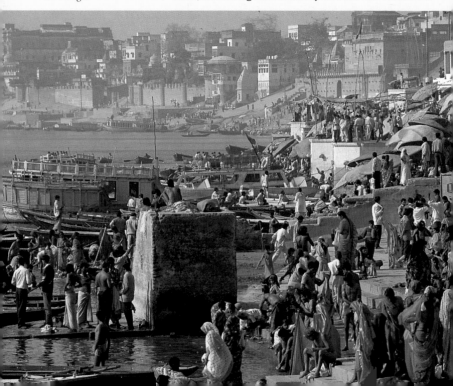

of bathing pilgrims who rub themselves with oil to mitigate the extreme cold. Simple people used to trek for weeks from their villages in the plains to realize their lifetime's ambition: a dip in the Ganges as it flows through the abode of the gods. It is the Hindu equivalent of Mecca. Today, most arrive by bus or car, their radios shattering the spiritual peace, but the highest reaches are still the preserve of determined sadhus.

Black spot Gushing through the Siwalik hills, which form the last humps of the Himalayas, the Ganges arrives at Haridwar, one of the seven sacred cities of Hindu India. From here it courses through Uttar Pradesh to Kanpur, the state's largest industrial center and the river's first source of major pollution: 80 percent of the city's sewage is dumped, untreated, into the Ganges to join toxic industrial effluents from textile, leather, and chemical factories. This was also one of the black spots of the Uprising (Indian Mutiny) of 1857, when several hundred British survivors of a siege were murdered on the banks of the holy river. Reprisals were no less ferocious.

Confluence Halfway between Kanpur and Varanasi lies Allahabad, exceptionally sacred as it lies at the prayag (confluence) of the Ganges and Yamuna rivers. Hindu mythology multiplies Allahabad's purifying powers by conjuring up the emergence of the underground river of enlightenment, the Sarasvati. In the Vedas, Sarasvati was a water goddess flowing west of the Himalayas through the first Aryan settlements. She was later identified with the holy rituals performed on her banks, and gradually became perceived as Brahma's wife, inventor of Sanskrit and goddess of all creative arts. A spit of land at Allahabad's confluence receives millions of pilgrims, particularly during the auspicious Magh Mela (lasting two weeks every January–February and even greater numbers during the 12-yearly Kumbh Mela.

River of death? Eastward from here, the increasingly overloaded Ganges traverses Varanasi (Benares), Patna and Calcutta, receiving human corpses, sewage, and industrial effluents on a seemingly unstoppable scale. Approximately 45,000 bodies are cremated yearly at Varanasi, while at Kanpur over 200 tanneries discharge chromium-rich effluents. Around Kolkata (Calcutta) some 150 factories pour untreated waste into the brown waters of the Hugli, a Ganga tributary. In 1985, India launched the Ganga Action Plan, which has been ineffectual. Meanwhile, fish die and riverwater laced with toxins irrigates farmland, eventually seeping into food and village borewells to cause untold disease, from cancer to renal failure and numerous skin complaints. Ganga water, once the only liquid thought fit for orthodox Brahmins, is undrinkable. The river of benediction has been transformed into a river of blight.

Hari ki Pairi, at Haridwar—one of India's seven sacred cities—is much revered by Hindus

▶ **Haridwar** 116B3

Lying at the base of the Siwalik hills on the edge of the Himalayas, Haridwar is one of India's seven sacred cities, for it is here that the holy Ganga (Ganges) leaves the mountains to start its lengthy course eastward across the plains. Every 12 years Haridwar hosts the incredible festival of Kumbh Mela, drawing millions of pilgrims to its *ghats*. The Dikhanti festival each spring also draws crowds, but at other times this mini-Varanasi has a generally placid, small-town atmosphere. The bazaars offer colorful wares, especially Moti Bazar along Railway Road and Bara Bazar in the northern part of town.

Heavy worship The center lies on the west bank of an area sliced by canals into a network of islands and bridges. *Ghats*, *ashrams*, temples, and the hovels of *sadhus* culminate at Hari Ki Pairi, the site of Vishnu's footprint (not accessible to non-Hindus). Every evening at dusk a moving ceremony takes place here, orchestrated by priests and accompanied by musicians. None of the temples is particularly memorable, despite the *Mahabharata's* numerous references to the spot, but it is worth taking the cable car to the hilltop **Mansa Devi temple▶** for good views and a glimpse of this form of the goddess Durga.

Ashram-land 16 miles north lies **Rishikesh▶▶**, associated with the Beatles and their guru, the Maharishi. This deeply spiritual center, where meat and alcohol are strictly prohibited, is a real eye opener on the immensely varied rituals and fervent nature of *sadhus* and yogis. Many stop in Rishikesh before continuing their lengthy pilgrimage northward to the source of the Ganges (Bhagirathi) at Gangotri, where the goddess Ganga is believed to have descended to earth. This small town is almost completely monopolized by *ashrams*, offering courses in yoga, meditation, Sanskrit, natural medicine, music, and countless spiritual paths. Not all is holy however: many loin-clothed *sadhus* are adept at the age-old art of trickery, particularly where tourists are concerned.

Evening worship with floating candles takes place at Triveni ghat, near the main concentration of low-key hotels. To the north, at the much frequented Swarg Ashram, *sadhus* wander out of forest caves to worship at modern temples lining the river.

▶ **Jhansi** 116B1

Situated in a remote finger of Uttar Pradesh that dips into Madhya Pradesh, Jhansi holds little interest apart from being a stopover on the way to Orchha. It does boast a crumbling 17th-century fort (*Open* daily dawn–dusk. *Admission: inexpensive*), but this is less exciting than the legends of the mid-19th century Rani who fought tooth

TOURIST OFFICES
UP Tourism, Rahi Motel, Station, Road, Haridwar (*Open* Mon–Sat 10–5; tel/fax: 0133 427370). GMVN, Lalta Rao Bridge, Upper Road, Haridwar (*Open* Mon–Sat 10–5; tel: 0133 424240, email: gmvn@nde.vsnl.net.in). UP Tourism, Nehru Park, 162 Railway Road, Rishikesh (*Open* Mon–Sat 10–1:30, 2–5; tel: 0135 430209),

and nail against the British to regain it (see panel). Her palace, the **Rani Lakshmi Mahal▶** (*Open* Tue–Sun 9:30–5:30. *Admission: inexpensive*) now houses a wide-ranging display, which includes panels about the 1858 massacre carried out by the British.

Orchha From Jhansi, it takes half an hour to cross the Madhya Pradesh border to reach the now deserted capital of **Orchha▶▶**, set on an island in the Betwa River in beautiful forested surroundings. It was founded in the 16th century by the Bundela Rajput ruler, Rudra Pratap, and then abandoned in the 18th century. Evocative palaces, temples, and *chhatri* cenotaphs stand next to a sleepy yet functioning village with a busy bazaar and a selection of accommodations.

Decorative riches The fort complex is approached by an arched bridge that leads to the Raj Mahal (*Open* daily 10–5. *Admission: inexpensive*) built by the devout Madhukar Shah. It has sober facades crowned by *chhatris*, and contains an extraordinary interior. The most striking decorative features are the subtle murals depicting Hindu myths and court life, many still in remarkable condition. Richer still in its ornamentation is the later Jehangir Mahal, built to commemorate the visit of the Mughal emperor in the 17th century. Strong lines are counterbalanced by delicate *chhatris*, trellis work, *jali* screens, and tiles, all introduced by two stone elephants at the main gateway. Other memorable monuments include the soaring spires of the Ram Raja temple, a former palace, the Chaturbhuj temple, and the Lakshminarayan temple, which is richly painted with murals.

LOCAL HEROINE
The Rani of Jhansi is feted as one of India's great heroines, for putting up a determined fight against the British. In 1853 her husband died, leaving a kingdom without a male heir, whereupon the British seized the town and fort. After recouping in Gwalior, the Rani launched a massive attack on the fort during the Uprising (Indian Mutiny) of 1857, and in a lengthy bout of bloody fighting some 5,000 of her soldiers died. The Rani, who had by then adopted a baby son who was strapped to her back, managed to escape through the British troops but eventually met her end "dressed as a man, holding her sword with both hands and her reins gripped between her teeth".

129

The Lakshman Jhula bridge over the Ganges at Rishikesh

The North

TOURIST OFFICES

Government of India, opposite Western Group (*Open* Mon–Fri 9–4:30, Sat 8–12:30. tel: 07686 2047/8). Basic map and information on nearby sights, cultural shows, and the Khajuraho Dance Festival held in the temple precinct in mid-March. Car rental and guide hire.

MP Tourism, Chandela Cultural Center, Tourist Village, north of Western group (*Open* Mon–Sat 10–5; tel: 07686 44051, fax: 42330, email: mail@mptourism.com). Also counter at bus-stand.

Khajuraho is one of the highlights of the northern trail, offering a feast of intricately carved "erotic" temples scattered over a tranquil, rural landscape. Although daily flights carry tour groups in and out from Delhi, Agra and Varanasi (Benares), it is well worth spending a couple of days here to bicycle around the sights and tour the lovely environs perfumed with *mahua* trees.

Background The creators of this stupendous legacy were the Chandellas, thought to be of Rajput origin, who became a powerful dynasty during the 9th century. Forgotten for centuries and engulfed by vegetation, the temples were rediscovered by a British engineer in 1835. Of the original total of over 80 temples, only 22 survive and the once thriving city has been reduced to a sprawling village highly dependent on the tourist trade.

Shakti style Although Siva dominates, some Khajuraho temples are dedicated to Vishnu and there are also traces of Buddhism, Jainism, sun worship, and animistic cults. All are carved in sandstone and were once coated in white gesso, their multiple towers clustered around the lofty main *shikhara* suggesting the holy mountain and strongly reminiscent of the Orissan style. Below is the sanctum enshrining the deity of the temple with a passage leading around side porches and a front *mandapa* (hall), all alive with sculpted figures and friezes. Each temple is on a high platform, allowing worshippers to circle the edifice and gain close views of the staggeringly complex carvings.

Khajuraho is famed above all for its erotica, but this constitutes only about a tenth of the total. It is thought that the temples were built to celebrate episodes from the marriage of Siva and Parvati (or *shakti*, the divine female force). From this stems the Tantric cult, worshipping the activation of male forces by sexual union with *shakti*.

Priorities The seven temples of the **Western Group**▶▶▶ (*Open* daily dawn–dusk. *Admission: inexpensive*, ticket includes museum) stand in a beautifully landscaped garden, their lace-like towers aligned in two rows. These are Khajuraho's most accomplished structures. The Lakshamana, Viswanath and Kandariya Mahadeva temples are outstanding. South of the enclosure is the unusually plain Matangesvara temple, containing a magnificent *lingam*, over 6.5 feet high and still worshipped today. Opposite, the museum (*Open* Sat–Thu 10–5. *Admission free*) exhibits related fragments and sculptures. Huddled around old Khajuraho is the **Eastern Group**▶▶, composed of three richly carved Jain temples within an enclosure and four scattered Hindu temples. The remote **Southern Group**▶, near the airport, has only two, later temples, one displaying a massive statue combining the head of Siva, the body of Vishnu and the legs of Krishna.

Excursions

Khajuraho is well placed for trips to Panna National Park (16 miles), Pandav Falls (21 miles), the Majhgaon Diamond Mines (35 miles) showing open-cast mining and, closest of all, the Rajgarh Palace, an atmospheric, isolated palace said to be connected by a tunnel to Khajuraho.

PURSUIT OF PLEASURE

"In a country where the linga cult is the source of religious belief and its manifestations are to be seen in very early periods of civilization the erotic sculptures are but a continuation of that tradition which accepts procreation as a major function of life. The presence of erotic sculptures show that there were no taboos or inhibitions against sex as we have now. *Kama*, or pursuit of pleasure, was deemed to be one of the four *purusharthas* or legitimate aims of life for a Grahast as it was regarded as a stepping stone to *moksha* (deliverance)."

Anonymous author, *Khajuraho*

Ancient erotica—carved pillars at Devi Jagadambi temple, in the Western Group, Khajuraho

TOURIST OFFICES
Government of India, 15B The Mall, Cantonment (*Open* Mon–Fri 9–5:30, Sat 9–4:30; tel: 0542 343744). Very helpful, also counter at airport. *Ghat* tours at 6 AM, finish at the university, afternoon tours to Sarnath.
UP Tourism, Tourist Bungalow, Kothi Parade, Cantonment (*Open* Mon–Sat 10–5; tel: 0542 343413/341162, fax: 344545, email: upstdc@lwl.vsnl.net.in). Well organized, with maps. Equally helpful at Cantonment train station (*Open* daily 6 AM–8 PM; tel: 0542 346370).
Visit one of the above to avoid the Varanasi touts and hustlers.

▶ Shivpuri 116B1

Once the summer capital of the Scindia rulers of Gwalior, Shivpuri has palaces, hunting lodges and marble-turreted cenotaphs in a landscape of wooded hills, grasslands and a lake, now designated the Mandhav National Park. It lies about 62 miles from both Gwalior and Jhansi, and includes a complex of ornate *chhatris*▶▶ set in a formal Mughal garden: the stone inlay is particularly striking on the Madho Rao Scindia cenotaph. Crowning a hilltop is the **Madhav Vilas palace**▶, a rose colored, colonial-inspired building with marble floors, cast iron pillars, and wide terraces.

▶▶▶ Varanasi (Benares) 117D1

The holiest of holy places in India is Varanasi, a city with a virtually unrivaled status in Hindu mythology. For Mark Twain "Benaras is older than history, older than tradition, older even than legend and looks twice as old as all of them put together". Even today, congested with thousands of tourists and pilgrims, Varanasi feels like this. More than any other Indian town, it incarnates the incomparable complexities of Hindu rituals and worship. Around two million inhabitants include an estimated 50,000 Brahmins, and each year the number of pilgrims easily rivals the resident population.

The holy city of Varanasi attracts sadhus *and pilgrims from all over India*

Intensity The extraordinary activity on the *ghats* starts before dawn (see pages 134–135). As the sun rises opposite over Mother Ganges, yogis plunge into meditation and pilgrims dip in the water. Varanasi's mysticism comes hand-in-hand with the less elevated life of hustlers, commissions, and drugs, and the city can be deeply unpleasant for independent travelers, who make obvious targets for con men. To escape unwelcome harassment, it is best to stay in the tree-lined avenues of the Cantonment area, about 2 miles from the vibrant but exhausting *chowk* and *ghats*.

South Varanasi Varanasi is also an important center of learning and the arts. **Banaras Hindu University►** occupies a huge landscaped campus to the south and includes an archeological museum, **Bharat Kala Bhavan►** (*Open* Mon–Sat Jul–Apr 11–4:30; May–Jun 7:30–12:30. *Admission: moderate*). Here too is the imposing New Vishwanath temple (1966), a cool marble edifice designed for use by all castes. Opposite the campus on the strangely empty east bank of the Ganga (Ganges) is only one sight, the dilapidated **Ramnagar Fort►►** (*Open* daily 9–noon, 2–5. *Admission: inexpensive*) where inlaid silver *howdahs*, dusty carriages, vintage cars, exquisitely carved ivory, and superb Rajput weapons are exhibited in a potent atmosphere of neglect. Along Durga Kund Road, linking this southern area with the center, stand two significant temples: firstly there is the Tulsi Manas Mandir, built in 1964 to commemorate the medieval poet, Goswami Tulsidas, and secondly there is the red-spired 18th-century Durga Temple (the inner sanctum is closed to non-Hindus).

ANCIENT REFERENCES
The earliest descriptions of Varanasi are found in Buddhist scriptures and in the Hindu epic, the *Mahabharata*. According to Sanskrit puranas, the Varuna and Assi rivers (running along the city's north and south perimeters respectively) originated from the body of the first man at the beginning of time. The sacred Ganga is the eastern perimeter. Varanasi was also known as Kashi (from *kas*, meaning "to shine") and is the "city of light", standing on the original ground created by Siva and Parvati.

133

The back streets of Varanasi are a maze of narrow alleyways

Holy cows are as much a part of Varanasi as pilgrims and tourists

POLLUTED WATERS

The sacred waters of the Ganga (Ganges) are visibly polluted. In 1985 the Ganga Action Plan was intended to achieve India's largest-ever clean-up, but poor monitoring, overspending, slow progress, and corruption have combined to produce abysmal results. In Varanasi, over 28,000 turtles were introduced into the Ganges to feed on the polluting corpses. Most were poached and the turtle farm is now without a single inmate. A specially designed *dhobi* (laundry) *ghat* lies empty, apart from being used as a public toilet. Sewage was diverted and discharged into the Varuna River, and now causes a rash of water-borne diseases such as jaundice, malaria, and skin diseases among local villagers.

Ghat-land Along the edge of the Ganga (Ganges) are over 100 *ghats*, a focus for living, dying, and dead Hindus alike. Some *ghats* have a social function, and are places where locals chat while performing their ablutions. Others are the sites for specific religious rituals. Old people are numerous, as anyone who dies in Varanasi on the banks of the Ganges achieves *moksha* (deliverance). A four o'clock start is the rule if you want to join the pre-dawn hordes of devotees and locals, bathing, performing *puja*, meditating, washing clothes, or in the case of a few emaciated hippies, striking out to the opposite bank. Boat-loads of tourists snap away at these images in the soft, pink light of dawn while hundreds of leaf-borne candles drift over the water. Boat tariffs are lower later in the morning, but rise again towards sunset. Whatever time you visit, bargain hard.

Magnetic forces A good starting point is the central Dasaswamedh Ghat, named after 10 horses sacrificed by Brahma and considered one of the holiest spots for bathing. Its confluence position has given it specific magnetic forces. To the south is Harishchandra Ghat, Varanasi's second crematorium. Walking or boating north from here brings you to the Man Mandir Ghat. Looming above the riverbank is the Man Singh observatory (*Open* daily 8–5. *Admission free*), housed in a palatial 1600s building containing frescoes and astronomical instruments. Immediately north of this is the tiger-fronted mansion belonging to the Dom Rajas, the "untouchable" family that runs Varanasi's lucrative crematoriums. Goats, buffaloes, *chai*-sellers, postcard-hawkers, boatmen, beggars, *sadhus*, and pilgrims all mix in a mesmerizing atmosphere that continues north to Panchganga Ghat.

Cremations Manikarnika Ghat, Varanasi's main crematorium and first stone *ghat*, was built in 1302 to replace earlier sand and clay versions. On the steps is a large *lingam* and behind is stacked the wood that is carefully weighed out for each pyre. Before cremation, the shrouded corpse experiences its last dip in the Ganges. If you arrive during a cremation, remember that photo-taking is strictly forbidden. Beyond the *ghat* is a stepped *tank* supposedly created from a divine earring, and in front, a lopsided, sinking temple, believed to have been cursed by the builder's mother 150 years ago. This main stretch ends beyond Ram Ghat at Panchganga Ghat, overlooked by a crumbling Maratha palace.

Heart of the past From Panchganga Ghat, wide steps lead up to the Alamgir mosque, built in 1669 by Aurangzeb from the debris of a Hindu temple. From here a fascinating maze of winding lanes lined with tiny stores, some mere cubicles on two storys, plunges you back into the Middle Ages. Jewelers, barbers, cobblers, and sellers of curd, spice, oils, herb, and betel are all packed in, while cows and bicycles filter through the crowds. Wider streets and more ornate buildings take over at the main *chowk* with its flower market and its tourist-stores displaying a glittering show of silks, sitars, brass, and copperware.

Sectarian rivalry Near the clock tower, along a heavily policed lane, are the Kashi Vishwanath (Golden) Temple, and a few yards away, the Gyanavapi Mosque. These epitomize India's ongoing Hindu–Muslim tensions, the armed guards protecting the mosque against Hindu extremists. Their visible presence is a response to threats against it. Muslims make up over 20 percent of Varanasi's population and this, set against Hindu orthodoxy, does not bode well for peaceful coexistence. The original Vishwanath temple was demolished by Aurangzeb to build his mosque but in 1776 the present Siva temple arose. In 1835 it acquired gold-plated spires and a dome (using one ton of gold leaf) that shelters the *lingam* below.

Seasonal flooding creates an annual need for repairs to the ghats

SILKS
Varanasi produces many stunning silks and brocades. Although much of the city's output is sold in Delhi, the stores of Varanasi have a huge range of high-quality scarves, saris, and bolts of cloth with gold borders or finely woven patterns that create shimmering brocades. The small store units on the upper floors opposite the Golden Temple deal mainly in well-priced scarves. You can watch the weavers at work at the Government Weaving Center at Chauka Ghat. Shop without guides or drivers, as commissions may boost the price by 40 percent. Good deals for silk, scarves, and saris can be obtained at Ali Handicrafts, C19, A-5 Lallapura, which is a wholesale store that welcomes retail buyers.

The North

136

Pilgrims often follow a purifying dip in the Ganges with a ritual shave

The original *lingam* is said to lie in the well that stands between the two rivals. Only Hindus and Muslims are admitted to the temple and mosque respectively, but good views can be had, for a tip, from the upper floors of the stores opposite.

Excursion

Sarnath▶▶ Buddha preached his first sermon at Sarnath, about 6 miles north of the center of Varanasi, and it became a major religious and study center in the 4th–9th centuries. Excavations were carried out in 1905–1910 when the museum was built, and since then the site has acquired Buddhist temples funded by China, Japan, Tibet, Myanmar (Burma), and South Korea, though these are of little interest.

The first monument encountered on the road from Varanasi is the 5th-century Chaukhandi *stupa*, crowned by an octagonal tower (1588) to commemorate the Mughal emperor Akbar's victory. The caretaker will unlock this for a tip. The next stop is the excellent **Archaeological Museum** (*Open* Sat–Thu 10–5. *Admission: inexpensive*) containing abundant Buddhist statues, among them Ashoka's Lion capital, famed as the national emblem of India. Four lions crown a 24-spoked wheel representing dynamism and continuity—the Buddhist wheel of law. The base is a lotus, a recurring symbol in Buddhism, Hinduism, and Jainism. Other marvels include a 1st-century Bodhisattva from Madura and a superb preaching Buddha (5th-century) from Sarnath.

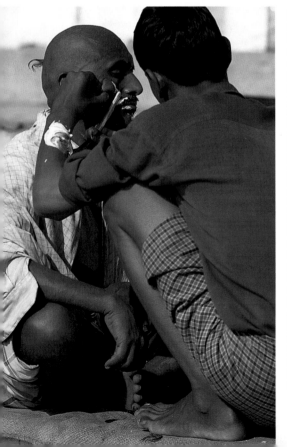

Main site The grounds opposite the museum are dominated by the magnificent Dhamekh *stupa*, elaborately carved by the 5th-century Guptas and marking the place where Buddha's first sermon was delivered. East of the *stupa*, by Sri Lanka's Mulagandhakuti Vihara—the temple of the Maha Bodhi Society—is a symbolic bodhi tree. It was planted in 1931, having been brought from Sri Lanka as a sapling. To the west, beyond the Jain temple, stand the remains of Ashoka's Dharmarajika *stupa* and, behind this, the base of the pillar of the Lion capital displayed in the museum. The main temple opposite, where Buddha used to meditate, is another Ashoka-Gupta relic leading to a succession of votive *stupas*. North of the main temple stretch the ruins of what were once 30 monasteries (according to 7th-century traveler Hsuan Tsang), rising to the Deer Park. This is all part of the mythological belief that saw Buddha as the King of Deer in a former life.

China invaded Tibet in 1950, and began a brutal campaign against Tibetan Buddhism in 1959. The Chinese occupation has driven some 200,000 refugees to live in the Indian Himalayas, including farmers, weavers, monks, and their spiritual leader, the Dalai Lama.

When China invaded Tibet, its ownership claim was based on Mongol imperial expansion throughout Central Asia in the 13th century, and on China's similar expansionism under the Manchu emperors in the 18th century. Buddhism had flourished in Tibet from the 7th century onward, absorbing characteristics of the earliest religion, Bön. It was finally blended with politics when the first Dalai Lama assumed power, in 1578. Tibetan national identity became indistinguishable from Buddhism, and by the 1950s there were over 6,200 monasteries inhabited by 590,000 monks and nuns in a total population of six million people.

Cultural annihilation In 1959, the Chinese government began their systematic destruction of Buddhism, desecrating monasteries and persecuting monks. The national uprising that followed was brutally crushed, forcing the Dalai Lama and his government into exile. Ever since, their base has been Dharmsala (see page 139), where Tibetans now outnumber local inhabitants, a source of some tension. Tibetan resistance groups, trained by the CIA, attacked the Chinese from bases in Nepal throughout the 1960s but in 1971 the warming of US–China relations ended this support.

Refugees continue to make the arduous journey over the mountains, seeking asylum in Nepal and India, while about 10,000 live in the West. Most still hope to return to a free Tibet with the Dalai Lama as their spiritual leader in a reformed democratic state, but little headway has been made since dialogue with China was initiated in 1979. Meanwhile, over one million Tibetans have died and there are regular purges of the religious community.

WORLD ATTENTION
Although criticised by some Tibetans for his conciliatory attitude towards China, the indefatigable Dalai Lama has been highly successful in gaining international, high-profile support for Tibet's cause. Constantly jetting around the world and being feted by luminaries such as Richard Gere, Björk, Harrison Ford, and Oliver Stone, he has helped inspire a number of films such as Martin Scorsese's *Kundun*, recounting the Dalai Lama's travails, and Jean-Jacques Annaud's *Seven Years in Tibet*, based on Heinrich Harrer's book.

137

India has become a home for thousands of Tibetans

Rice terraces near Chamba

Western Himalayas

▶▶ Chamba   116A4

Perched in the northwestern corner of Himachal, Chamba is well off the beaten track but offers an array of superbly carved temples in a setting of terraced meadows, oak and pine-clad slopes, lakes and the Ravi river valley. Its isolation encouraged unique forms of painting, sculpture, and crafts, including delicate, finely worked *rumal* (double-sided embroidered panels). At barely 3,280 feet, it is considerably warmer than Dalhousie, the main access point via the higher, more scenic road (27 miles). About 12 miles before Chamba is **Khajiar▶**, an attractively sheltered lake with an island temple.

Temples Dominating the elongated *maidan* or *chaugan* (open grassy space) is the Mughal-influenced Rang Mahal palace, now a college. Chamba's main legacy is its cluster of 10th-century **Lakshmi Narayana temples▶▶**, whose curved, ribbed stone towers have slate-tiled eaves and porches. Bas-reliefs and sculptures, some inlaid with brass, copper, and silver, depict the Hindu pantheon. High up at the northern end of town is the 10th-century Chamunda Devi, a timber construction with illustrative carved wood panels. South of the *chaugan* stands the Bhuri Singh museum (*Open* Mon–Sat 10–5. *Admission free*), displaying an intriguing selection of Kangra miniatures, palace murals, temple statues, and some beautiful *rumal*. A scenic drive 40 miles east reaches **Brahmaur▶**, the idyllic ancient capital, with 8th- to 10th-century temples built in the classic Pahari style of these hills.

▶ Dalhousie   116A4

The erstwhile Marquis of Dalhousie, Governor-General (1848–1856), retreated here for his health, and gave his name to this quiet town. It became a popular colonial sanatorium and hill station that, by the 1920s, rivaled Shimla. It commands imposing views from a lofty site 6,562 yards high, with rugged mountains to the west and the gentle valley of Chamba to the east. Although there are no specific

TOURIST OFFICES
HP Tourism, near bus-stand, The Mall, Dalhousie (*Open* (in theory) Mon–Sat 10–5, plus (in season) Sun 10–1; tel: 01899 42136).
HP Tourism, Kotwali Bazar, Dharmsala (*Open* Mon–Sat 10–1:30, 2–5; tel: 01892 24928).
HP Tourism, Scandal Point, The Mall, Shimla (*Open* daily in season 8–8, at other times 9–6; tel: 0177 252561/258302, fax: 0177 252557, email: infor@himachaltourism.com). Maps, tours, buses
HP Tourism, near the Maidan, Dhalpur, Kullu (*Open* Mon–Sat summer 9–7, winter 10–5; tel: 01902 24605). Maps, information.
Jammu & Kashmir Tourism, Airport Road (*Open* Mon–Sat 10–4; tel: 01982 52297).
Leh Tourist Information counter, Fort Road (bazaar), Leh. (*Open* Mon–Sat 10–4). Helpful.

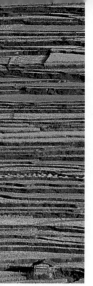

sights, the fresh mountain air attracts an increasing flow of tourists who use it as a base for trekking and horseback riding. English bungalows dot the town, but the foreign population now consists mainly of Tibetans, who make and sell hand-made crafts and woolen garments.

▶▶ Dharmsala　　　　116A4

Site of the Dalai Lama's residence and monastery ("Little Lhasa"), Dharmsala is a magnet for Western Buddhophiles, backpackers and New Agers, whose presence has spawned countless meditation, yoga, and music courses. There are 7–8,000 Tibetans here, forming half the population. The main concentration of hotels, "travelers" restaurants, temples and Tibetans is in Mcleodganj, a sprawling village tucked dramatically into the shadow of snowy peaks and about 1,948 feet higher than Dharmsala. Between the villages are two steep, twisting roads used by buses, jeep taxis, hikers, Tibetans, and maroon-robed Buddhist monks and nuns. Dharmsala itself is useful only for the large Kotwali bazaar and transportation facilities.

Mcleodganj The commercial center of Mcleodganj, dominated by Tibetan culture and shops, clusters around the bus stand, bazaar, and prayer wheels of the Namgyalma temple. From here Temple Road runs downhill past stores, tour agencies and craft workshops to the **Namgyal monastery▶**, a modern replica of the one in Lhasa and standing opposite the Dalai Lama's residence. Inside the elevated temple (*tsuglagkhang*), the main altar is flanked by 100 volumes of the Tibetan translations of Buddha's teachings, surveyed by a fearsome Guru Padma Sambhava, the 8th-century Indian who propagated Buddhism in Tibet. The peaceful atmosphere of wind chimes, flags, and pine trees is interrupted every afternoon by the vociferous "one-hand-clapping" of debating monks, well worth observing. The monastery bookstore and canteen are open to everyone. The road continues downhill to the **Tibetan Library▶▶** (*Open* daily 9–5, cloded an hour for lunch. *Admission free*), containing a wealth of archives, manuscripts, books, and old photos as well as a small museum. Lectures and courses on Tibetan Buddhism and language are held here.

Peace and wildlife From Mcleodganj's bus stand, another rough road runs a couple of miles northeast to **Bhagsu▶▶**. This makes a beautiful walk that culminates at a walled Siva temple with a waterfall plunging into a deep valley just beyond. Kites, hoopoes, eagles, butterflies, and monkeys are constant companions on the way.

Above: the exiled Dalai Lama
Below: Tibetans in Dharmsala

Tripura Sundri Devi Temple at Naggar in the Kullu Valley

BEYOND LEH
A day trip south by car or jeep with a local guide can cover the following sights: the royal palace at Stok (6 miles); an older one at Shey (9 miles); the huge monastery complex of Tiske (15 miles); the immaculate little monastery at Stakna (19 miles), and the spectacular 17th-century monastery of Hemis (28 miles). Other monasteries lie along the road west towards Srinagar, notably Spituk (5 miles), Phyang (10 miles), which hosts a compelling festival in July, and the richly decorated Akhi (43 miles), a massive monastery complex founded in the 11th century at the same time as neighboring Lekir. Countless trekking destinations include Changthang and the Hemis sanctuary across the Zanskar range.

▶▶ Kullu Valley   116B4

Celebrated with the epithet "Valley of the Gods" and mentioned in the *Mahabharata* and *Ramayana*, Kullu is one of Himachal's most delightful regions. In spring, this narrow, 50 mile-long river valley blossoms between pines and cedars while snow tops the peaks above. Mountain villages, terraced apple orchards, hot springs, and forests invite endless trekking, and there are numerous Hindu temples to visit. Despite centuries of being exposed to outside influences, due to its position on a Central Asian trade route, and more recent influxes of Tibetans and tourists, local traditions remain strong among the *paharis* (hill people) and nomadic shepherds who roam the hills.

A smoke? Among the crops are cannabis (*charas*) plantations, that have made the valley, especially **Manali▶**, a favorite haunt for Westerners wanting inexpensive and abundant dope. This oversubscribed resort at the foot of the Rohtang Pass is definitely past its best, (most of the Westerners on a permanent high who once monopolized the place have moved on, to be replaced by Indian vacationers) but offers a wide selection of accommodations, beautiful surroundings and buses that cover the gruelling 25 to 30-hour trip to Leh.

To the castle In the south, the market town of Kullu itself is hardly inspiring, having succumbed to the glories of concrete. It is however a transportation hub and a necessary stopover en route to better things. Far more interesting is **Naggar▶▶** 17 miles north, the local capital for 1,400 years. Beautifully situated on wooded slopes and commanding sweeping valley views, the town offers several ancient temples, and on a high outcrop, a castle that is now partly a hotel and museum. Naggar's most illustrious foreign resident was a Russian artist and mystic who died in 1947 and is commemorated by the Nicholas Roerich Gallery (*Open daily 9–1, 2–5. Admission: inexpensive*). Paintings and photographs in the gallery give a taste of his wide-ranging interests.

▶▶▶ Leh   116B5

The remote, bleak and dramatic moonscapes of Ladakh, sharpened by their unusual crystalline light, center on Leh. The fortunes of this once flourishing market town on the Silk Road into China plummeted in the 1950s when the Chinese border was closed, but revived in 1974 when Ladakh was opened to tourism. The brevity of the warm season means that in summer tourists far outnumber the colorful local mixture of Muslims, diminutive Ladakhis, Tibetans, Baltis and mercantile Kashmiris. Despite this invasion, Leh's infrastructure is appalling: power cuts, dirt, sewage and notoriously unhygienic food add to the problems of altitude sickness. Yet this unique and perceptibly isolated region captivates most visitors, whether they are investing in fabulous Ladakhi and Tibetan handmade crafts, trekking or tracking down remote *gompas* (monasteries).

Above Overlooking the northern town is the ramshackle nine-story **palace▶** (*Open* daily 7–9 AM. *Admission: inexpensive*), built in the 16th century with jutting wooden balconies, buttresses and a roof terrace with amazing views. Badly deteriorated, with perilous holes in some floors and flaking murals, it is rather a sad testimony to Leh's royal family, though a small museum exhibits a few heirlooms. Rising high above the palace, and requiring an arduous climb to reach it, is the 15th-century **Namgyal Tsemo gompa▶▶** (*Open* daily 7–9 AM. *Admission: moderate*), comprising two temples. The first, with repainted murals, houses a gigantic Buddha, and the second temple preserves some beautiful wall paintings.

Below Huddled at the base of this hill is the **old town▶▶**, an atmospheric maze of narrow lanes that ends at the Jama Masjid and the main bazaar. You can buy Tibetan, Ladakhi and Kashmiri handmade crafts here. Beyond the church, is the **Ladakh Ecology Center▶** (*Open* daily 10–5. *Admission free*), dedicated to encouraging sustainable local crafts, agriculture and small industries. In an idyllic rural setting 2 miles north is the **Sankar Gompa▶▶** (*Open* daily 7–10, 5–7. *Admission: inexpensive*), a monastery dating from the 17th century and rimmed by *chortens*. This is Ladakh's center for the "yellow hat" sect (a branch of Buddhism). The large prayer hall in particular is a riot of colors, filled with gilded statues and eye-catching murals.

Ladakhi women selling vegetables on the streets of Leh

Cultural diversity in northern India; an English church in Shimla (top) and a Ladakhi woman

► **Shimla** 116B4

Shimla, at 7,218 feet, is the capital of Himachal. Until 1819, when the British uncovered its charms, Shimla was a mere village. From 1865 to 1939, it was the summer seat of government, which would move here lock, stock, and barrel each year from Calcutta and subsequently Delhi. Rudyard Kipling was one of its many admirers. This long British presence has left a wealth of atmospheric old hotels, bungalows, and municipal buildings strung along a ridge overlooking the "Indian" maze of twisting lanes, weathered corrugated iron, and **bazaar►** that huddles below. The Mall, once off-limits to most Indians, is the main promenade. It runs from the canary-yellow Christ Church (1844) and the Library (1910) at its eastern end to join The Ridge at Scandal Corner (a name derived from the elopement of a British official's daughter with an Indian prince). Just before this much-frequented crossroads is the Gaiety Theatre (1887), which is still in use.

A half hour walk west is the **state museum►** (*Open* Tue–Sun 10–5. *Admission: inexpensive*) housed in an elegant mansion. Exhibits range from miniatures to colonial watercolors, Kullu masks, and bronzes. From here, a short walk up Observatory Hill takes you to Rashtrapati Niwas PP, once the Viceregal Lodge and now the Indian Institute of Advanced Studies (*Open* Tue–Sun 10–5. *Admission: inexpensive*), an impressive mock-Tudor mansion, built in a luxurious fashion in 1888. It is well worth seeing, but permission is needed from the officer in charge. Shimla also offers some rewarding walks, to the Jakhu temple (1 mile), high on the ridge with superb views, the Glen (2 miles), and Prospect Hill with its Kamna Devi temple (3 miles).

► **Srinagar** 116A5

What was once the paradisical playground of the Mughals and the British is now an army encampment, plunged into militancy and turmoil since the late 1980s. Tourists have been replaced by soldiers, armed police, and paramilitary groups, while the more enterprising Kashmiris have fled to safer pastures. The legendary Vale of Kashmir is now occupied by an estimated 300,000 troops, who warily watch Pakistan over the border and the JKLF (Jammu and

Kashmir Liberation Front) at home. The latter seeks *azadi* (independence), while other factions support integration with Pakistan, which has actively trained and armed them. Islamic fundamentalists and the Hindu majority of Jammu are other ingredients of the unease.

Terrorism Since 1988, bombs and assassinations have killed tens of thousands of people, and Kashmir underwent seven years of direct rule (and military control) from Delhi, which imposed curfews, brutality, and imprisonment without trial. A marginal improvement in the tense situation came in September 1996, when state elections restored Farooq Abdullah's National Conference party to power with promises to negotiate greater autonomy and rebuild the disastrous economy. Kashmir's historical complexities are many, not least the paradox of a fervently Muslim population that in 1846 was sold by the British to a Hindu ruler. In 1947, the last maharaja, an autocratic hedonist who languished happily by his palace swimming pool, or shot ducks over the lake at sundown, vacillated between joining India or Pakistan. Wars and the drawing of new borders followed, but the promised referendum has never been held, and today the rest of the world can only hope that nuclear tests by both countries will prove to be no more than sabre rattling.

With caution Nowadays, it is hard to recommend Srinagar. Gone are the days of hiking through fruit orchards to the mountains, haggling with boat wallahs to cross Dal Lake or explore the canals, and relaxing in luxurious houseboats. No longer can you safely bargain your life's savings for a pashmina shawl, visit the once beautiful Mughal gardens, or go to the mosque of Hazratbal that houses a quartz vial containing one strand of the Prophet Mohammed's hair. Although it is still possible to fly there and stay on a Lake Dal houseboat, consular advice is that it is not safe to do so.

What is certain is that the moment the situation improves, the highly motivated Kashmiris will set the wheels of tourism back into motion immediately and welcome back the many tourists who want to explore this region.

KASHMIR SHAWLS

Shawls were first produced in Kashmir around 1450 by weavers from Turkestan, and a century later were being used by Akbar as valuable diplomatic gifts. Through the Portuguese and the British, Kashmir shawls became fashionable in Europe: Empress Josephine, wife of Napoleon, is said to have owned some 400. The simple floral motifs of 18th-century shawls developed into the heavy, swirling patterns popular in Georgian Britain, where the manufacture of copies began. By 1870, Jacquard-woven paisley shawls (made in Paisley, Scotland, and elsewhere in Britain) had swamped the market, leaving work only for Kashmir's deft embroiderers. Pashmina wool comes from the soft underbelly fur of mountain goats and produces feather-weight shawls fine enough to be pulled through a ring. The best quality of all, more common in Ladakh, is *shahtush* from the Tibetan gazelle.

143

Dal Lake at Srinagar is deceptively tranquil in this troubled land

The Northeast

 REGION HIGHLIGHTS

RC

NP

8598m
Kanchenjunga
Dzongri **SIKKIM**
Pelling **Phodong**
Pemayangtse **Gangtok**
Rumtek
Darjiling Kalimpong
Ghoom
Karsiyang **Shiliguri**
Baghdogra

BT

Manas
Wildlife
Sanctuary

Gorakhpur
Bettiah
Motihari
Deoria Gopalganj Sitamarhi Madhubani
Azamgarh **Muzaffarpur** **Darbhanga** Araria Kishangani
Siwan Samastipur Saharsa **Purnia**
UTTAR **Chhapra** Hajipur Khagaria
PRADESH Ballia **Patna** **Munger** **Katihar**
Ghazipur **Ara** **Bhagalpur** Sahibganj **Ingraj**
Varanasi **Bihar Sharif** **Bazar**
Sasaram Nalanda
Robertsganj Dehri **Gaya** Nawada Godda
Aurangabad Bodh Gaya Devghar
Daltenganj Giridih Dumka
BIHAR
Hazaribag
Samri **Dhanbad** Siuri
Hazaribagh Range Lohardaga **Asansol**
Ambikapur Gumla **Ranchi** Puruliya **Durgapur** **Navadwip**
Jashpurnagar **Bankura** **Bardhaman**
MADHYA Chaibasa **Jamshedpur** Chunchura
PRADESH **Medinipur** Barakpur
Raurkela Bally
Sundargarh **Kharagpur** Haora
Raigarh Jharsuguda Baripada Haldia
Hirakud Kendujhargarh **Sambalpur** *Similipal* Baleshwar
Bargarh **National**
O R I S S A *Park*
Balangir *Mahanadi* Dhenkanal **Bhadrakh**
Phulabani **Cuttack** Palmyras Point
Bhawanipatna **Bhubaneshwar** Kendrapara
Aska Pipli Paradwip
Puri
Chilika Lake
Rayagada Brahmapur Chhatrapur Konark

Jalpaiguri Kokrajhar
Barpeta
Dhuburi Goalpara
William
Nagar
MEGHA
Tura *Khasi*

Ganga

BD

Agartala

Hugli
Krishnanagar
Basirhat
Dum Dum
KOLKATA
(CALCUTTA)

Kakdwip

Mouths of the Ganga

Bay of Bengal

Northeast For all the difficulty of making comparisons in India's kaleidoscope of cultures and landscapes, the northeast is arguably the most diverse and certainly the least frequented region of all. Sweeping through the parched plains of Bihar and West Bengal, the increasingly polluted Ganga (Ganges) finally ends in the flood-prone delta of Bangladesh, just east of Kolkata (Calcutta). To the south lies verdant Orissa, a prosperous state whose unique temples culminate at Konark's superlative Sun

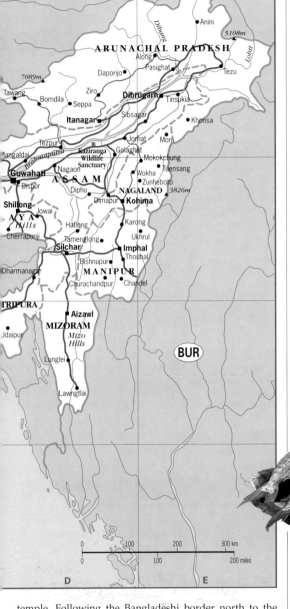

An Orissan fisherwoman carries fish in a turtle shell

temple. Following the Bangladeshi border north to the Himalayas, the trail leads to the beautiful state of Sikkim, where snowy peaks tower over Buddhist monasteries. Finally, on India's easternmost frontier, there are the seven troubled states around Assam, which suffer from chronic insurgency—take local advice before visiting.

The magnificent The logical starting point and base for visiting this region is the city of Kolkata (Calcutta),

RAILROAD HAZARDS

"At Sukhna station in the winter of 1900 the staff was held up one bright morning by a tiger which had spent the early hours lying on the cool, cemented surface facing the ticket office. Needless to say, its days were numbered, for a soldier happened to be at the Forest bungalow, and at the earnest solicitations of the staff came across and dispatched it. Again, early in 1915, the rumble of an incoming train awoke a tiger which had been asleep under the first railway culvert outside the station limit, which in its mad rush out knocked over an Indian wayfarer who just managed to crawl into the station, shaking like an aspen leaf... On another occasion, a herd of wild elephants caused a little flutter among the station staff and also compelled the driver of a train to back right into Sukhna..."
E. C. Dozey, *A Concise History of the Darjeeling District since 1835*

Calcutta still has hand-pulled rickshaws

"the many-sided, the smoky, the magnificent" in Rudyard Kipling's words. Kolkata is bursting at the seams with a ceaseless influx of impoverished peasants from Bangladesh and from West Bengal itself, and is best known in the West for its extreme misery, yet it has an incomparable spirit of survival. This was British India's first capital, the greatest colonial city of the East, whose cosmopolitan middle class experienced a sociocultural boom unique in India. Bengali intellectuals set the example, from the prolific Rabindranath Tagore (see pages 150–151) to, more recently, the movie-maker Satyajit Ray. From the 1930s onward, many turned to Communism, and West Bengal is now governed by a Marxist party. Despite the chaos, the straining infrastructure and the poverty, Kolkata is full of surprises, boasting, for example, India's only road subway, and a cricket stadium whose scale reflects the Bengalis' greatest passion.

Hindu might From the 8th to the 13th centuries, when Calcutta was a mere cluster of mud-flat villages, glorious temples were being built in Orissa, a strikingly fertile, subtropical region rich in tribal people and with a strong crafts tradition. Its beautiful, unspoiled sandy beaches were discovered long ago by Pacific ridley turtles. Bhubaneshwar, Puri and Konark are the temple centers, and are dominated by superbly carved beehive-shaped structures rising to celestial heights; in some cases they are behind walls that restrict entry to Hindus only (notably in Puri). Earlier still, in the 3rd century BC, Orissa's powerful Kalinga dynasty was routed by Ashoka in a battle so ferocious that it led to his conversion to Buddhism. Many of Ashoka's rock edicts survive here, particularly at Dhauli, near Bhubaneshwar.

Nirvana? The heart of Buddhism, ironically, lies in Bihar, an uninspiring, near-destitute state whose main claims to fame are its caste wars, uncontrolled crime, slums, widespread poverty, and corruption. If you can brave the *dacoits* who sporadically attack trains, your destination should be Bodh Gaya, the site of Buddha's enlightenment and now a major Buddhist pilgrimage center.

Rising higher Far more welcoming are the delightful, atmospheric hill stations of the Himalayas: Darjiling and Kalimpong, where remnants of colonial days mix with a cross section of Lepchas, Nepalese, Bhutanese, and Tibetans in idyllic, undulating landscapes carpeted with tea plantations or pine forests. To the north rises the rugged emptiness of Sikkim, watched over by the awesome peak of Kanchenjunga. Buddhism and commerce coexist easily in the bustling capital of Gangtok, where red-robed monks drop into cafés to eat *momo* (dumplings) beside newly thriving entrepreneurs. Beyond this unfolds a restricted area, only open to permit holders for trekking or visiting the western mountains, where the jewel is the monastery of Pemayangste. Restrictions are applied equally strongly in the turbulent states of the far flung northeast. This is a region of great ethnic diversity where dance, music, and crafts traditions have been preserved in isolation from the rest of India.

Above: Bodh Gaya, a place of pilgrimage for Buddhists from around the world
Below: Buddhist monks

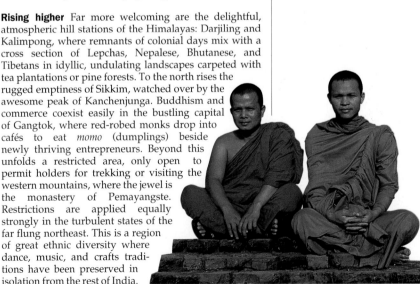

Three generations of the Tagore family left an indelible mark on Bengali society and, eventually, on India. The last and most famous was Rabindranath who attained international readership and esteem. The Tagores' lives and philosophies represented a renewed dynamism of spirit after centuries of dynastic, Mughal, then British control.

RAJA RAMMOHUN ROY
Rammohun Roy (1772–1833) was a highly influential figure in the Bengali intelligentsia. Although born a Hindu, he became critical of aspects of Hinduism. In 1828 Roy founded *Brahmo Sabha*, a reformist religious association that welcomed all castes and races. This later became a dynamic monotheist faith, the *Brahmo Samaj*, developed by Debendranath Tagore.

The Tagore Museum in Kolkata

Bengal in the 19th century was a hothouse of reformist and progressive movements that culminated in the humanist approach of the poet-philosopher Rabindranath Tagore (1861–1941). His ideas subsequently inspired the leaders of the Indian independence movement, Gandhi and Nehru, and his experimental, international university at Santiniketan still functions today.

Eclectic role model Rabindranath's grandfather, "Prince" Dwarkanath Tagore (1794–1846), was a Calcutta merchant who lived in opulent style thanks to his extensive business, agricultural, and shipping interests. True to his time, he lived a double life, following Hindu traditions at home (now the Tagore Museum), and in his entertainment annex, laying on lavish receptions. Dwarkanath was also a philanthropist: the first Indian member and patron of the Asiatic Society, he helped found the National Library. He was also involved in the creation of India's first center of modern education, the Hindu College, and its first medical college and hospital, in 1835.

This extraordinarily astute and generous man supported the progressive movements of his day, whether religious, social or political, and was much inspired by his friend Rammohun Roy (see panel), the visionary social and religious reformer. Dwarkanath twice broke the Hindu taboo against sea voyages by crossing the ocean to visit Europe and England, where he died prematurely.

The saint and sage Born in 1817, Dwarkanath's eldest son, Debendraneth, was no less remarkable. Brought up in a cocoon of luxury, he went through an existential crisis at the age of 18, experiencing a sudden aversion to wealth and its trappings. From then on, he spent his life searching for a spiritual truth. He studied the Vedas, Sanskrit texts and Western philosophy, and

finally united his ideas in a new religion dedicated to the worship of a universal and formless divinity. On his father's death, Debendraneth was played a strange card by fate: it was discovered that the debts of the family firm far exceeded its assets and so, with great joy, he found his inheritance reduced to zero. Yet he was shrewd enough, over the years, to rebuild a material base for his large family and integrate his peripatetic spiritual leanings. His favorite destinations were the Himalayas and Santiniketan ("abode of peace"), where he contemplated nature as a mystic and came to be known as the Maharshi (saint and sage).

Universal man In 1861 the Maharshi's 14th child, Rabindranath, was born. This child prodigy who wrote his first verse at the age of eight was nurtured by his father and never obstructed: freedom and truth were the guiding ethics. Over the years, his poetry, songs, lyrical drama, novels, and social comedies won him international recognition but he was also deeply concerned by the plight of Indian peasants and actively helped rural communities. In 1913, his Nobel Prize check went straight to his experimental school and to an agricultural bank that he had set up. His love for India had no room for xenophobia and he held responsible both the oppressors and the oppressed for the ills of the land.

Roving ambassador Although in basic sympathy with Gandhi, with whom a lifelong friendship started in 1915, Tagore had a more humanist, less ascetic approach. The contrast between the two was best described by their mutual English friend, C.F. Andrews: "Tagore is essentially a modern; Mahatma Gandhi is the St. Francis of Assisi of our own days." Their differences became more apparent in the 1920s when Tagore became India's roving spiritual ambassador, preaching cooperation between East and West, while Gandhi was advocating non-cooperation. Rabindranath's brilliance sparkled until the very end, as he dictated poetry on his deathbed.

AFTER THE CATACLYSM
"The wheels of Fate will one day compel the British to give up their Indian empire. But what kind of India will they leave behind, what stark misery? When the stream of the last two centuries' administration runs dry at last, what a waste of mud and filth they will leave behind them!... As I look around I see the crumbling ruins of a proud civilization strewn like a vast heap of futility. And yet I shall not commit the grievous sin of losing faith in Man. I would rather look forward to the opening of a new chapter in his history after the cataclysm is over and the atmosphere rendered clean with the spirit of service and sacrifice."
From *Crisis in Civilization*, Tagore's last public address, in April 1941.

Rabindranath Tagore (below); his study (above)

151

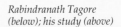

Monsoon season in Kolkata, when the heavy rains cause floods

Kolkata (Calcutta)

Kolkata, India's second metropolis, with over 14 million inhabitants, hits new arrivals with an incomparable blast of fumes, humid heat, dirt, tumbledown buildings, broken pavements, and human misery. What must be the world's most decrepit cars maneuver and honk past hand-pulled rickshaws and buses fit for the city dump, while men clad in *dhotis* soap themselves under roadside water-pumps and rats scuttle through the garbage. This looks like a shattered, paralyzed city, abandoned to a strange destiny. And yet among the squalor and neglect are more bookstores, fax and email offices, and speakers of English than anywhere else in India. Kolkata's cultural life beats anything that Mumbai (Bombay) or Delhi has to offer and the stately colonial edifices seem, for once, an integral part of this city of paradoxes. Startling decay and rampant overcrowding cannot detract from a specific fascination and excitement found only in Kolkata.

Rise to power Named after the ferocious goddess Kali worshipped by local villagers, the city was founded in 1690 by an English trader, Job Charnock, who chose the Hugli estuary as the site for an East India Company trading post. Bengal's muslin, grain, silk yarn, tobacco, and saltpeter gradually created a dual city: the palatial British settlement of Chowringhee, ranged around the huge open space of the Maidan bordering the Hugli River, and the "native" quarter of filthy lanes and chaotic hovels beyond.

By 1772 Fort William was built and Calcutta had become the capital of the British Empire in India. From then until 1911, when the capital was moved to Delhi, Calcutta boomed. Imposing municipal buildings that earned it the

TOURIST OFFICES
Government of India, 4 Shakespeare Sarani (*Open* Mon–Fri 9–6, Sat 9–1; tel: 033 242 1402/1475/5813, fax: 033 242 3521, email: caltour@cal2.vsnl.net.in). Very helpful information. WBTDC, 3/2 BBD Bagh East (*Open* Mon–Fri 10:30–1:30, 2:15–5:30; tel: 033 248 8271, fax: 033 248 5168, email: wbtdc@cal2.vsnl.net.in). Tours, boat trips, permits, guides, and car rentals. Also counters at the airport and Howrah station.

sobriquet "city of palaces" were erected, and in 1876, even filtered drinking water and drainage systems were installed in the city.

New thinking Parallel to the expanding British infrastructure, a new class had been created, the Babu. These *nouveau riche* merchants built fabulous mansions and became famed for their decadence: one would light his cigars only with ten-rupee notes (twice the monthly earnings of a coolie). Equally important was the development of the Bengali intelligentsia; reformist luminaries such as Rammohun Roy, Vivekananda and Dwarkanath Tagore (see pages 150–151) greatly contributed to the liberal thinking that eventually brought independence and democracy.

Radicalism This overtly cosmopolitan city (its ethnic groups include Armenians, Chinese, northeast tribal people and Gurkhas) has been controversially run since 1977 by the CPIM (Communist Party of India Marxist). Desperate Bangladeshis and Bengali villagers continue to pour in, crowding the city even more, and charitable efforts by Mother Theresa's successors, the Kali temple, and individual citizens are mere drops in the vast ocean of poverty. In the mid-1960s Kolkata's problems provoked another extremist movement, the Naxalites, who sought to eradicate social inequality through what eventually became anarchic assassinations.

Layout The center lies east of the Hugli's cantilevered Howrah Bridge, that groans under traffic crawling towards the main train station (Howrah) on the west bank. To the south a newer bridge, the Vivekananda Setu, said to be India's longest, offers an easier route to the beautiful Indian Botanical Gardens, also in the west. Crowning the center is the vast Maidan, edged to the east by J Nehru Road (formerly Chowringhee), whose restored glory is the stunning Oberoi Grand hotel. Halfway down, beside the Indian Museum, is Sudder Street, crammed with budget and some mid-range hotels, travelers' cafés and travel agencies. South of here are more salubrious, modernized streets lined with clubs, embassies, expensive stores, hotels, and airline offices. Park Street has the Asiatic Society at one end (No. 1), and at the other the atmospheric Park Street cemetery (dating from 1767).

North of the Maidan sprawls old Calcutta, where British monuments are juxtaposed with mosques and mansions, the university, bazaars, and the red-light district. The Parasnath Jain temple is the farthest sight of major interest.

153

Goats, a common sight in the streets of Kolkata

Bagbazar

Belgachia
Dum Dum'

Shyam-
bazar

SHYAMBAZAR

BOSE AVE

MOHAN AVE

AUROBINDO SARANI

BENIATOLA

SHOBHA-
BAZAR

MANIKTALA

Girish
Park

Parasnath
Jain Temple

TAGORE ST

VIVEKANANDA RD

A P CHANDRA ROAD

MANIKTALA
ROAD

STRAND ROAD

Rabindra Bharati
Museum
(Tagore House)

Marble
Palace

MG Road

MACHUABAZAR

HAORA
(HOWRAH)

HOWRAH
BRIDGE

COTTON ST

MAHATMA

K C SEN STREET

Howrah
Railway
Station

Armenian
Ghat

Barabazar

BARABAZAR

Central

TIRETTA

Calcutta
University

BAITAKKHANA

Sealdah
Railway
Station

GANDHI ROAD

CHITTARANJAN AVE

GANGULI STREET

BEPIN BEHARI

BBD
BAGH

St John's Church

Raj Bhavan

Chandni Chowkh

Esplanade

BOW BAZAR

DR S C BANNERJEE RD

HAORA
(HOWRAH)

(Hooghly)

STRAND ROAD

Babu and
Chandpal Ghat

High
Court

Hugli

Eden
Gardens

LENIN SARANI

Oberoi
Grand Hotel

New Market

TALTALA

A J C BOSE ROAD

Indian
Botanical
Gardens

VIVEKANANDA SETU
(Second Hooghly
Bridge)

Ranji
Stadium

INDIRA GANDHI RD
(RED RD)
DUFFERIN RD

SUDDER
ST

St
Indian Museum

Asiatic Society

Fort
William

Maidan

ST GEORGE'S GATE

KHIDIRPUR RD

HOSPITAL ROAD

NEHRU ROAD (CHOWRINGHEE)

Park
Street

Maidan

PARK STREET

HASTINGS

GARDEN
REACH
RD

Victoria
Memorial

St Paul's
Cathedral

i

Rabindra Sadan
& Nandan

Park Street
Cemetery

PARK
CIRCUS

KARL MARX SARANI

A J C BOSE ROAD

Rabindra
Sadan

A J C BOSE ROAD

KHIDIRPUR

Zoo

BHAWANIPUR

ASHUTOSH MUKHARJI ROAD

SARAT BOSE ROAD

BALLYGUNGE

GARIAHAT ROAD

ALIPUR

Bhawanipur

JUDGE'S COURT ROAD

DIAMOND HARBOUR ROAD

Jatindas
Park

HAZRA ROAD

KALIGHAT

Dakshineswar
(Kali Temple)

Kalighat

SHYAMA PRASAD MUKHARJI ROAD

RASH BEHARI AVENUE

CHETLA CENT RD

Birla Academy of
Art and Culture

DHAKURIA

CHETLA

Rabindra Sarovar

TARATALA

TOLLYGUNGE CIRCULAR

Rabindra
Sarobar

ROAD

1 km

1 mile

Tollygunge

B PRINCE ANWAR SHAH ROAD

A

B

C

▶▶ BBD Bagh 154B4
(formerly Dalhousie Square)

Kolkata's administrative center was created in the late 18th century and still has the original red brick Writers' Building (1780) on the north side. It was once the headquarters of the East India Company, and is now the State Secretariat. East of here stands St. Andrew's Kirk (1818), evidence of the large Scottish community that once monopolized the trading houses of the commercial district surrounding the Stock Exchange.

On the west side stands the unusual Customs House, next to the domed white Post Office (1868) and, one block south, St. John's Church (*Open* daily 9–noon, 5–6. *Admission free*) built in 1787 to resemble London's St.-Martin-in-the-Fields church. The cemetery contains Job Charnock's tomb and a monument to victims of the Black Hole of Calcutta (see panel); inside is *The Last Supper* by Johann Zoffany. South of this is the large walled Raj Bhavan, the magnificent Governor's residence built in 1802 (*Open* only with special permission) and, southwest, the High Court. Beyond are the Eden Gardens in the Maidan, where a pretty landscaped park is crowned by a pagoda. The neighboring cricket stadium accommodates 100,000 spectators, and is Kolkata's favorite institution.

▶▶▶ Dakshinieswa (Kali Temple) 154B2
Near Belur Math Metro: Kalighat or Jatindas Park
Open dawn–dusk. Admission: free

Founded in 1602, this temple represents the heart and soul of Kolkata. Some 2,000 poor are fed twice a day by its kitchens, and mothers with newborn babies flock to give thanks to the "tree of life", an ancient cactus hung about with black stones donated for fertility. At the back of the temple is a shrine dedicated to Brahma, near the slaughter area for black kid goats. Considered representatives of evil, these squealing creatures meet their end with long *pujas* carried out in the main hall facing the sanctum. The statue of Kali herself, fearsome and black-faced with three eyes, is always surrounded by a dense crowd of heavily garlanded worshippers. To escape from this intensity, take the side entrance leading to the peaceful *tank*. The resident Brahmin guides are very informative, but they are extremely insistent in their demand for donations.

Men bathing in the Kali Temple tank

▶▶▶ Indian Museum (Jadu Ghar) 154B4
27 Jawaharlal Nehru Road
Metro: Park Street. Open: Tue–Sun 10:15–4:30.
Admission: moderate

India's oldest museum started life in 1814 as part of the Asiatic Society, and in 1875 opened its doors to the public. It houses a stunning collection of archeological treasures, starting in the lobby with two superb 2nd century BC statues that came from a Buddhist *stupa*. The *stupa* is partly reconstructed in the adjoining Sunga Room (to the right). Gandhara, Mathura, Hoysala, and Chola (see pages 36–39) sculptures follow on from this and across the cool, verdant courtyard are prehistoric, anthropological and geological exhibits. The second floor, mainly zoological, leads to a wing with a rich display of textiles and decorative arts and, above it, paintings from Bengal, Rajasthan, and Southeast Asia.

THE OBEROI GRAND
Kolkata's most prestigious hotel, the Oberoi Grand, was raised from the ashes of the old Theatre Royal in 1911 by Arathoon Stephen, an Armenian who started life as a barrow boy and ended as one of Kolkata's real-estate barons. With additional floors eventually providing 500 rooms, it became India's most luxurious hotel and the city's most fashionable watering hole. It enjoyed two glorious decades—until polluted water killed six hotel guests. In 1937, the ageing institution was forced to close down. It was resurrected by Rai Bahadur Mohan Singh Oberoi, ebullient from his success with Simla's legendary Cecil Hotel. Within a year, he had renovated and reopened the hotel. After requisitioning during World War II, it thrived again in the 1950s, Kolkata's last period of brilliance. It is still one of Kolkata's most sumptuous and expensive hotels.

▶▶ Marble Palace 154B5

Muktaram Babu St. Metro: Girish Park. Open: Tue, Wed, Fri, Sat, Sun 10–4 with permit from Government of India Tourist Office. Admission free

This extraordinary colonnaded edifice crumbles gracefully in a walled garden. It is a relic of a wealthy Muslim landowning family, some of whom still live here, bound by a trust not to sell. Built in 1835 during the city's heyday, it reflects the opulence and Anglophilia of that period: Queen Victoria is honored with a huge wooden statue. Inlaid Italian marble floors lead past Belgian glass chandeliers, gilt-framed mirrors, and French clocks, and the painting gallery (wide open to Kolkata's dust and humidity) displays no lesser artists than Rubens, Murillo, Reynolds and Titian. Dustcovers and caged birds add to the theatrical atmosphere.

▶▶ Rabindra Bharati Museum 154B5

6/4 Dwarkanath Tagore Lane
Metro: Girish Park. Open: Mon–Fri 10–5, Sat 10–2, Sun 11–2. Admission free

Housed in the attractive family home of the Tagores, this fascinating museum covers Bengal's 19th-century progressive movement (spearheaded by Dwarkanath Tagore), and Rabindranath Tagore's life, prolific writings and associations, with paintings, photos and old furniture.

▶▶ Victoria Memorial 154B3

Queen's Way
Metro: Maidan. Open: Tue–Sun Nov–Feb 10–3:30; Mar–Oct 10-4:30. Sound-and-light show 7:15 or 8:15. Admission: inexpensive

This enormous building (1906) reigns supreme over the southern end of the Maidan, fronted by large ponds and a huge statue of a glowering Queen Victoria. Inside, the lofty atriums and upper galleries have changed little, displaying huge Victorian oils, commemorative busts of colonial heroes, drawings of the Himalayas, colonial watercolors, East India Company documents, arms, and diverse British Raj memorabilia. More dynamic in style is the Kolkata Gallery, admirably spelling out the rise (and to a lesser extent the fall), of the city, with superb aquatints of the 1780s, photos and well-presented panels, culminating in a lifesize replica of an old street.

Victoria Memorial, a white marble masterpiece

Practical details

Transport Kolkata surprisingly boasts an immaculate 1980s subway system, unique in India, that runs Mon–Sat 8 AM–9:15 PM. Sun 3 PM–9:15 PM from Dum Dum (2 miles from the airport) in the north to Tollygunge in the south. By far the best way to reach the city's principal sights, although its empty marble platforms hardly reflect the city's teeming masses above ground. Keep your ticket until the end of the journey as you need it to get out.

Double-decker and minibuses travel countless routes, but are often crowded and are fertile ground for pickpockets. unless you can use the women-only carriages, trams are not a comfortable experience for female visitors.

Kolkata's inexpensive, beaten-up taxis actually use their meters, with charts to calculate fare adjustments (which double the fare at least), but it is often quicker to walk.

Auto-rickshaws are also available, but mainly outside the center. Kolkata's specialty, human-pulled rickshaws, are used by locals, but many visitors prefer to avoid them.

Tongas (horse-drawn carriages) trot around Victoria Memorial, but they are purely for pleasure jaunts.

The Hugli ferry service has been suspended and it is possible that it has gone for good.

Shopping New Market, one block north of Sudder Street, is the obvious shopping destination. Its 1874 structure shelters a vast, labyrinthine general market selling food, household goods, jewelry, handmade crafts, and clothes, but beware of the numerous touts and pickpockets. Russel Street offers auction houses, home decoration stores, jewelry, and upscale boutiques, while at dusk J Nehru Road's general souvenir and handmade craft stores compete with a mass of sidewalk vendors selling watches, sunglasses, and immaculate white shirts. The Central Cottage Industries Emporium at No. 7 has products from all over India, and Handloom House offers good *khadi* (handwoven, handprinted cloth), at 2 Lindsay Street. Bazaars exist all over Kolkata, such as Jagannath Ghat (a flower market), Shyambazar (the coconut market) and Bentinck Street (for tailors, shoemakers, and sweetmeats). The Oxford Bookshop, Park Street, offers a good selection of English-language books.

157

Porters carry immense loads through the city streets

Plum in the middle of the arid, poverty-stricken state of Bihar is Buddhism's holiest site, Bodh Gaya, where Buddha reached enlightenment. Together with nearby Nalanda, this has become a major pilgrimage destination, visited and invested in by East Asian Buddhists, in complete contrast to its miserable environs.

158

TRANSMITTING THE WORD
Buddha's disciples met at Rajgi to draw up a definitive version of *dharma* and *vinaya* (rules of monastic conduct). They memorized their conclusions, using complex mnemonic devices, but wrote nothing down. The only Buddhist text to have survived in an ancient Indian language is the Pali Canon, produced in Sri Lanka around the 1st century BC.

A depiction of Buddha, Bodh Gaya

The Buddhist monuments of Bihar are redolent with the spirit of Gautama Buddha, born as Prince Siddhartha in the mountains of what is now Nepal, around 560 BC. After marrying and fathering a son, at the age of 29 he decided to abandon his life of luxury and search for a more engaging truth. For six years he wandered as an ascetic and beggar, before finally reaching the bodhi tree at Bodh Gaya. Here, at full moon on his 35th birthday in May, he plunged into a night of meditation that was to be his path to enlightenment. According to Buddhists, this involved first examining his previous existences to gain knowledge of himself, then seeing the endless cycle of birth and death that humans were caught in (*kharma*), thirdly understanding the causality and interdependence of the world (the cycle of *samsara*), and finally, with this newly gained perception, transcending the greed, hatred and delusion that had previously tied him to rebirth and suffering.

The truth At the moment of maturing from *Bodhisattva* ("on the path to Buddhahood") to Buddha ("the awakened one"), his knowledge thus crystallized into the four truths concerning the essence, origin, cessation, and path to the cessation of *dukha* (suffering). These encapsulate the teaching of Buddhism. After spending 49 more days under the tree meditating on this, Buddha set off to teach the world about his discoveries. His first sermon took place at Sarnath, near Varanasi, and from there he built up a group of followers, the *sangha*, a community of monks and nuns who continued to teach after his death around 486 BC.

Bodh Gaya Indelibly marked by all this is the village of Bodh Gaya where Buddha not only reached *nirvana* (the extinction of desires) but also spent the rest of his life preaching. A pipal tree which is a descendant of the original bodhi tree stands near the Mahabodhi temple. The temple was built in the 7th century over a 3rd-century BC shrine established by Emperor Ashoka (but heavily altered and restored in the 19th century).

Tibetan monks praying under the bodi tree at Mahabodhi temple

Its soaring pyramidal tower rises more than 160 feet above the sanctuary which contains a large gilded statue of Buddha, in the *asana* (yogic posture) signifying enlightenment. This temple is now rivalled by numerous others of varying sizes and styles, erected over the last decades by the Buddhist nations of Myanmar (Burma), Thailand, China, Japan, Tibet, Bhutan, Sri Lanka, and Vietnam. All are watched over by a gigantic and graceless stone Buddha installed in 1989.

Although most of the year Bodh Gaya sees only a steady trickle of pilgrims joining the resident monks, it springs to life between November and February, when a general forum of international Buddhists takes place, partly led by the Dalai Lama. Commercial enterprises flood the village and the environs are invaded by ceremonies, meditation courses, and lectures by the different Buddhist schools, activities that create an animation that seems far from *nirvana*—a state of total peace.

Universal university Anyone visiting Bodh Gaya also goes to Nalanda, about 37 miles northeast. This was the site of one of the world's earliest universities, originally a monastery built during Buddha's lifetime. It developed into a celebrated center of learning from the 5th to the 12th centuries, attracting students and scholars from Tibet, China, Korea, Japan, and Indonesia. The 7th-century Chinese pilgrim-scholar, Hsuan-Tsang, described Nalanda as catering for 10,000 studious monks with 2,000 teachers and 9 million manuscripts—possibly an exaggeration. He praised its "carved and ornamented, pearl-red pillars, richly adorned balustrades", towers and turrets. Mercilessly sacked by Afghan invaders in the 12th century, Nalanda's *stupas*, temples, and monasteries now stand in ruins, and most of the surviving statues are to be found in museums.

BUDDHA'S PROGRESS
With adherents throughout Asia for 2,500 years, Buddhism has survived inroads from Islam and the resurgence of the far older beliefs of Hinduism. It remains the world's most practiced religion, whether in Himayana (Lesser Vehicle), Mahayana (Greater Vehicle), Tantric, or Zen interpretations. Its widespread influence throughout China, Indochina, Southeast Asia, and Japan is directly due to one of Buddhism's fundamental obligations, the need to spread the word or Buddhist law known as *dharma*. It is becoming increasingly popular in the West, partly as a result of the proselytizing of the charismatic Dalai Lama.

TOURIST OFFICES
WBTDC, Hill Cart Road,
Shiliguri (tel: 0353
431974). Also information
counters at New Jaipalguri
train station and at
Baghdora airport.
WBTDC, Bellevue Hotel,
1st floor, 1 Nehru
Road/The Mall, Darjiling
(tel: 0354 54050). Basic
maps, information about
trains, treks. Local tours.
Darjiling Gurkha Hill
Council, Ghorka Ranga
Nanch Bhawan, between
Chowrasta and Jawarhar
Road, Darjiling (tel: 0354
54214/54879). Enquire
at either of these offices
about the exceptional
Ropeway Cable Car that
crosses the northern
valley: sometimes it
works, sometimes it
doesn't. Both also give
information about visiting
tea estates.

TOY TRAIN
The train puffs and
zigzags up its narrow-
gauge track from New
Jalpaiguri and Shiliguri
through Karsiyang and
Ghoom to Darjiling, a feat
of 1880s engineering not
to be missed. Taking
8–10 hours to cover the
56 miles from the plains
to Darjiling's 7,000-foot
altitude, it is slow, dirty,
frequently breaks down,
and majestically accom-
plishes a complete circle
at Batasia Loop between
Ghoom and Darjiling. The
rewards are a unique
experience, the tinkering
of the accompanying engi-
neers, and stupendous
views. Rather than
attempt the full-blown trip,
make the four-hour ride to
Karsiyang (twice-daily) or,
even shorter, to Ghoom,
then return by bus or jeep.
The train does not func-
tion in winter or during
the monsoon.

Eastern Himalayas

Rising from the dusty plains of West Bengal and Bihar is a
tiny Indian chunk of the eastern Himalayas, squeezed
between Nepal and Bhutan with Tibet unfolding to the
north. This sparsely populated, captivatingly beautiful
region is dominated by the mighty Kanchenjunga, at 27,887
feet the third highest mountain in the world, with Everest
looming to the west. In the foothills, at a lofty 6,890 feet, lies
Darjiling, renowned for its Gurkhas, tea estates, narrow-
gauge train (the "toy train") and enduring Anglo-Indian
atmosphere. To the east, in lush, warmer surroundings, is
less well-known Kalimpong, with strong Bhutanese and
Tibetan influences. To the north lies the magical state of
Sikkim, strongly Buddhist, replete with orchids and
rhododendrons, and requiring a special entry permit.

Power struggles This entire area was once ruled by its
own monarch, but in recent centuries control has been
lobbed between Bhutan, Tibet, Nepal, and British India.
Britain obtained Darjiling from Sikkim in 1835 and
acquired control over Sikkim in 1890, through a treaty
with China that defined the nebulous Sikkim–Tibet
border. Kalimpong, originally a strategic Sikkimese trading crossroads, was occupied by Bhutan in 1706, then
gained by British India in 1865. At Indian Independence,
Sikkim remained a protectorate of India, keeping its king,
but in 1975 widespread domestic dissatisfaction led it to
become a fully fledged state of India. Darjiling's Nepalese
majority (Gurkhas) is now run by a Gurkha Council, and
there are increasing demands for special, "Gurkhaland"
status, independent of West Bengal.

Access to any of these points is through the unpleasant
little town of Shiliguri. Trains from Delhi or Kolkata
(Calcutta) stop at New Jalpaiguri (3 miles away), and the
only airport in the region, Baghdora, is 7 miles west.
Buses, jeeps, and taxis leave from
Shiliguri's Tenzing Norgay bus station,
taking three to four hours to Darjiling or
Kalimpong and six or seven hours to
Gangtok, capital of Sikkim. Make sure
you arrive in Shiliguri by early afternoon, or you will have to stay
overnight—something to be avoided.

▶▶▶ **Darjiling (Darjeeling)** *146B4*
Whether you brave the tortuous railway
or the equally nerve-wracking road that
switchbacks up to Darjiling, you will be
rewarded on arrival by the sight of a
vast pine-clad valley, with the town
tumbling steeply downhill from
Chowrasta, the highest point, to the bus
stand far below. Colonial bungalows
and newer concrete edifices line alleys,
steps and the main street (for pedestrians only from halfway up). Nights can
be extremely cold and damp, and you
will have to get up early if you want to
glimpse Kanchenjunga before clouds
descend. The lively Nehru Road

(formerly The Mall), offers good retreats for tea, snacks and meals, with abundant handmade craft stores.

From Chowrasta a circular walk leads north, past the delightful Windamere Hotel to Observatory Hill, good for mountain views at dawn. St. Andrew's, Loreto School, and the Gymkhana Club are colonial relics on its western flank. Signposted downhill (west) from Woodland Hotel is the **Natural History Museum**▶ (*Open* Fri–Wed 10–4. *Admission: inexpensive*), founded in 1903 and a timewarp of stuffed local birds and animals, including some 4,000 specimens altogether. From here, Jawahar Road continues north, downhill to the **Zoo**▶ (*Open* Fri–Wed 10–4. *Admission: inexpensive*), home to yaks, Siberian tigers, snow leopards, red pandas, Tibetan wolves, and more. Beyond is the **Himalayan Mountaineering Institute**▶▶ (*Open* daily 9–1, 2–4. *Admission free*). Outside stands a hilltop statue of Tenzing Norgay, the sherpa who accompanied, among others, Sir Edmund Hillary to the summit of Everest in 1953 and was the Institute adviser until his death in 1986.

▶ Ghoom
146B4

Ghoom, reached from Darjiling by train, bus, taxi or on foot (5 miles), has a 19th-century Buddhist monastery, **Yiga Choling**▶, with a lavishly painted interior. The monastery, where yellow-hat Buddhism is practiced, is now masked by an ugly resort hotel. **Tiger Hill**▶▶, 3 miles beyond Ghoom, is a very popular predawn destination (jeeps leave Darjiling daily at 4 AM, book in advance) where a tower gives wonderful views from the plains of Bengal to Everest.

Tea growing in Darjiling Inset: a monk at Ghoom's Yiga Choling monastery

161

The Northeast

PERMITS AND TOURIST OFFICES
Sikkim Tourist Center, MG Marg, Gangtok (*Open* Mon–Sat 10–4, closed second Sat of month; tel: 03592 22064, fax: 03592 25647, email: sikkim@sikkim.ren.nic.in).

15-day permits should be obtained either while applying for your Indian visa or at Sikkim Tourism offices in Delhi (tel: 011 611 5346), Kolkata (tel: 033 226 8983) or Shiliguri (tel: 0353 432646).

Kalimpong has no tourist office but hotels, particularly Kalimpong Park and the Himalayan, have a wealth of information. A useful publication covering the entire area, regularly updated and obtainable at the excellent Oxford Bookshop in Darjiling, is *Sikkim, Darjiling, Bhutan* by Rajesh Verma.

►► Kalimpong   *146B4*

This well-kept secret is an isolated hill town, at 4,101 feet considerably warmer than its neighbors and still preserving a relaxed, friendly atmosphere as a crossroads for Tibetans, Bhutanese, Sikkimese, and Gurkhas. From Darjiling, a three-hour jeep ride winds through rolling tea estates then down to the subtropical vegetation of the **Tista River**►► before ascending again through forests, bamboo and flower nurseries to Kalimpong.

Sights The main Rishi Road cuts along a ridge, roughly north–south. The large market, bus and jeep stand, restaurants and a few craft stores are midway on the eastern side, monasteries to the northeast and better hotels joining colleges to the south. Like Darjiling, Kalimpong saw many Christian missionaries, including Reverend Macfarlane who by 1873 had founded 25 primary schools, with lessons in Hindi. An attractive church (1881) is named after him. Near here is the Arts and Crafts cooperative, founded in 1897 to promote local crafts. Uphill is the **Thorpa Choling**►, a Tibetan monastery founded in 1937, with an important library of ancient scripts. Below stands the much older **Bhutanese Thongsa Gompa**► (1692), faced with prayer wheels and home to around 60 monks. Its beautiful old murals have sadly been repainted in less refined style. Immediately south stands the massive new Parnami Mandir, a Hindu temple devoted to Krishna.

Towering to the southeast is Durpin Hill, with fabulous Kanchenjunga views. To the north of town is Deolo Hill, site of Dr. Graham's Home (1900) which combined an orphanage, school, dairy, and bakery. There are endless walks around Kalimpong and good treks to Samthara through Lepcha villages and forests.

►► Sikkim   *146B4*

Still very restricted for foreigners, Sikkim's destinations for individual visitors are limited to Gangtok, Rumtek, **Phodong Monastery**►, Dzongri, and Pemayangtse. Groups (4–20 people) can get 15-day permits to travel to and trek in other regions (available through Gangtok travel agents). Accessibility varies with the political situation and it is never advisable to stray from the designated routes, which provide spectacular scenery dotted with monasteries.

Starting point Sikkim's capital, **Gangtok**►, sprawls like Darjiling down a high valley at 4,921 feet, but has far more concrete and traffic, a palpably more mercantile attitude and less character. At its commercial heart are the stores, accommodations and restaurants of MG Marg, with Lal Bazar at its southern end and the noisy Highway 31A slicing uphill to the north. Farthest up the highway,

Sikkimese woman

at zero point (from where kilometres north of Gangtok are measured), is the Cottage Industries Institute. From here a side road meanders uphill to the **Enchey Monastery**▶ (1901), blessed by a Tantric Lama known for his power of flying, a useful talent here. (*Open daily. Admission free.*) Visitors can join prayer sessions at 5–7 AM and 5–7/8 PM.

Gangtok's most interesting sights lie to the south. The **Chogyal Royal Palace and Chapel**▶ are seldom open but about 1.2 miles south, on a wooded bluff, the **Research Institute of Tibetology**▶▶ (*Open Mon–Sat 10–4. Admission: inexpensive*) welcomes visitors. Founded in 1958 to further knowledge of Tibetan and Mahayana Buddhism, it stores the 24 volumes of writings by the 5th Dalai Lama (1617–1682). Exhibits also include Buddhist scrolls, statuettes, and ritual objects. A short distance along the ridge is the reliquary **Do-Drul Chorten**▶ (1960s), a gold-topped *stupa* surrounded by prayer-wheels, flags, and young monks from the neighboring monastery. Far below lies an orchid sanctuary nurturing some 500 species.

Rumtek The majestic **Rumtek monastery**▶▶ (*Open daily dawn–dusk. Admission free*; take your passport) lies 15 miles away on the opposite hill. It was founded by the head of Kargyugpa Buddhism when he fled Tibet in the 1960s, and built as a replica of the original headquarters. This huge, terraced, monastery and prayer hall is part of a self-sufficient community that continues outside the gates. A short distance farther on a bluff stands the smaller **Old Rumtek monastery**▶▶ (1730), beautifully reconstructed after a disastrous fire.

HANDMADE CRAFTS
Sikkim offers few handmade crafts apart from carved wooden *choksees* (tables), beautiful but expensive silverware and Chinese-style tufted-wool carpets. Recent prosperity, much aided by government projects, seems to have relegated traditional crafts to second place. Far more interesting are the goods found in tourist stores in Darjiling and Kalimpong, whose owners net the entire region. *Thangkas* (Buddhist scrolls), Tibetan jewelry, Sikkimese silver, ceremonial robes, Bhutanese weavings, tribal art from Nagaland, local handknitted sweaters and scarves, rabbit-fur gloves... the list is endless. Search out Soni Emporium, Mani Link Road, Kalimpong, which has enticingly unusual selections. Manjusha Emporium, Nehru Road, Darjiling, is West Bengal's fixed-price outlet for all manner of Himalayan crafts.

163

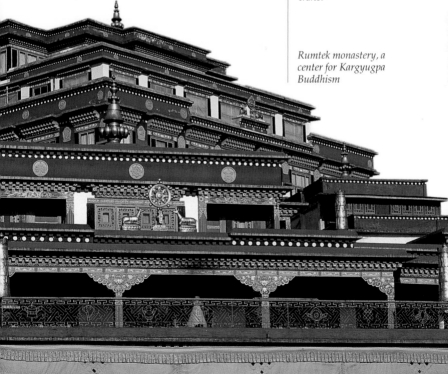

Rumtek monastery, a center for Kargyugpa Buddhism

UDAYAGIRI AND KHANDAGIRI CAVES

These much-promoted Buddhist and Jain cave temples, 5 miles from town, are in no way comparable to the Ajanta and Ellora Caves of Maharashtra (see pages 178–179), they are best regarded as providing an interesting backdrop to a peaceful ramble enlivened by monkeys and views. Dating from the 2nd century BC, the cave temples punctuate the sandstone and vegetation in two facing hills. The best preserved are Udayagiri's Cave 1, the Rani Nur; Cave 10, Ganesh Gumpha; and Cave 14, Hathi Gumpha, which contains an inscription of King Kharavela of the 2nd-century BC Chedi dynasty. The modern Jain temple crowning Khandagiri has panoramic views of the area.

164

Orissa

The state of Orissa (frequently written "Odisha") nestles on the Bay of Bengal between West Bengal and Andhra Pradesh. This often bypassed gem, protected by the Eastern Ghats, has a heavy rainfall from May through November, and is a beautifully lush, fertile region. Rice fields stand bordered by banana and coconut palms, and the thatched, hand-painted mud huts are fronted by large ponds. Coal, bauxite, and iron ore-mines function profitably here, and there are rich veins of gems and nickel, still virtually untapped. It is the industrial centers that have produced Orissa's recent upsurge in prosperity, in contrast to its former status as one of India's poorest states.

Temples and turtles Orissa's main attractions are its elaborate temples. There are no fewer than 500 from the 8th to 11th centuries in Bhubaneshwar alone, as well as the historical colossi of nearby Puri and Konark. Less well known are the 62 tribes of varying culture, size and dialect, whose traditions can be witnessed only on a guided tour. Handmade crafts are much in evidence, as Orissa is renowned for a wealth of unique techniques, producing metalwork animals, Pipli appliqué (see panel, page 166), *ikat* silk and cottons, and incised palm-leaf manuscripts. Further enticement lies in the crocodiles and birdlife of the coastal mangrove forests, the Pacific ridley turtles at Bhitar Kanika National Park (north of Konark), and the white tigers of Similipal National Park in the north. Magnificent, unspoiled beaches sweep down the coast past Konark to Puri, where tacky domestic tourism takes over.

▶▶ Bhubaneshwar   146A1

The modern services center of Bhubaneshwar is, at first sight, hardly inspiring. Hotels, banks, and markets radiate from Rajpath, which crosses the railroad track to a junction with Jaidev Marg. South from here are the museum, tourist office and a string of craft stores. About a mile farther on is the temple area and old town. The scattered temples are best visited by rickshaw.

Temple style Orissan temples have a distinctive *deul* that rises from a square base to form a ribbed, bell-shaped structure, crowned with a flat, round stone and surmounted by a *kalasa* ("vase of plenty"). They have complex, refined sculpture, including geometric patterns, *chaitya* windows, latticework, scrolls, animals, dancers, dwarves, gods, and sometimes erotic figures. The farthest south and the most elaborate and mature in form is the **Lingaraja temple▶▶▶** (11th century) whose multiple towers, the highest reaching 131 feet, can be viewed by non-Hindus only from a platform overlooking the wall.

More accessible is the midway group. It includes the **Parasurameshvara temple▶▶** (*ca*750), displaying numerous images of Siva, and elements that reach perfection in later neighboring temples, such as the superb 10th-century **Muktesvara temple▶▶▶**. This temple, still in use today, represents a transition point in South Orissan architecture, and the niches of the compound wall include Buddhist and Jain images alongside Hindu ones. Of note are the richly sculpted archway, shrine, and *tank*.

TOURIST OFFICES

Government of India, BJB Nagar (*Open* Mon–Fri 10–6, Sat 10–2; tel: 0674 412203). Helpful. OTDC, 5 Jaidev Marg. Next to Panthanivas Hotel. (Open Mon–Sat 10–5; tel: 0674 431299; fax: 0674 431053). Counters at the airport and train station.

East from here along Tankapani Road is the **Raja Rani temple▶▶▶**, another 11th-century gem standing in a large garden that sets off the lofty main tower. The farthest east is the **Brahmesvara temple▶▶** (1060), isolated in a peaceful, semirural setting. It is still frequented by devout worshippers of Lakshmi, whose image is set into the outer wall, and of the Sivalinga inside the shrine. Crowning it is a magnificent, lavishly sculpted tower. Non-Hindus are not particularly welcome here, so be sensitive.

Museums Exhibits at **Orissa State Museum** (*Open* Tue–Sun 10:30–5:30. *Admission: inexpensive*) include reproductions of lovely *chitra muriya* (flourpaste wall drawings) and 50,000 palm-leaf manuscripts. Tribal crafts are exhibited in traditional huts at the Tribal Research Museum (*Open* Mon–Sat 10:30–5:30. *Admission free*), northwest of the center.

Detail from the Parasurameshvara temple at Bhubaneshwar

▶▶▶ Konark

An idyllic rural route runs 37 miles southeast of Bhubaneshwar to the outstanding Surya (Sun) temple (*Open daily dawn–dusk. Admission: inexpensive*). This crowning glory of Orissan—or indeed of Indian—medieval art once dominated the coast, but the sea has since retreated behind the white dunes and the temple now stands in a large compound fronted by coconut and *chai* (tea) stands, persistent "guides" and postcard-sellers, cafés, low-key hotels, and a small museum (*Open Fri–Wed 10:30–5. Admission free*).

Erotica fantastica The Surya temple was constructed in 1238–1264 out of khondalite and chlorite (sandstone) that together create a remarkable palette of yellow, ocher, green, and black. This masterpiece was sacked by Muslim invaders in the 17th century, and was soon buried under sand. It was not excavated until the early 1900s, whereupon its gigantic representation of the Sun God's chariot was revealed in all its glory, with 12 pairs of intricately carved wheels pulled by seven horses. Equally astonishing was the abundance of erotic sculptures that peppered the facade, more realistic and visible than at Khajuraho (see pages 130–131). In 1903, the *jagamohana* (antechamber) was bricked up to prevent further collapse, but the exterior walls have been superbly restored, displaying a profusion of groups and couples engaged in explicit, acrobatic performances straight from the *Kama Sutra*. Ecstatic bliss is linked to the Tantric concept of the female force or *shakti*, and Konark may have been a center for this particular cult that was later suppressed by Hindu orthodoxy.

Structures The first structure encountered is the Nata Mandir, a raised, colonnaded platform probably used for dance and music performances. Carved into the plinth are dancers, musicians, and erotic couples. West of this is the main temple, fronted by the magnificent Jagamohana, whose pyramidal roof rises nearly 131 feet above a lavishly carved platform. This incorporates the famous wheels beside friezes of elephants, battles, human figures, scrollwork, *chaitya* windows, and *nagas* with human heads. At the back are the ruins of the sanctuary tower, where three statues of Surya survive; the most striking stands, life-

Pilgrims and tourists visit the Surya temple at Konark

ORISSAN CRAFTS
Brilliantly colored appliqué parasols, bedspreads, bags, and other items are made at Pipli, a large crafts village on the road between Bhubaneshwar and Konark. Other Orissan specialties are palm-leaf miniatures and scrolls (including erotica), *tarakashi* (woven wire), used to create beautiful little ornaments and filigree jewelry, and *dhokra*, a lost-wax casting method that produces delightful figures. Orissan textiles, both silk and cotton, have strong, bold colors and designs. There are textile stores near Puri's temple which have wide selections.

size, in a shrine on the south side. Visitors clamber over the back to enter the remains of the sanctum. The deity was spirited away to Puri long ago, but the sanctum preserves a profusely carved platform with a kneeling figure thought to be King Narashimadeva, the temple-founder. It is worth while to walk round twice, once at the lower platform level and again above, in order to appreciate the structure and sculptures. In the grounds stand the raised colossi: elephants to the north and rearing chargers to the south.

▶ Puri

146B1

Sadly, the great Jagannath temple of Puri, one of India's most visited pilgrim centers, is out of bounds to non-Hindus. Built in the early 12th century, inspired by Bhubaneshwar's Lingaraj temple, it is the abode of Lord Jagannath, the Lord of the Universe. The main *deul* rises 213 feet above numerous surrounding *mandapas*, together creating an impressive sea of towered roofs. To the left is a vast kitchen and restaurant area, easily the largest in the world, said to feed 25,000 people daily. Prepared according to strict Brahmin rules, the food is distributed to pilgrims and to the 6,000 temple administrators and priests. To glimpse the animated life within the walls, visit the Raghunandan Library (*Open* Mon–Sat 8–noon, 4–7. *Admission free*) opposite the main, eastern gateway where a guardian will accompany you to the rooftop for a tip.

Puri's grand market street is lined with incongruously ornate buildings that act as a backdrop to armies of beggars and polio or leprosy victims. To the south lies the endless white-sand beach, whose central stretch has pony and camel rides, cheek-by-jowl accommodations, restaurants, and garbage. The currents can be dangerous.

THE LORD'S ANNUAL OUTING
At full moon each July, the three statues of Lord Jagannath, his brother and his sister are wheeled out of the temple on huge canopied chariots and dragged by thousands of devotees to their summer residence which is just under a mile away. This *Rath Yatra* ("car festival") is the high point of the year, and the procession is accompanied by musicians, elephants, and teeming millions. At the gods' summer temple, new costumes are worn daily, and eight days later the whole proceedure is reversed as the procession moves the statues back again. Despite his status, Lord Jagannath is said to be in crisis, as temple finances are allegedly running at a deficit.

167

Jagannath temple, a prominent feature of Puri's skyline

Striking east out of West Bengal brings you to a remote corner of India that exists in a constant state of flux between insurgency and traditional tribal life. Immensely scenic, sometimes danger-ous, the far northeast does not make for easy traveling, but the rewards can be great.

PERMITS AND TOURIST OFFICES

Entry restrictions for the seven states change so make enquiries at Indian consulates before making any travel arrangements. At the time of writing, Assam, Manipur, Meghalaya and Tripura are completely open, but check with the consulate before traveling there. Arunachal Pradesh, Mizoram and Nagaland require Restricted Area Permits, which means travel in minimum groups of four, following specific itineraries and with a maxi-mum stay of ten days. Apply to the Ministry of Home Affairs, Foreigner Division, Lok Nayak Bhavan, Khan Market, New Delhi 110003 (tel: 011 469 3334). Allow at least four weeks. Government of India, B K Kakati Road, Guwahati, Assam (tel: 0361 547407) provides information.

India's isolated and politically sensitive far northeast consists of seven states clustered around Assam; all one state until the 1960s. This is a wildly beautiful region of mountains, tropical rainforests, and plains of rice fields bisected by the mighty Brahmaputra River. Among its many extremes, it boasts astonishing amounts of rain, enjoyed by a fantastic patchwork of ethnic groups more closely related to peoples in Tibet and Southeast Asia than the rest of India. Of the seven states, only three enjoy relative normalcy: Mizoram, Meghalaya and Arunachal Pradesh. The others, Nagaland, Manipur, Tripura and Assam itself are in a state of constant insur-gency, with governments that are neither competent nor powerful enough to maintain order. Corruption is endemic and there is little let up in violence, looting, extortion, and murders, often related to inter-ethnic conflicts.

Not just tea At the heart of this northeast region is Assam, home of high-grade tea and two of India's finest wildlife sanctuaries, Kaziranga and Manas. Although at present Assam has no entry restrictions for visitors, militancy and terrorism led by the United Liberation Front of Assam (ULFA) simmer dangerously. Guwahati, the capital and gate-way to the region, offers fascinating old temples and tea-auctions, besides a good infrastructure that caters to visitors to the wildlife-rich sanctuaries. North of Assam is a botanist's dreamland, the mountainous, often cloud-shrouded state of Arunachal Pradesh, where dense tropical jungle gradually gives way to alpine flora at altitudes of over 16,404 feet, on the border with Bhutan and China.

Waterlands Meghalaya and Tripura lie to the south of Assam, bordering Bangladesh. Both are open to visitors. Tiny Tripura, picturesque, hilly, and full of lakes and bamboo groves that produce interesting cane crafts, was once a princely state, and the capital, Agartala, has a wonderful Indo-Saracenic palace set in Mughal gardens. There is tension in Tripura between the Bengali (Bangladeshi) majority and tribal minorities who are attempting to reclaim their power. Dubbed the "abode of clouds," Meghalaya has the world's highest rainfall, and decades ago drew many Scots to inhabit its lush, rolling hills. Former colonial hill resorts include fantastically wet Cherrapunji and the 4,921-foot lakeside capital, Shillong, now decidedly past its best. This is another region for naturalists, full of thundering waterfalls favored by hundreds of butterfly species, where orchids, ferns, bamboos, and palms sprout exuberantly. Militants from neighboring states frequent Meghalaya for rest and recreation purposes.

Sidestep Snaking down the border with Myanmar (Burma) are the states of Mizoram, Manipur, and Nagaland, the latter being the thorniest point of the far northeast. Mizoram's friendly, peaceful, and colorful capital, Aizawl, rises like a citadel over pastoral valleys inhabited by the Christianized Mizos. Originally from Myanmar the Mizos preserve strong egalitarian, agricultural, and musical traditions. In the Mizo Hills lies the Dampa Sanctuary; its bamboo and semi-deciduous forest contain swamp deer, tigers, leopards, elephants, and gibbons. Mysterious Manipur and its capital, Imphal, has an isolated, independent past. The Meithei inhabitants invented polo and developed their own form of Hinduism as well as dance, music, and weaving traditions. In the last few years underground organizations have multiplied, creating an anarchic situation in which massacres of Kuki and Naga minorities occur.

Land of the Nagas Most fascinating of all is the state of Nagaland. This fertile strip of hills is home to 16 ethnic groups, which were described in ancient Sanskrit literature as "hillpeople living on nature's gifts, warlike and possessing formidable weapons." Their superlative and deep-rooted craft traditions still survive, making this an enticing destination whenever things are quiet enough for visits to be possible.

Opposite page: Aizawl in Mizoram
Above: Mosmai waterfall in Meghalaya
Below: the high landscape of Arunachal Pradesh

▶▶▶ REGION HIGHLIGHTS

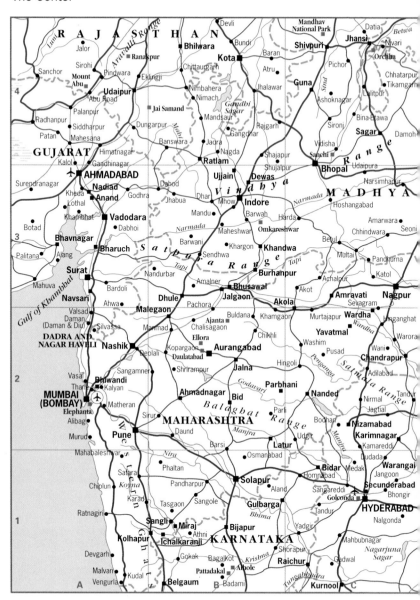

*Previous pages:
a busy vegetable market
in the heart of Mumbai
(Bombay)*

CENTER For many visitors, this region is the stepping-stone into the subcontinent. India's largest city, Mumbai (Bombay), arrogantly and dynamically occupies a west coast isthmus, protected by the Western Ghats. These mountains unfold into the arid Deccan plateau, comprising the states of Maharashtra, Andhra Pradesh, and the south of Madhya Pradesh. Bijapur, though just inside Karnataka, has been included here as its Mughal history and architecture relate to this region. To the east lies the sprawl of Hyderabad, rich in the relics of its outrageously wealthy Nizam rulers, and to the north the ghost town of Mandu, with a wealth of Mughal monuments. The fabulous

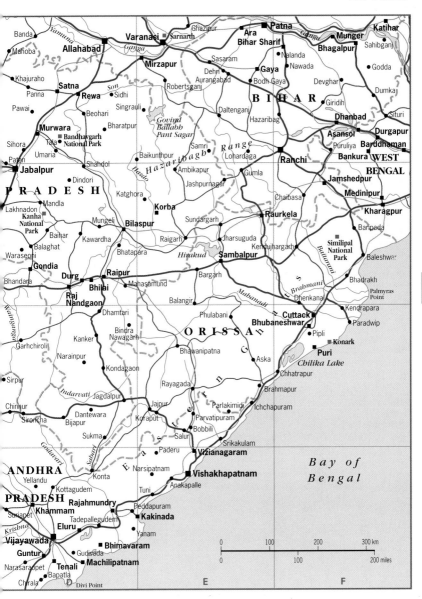

national parks of Kanha and Bandhavgarh, in the remote east of Madhya Pradesh, offer a slim chance of glimpsing a tiger, and a much better one of seeing plenty of other mammals and exotic birds.

SPIRITUAL GLORIES The glories of the center are undoubtedly its ancient spiritual sites, including the Buddhist *stupas* of Sanchi, dating back to Ashoka (3rd century BC), the rock-cut temples of Ajanta and Ellora, and, not quite in the same league, Mumbai's Elephanta. The cave temples were chiseled directly out of the rock (usually basalt) to create massive monoliths, reliefs, friezes, towers, and

174

*Mumbai (Bombay) is still
a busy seaport*

arches; some are over 2,000 years old. At Ajanta, superb sculptures share their glory with a wealth of frescoes depicting not only Buddha and his life but also courtly and monastic customs and characters. At Ellora the caves were initiated by Buddhist monks in the 7th century then developed by Hindu and Jain priests over the following three centuries. The result is one of the world's greatest sights, Cave 16, the Kailasanath temple. The base for visiting these caves is Aurangabad, which has several other major sights, not least the fiendishly labyrinthine fortress of Daulatabad, and the Bibi-ka-Maqbara, like a less grand Taj Mahal. Aurangabad, Bijapur, Hyderabad, and Mandu were all Muslim-controlled cities, where Islamic architecture reached its zenith.

OLD BATTLES Today, Maharashtra is India's most industrialized state, but its past is rife with battles and opposition to the reigning Mughals. The greatest Maratha warrior, Shivaji (1627–1680), was renowned for his astute guerrilla tactics and for decades terrorized the Mughal emperor Aurangzeb. At the same time Shivaji created unity and pride among the Marathi-speaking population, whose control gradually extended east to Orissa. By the time the British arrived, Maratha power was diminishing but it was Mumbai (Bombay) that, in 1885, saw the birth of the Indian National Congress, subsequently a forceful influence in the move towards Independence.

NEW BATTLES Since 1966 the Marathas have launched another crusade, this time under the banner of "Maharashtra for the Maharashtrian". Using the 17th-century hero Shivaji as a figurehead and the tiger as its emblem, the Shiv Sena ("Shivaji's army") has been astutely guided by newspaper owner Bal Thackeray. Its neo-fascist net now encourages Hindu fundamentalism throughout the nation, and appeals especially to the poorly educated lower Hindu castes. In the 1996 Maharashtra state elections, Shiv Sena swept to power in coalition with the

right-wing Hindu BJP (Bharatiya Janata Party), a dangerous result only two years after fatal confrontations between Hindus and Muslims. The Mumbai stock exchange plunged, as the business community is dominated by Gujaratis and Parsis (traditionally supporters of the Congress party), and Thackeray was forced to declare that the state still welcomed foreign investments.

DECCAN HEARTLAND Southeast of Mumbai, beyond the popular hill station of Matheran high in the forested Ghats, lies the increasingly industrialized city of Pune. Automobile factories and engineering companies coexist with the bizarre Osho Commune, an internationally renowned *ashram* that has more to do with creature comforts than the benefits of the spirit. From here the dry Deccan plateau of central India takes over, where villagers eke out meager livings cultivating sugarcane, cotton, wheat, and millet. In some areas tribal people provide a splash of color, and rocky outcrops and boulders give shape to the otherwise monotonous, flat landscape, but it is essentially the cities that are of interest to outsiders.

The Kailasnath temple at Ellora represents Siva's Himalayan home

WORSHIPPING THE LAND
Rural India formed the basis for Gandhi's political philosophy, and it was in the northeast corner of Maharashtra, at Sevagram, near Nagpur, that he chose to set up a model village and *ashram* in 1933. Today men and women still sit on the verandas of their huts, spinning and singing in memory of the Mahatma, and the hospital continues to offer low-price treatment to local farmers.

The Center

TOURIST SERVICES

Government of India Tourist Office, Krishna Vilas, Station Road East J180 (*Open* Mon–Fri 8:30–6, Sat 8:30–1:30; tel: 0240 331217; email: gitoaur@vsnl.com). Also counter at airport. Helpful. MTDC, Holiday Camp, Station Road East (*Open* Mon–Fri 9:45–5:30; tel: 0240 331513; fax: 0240 331198). Information and daily tours of city sights. Classic Travel shares MTDC office (tel: 0240 335598/336110; fax: 0240 338556). Private travel company operating in conjunction with MTDC (Open Tue–Sat 7 AM–10 PM). Ticketing, tours, car rentals.

Right: Chand Minar at Daulatabad Fort. Below: Bibi-ka-Maqbara, reminiscent of the Taj Mahal

▶ Aurangabad 172B2

This sprawling industrial city still feels like a village, with unsealed, unlit streets and quarters that are distinctly medieval in atmosphere. Investment is now pouring in thanks to a Japanese mining company and the infrastructure (including the highway to Ajanta) should be vastly improved in the next few years. Aurangabad is mainly of interest as a base for Ajanta and Ellora but it, too, has its own cave temples, as well as relics of Aurangzeb, the last of the six great Mughal emperors, who gave his name to the town. There are good air connections with Mumbai (Bombay), Delhi and Rajasthan, and trains to Mumbai and Hyderabad. Accommodations, scattered around the "new" town, span the full spectrum.

City sights Aurangabad's atmospheric old center is well worth a half-day's exploration. Fourteen gates surround its walled perimeter and ox carts trundle along narrow streets, some lined with *mahari* (traditional carved wooden facades). The city is still home to a substantial Muslim population and veiled women flit past domed mosques (closed to non-Muslims). In the main square stands the early 18th-century Shahganj mosque, partly concealed by stores and a market, with the main City Chowk (market) immediately to the west. Beyond this is the Kali Masjid, dating from the founding of Aurangabad in the early 1600s. Just north is the Jama Masjid, whose 55 domes rise above a delicately worked stucco facade.

Over the river Northwest of the old city, across the Kham River, are Aurangabad's main monuments. **Panchakki▶** (*Open* daily 8–8. *Admission: inexpensive*) is an ingenious Mughal mill whose large grinding stones were powered by water channeled underground from a spring located about 4 miles away, then raised by siphon to a large reservoir.

The pretty gardens at the back contain the tomb of Baba Shah Musafir, the *Sufi* adviser to Aurangzeb (Muslims only). Another 2 miles north is the **Bibi-ka-Maqbara**►► (*Open daily dawn–10 PM. Admission: inexpensive*), a Taj Mahal lookalike built in the late 17th century as the mausoleum for Aurangzeb's wife and now considered the finest Mughal monument in the Deccan. Gleaming white domes and minarets crown a high platform set in beautiful walled Mughal gardens that are bisected by a long water channel spouting fountains. Although it is beautifully laid out, superbly situated against a backdrop of hills, and at a distance looks as grand as the Taj Mahal, its materials, details, finish, and even proportions are in no way comparable with the original.

Rock temples From here the road crosses undulating scrubland to the **Aurangabad Caves**►► (*Open Tue–Sun dawn–6 PM. Admission: inexpensive*). These are divided into two main Buddhist groups and date mainly from the 4th to the 8th centuries. The most interesting are in the eastern group, where the lavish colonnaded shrines of Cave 7 include a preaching Buddha flanked by high-relief carvings of voluptuous *apsaras* (dancers), and musicians. In Cave 6, one Buddha is surrounded by kneeling disciples and another meets Ganesa.

Military might The magnificent **Daulatabad Fort**►► (*Open daily dawn–6 PM. Admission: inexpensive*) stands 8 miles northwest of Aurangabad, on the road to the Ellora Caves. It crowns a seemingly impregnable volcanic hilltop rising dramatically out of farmland. One of India's oldest forts, it was built by Bhilam Raja of the Yadava dynasty in 1187, when it was known as Deogiri. In 1327, Emperor Mohammed-bin-Tughluq attempted to transfer his capital here from Delhi. During this tragic experiment thousands of Delhi migrants perished on the 684-mile march, or, if they survived the journey, succumbed to famine and drought later. The formidable fort itself was continuously occupied by Muslim rulers until Independence, and Mughal tombs dot the surrounding countryside. At the base of the sheer rock walls stands the victory tower, the **Chand Minar**, opposite the Jama Masjid (1318). From here bastions, walls and moats end at the Chini Mahal, beyond which dark, maze-like passageways finally emerge into daylight at the Baradari, a royal pavilion used by Shah Jahan. The citadel is reached by more steep stairways, worth climbing for the fabulous views.

Excursions

Ajanta►►► (*Open* Tue–Sun 9–5:30. *Admission: inexpensive*). The Ajanta caves are a landmark in Indian art and culture, illustrating the evolution of Buddhism from the 2nd century BC to the 7th century AD. In all, 27 caves were sculpted and chiselled out of the layered granite rock of a spectacular semicircular ravine in the Sahyadri hills, 68 miles northeast of Aurangabad. These are India's earliest surviving shrines, whose structures, whether *viharas* or *chaityas*, inspired numerous later dynasties. They clearly reflect the two schools of Buddhism that emerged in the 2nd century AD: Himayana (the original purist faith) and Mahayana (the more liberal version aimed at the masses). The colors, concepts and designs of their murals are unique. During its heyday, Ajanta is thought to have been home to over 200 monks and numerous artists and craftsmen; today these have been replaced by aggressive hawkers selling postcards and local minerals to busloads of tourists. The caves were forgotten after the 7th century, until a party of British officers hunting tigers discovered them in 1819.

Highlights Cave 1, a huge late 5th-century *vihara*, combines magnificent *Jatakas* (illustrations of the life of Buddha and social and court life) with monks' cells and several sculptural masterpieces. Cave 2, a more intimately scaled *vihara*, has superbly decorated shrines, and ornate, 6th century columns. Ajanta's fragmented earliest paintings (2nd century BC to 2nd century AD), are in the *chaityas* of Caves 9 and 10, with their magnificent *stupas* and rows of octagonal pillars. The 5th-century *vihara* style can be seen again in Cave 16, where a giant statue of the teaching Buddha dominates the 65 foot long hall and its murals of the "Dying Princess" and Siddhartha (Buddha pre-enlightenment). Cave 17, slightly later and showing the transition to Mahayana Buddhism, contains some of Ajanta's liveliest murals, depicting *apsaras* and spirits floating across the sky, a royal procession, blissful lovers, animals, and vegetation. Ajanta's most elaborate facade is at Cave 19, a Mahayana *chaitya* rich in paintings and sculptures surrounding a huge central *stupa*. The lofty window of Cave 26, flanked by high relief statues, fronts an enormous *chaitya*, remarkable for a 29 foot "sleeping Buddha."

Ellora►►► (*Open Tue–Sun 9–5:30. Admission: inexpensive*). Equally inspiring are the 34 cave-shrines of Ellora, created between the 7th and 10th centuries AD to honor Buddhist, Hindu and Jain beliefs. They stud a granite escarpment about 19 miles from Aurangabad, on an old trading route and so, unlike the more remote Ajanta, were much used by travelers. The highlight here is the 8th-century Cave 16, the extraordinary Kailasnath temple, conceived as a temple mountain dedicated to Siva. Measuring 164 feet in length and 98 feet high, this unique creation incorporates a *gopuram*, pavilion, courtyard, assembly hall, sanctum and towers, all lavishly carved but blending with the natural shape of the rock. To the right of the entrance, a path leads up to the clifftop, offering a clear and remarkable view of the ambitious structure. Most interesting among the other Hindu temples (nos 13–29) are Cave 14, with statues of Vishnu, Lakshmi and Siva; Cave 21, with sophisticated figures of Ganga and a dancing Siva; and Cave 29, with superb bas-reliefs depicting Siva legends.

Back to Buddha South of here are the 7th- to 8th-century Buddhist caves (no.s 1–12). Outstanding are Cave 5, with a superb trio of statues, and Cave 10, a *chaitya* with a spectacularly ribbed "ship's hull" ceiling and a Buddha emerging from the shadows of the ambulatory around the stupa. Overlooking the main hall is an upper gallery decorated with amorous couples and offering close views of the lively friezes of dwarves and *naga* queens below. Cave 12 has rows of Buddhas in three stories.

The Jain Caves (nos. 30–34) are some distance north of the Hindu Caves but should not be overlooked. Here, the finest is undoubtedly the early 9th-century Cave 32, dominated by a pot-bellied Mahavir. On the gallery above, there are rich wall carvings and traces of murals.

VISITING THE CAVES
The original way into the Ajanta caves was from the riverbed at the base of the cliffs, where stairs lead up at intervals to the cave temples above. This route can still be followed, but the main entrance is up a long flight of stairs that reaches the level of the caves. Bring adequate water and a powerful torch as, although some caves have electric illumination, many remain unlit. Remember that in order to preserve the priceless murals, flash photography is forbidden. Some cave-guardians offer to turn a blind eye for a tip—ignore them.

179

Inside Cave 26 (left) and (inset) a mural depicting Buddha in Cave 1, Ajanta

MURAL TECHNIQUES
The rock was chiseled to roughen it, then a layer of clay mixed with cow dung and powdered rice husk was applied. This was left to dry before being given a coat of smooth white lime plaster. The surface was then smoothed with a trowel, ready for the artists, who sketched their pictures using cinnabar (a bright red mineral). The paint was made with pigments from the mineral-rich surroundings, and the brushes were generally of squirrels' hair. A last burnishing left a lustrous surface. Mistakes have been made in restoration, but now UNESCO and the Archaeological Survey of India appear to have devised a suitable modern technique.

A leopard at Bandhavgarh National Park

▶▶ Bandhavgarh National Park   173D4

Open: Nov–Jun; daily dawn–noon, 3–dusk with seasonal variations. Admission: expensive.

This 40 square miles park offers the best chance in India of spotting a tiger, (there are around 50—and 27 leopards), among massive rocky hills that rise abruptly from swamp and thick forest. The most striking outcrop is Bandhavgarh, crowned by a fort thought to be some 2,000 years old, according to ancient texts and Sanskrit inscriptions etched into the sandstone of surrounding cave shrines. The dynasties that inhabited it included the Chandellas, creators of the fabulous temples of Khajuraho. The 16th century Rewa dynasty moved north, leaving the fort to be engulfed by vegetation.

Splendid isolation Bandhavgarh's relative isolation makes access difficult, but trips can be arranged from Khajuraho, Varanasi, or Jabalpur to the park headquarters at Tala, where accommodations are located. Even here, outside the park perimeter, it is common to see elephants and monkeys, and great gaur (Indian bison), sambar, barking deer, and nilgai often graze in the grasslands at dusk. The elusive white tiger of Rewa was discovered here, but none have been seen in the park since one was captured by a maharaja in 1951. Birdwatchers may spot hornbills, drongos, flycatchers, parakeets, and eagles among the 150-odd known species. Jeeps are the only way to get around and can be rented through a hotel or at the park headquarters. The luxury alternative is to ramble through the outer edge of the park on an elephant.

▶▶ Bijapur   172B1

Nudging the Maharashtra border from Karnataka, the small town of Bijapur has superlative 15th- to 17th-century Islamic architecture. Mosques, mausoleums, palaces, and forts, built with wealth gained from conquering the Vijayanagar at Hampi, fill the skyline within a compact walled center punctuated by five gates and 100 bastions. Muslim orthodoxy is the rule here, so behave respectfully.

Big dome The star of Bijapur is the **Gol Gumbaz▶▶** (*Open daily 6–6. Admission: inexpensive,* free on Fri) containing the tomb of Mohammed Adil Shah under one of the world's largest domes. Left unfinished in 1660 when the Adil Shah dynasty was in serious decline, the squat stone structure lacks majesty, but the spacious "whispering gallery" preserves startling acoustics, best experimented with early in the morning before the crowds arrive. Access is by stairs in a corner tower that gives sweeping views over the town. A gatehouse museum (*Open* Tue–Sat 10–5) displays some exceptional Chinese porcelain, Deccani miniatures and Bijapur carpets.

Facing Mecca Far more restrained is the **Jama Masjid▶▶**, one of the Deccan's most beautiful mosques. This dates

Gol Gumbaz, in Bijapur

from the mid-16th century, when Bijapur flowered under Ali Adil Shah; he was also responsible for the city walls and water systems. The elegant, colonnaded prayer hall features a marble floor decorated with a grid representing a prayer space for each of the 2,000 or so worshippers. The mosque roof covers the entire courtyard and is crowned by a series of domes, the largest located over the central *mihrab* (prayer niche facing Mecca).

Other sights The modestly scaled but delightful **Mehtar Mahal and mosque►** (*c.*1620) has delicate minarets of carved stone. Also worth a look are the dilapidated Asar Mahal (1646) and the central citadel. The **Ibrahim Rauza►►** was designed by a Persian architect in the early 17th century as the tomb of Ibrahim Adil Shah and was possibly the inspiration for the Taj Mahal. Again, exquisite stonecarving skill is exploited to its utmost in the minarets, domes and screens that decorate the mausoleum and mosque opposite.

TOURIST OFFICE
KSTDC tourist office, Hotel Mayura Adil Shahi, Anandamahal Road, Annexe Bijapur (*Open* Mon–Sat 10:30–1:30, 2:15–5:30; tel: 08352 20359/20934).

 The best way to get around the compact center of Bijapur is by bicycle, available for rent at several places near the bus station or from the Mayura Adil Shahi hotel. Auto-rickshaws are also readily available.

For four centuries the state of Hyderabad was the hub of Muslim power in the Deccan. From the 18th century until Independence it was governed by a succession of fabulously wealthy rulers, named the Nizams of Hyderabad. The seventh and last in line was one of the world's richest men, but also one of its most miserly.

The interior of the lavish Italianate Falaknuma Palace, home of the Nizams of Hyderabad

FALAKNUMA PALACE
The last Nizam never lived in Hyderabad's magnificent Falaknuma Palace (1883) after his father met his death there. From then on it functioned as a guest-house for state visitors and royalty, from George V and Queen Mary to India's first President, but the days of dinners for 100 people, eaten off gold plates, were over. Its Italian marble, stained glass, chandeliers, interior fountains, murals, case-ment ceilings, gilded cornices, and embossed camel-hide upholstery are all still pristine and it is being converted into a luxury hotel.

The last days of the British Raj also constituted the death throes of power for India's 565 princely rulers. Renowned for their exotic ways of life, their hunting, palaces, Rolls Royces, elephants, and concubines, they had become an anachronism in a world reeling from the shock of World War II. Not all lived up to this image: some held sway over only a few cow pastures, others ruled efficiently in the interests of their subjects. Others still, notably the Nizam of Hyderabad and the Maharaja of Kashmir, headed states that easily rivaled European countries in size and population. They both enjoyed the privilege of the 21-gun salute (as did the rulers of Gwalior, Mysore and Baroda), an accolade directly related to the ruler's loyalty to, and funds expended for the British.

Last call Mir Osman Ali Khan (1886–1967) was the seventh in line of a dynasty that emerged in 1724 during the chaotic period of Mughal decline. In 1800, after decades of divided loyalties, the second Nizam was finally persuaded to allow British forces a garrison in Secunderabad, so opening the gates to the influence of the British. In 1911, the young Osman came to the throne unexpectedly when his gregarious and alcoholic father toppled off a veranda of the fabled Falaknuma Palace, went into a coma and died. Raised in an atmosphere of palace intrigue and sycophancy, Osman paraded in magnificent costumes and jewelry, and used one of the world's largest diamonds as a paperweight. He rapidly entered the good books of the British by contributing US$100 million to their World War I coffers. He also appealed to India's Muslims to support the British rather than Ottoman Turkey, allied to Germany. As a result he was given the title "His Exalted Highness", unique among India's princes.

Mr Avarice Osman's character became ever more volatile, partly due to an opium habit that he had adopted to calm his violent temper. "His Exalted Highness" suffered from pyorrhoea, had decaying teeth and became increasingly oblivious to his scruffy appearance, wearing the same dirty fez for 35 years. Holed up in his palace, where garages were filled with unused cars and cellars were stuffed with bins of priceless emeralds, diamonds, and rubies, the Nizam lived in a filthy bedroom where he ate off a tin plate, squatting on a mat. He was in constant dread of being poisoned, and obliged a food taster to share his unvarying diet of cream, sweets, fruit, betel nuts, and nightly opium. He smoked cigarette butts left by his guests, and cut back the electric current in the palace to save on bills. Meanwhile, some 10 million dollars in cash were stuffed away in his dusty attics, and eventually chewed up by rats. His early prudence in financial matters had developed into an all-consuming obsession.

The end At Independence, in 1947, the last Nizam presided over India's most populous state, composed of 20 million Hindus and 3 million Muslims. Reluctant to read the writing on the wall, this frail, diminutive old man dreamed of an independent sovereign state and for a full two months resisted signing any agreement with the new Indian government. Finally, under great pressure, he capitulated, but filed a case with the U.N. Security Council against India for intervening in the internal affairs of Hyderabad. The Indian army was put into action, and from 1948 to 1956 the Nizam played the role of constitutional ruler, preserving his fortune and privy purse (see panel). In 1956, the state of Hyderabad ceased to exist and the city became capital of Andhra Pradesh. Until his death in 1967, Osman Ali Khan lived on in the crumbling King Kothi palace.

PRINCELY PRIVILEGES
When India became independant in 1947, its princes gave up power in return for privileges such as free medical treatment and exemption from paying water and electricity rates. In 1971 Indira Gandhi introduced a bill abolishing these privileges, but the Supreme Court declared it illegal. As a result, she was forced to call new elections. She was overwhelmingly returned to power, and the princes' last privileges were lost forever.

His Exalted Highness, the Nizam of Hyderabad

*Mughal gateway in
Hyderabad*

BUYING TEXTILES
A good place to snap up
superb textiles and saris,
in particular beautiful
Andhra *ikats*, is Kalanjali,
a large air-conditioned
emporium opposite the
Public Gardens on Hill
Fort Road.

▶▶ Hyderabad/Secunderabad　　172C1

Burgeoning, buzzing and polluted, the capital of Andhra
Pradesh is rich in Islamic monuments. As a bonus, it offers
a delicious non-vegetarian cuisine that comes as a relief for
meat eaters emerging from the vegetarian south. Known
for its Bidri ware (engraved or inlaid metalwork), pearls,
diamonds, and highly colored glass bangles, Hyderabad is
also developing high-tech industries. The population of
five million, mainly Telugu speaking, has a large proportion of Muslims, reflecting the city's importance from the
16th century onward, when it replaced nearby Golconda
as a seat of Muslim power.

Layout The old city lies south of the Musi River, spreading
out in a grid pattern from the Charminar, the magnificent
arch that has become a symbol of Hyderabad. Under Asaf
Jahi in the 18th century, the increasingly wealthy town
expanded north of the river, then in the early 1900s gained
the administrative and residential settlement
of Secunderabad that lies northeast of the
immense Hussain Sagar lake. Today,
wealthier residents prefer the airy hills scattered with stark boulders on the western
side of the city towards Golconda Fort; this
too is where the better accommodations
are located. The airport is at the northern
end of the lake close to the train stations.

Old city Hyderabad's Islamic heart beats
in the narrow lanes of the Lad Bazar and
the arcaded streets leading to the imposing **Charminar▶▶**. This square arch with a
fifth-floor mosque, corner minarets and a
small Hindu shrine below, was built in
1591, probably to celebrate the end of a
plague epidemic. Immediately southwest
looms the **Mecca Masjid▶▶**, where
construction started in 1614 but was not
completed until 80 years later, by
Aurangzeb. Accommodating 10,000
worshippers, with huge arches and

pillars made from single slabs of black granite, and bricks from Mecca embedded in its red brick gateway, it is a potent religious and architectural symbol. An open-sided structure to the left contains the tombs of the Nizams of Hyderabad (see pages 182–183). The city's oldest mosque, the **Jama Masjid▶** (1597), lies northeast of the Charminar. Running west from the arch is the fabulous **Lad Bazar▶▶**, strongly reminiscent of an Arab *soukh*, with stalls full of glittering glass bangles, cut-glass bottles, perfumes, wedding outfits, water pipes, and other wonders. Alleyways around Mitti Ka Sher and Charkaman specialize in antique silver filigree, Bidri-ware, and crystal, while Japanese cultured pearls, graded and finely strung in Hyderabad, are sold by dealers on Sadar Patel.

Museums The rambling **Salar Jung Museum▶▶** (*Open* Sat–Thu 10–5. *Admission: inexpensive*) stands north of this area on the riverbank and houses the extravagant collection of Salar Jung III (1889–1949), the Nizams' Prime Minister. Its 35,000 *objets d'art* range from the sublime to the ridiculous, and among the paintings, jewelry, textiles, swords, glass, South Indian bronzes, Italian marbles, and Indian miniatures are some extraordinary items, including jade, ivory, and Marie-Antoinette's dressing table. Across the Afzal bridge are the broad avenues of the commercial district, with jewels of 1920s and 1930s architecture, including the State Library and the General Hospital. In the Public Gardens stands the **Archaeological Museum▶** (*Open* Sat–Thu 10:30–5. *Admission: inexpensive*), converted from one of the Nizams' mansions and counting among its displays some superb early bronzes, reproductions of the Ajanta frescoes and stone sculptures.

Golconda It is 6.5 miles west of Hyderabad at **Golconda Fort▶▶** (*Open* Tue–Sun 10–4:30. *Admission: inexpensive*) that the might of the city's founders resounds. The fort, which dates from the 13th century, was expanded under the Qutb Shahi kings (*ca*1512–1687) until finally three tiers of walls stretched 4 miles around it. The city of Golconda inside was famed for its diamond trade, mosques, harems, royal palaces, dungeons, and the vault that contained the coveted Koh-i-noor diamond. Much is now ruined but the fort's scale, complexity and military might remain apparent. Immediately north lie lovely gardens containing the impressive tombs of the **Qutb Shahi▶▶** (*Open* Sat–Thu 10–4:30. *Admission: inexpensive*), with stuccoed arches and minarets.

TOURIST OFFICES
Government of India, Sandozi Building, 2nd floor, 26 Himayat Nagar (*Open* Mon–Fri 6 AM–7 PM; tel: 040 163 0037).
AP Travel & Tourism Development, Tankbund Road, Hyderabad (*Open* Mon–Sat 10:30–5, closed 2nd Sat each month; tel: 040 345 2492/3086/3036, fax: 040 345 4514, email: aptourd@ap.nic.in). Information on tours, and the sound and light show at Golconda Fort (in English daily Nov–Feb 6:30 PM, Mar–Oct 7 PM. *Admission: moderate*). Information counters at the airport and train station.

185

Inscription on a cannon at Golconda Fort

AROUND INDORE
Indore, at the heart of the Malwa plateau, was the seat of the Holkars and later became a major textile trading center. Cricket heroes rather than kings are idolized now, and the town itself is smothered in a blanket of industrialization. Avoid it if you can, but it may be a necessary stopover on the way to Mandu or to Ujjain (see page 197). Indore is regularly thronged with pilgrims heading for the sacred shrines that surround it, at Ujjain, Maheshwar and the holy island of Omkareshwar. The last two are situated 43–56 miles south of Indore. An intriguing offbeat circuit can be made by car, combining these major temple sites with Mandu.

▶▶▶ **Kanha National Park**   173D3

Open: Nov–Jun; dawn–dusk. Visitors' centres daily 7–11 AM, 3–6 PM. Admission: expensive.

This fabulous reserve is Rudyard Kipling country, encapsulated in his *Jungle Book*, written a century ago. Already protected in the 1930s, Kanha achieved national park status in 1955 and in 1974 became one of the first participants in Project Tiger (see page 100). Today, there are few tigers in this 772-square-mile park but it is densely inhabited by 22 other species of mammal. Palm squirrels, langurs, jackal, wild pigs, spotted and swamp deer (the latter unique to this park), sambar, and black buck are all easily seen. More elusive are the Indian hare, wild dog, barking deer, Indian bison, fox, sloth bear, striped hyena, jungle cat, panther, four-horned antelope, and Indian porcupine. Over 200 bird species also inhabit the deciduous forest and savannah that clothe hills and meadows crossed by streams. These include bee eaters, golden orioles, paradise flycatchers, egrets, grey hornbills, kingfishers, minas, parakeets, and Indian rollers.

Practicalities Isolated Kanha is best reached from Jabalpur (a bumpy five-hour drive), which has train connections with Varanasi (Benares) and Bhopal. The nearest airport is at Nagpur, about 136 miles to the southwest. Park headquarters are at Kisli, with visitors' centers at Khatia and Mukki, where there are also accommodations. All hotels organize jeeps with guides in conjunction with the Forest Department, as this is the only way to explore the park. Observation towers are judiciously placed along the main circuit. The only drawback is the large number of visitors, particularly in the early months of the year. In winter, night temperatures descend to just above 32°F, so come prepared with warm clothing for dawn expeditions.

▶▶ **Mandu**   172B3

This deserted hill town 62 miles southwest of Indore once inspired the Mughal emperor Jehangir to write, "I know of no place so pleasant in climate and so pretty in scenery as Mandu during the rains." This by no means precludes a visit during the dry season, as it offers a refreshing escape from the plains, being 1,968 feet up in the rugged Vindhya hills. The 28 miles of parapets and walls are entered by 12 gates (the Delhi Gate being the most impressive), and surround ruined palaces, pavilions, mosques, *tanks*, and gardens. Accommodations are limited but perfectly adequate, and bicycles can be rented to get you around the sights of the fort.

Crumbling glory As the fort capital of the Parmar rulers of Malwa it was called Mandapa-Durga ("hall of the goddess Durga", a name that became Man-du). Towards the end of the 13th century the town fell to the Muslims. A century later it was promoted from a mere pleasure resort to royal capital of the Sultans of Malwa. Renamed Shadiabad (the original "city of joy"), it nurtured the arts and tolerated Hindu, Jain, and Muslim beliefs. Mandu's heyday came in the late 15th century when Sultan Ghiyas-ud-din built the Jahaz Mahal for his harem of 15,000 women, creating a highly influential style of Islamic architecture. From then on Mandu shuttled between various rulers before being abandoned in the early 18th century, the time of the demise of the Mughals.

Sights Numerous and fascinating to explore, Mandu's monuments are dominated by the magnificent Jahaz Mahal, a 394 foot-long, two-story palace with balconies and open pavilions that rises between two lakes and resembles a floating ship. Close by are the sloping walls of the Hindola Mahal ("Swing Palace"), also built by Ghiyas-ud-din, who would enter astride an elephant up a long ramp. Towering over the village group on a high platform is the domed Jami Masjid, inspired by the great mosque of Damascus. Original tiles, Koranic inscriptions and *jali* screens remain intact. Hoshang Shah's spectacular Afghani marble tomb stands just behind this. Other, much earlier, sights can be found at the sacred Hindu site of Rewa Kund, where Baz Nahadur's palace and the lovely Roopmati Pavilion overlook an ancient reservoir.

Above: Jahaz Mahal at Mandu
Below: Roopmati Pavilion at Rewa Kund

TOURIST OFFICES
For Kanha, contact MPSTDC, Regional Office, train station, Jabalpur (*Open* Mon–Fri 10–5; tel: 0761 322111, fax: 0761 321490). Car rental, runs bus to Kanha Park daily—phone to check times and to make reservations. Mandu can be reached by bus or taxi from Indore. MPSTDC Regional Office, Tourist Bungalow, behind Ravindra Natya Griha, Rabindranath Tagore Road, Indore (*Open* daily 10–5; tel: 0731 528653). Organizes car trips to Mandu.
Information in Mandu itself at MP Tourism's Tourist Cottages and Travelers' Lodge.

Mumbai Chhatrapati Shivaji, formerly known as Victoria Terminus, is composed of many architectural styles

Mumbai (Bombay)

The capital of Maharashtra is India's brashest, most confident and most populous city, displaying all the contrasts spawned by rampant corruption, social chasms and political extremism. This cosmopolitan metropolis of 15 million people sprawls some 25 miles down a narrow peninsula and encompasses both the flashy villas of the *nouveaux riches* and the pathetic encampments of the indigent, strung out between the airport and the highrises of Juhu and Bandra. In the historical heart of Mumbai are colonial buildings, exclusive clubs, and the modern blocks of India's largest commercial center. They line broad avenues choked with beat-up double-decker buses beside the latest Japanese cars. A few streets away, pubescent prostitutes drape themselves in doorways, while in

Colaba, well-heeled tourists flock to the venerable Taj Mahal Hotel with its unbeatable view of Mumbai's emblem, the Gateway of India.

Waterfront magnificence—Gateway of India and the luxurious, red-tiled Taj Mahal Hotel

Slow start This cosmopolitan city started life as seven islands inhabited by Koli fishermen who worshipped the goddess Mumbadevi (hence "Mumbai"). When the Portuguese assumed the reins in 1534 they changed the name to Bom Bahia ("beautiful bay") but little else changed in this backwater. In 1661, Charles II of England received the islands as part of a royal dowry; hardly impressed, he sold them for a pittance to the East India Company. Reclamation work commenced and within a short time Mumbai was offering a large protected harbor for trading ships ducking the monsoon. Commerce blossomed along with shipbuilding (a Parsi undertaking), and was boosted in 1853 by the opening of India's first railroad line, which started in Mumbai. The subsequent opening of the Suez Canal in 1870 assured Mumbai's pivotal role in trade across the Arabian Sea.

Stars and strikes Traders, merchants and entrepreneurs flocked to the booming city, and in the 20th century it embraced the movie business, creating "Bollywood" and a star struck following of millions. In the last few decades, Mumbai has repeatedly hit the headlines with frauds, gang wars, violent strikes, and deadly sectarian violence, including bombings (most recently in 1992–1993). The Shiv Sena, an extreme right-wing Maharashtran political movement emerged (see pages 174–175), and in 1996 wrested state power from the Congress Party, but Congress regained power in 1998.

Strung out Love it or hate it, Mumbai does not care. India's largest economic power, materialist and westernized, is not particularly concerned with nurturing its

END OF AN ERA
On February 28, 1948, Bombay witnessed the departure of the last British troops, who ceremonially left the newly independent subcontinent through the Gateway of India. Saluted by a guard of honor of Sikhs and Gurkhas to the tune of an Indian Navy band, the soldiers of the Somerset Light Infantry slow-marched through the arch to the barges moored below. Centuries of collaboration, confrontation, tragedy, and, finally, negotiation were wrapped up in that emotion-charged moment. And then, unexpectedly, from the huge crowd amassed along the waterfront emerged the strains of *Auld Lang Syne*.

The Center

TOURIST OFFICES

Government of India, 123 M Karve Road–opposite Churchgate Station (*Open* Mon–Fri 8:30–6, Sat and holidays 8:30–2; tel: 022 203 3144/6854/207 4333, fax: 022 2014496, email: gitobest@bom5. vsnl.net.in). Will arrange city tours and excursions. Also counters at the airports (international open 24 hours, domestic manned 7 AM–last flight), MTDC, Madame Cama Road, near Nariman Point (*Open* daily 9–7; tel: 022 202 6713/4627/7784, fax: 202 9122/285 2812, email: info@mumbainet. com). Counters at airports and train stations.

Red double-decker buses complement the British building styles that still dominate the city

Map labels

Haji Ali Dargah

Mahalaxmi Temple

TATA LA PATRAI MARG

KESHAVRAO

Willingdon Golf Course

CUMBALLA HILL

TARDEO

Grant Road Railway/ Station

BHULABHAI DESAI MARG

DR D DESHMUKH MARG (PEDDER RD)

TARDEO ROAD

AUGUST KRANTI MARG

Towers of Silence

Mani Bhavan

SITARAM PATKAR MARG

JAGMOHANDAS MARG

NEPEAN SEA ROAD

Hanging Gardens (Pherozeshah Mehta Gardens)

BRIDGE ROAD

Babulnath Temple

PURANDARE MARG

Opera House

Kamala Nehru Park

MALABAR HILL

Jain Temple

BAL GANGADHAR

WALKESHWAR ROAD

Chowpatty Beach

Taraporevala Aquarium

LAKSHMIBAI

Walkeshwar Temple

WALKESHWAR ROAD

Back Bay

Banganga Tank

Malabar Point

Raj Bhavan

A

Nariman Point

World Trade Centre

CUFFE PARADE

Afghan Memorial Church

B

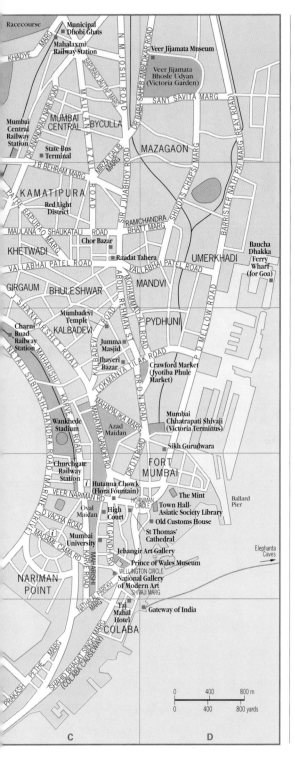

Statue of King George V outside the Prince of Wales Museum

THUS SPAKE ZARATHUSTRA

Zoroastrians, or Parsis, originated in Persia as followers of the prophet Zoroaster (Zarathustra, *ca*800 BC), who taught of the opposing forces of good and evil and an after-life in heaven or hell. After the Islamic conquest of Persia in the 10th century, many Parsis went to Gujarat, from where they later moved to Mumbai for its entrepreneurial poten-tial. Parsis contributed greatly to the city's economic momentum and education but their numbers have fallen, to less than 60,000 today. Foremost among them is the Tata family (with inter-ests in watches, hotels, trucks, pharmaceuticals, and more). Their ances-tors Sir Ratan Tata and Sir Dorab Tata donated valu-able art collections to the Prince of Wales Museum.

An artisan at Chor Bazar, the city's principal antiques and junk market

visitors (helpful tourist offices apart), and historical sights are hardly numerous. The main concentrations of hotels, restaurants and tourist stores are in the pretty, tree-lined streets of Colaba and along Marine Drive, respectively the east and west of the southern peninsula. Immediately to the north, west of a string of *maidans*, are Fort Mumbai's neo-Gothic and Byzantine buildings. These include Churchgate Station, Victoria Terminus (now renamed Mumbai Chhatrapati Shivaji) and Crawford Market, (now Jyotiba Phule Market), all Victorian relics. North of Marine Drive and Chowpatty Beach is the exclusive Malabar Hill, beyond which lie Haji Ali's offshore tomb and, east of the race track, the municipal *dhobi ghats* (see panel, page 194) the northernmost point of interest before the suburban sprawl.

▶▶ Fort Mumbai   191D2
The historical heart of Mumbai has a wealth of idiosyncratic Indo-Saracenic and neo-Gothic monuments, though few are open to the public. Notable facades are the High Court (1879), the Secretariat (1874) and Mumbai University (1857), the last partly financed by Parsi and Jewish businessmen. Horniman Circle is the place for neo-classical architecture, exemplified in the Doric Town Hall (1823) which houses the Asiatic Society Library, the Old Customs House (incorporating a Portuguese section) and the Mint (1829). At Fort Mumbai's southeastern point looms the **Gateway of India▶**, a massive stone arch built in 1924 to commemorate a visit by George V and Queen Mary. It is now used principally as the embarkation-point for ferries to Elephanta, and well frequented by hustlers.

▶ Malabar Hill   190A3

Rising on a headland overlooking the popular evening haunt of Chowpatty Beach, this exclusive residential area is best visited by taxi. At the less salubrious southern tip is an ancient Hindu site marked by the Walkeshwar Temple, rebuilt in 1715, with the **Banganga tank▶** below. Farther up the promontory is the **Jain temple▶**, between film stars' mansions and businessmen's apartment blocks. Although relatively new, it gives a good idea of the strict rituals and prosperity of its masked worshippers, seen crossing marble floors and passing through silver-plated doors to the central sanctum to honor Adinath, the first teacher saint. Farther north and higher up the hill are the Hanging Gardens, a park built over a reservoir. Opposite this is the Kamala Nehru Children's Park, interesting only for fine views over the city.

Bone-cleaners Most visitors to the hill come to stare at the Towers of Silence—though hidden inside a walled enclosure they are hardly a spectacle. This is where the Parsis dispose of their dead by leaving the corpses to vultures; men lie atop the black tower, women on the yellow tower and children on the green tower. Only pallbearers are allowed inside, though the odd toe has apparently found its way onto the balconies of nearby appartments.

▶▶ Mani Bhavan (Gandhi Museum)   190B4

19 Laburum Road, Gamdevi
Open: daily 9:30–6. Admission: inexpensive
It may not be the first Gandhi Museum on your itinerary, but this one has a special atmosphere that justifies a visit. It lies in an attractive residential area northeast of Malabar Hill and is where Gandhi lived sporadically between 1917 and 1934. The house has barely changed since then, and its simple furniture makes a peaceful setting for a comprehensive display of photographs, letters, the Mahatma's spinning wheel, and an antiquated phone. An extensive library is used by researchers.

▶▶ National Gallery of Modern Art   191C2

SP Mukharji Chowk (Wellington Circle),
opposite Prince of Wales
Open: Tue–Sat 11–6, Sun 11–4. Admission: inexpensive
This airy, museum offers an overview of Indian post-Independence art, with strong emphasis on the Progressive Artists Group that included Husain, Souza, Raza, and Ara. The upper floors complete the display with self-assured images from the 1990s, and an auditorium shows related movies. There are more contemporary art exhibitions, of varying quality, at the Jehangir Art Gallery, next to the Prince of Wales Museum (*Open* daily 9–7. *Admission free*).

▶▶▶ Prince of Wales Museum   191C2

159–161 Mahatma Gandhi Road, Fort
Open: Tue–Sun 10:15–5:30. Admission: expensive
This impressive, domed structure set in lovely gardens is the highlight of Mumbai's historic and cultural sights. Inaugurated in 1923, it houses a vast collection acquired through public and private donations. Indus Valley relics (2500 BC) and Assyrian palace reliefs (9th–8th century BC)

AN OCEAN OF STORIES
"Bombay was central, had been so from the moment of its creation: the bastard child of a Portuguese–English wedding, and yet the most Indian of cities. In Bombay all Indias met and merged. In Bombay, too, all-India met what-was-not India, what came across the black water to flow into our veins. Everything north of Bombay was North India, everything south of it was the South. To the east lay India's East and to the west, the world's West. Bombay was central; all rivers flowed into its human sea. It was an ocean of stories; we were all its narrators, and everybody talked at once."
Salman Rushdie, *The Moor's Last Sigh*, 1995.

193

The dhobi wallahs *provide a manual laundry service for the city*

are the earliest exhibits, followed by Gandhara, Gupta, and Maharashtran sculptures. On the second floor over 200 superb miniatures are displayed next to decorative arts, and other halls cover Nepal and Tibet. Top floor exhibits include jade, ivory, European glass, and china.

Excursion

Elephanta▶▶▶ (*Boats with guide* half-hourly 9–2, last return 6 PM. Faster catamarans: depart at 10:30, return at 2. Private boats only during monsoon. *Boat and admission: expensive*). The magnificent cave temple of Elephanta lies less than an hour from the Gateway of India by "luxury" boat. It offers a foretaste of Ajanta and Ellora (see pages 178–179) plus a unique image of Siva in his triple form. The island, originally Gharapuri, was named Elephanta by the Portuguese after the huge elephant sculpture that now stands in the Victoria Garden. There are several rock-cut shrines here but only the most elaborate is open. This dates from the early 8th century and is ascribed to the Rashtrakutas, who artfully combined late Gupta and Chalukyan styles. It lies at the top of a long, steep climb from the jetty that entails dodging vendors before you arrive at what has become a favorite site for weekend picnics. These, and the island girls who for a small fee will pose for photographs with copper pitchers, tend to dissipate one's sense of the divine.

Multi-faceted Siva Just inside the main entrance porch are two images of Siva; on the left he appears as Yogishwara (Great Ascetic) and on the right as Nataraj (Lord of the Dance). Beyond stretches the gloomy, pillared interior, with reliefs of other incarnations of Siva along the back walls. Side courtyards contain subsidiary shrines. The focal point is the platform of the *lingam* shrine, round which devotees walk seven times clockwise. Remove shoes before entering this shrine. At the center of the back wall is Elephanta's most remarkable sight, the triple-headed Siva Mahesamurti. This superb 20 foot-high relief depicts the god as destroyer (left), protector (center) and creator (right). To the left of this masterful depiction of moods is Ardhanarishvara (Siva in languid style as the embodiment of male and female). To the right is Gangadhara (the descent of the Ganga [Ganges] to earth through Siva).

DHOBIS AND TIFFIN-WALLAHS

In the warren of municipal dhobi ghats next to Mahalakshmi station, some 4,000 *dhobi wallahs* (washermen) work in shifts starting at 4 AM, thwacking and pounding the city's dirty laundry in low walled areas connected by water channels. Behind, steam billows from sheds containing huge boiling vats. Another Mumbai speciality are the 3,500 or so *tiffin wallahs* who daily handle 100,000 lunchboxes collected from dutiful suburban wives, transported by train, then whisked from the central stations to the desks of the individual office workers. An organizational *tour de force*.

Practical details

Transportation If arriving at Mumbai's domestic or inter-national airport, use the prepaid taxi service to go down-town. For travelers making a connection, airport accommodations are plentiful and span the full price range. There are regular shuttles between the two airports.

In the city, black and yellow cabs are easy to find, but drivers rarely use meters and bargaining is necessary. Auto-rickshaws function only in the suburbs. Horsedrawn carriages operate around the Taj Mahal Hotel and along Marine Drive; again, bargain hard.

Mumbai also has efficient though overloaded suburban train services from Mumbai Chhatrapati Shivaji/CST (formerly Victoria Terminus/VT), Mumbai Central and Churchgate Station. Go to the latter for trains to the Buddhist Kanheri Caves, which are about 50 minutes away. Long-distance train journeys can be reserved at the Foreigners' Counter at CST (*Open* 8:30–4); go early.

Shopping Food and traditional goods are sold at the riveting Jyotiba Phule (Crawford) Market, just north of the train station, Mumbai Chhatrapati Shivaj. Opposite this Victorian complex, *kurtas* (traditional loose tunics), saris, Kashmir shawls, and embroidered textiles fill the labyrinthine network of booths in Mangaldas Lane. Here too is the Jhaveri Bazar, full of dazzling new gold and diamond jewelry, and much frequented by young brides-to-be. Antiques, fakes, and dusty junk are the specialty of the legendary Chor Bazar in Maulana Shaukat Ali Road. The best day to go shopping is Friday, when the streets fill with "antique" vendors, though the stores are open daily except Sunday.

The city's other shopping hubs are the Oberoi shop-ping arcade and the Taj Mahal Hotel, where prices are more obviously geared to plump western purses. The widest selection of hand-made crafts is to be found at the Central Cottages Industries Emporium, 34 Shivaji Marg, which stocks furniture, textiles, minia-tures, and many other prod-ucts in between. The Taj itself has the excellent Nalanda Bookshop, with a vast selection of art books and fiction.

The city's tiffin wallahs *take home-cooked lunches to office workers*

The Center

OSHO AND RAJNEESH
The main attraction for young westerners in Pune is Osho Commune International. It was founded in 1974 by the now legendary Bhagwan Rajneesh, known for his predilection for Rolls Royces. Rajneesh was at one point accused of crimes that included tax evasion, drug abuse, and fraud, all apparently committed while he was setting up an eccentric utopian project in Oregon. His teaching combined *Sufism*, Buddhism, meditation techniques and yoga with more West-inspired sexual liberation and computer technology. Rajneesh's spirit lives on, and Pune's luxury lair continues to attract followers—at a price and on production of an HIV-negative certificate.

▶ Pune 172A2

Pune was for a long time the heart of Maharashtra and this history, together with its altitude and closeness to Mumbai (Bombay) made it a favorite hill station in colonial days. Industrialization has taken its toll but there are enough sights to justify a short visit. Foremost is the **Raja Dinkar Kelkar Museum**▶▶ (*Open* daily 8:30–6. *Admission: moderate*), a mansion housing an unusual, idiosyncratic collection of functional objects amassed over several decades by its late founder, who was also a poet. Carved wooden doors, inkpots, nutcrackers, textiles, toys, and brass lamps are displayed, and there is a section on the role of Indian women. The Gandhi National Memorial, in what was the **Aga Khan Palace**▶ (*Open* daily 9–12:30, 1:30–5:30. *Admission: inexpensive*) was once the residence of the Muslim Bohra leader and was subsequently used by the British as a prison for dissidents. These included Gandhi and his wife Kasturba, who died here. Her memorial stands in the garden, and a photo exhibition is devoted to him. His Hindu assassin came from Pune.

It is well worth touring the **Osho Commune International**▶▶ (*Open* daily. Tours start at 10:30 and 2:30. *Admission: moderate*; tel: 022 628562, fax: 624181, email: commune@osho.net). This New Age community offers endless esoteric courses and a vast residential complex with facilities worthy of a luxury hotel.

▶▶▶ Sanchi 172C4

One of India's most significant Buddhist sites lies nearly 30 miles northeast of Bhopal. It encompasses *stupas*, monasteries, temples, and pillars dating from the 3rd century BC to the 11th century AD. Like many of Madhya Pradesh's spiritual centers, it is well off the main tourist circuit. A museum (*Open* Sat–Thu 10–5. *Admission: inexpensive*) at the entrance displays exceptional sculptures and fragments. and sells useful guidebooks. Allow a half day to explore this superb World Heritage site.

Heavenly structures Dominating the main walled precinct is the 131 foot diameter Great Stupa. It was built by Ashoka, as was the nearby pillar inscribed with his edict warning against a schism among Buddhists. Additions to

Buffalos in Pune

the *stupa* were made by subsequent rulers, notably the Andhras (1st century BC); these include the gloriously carved sandstone *toranas* situated at the four cardinal points. Their magnificent carvings (some now in foreign museums) illustrate the lives of Buddha and inspired many subsequent Indian art forms. Devotees would enter at the eastern *torana* and walk clockwise, following the passage of the sun, in order to harmonize with the cosmos. Crowning the *stupa* itself is the three-tiered umbrella (*chattra*). This is seen as the sacred tree to heaven standing above the holy reliquary buried deep in the mound.

▶ **Ujjain**   172B3

Ujjain, one of India's most sacred cities, lies 33 miles north of Indore. It has origins that go back to the ancient Sanskrit texts of the *Upanishads* (the philosophical basis of Hinduism) and the Puranas and attracts thousands of pilgrims. They come to bathe in the sacred River Shipra or perform *puja*, and numbers reach around 15 million during the 12-yearly Kumbh Mela. Sadly the **Mahakaleshwara temple**▶ is a modern (though traditionally designed) replacement of the original, one of India's 12 *jyotirlingas*, but its extensive and colorfully populated complex of shrines, courtyards, and *tanks* compensates for this. Other attractions include the **Gopal Mandir**▶, a 19th-century temple devoted to Ganesa and the still-functioning 18th-century observatory, the Vedha Shala. On the outskirts stands the Kaliadeh Palace (1458), superbly located on a river island but closed to the public. The **Bhartrihari Caves**▶▶ are much favored by *sadhus* and a sect of yogis who honor the 5th-century scholar-poet, Bhartrihari.

Eastern gateway of the Great Stupa at Sanchi

STUPA **SYMBOLISM**
Stupas are dome-shaped Buddhist monuments, said to take their shape from an upturned begging-bowl used by the Buddha to symbolize the sacred mountain. Some 84,000 were allegedly erected by Emperor Ashoka to spread *dharma* throughout his empire. Sanchi's Great Stupa, when doubled in size by the Andhras in the 2nd century, became India's largest Buddhist monument. These early stone *stupas* were burial mounds and contained a reliquary. At Sanchi, Stupa 3 has revealed caskets containing the bones of some of Buddha's disciples. The three tiers of the *chattra* represent the Buddha himself, the Law and the community of monks.

Entire families encamped in lean-tos beside Mumbai's highways, legless beggars, sleeping bodies on pavements, child labor: poverty is the unavoidable face of India. Despite visible progress in recent years, India remains handicapped by a web of socio-religious conflicts and a population that is multiplying fast.

Above: shanty towns are a feature of every Indian city

TROUBLE FOR THE COUNTRY

"Our newspapers, for instance, are very much class oriented. When we say we want to remove poverty it is not simply because poverty is bad—it is bad, evil and ugly and a very big human problem— but also because it will create trouble for the country: if poverty and richness co-exist there will be social tension. Either you kill off the poor people, or you learn to live together, and you can only learn to live together if the poor feel there is some amount of sharing... Everyone is conscious of his rights, whether he is brown skinned, black skinned, a woman, a youth or a poor person."
Indira Gandhi, *My Truth*, 1981

"Poverty and uttermost misery have long been the inseparable companions of our people", wrote Jawaharlal Nehru, who felt much of the blame could be laid on the colonizing British. By forcing India to import British-made products such as textiles, and keeping monopolies on basic necessities such as salt, the British Raj had prevented the development of local industries and employment. In the post-Independence years, Nehruvian socialism built up domestic industry and technology through protectionism and five-year plans. The aim was to eradicate illiteracy, disease, and poverty. Today, over 50 years on, industry employs over 28 million people (with some 20 million employed by the state railroad), but unemployment still affects over 36 million people.

Manipulation The reasons for these figures are many and complex. Corruption is high on the list, as are enduring caste divisions that lead to confrontation, envy, or passive fatalism. India is the world's 20th biggest economy, yet members of low castes still toil their lives away in bondage to a landowner. Add to these factors a deep antipathy between Hindus and Muslims, and the incendiary nature of the situation becomes apparent. In 1992–1993, some 1,400 Mumbai citizens died as a result of bitter clashes following the destruction of the Ayodhya mosque by Hindu extremists. Both Muslims and Hindus were involved, but victims were all from the lower levels of society, in a city that soon after registered the world's highest real-estate prices. Paradoxes such as these lead to movements spearheaded by politicians who, whatever their professed beliefs, are often sucked into the vortex of corruption.

Caste system Gandhi and the Indian constitution demanded that caste discrimination be outlawed. The untouchables were renamed *harijans* ("children of God"), and quotas were set to aid their integration into society. The constitution was drafted by India's first Minister of Law, Dr. Ambedkhar, a great supporter of the *harijan* cause who later took the radical step of encouraging them to abandon the caste-ridden system of Hinduism in favor of Buddhism. He died in 1956, before this policy could be developed, but is still a figurehead for *harijans*.

Today the harijans, who prefer the label of *dalit* ("oppressed"), are a fast-growing force. The government, previously dominated by *Brahmins* (the educated, priestly caste) has, since 1995, seen a huge influx of *dalits*, and in 1996 only one cabinet member was a *Brahmin*. In Bihar, India's poorest and most lawless state, marauding caste armies wage war against *Brahmins*. They were encouraged in this by their Chief Minister, Laloo Prasad Yasav, until his imprisonment for corruption in 1997. Elsewhere, the anarchic, neo-Maoist Naxalites carry out sporadic assassinations of landowners or police.

Moving forwards Famine is now relegated to the past, thanks to the Green Revolution instigated in the mid-1960s by Prime Minister Indira Gandhi. This policy introduced new high-yield grain and expanded irrigation projects. Today Indian farmers not only feed the nation but also export their produce, earning nine percent of total export revenue. Things are changing and the wealth of India's new middle class (estimated at around 350 million people) does seem to be trickling downwards. Current impressions are that poverty is retreating, but rising prosperity is offset by a growing population. While the percentage of the population suffering from poverty decreases steadily, the number of individuals affected remains approximately the same.

Plump women in saris and trainers jog along Marine Drive or frequent one of the city's many diet clinics while others live 10 to a room in tenement houses.

THE DREGS
"In the villages, the untouchables were virtually helpless; almost none of them owned that eventual guarantor of dignity and status, land. Few worked it as tenants, and of those tenants fewer still would be able to make use of the paper guarantees of the forthcoming land reforms. In the cities too they were the dregs of society. Even Gandhi, for all his reforming concern, for all his hatred of the concept that any human being was intrinsically so loathsome and polluting as to be untouchable, had believed that people should continue in their hereditarily ordained professions: a cobbler should remain a cobbler, a sweeper a sweeper."
Vikram Seth, *A Suitable Boy*, 1993 (referring here to the early 1950s)

199

The South

▶▶▶ **REGION HIGHLIGHTS**

Karad
MAHARASHTRA
Ratnagiri
Sangli
Kolhapur **Miraj** Athni
Ichalkaranji
Gulbarga Tandur
Bhima
Bijapur Yadgir
Shorapur
Gokak Bagalkot *Krishna* **Raichur**
Devgarh **Aihole** Gadwal
Pattadakal Badami
Malvan Kudal
Vengurla **Belgaum**

Panaji **Dharwad** Hampi **Adoni**
GOA ✈ **Hubli** **Gadag** Kamalapuram
Margao **Hospet** Guntakal
Palolem Haveri **Bellary**
Karwar
A r a b i a n Sirsi **KARNATAKA** Rayadurg
S e a Kumta Ranibennur Harihar **Anantapur**
Honavar **Davangere** Dharmavaram
Linganamakki Chitradurga
Bhatkal **Shimoga** Bhadravati
Kundapura Tarikere Kadur Sira Hindupur
Bhadra Chik
Udupi *1892m* Arsikere **Tumkur** Ballapur
Karkal Chikmagalur Tiptur
Mangalore Bantval **BANGALORE** ✈
Hassan
■ Shravanabelgola
Kasaragod Madikeri **Mandya**
Shrirangapattana *Kaveri*
Mysore Kollegal
Nanjangud
L a k s h a d w e e p Kannur Nagarhole Bandipur
Chetlat National National Park
Thalassery Park
Mahe Mudumalai *2636m* Bhavani
Kiltan Wildlife Sanctuary ▲ **Erode**
Amindivi Kadmat **Kozhikode** Udagamandalam Coonoor
Islands **(Calicut)** ✈ (Ooty) Tiruppur
Bangaram *Nilgiri Hills*
Androth Manjeri **Palakkad** **Coimbatore**
Agatti Pitti Ponnani Pollachi
Kavaratti Palani
Laccadive Islands Thrissur **KERALA** **Dindigul**
Cannanore Is *2695m* Kodaikanal
Suheli Ernakulam Teni
Kochi Painavu
LAKSHADWEEP **(Cochin)** Thekkadi Virudunagar
Kottayam Periyar Sivakasi
Nine Degree Channel **Alappuzha** National Park
Pathanamthitta **Rajapalaiyam**
Kollam
Varkala **Tirunelveli**
Minicoy **Thiruvananthapuram** ✈ Palayankottai
(Trivandrum) Kovalam
Vizhinjam **Nagercoil**
Padmanabhapuram
Kanniyakumari Cape
Comorin

Eight Degree Channel

MV

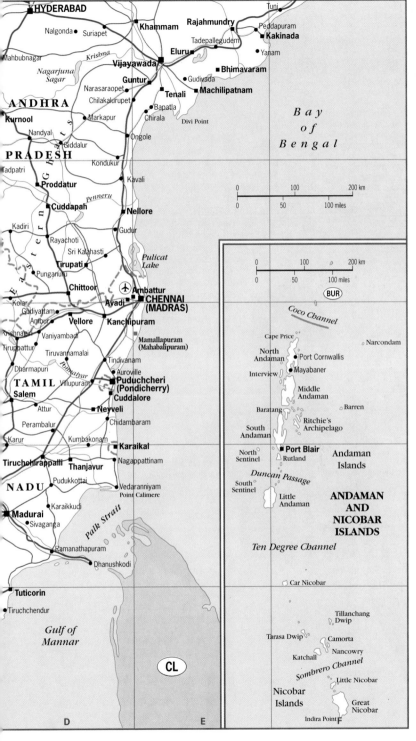

HYDERABAD
Nalgonda • Suriapet
Khammam
Rajahmundry
Tuni
Mahbubnagar
Peddapuram
Kakinada
Krishna
Tadepallegudem
Eluru
Yanam
Nagarjuna Sagar
Vijayawada
Bhimavaram
Guntur
Gudivada
Narasaraopet
Chilakalurupet
Tenali
Machilipatnam
ANDHRA
Bapatla
Chirala
Divi Point
Kurnool
Markapur
Nandyal
Giddalur
Ongole
PRADESH
Kondukur
Tadpatri
Kavali
Proddatur
Penneru
Cuddapah
Nellore
Kadiri
Gudur
Rayachoti
Sri Kalahasti
Tirupati
Punganuru
Pulicat Lake
Chittoor
Ambattur
CHENNAI (MADRAS)
Kolar
Avadi
Gudiyattam
Ambur
Vellore
Kanchipuram
Krishnagiri
Vaniyambadi
Mamallapuram (Mahabalipuram)
Tiruppattur
Tiruvannamalai
Dharmapuri
Tindivanam
Auroville
TAMIL
Villupuram
Puduchcheri (Pondicherry)
Salem
Cuddalore
Attur
Neyveli
Perambalur
Chidambaram
Karur
Kumbakonam
Karaikal
Tiruchchirappalli
Thanjavur
Nagappattinam
Pudukkottai
NADU
Vedaranniyam
Point Calimere
Karaikkudi
Madurai
Sivaganga
Palk Strait
Ramanathapuram
Dhanushkodi
Tuticorin
Tiruchchendur
Gulf of Mannar
CL

Eastern Ghats

B a y   o f   B e n g a l

0   100   200 km
0   50   100 miles

0   100   200 km
0   50   100 miles
BUR

Coco Channel

Cape Price
North Andaman
Port Cornwallis
Narcondam
Interview
Mayabaner
Middle Andaman
Baratang
Barren
South Andaman
Ritchie's Archipelago
North Sentinel
Rutland
Port Blair
Andaman Islands
Duncan Passage
South Sentinel
Little Andaman
ANDAMAN AND NICOBAR ISLANDS

Ten Degree Channel

Car Nicobar

Tillanchang Dwip
Tarasa Dwip
Camorta
Katchall
Nancowry
Sombrero Channel
Little Nicobar
Nicobar Islands
Great Nicobar
Indira Point

D   E   F

The South

ESCAPING THE MONSOON
When the long-awaited monsoon finally breaks over India in early June, it is Thiruvananthapuram that sees it first. The downpours slowly move north from Kerala to reach Rajasthan in July, by which time rainfall has greatly diminished. Meanwhile, to the east, a separate branch sets in from the Bay of Bengal, sweeping across Calcutta and the Gangetic plain to Delhi. Tamil Nadu is different. Unlike the rest of India, this southeastern state receives its highest rainfall in October–December, during a tempestuous season of often destructive cyclones.

SOUTH As it narrows to its final point at Cape Comorin (Kanniyakumari), southern India traverses an incredible diversity of landscapes, cultures, and architectural styles. This is India's gentle half, where hours can be spent in temples watching fervent devotees or flower sellers stringing garlands. Or you can pass the time stretched out on glistening white sands, meandering in a boat through the Keralan backwaters, walking in the refreshing Nilgiri Hills, or riding astride an elephant in a wildlife sanctuary. Women in bright saris with jasmine in their hair and men in white dhotis invariably bear the sign of the gods in ash or yellow sandal paste on their foreheads, a sign of their strong Hindu beliefs. The bewitching and intriguing people of the south speak Tamil, Malayalam, Kannada or Konkani. They are trusting and open, making most interactions a pleasure illuminated by smiles.

RURAL SOCIETY This section covers the states of Tamil Nadu, Karnataka, smaller Kerala, and tiny Goa. There are few large towns, Chennai (Madras) and booming Bangalore being the exceptions. Kochi (Cochin), Mysore, Madurai, and Thiruvananthapuram (Trivandrum) remain small-scale, rewarding stopovers between the rural wilds. Unlike the north, this region was hardly touched by Muslim invaders until the 16th century, and preserves a wealth of Hindu temples and traditions. The dark-skinned Dravidians of Tamil Nadu are descended from India's original inhabitants and perpetuate 3,000-year-old beliefs. The Keralans claim India's highest literacy rate and these standards of education encourage a sense of professionalism that permeates society. Karnataka has a fascinating mixture of hill tribes and stretches of unspoiled coast that continue into Goa. In the former Portuguese colony of Goa Catholicism comes into conflict with partying Western youth and haphazard tourist developments.

A temple guard at Padmanabha Swami temple in Thiruvanantha-puram

AGES PAST The south is rich in the relics of a string of powerful Hindu dynasties whose influence was spread throughout Southeast Asia: the Pallavas (at Mamallapuram and Kanchipuram), Chalukyas (Badami), Cholas (Thanjavur), Nayaks (Madurai), Hoysalas (around Mysore), and Vijayanagar (at the sublime Hampi). Karnataka has a circuit of Jain sites, including the unforgettable high point of the shrines and towering statue at Shravana Belgola. The labyrinthine recesses of the major and still-functioning temples at Madurai, Thanjavur and Tiruchchirappalli provide mesmerizing sights, even though their inner sanctums are inaccessible to non-Hindus.

A devout attitude extends to food and drink: the south is predominantly vegetarian and *thalis* are the rule. Alcohol is not easily available in religious towns, although tea and excellent locally grown coffee are accepted stimulants.

COLONIAL IMPRINTS The Malabar Coast (from Goa to Kochi) was the stepping stone into India. Spices, ivory, and silk drew traders from the 16th century onward, and major ports arose such as Portuguese Goa and Kochi (later Dutch), British Chennai (Madras) and French Pondicherry. Catholic and Protestant missionaries arrived but they did not introduce Christianity—Syrian-Christian communities had been here from the 5th century, and the Apostle Thomas is reputed to have made converts and been martyred here. The British developed Chennai, and hill stations such as Udagamandalam (Ooty) and Kodaikanal.

ON THE WILD SIDE There are several national parks and sanctuaries in the Western Ghats, with tigers at Bandipur and Periyar. These reserves harbor elephants, sambar, sloth bears, and langurs, also found at Nagarhole, Mudumalai, and in the tropical jungles of the Silent Valley. The reserves are easily accessible from the coast and are generally well run with good accommodation, and guide services. Their popularity mounts in the dry season, so reservations are advisable. Then there are the highly developed resorts at Goa, less so at Kovalam and beachside pilgrimage sites such as Varkala and Mamallapuram (Mahabalipuram), where sybaritic pursuits combine with a backdrop of temples and swaying coconut palms.

Left: temple guardian on the Brihadeshwara temple at Thanjavur
Above: Maharaja's Palace, Mysore

PECULIARLY INDIAN
"The chain of the Ghats... divides the west from the plains; a dark violet color, it stands out with unbelievable clarity against the red strip of sunset that still lingers on the horizon; its granite peaks have shapes that are peculiarly Indian and exist nowhere else, simulating towers, pyramids, domes of pagodas. And the spindly palm trees which are, besides a few cruel-looking aloes, the only plants here, rise from the ground in hard lines, silhouetted against what is left of the light, scratching the pale gold of the sky with their dark sticks."
Pierre Loti, *India (Without the English)*, 1903.

Carved stone figure at Malegitti Sivalaya temple

CHALUKYAN TEMPLES
Although Vishnuites, the Chalukyans (see page 38) encouraged Jain and Siva worship and supported the artisans who labored over the centers of worship. Under them, a wealth of architectural experiments took temple-building from the simplicity of Buddhist rock-cut *chaityas* and *viharas* to a more sophisticated style. This became the prototype of southern temple structures under the Pallavas.

▶▶ Badami   *202C5*

In the fertile heart of the Deccan, over 150 temples were erected by the Chalukyan dynasty in the 5th to 8th centuries. Their most dramatic setting is at Badami, where steep red sandstone cliffs are studded with cave temples and freestanding structures. The main accommodations are located here, making it an ideal base for exploring the environs. For the moment it remains low key and well off the main tourist circuit, a peaceful stopover between Hampi and Bijapur, or an excursion from Goa.

To the lake This small town curls around a lake that is said to have healing properties and has a dramatic backdrop of striking rock formations. From the utilitarian main road, with bank, post office, bus station, hotels, restaurants, and funkily decorated *tongas* (pony carts), narrow lanes lead through a maze of whitewashed houses with ornately carved doors, packed between Hindu temples, mosques, and Chalukyan ruins. At the back of the village is the **Medieval Sculpture Gallery▶** (*Open* Sat–Thu 10-5. *Admission free*), which houses items recovered from Aihole, Pattadakal, and Badami, including exhibits connected with an ancient fertility cult. Following the path eastward round the lake, you pass the **Nagamma shrine▶**, devoted to the serpent goddess, before reaching the two beautiful **Bhuthanatha temples▶▶**, where Siva is worshipped as the God of Souls. The temples become magical towards sunset when watery reflections invade the sanctuary.

Rock sights Far above loom the ruins of the fort built by the later Vijayanagar Empire. This can be reached through a gateway next to the museum. From here a steep climb through dramatic rock fissures eventually reaches the clifftop "gun point", with fabulous views. At the far western end is the 7th-century **Malegitti Sivalaya temple▶▶**, magnificently carved with figures of Siva and Vishnu. A long but scenic walk overlooking the lake or a *tonga* ride along the main road brings you to the South Fort. Immediately below are Badami's **cave temples▶▶▶**, the oldest of which date from the 6th century. Cave 3 is outstanding, with carved statues of Siva, Hanuman, and Vishnu reaching 16 feet in height, and fragmented frescoes. Cave 4, Badami's only Jain temple, houses several statues of Mahavir, and Cave 1 has a statue of Siva as the 18-armed Natarja. Sweeping views over the lake and town are usually enlivened by monkeys.

Excursions

At least a half day should be spent exploring the idyllic rural surroundings of Badami for other Chalukyan experiments in temple building. **Aihole▶▶**, about 25 miles away, was the first Chalukyan capital and has some 125 scattered structures. These include the exceptional Durga Temple (named after the nearby fort wall, not the goddess) lying within a landscaped area (*Open* dawn–dusk. *Admission: inexpensive*) at the center of the village. Its unusual semi-circular apse and colonnaded ambulatory have superb sculptures dating from the late 7th century. Older still is the Lad Khan Temple (named after a Muslim prince who lived here), with a *shikhara*, a common feature of later Hindu temples. Here too is a small archeological museum (*Open* Sat–Thu 10–5. *Admission free*). Aihole's oldest structure is thought to be the severe Meguti Temple (AD 634), a Jain temple on a hilltop above a simple Buddhist temple. Both temples afford excellent views of the surroundings.

World Heritage Site Halfway between Badami and Aihole is **Pattadakal▶▶▶**, the Chalukyan capital during the 7th and 8th centuries and now a World Heritage Site. Enclosed in the archaeological park (*Open* dawn–dusk. *Admission free*) is a succession of intricately carved sandstone temples; some have gently curved towers crowned by lotuses and all are inhabited by agile monkeys. The Virupaksha Temple (AD 740) is exceptional, with its lively carvings and beautiful green stone *nandi*.

Closest to Badami is **Mahakut▶▶**, a temple compound built around a *tank* and dotted with shrines and statues, all shaded by huge banyans. The whitewashed 7th-century Mahakuteswara temple dominates, and the activities of swimmers and devotees create a unique atmosphere.

Woman with laundry at Badami

207

BANGALORE TOURIST OFFICES

Government of India Tourist Office, KFC Building, 48 Church Street (*Open* Mon–Fri 10–6, Sat 9–1; tel: 080 558 5417, fax: 080 558 5417, email: goitoblr@satyam.net.in). KSTDC information booths at the airport and train station and two downtown offices: Badami House, N R Square (tel: 080 227 5869/5883) and 10/4 Mitra Chambers, Kasturba Road, Queen's Circle (*Open* Mon–Sat 10–5:30; tel: 080 221 2901–3, fax: 080 223 8016, email: infn@kstdcbng.karnataka. nic.in).

Opposite: a painted statue of Krishna at the Parthasarathy Temple at Triplicane in Chennai (Madras)

CHENNAI TOURIST OFFICES

Government of India, 154 Anna Salai (*Open* Mon–Fri 9:15–5:45, Sat 9:15–1; tel: 044 852 4785/4295 /1913, fax: 044 852 2193, email: goito@md3.vsnl. net.in). Helpful. TTDC, 4 EVR Road, (*Open* Mon–Fri 10–5:30; tel: 044 561385/589132/58291 6/560294, fax: 044 432 0949, email: ttdc@md3. vsnl.net.in). Also at 25 Radhakrishnan Road (tel: 044 854 7335/7344) (*Open* daily 6 AM–9 PM). ITDC, 29 Victoria Crescent, C-in-C Road (*Open* Mon–Sat 6 AM–8 PM, Sun 6–2; tel: 044 827 8884).

▶ Bangalore   *202C3*

Karnataka's capital is a crossroads for connections between Mysore, Chennai (Madras) or Hampi, and few travelers will escape a transit here, whether traveling by plane, train, or bus. Bangalore is rated as India's (if not Asia's) fastest developing city thanks to its booming computer and software industries, but in the process has become unpleasantly polluted and westernized. Once dubbed a "garden city", it now has only a few historical green spaces: Cubbon Park (1864), with a rather mediocre museum (*Open* Thu–Tue 10–5. *Admission: inexpensive*) and the **Lalbagh Gardens▶** (*Open* daily 8–8. *Admission free*), laid out in 1760 by Hyder Ali. The latter has a copy of London's Crystal Palace brought by the British together with gardeners from Kew. Sightseeing diehards can dodge traffic to reach the southern side of the city and **Tipu Sultan's Summer Palace▶** (*Open* daily 9–5. *Admission: inexpensive*), but this is a pale shadow of his main palace in Shrirangapattana (see page 238).

▶▶ Chennai (Madras)   *203E4*

The recent transformation of the name Madras into Chennai has left many of the city's admirers dismayed. This stately old port nevertheless retains a distinct atmosphere that combines Tamil traditions with a long and still visible British legacy. Its airport may be international and its one-way systems highly regulated, but cows frequent the highway into town and water buffaloes with bells on their painted horns stop at traffic lights. Despite the disadvantages of a sprawling city with a population of around six million, Chennai's rich past makes it interesting enough to fill a couple of days.

History Founded in 1639 by the East India Company, the capital of Tamil Nadu stretches along the Bay of Bengal. When the British arrived, they found a community of Portuguese Jesuits around San Thome (there since around 1520), a few Armenian traders, and a weavers' colony at Chennapatnam. Lured by the cheap local cloth but wary of a Dutch trading post at Pulicut to the north, the British established themselves at Madrasapatnam, a settlement which expanded around Fort St. George. Over the centuries Madras gradually absorbed surrounding villages, survived partial destruction when it was captured by the French in 1746–1748, and grew to become a key commercial city of colonial days, generously endowed with striking Indo-Saracenic public buildings. Today its commercial services are located along Anna Salai (formerly Mount Road), a broad avenue that cuts diagonally across the city southwest of the Fort, while the sights generally lie on or just off the 7.5 mile beach road.

Spiritual sights At the southern end of Marina Beach is Mylapore, one of the busiest quarters of the city, full of traditional housing. Mylapore is dominated by the **Kapaleswarar temple▶▶**, a Dravidian temple with a huge *tank*, dating from 1250 but rebuilt in the 16th century. Though non-Hindus may not enter the main sanctuary, they are allowed through the colorful 121-foot *gopuram* into the compound to join the peacocks after which the district of Mylapore is named. Countless festivals are held

here, the greatest being the annual temple celebration in March–April. Surrounding streets, packed with fruit and flower sellers, are a delight to wander in. On the seafront nearby towers the neo-Gothic **San Thome Basilica▶**, built in 1896 to replace an earlier Portuguese structure honoring the relics of Thomas Didymus (the doubting apostle). Farther north, just off the seafront in Triplicane, is the **Parthasarathy Temple▶**, dedicated to Krishna. The temple dates from the 8th-century Pallavas, though it was rebuilt in the 16th century.

Fort St. George The beach road continues north past grand old structures in verdant grounds, above all the impressive red-brick University (1870). It then crosses the estuary to the symbolic heart of colonial Madras, Fort St. George (1640). This striking military complex now houses the Tamil Nadu state government, located beside the atmospheric **Fort Museum▶** (*Open* Sat–Thu 9–5. *Admission: inexpensive*); which has portraits of Queen Victoria and of local nawabs dripping with pearls, as well as displays on Chennai's military history. Behind the museum is the evocative **St. Mary's church▶▶** (*Open* daily 9:30–5:30. *Admission free*), the oldest surviving Anglican church east of Suez, dating from 1680. The solid, simple stone building has a bomb-proof roof, and inside is a superb collection of wall sculptures of soldiers and traders who died in the city, generally abruptly and often young. Robert Clive (see page 46–47) was married here and in 1753 inhabited the house opposite.

North of the fort lies Georgetown, an ordered grid of streets that is Chennai's commercial center. The chief reminder of colonial days is the Indo-Saracenic style **High Court▶▶**; contact the Commissioner of Police for permission to visit the courtrooms and climb the red tower (a former lighthouse) for great views. Armenian traders used the pleasing **Armenian church▶** (1772) that stands nearby, and behind it is the Catholic St. Mary's Cathedral (1675).

Egmore West of here, beyond the central train station, lies Egmore, designed as the cultural and social hub of Madras in the late 18th century. At Egmore's heart is a large complex once occupied by the Pantheon. This was a European social center which was replaced in

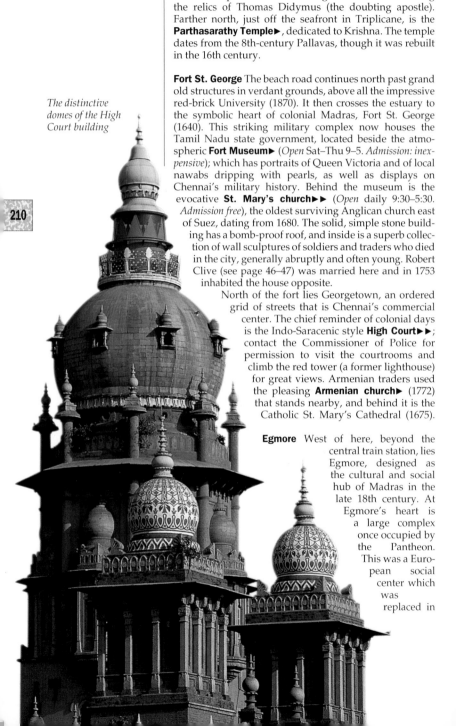

The distinctive domes of the High Court building

the 1880s by the **Government Museum►►►** (*Open* Sat–Thu 9:30–5. *Admission: inexpensive*). The museum has an exceptional collection of over 2,000 South Indian bronzes, Hindu sculpture, and Buddhist marble sculptures from Amaravati, some dating from the 2nd century BC. The architectural highlight of Pantheon Road is the **National Art Gallery►►** (*Open* Sat–Thu 9–5. *Admission: inexpensive*), another of Chennai's Indo-Saracenic gems. Designed by Henry Irwin in the early 1900s as the Victoria Memorial, it changed function after Independence and now houses 10th- to 13th-century bronzes, Mughal miniatures, Deccani painting, and crafts. Also here are sections on botany, archeology, anthropology, and art, the Connemara Public Library, and a Children's Museum.

South of the Adyar Chennai's two rivers give the city an easily comprehensible layout. To the north, the Cooum River divides the Fort area from Chepauk and Triplicane, while to the south the Adyar River fringes a more verdant residential area where some important institutions are located. Most prominent is the **Theosophical Society►►** (*Open* Mon–Sat 8:30–10, 2–4. *Admission: inexpensive*), set in 296 acres of magnificent gardens shaded by centennial trees and dotted with shrines. This world headquarters was founded in 1882 by Annie Besant and includes a school, museum, library and meditation center. Immediately east is Elliots Beach, quieter than Marina Beach but still not advisable for swimming. Another important cultural complex, the **Kalakshetra►** ("Home of Arts") lies south of here, again in a lovely garden. Dedicated to reviving the traditional arts of dance, music and painting, it has an unusual theater where a festival is held every December.

West of here lies Guindy National Park, with a race track, the Raj Bhavan (Government House, built in 1817) and Snake Park (*Open* Wed–Mon 8:30–5. *Admission: inexpensive*). By the Armenian Bridge, in the cave where St. Thomas lived, is the Little Mount shrine (Chinnamalai). Nearby are two commemorative churches to "Doubting Thomas"; one was built in 1551 by the Portuguese, while its modern counterpart was erected in 1971. Farther southwest, on the airport road, is **St. Thomas Mount►**, site of the apostle's martyrdom. Crowning this hillock is another 16th-century Portuguese church with a much-venerated cross (it is reputed to have bled) inserted into a wall.

Across the sea Far into the Bay of Bengal about 870 miles due east of Chennai are the **Andaman Islands►►►**, a slice of Eden dropped into an emerald sea. These, and the off-limits Nicobar Islands to the south, are home to some of the world's oldest and most isolated tribal peoples, who are largely protected from outside influences. Water sports are also a big attraction, as are the rich forest wildlife and nearly 250 bird species. Port Blair, the capital, was established by the British in 1789, became a penal colony the following century and is now the entry point, with the bulk of accommodations and services. A 30-day permit is required, obtainable at the same time as your Indian visa, or at Foreigners' Registration Offices in Chennai (Madras), Delhi, Kolkata (Calcutta) or Mumbai (Bombay). The Port Blair Immigration Officer can grant permission for short visits to a few of the other Andaman islands.

THE THEOSOPHISTS
In 1875, the Theosophical Society was founded in New York by Madame Blavatsky, Colonel Olcott and Annie Besant. A decade later its headquarters were established in Adyar. Here, Annie Besant soon assumed the reins and at the same time became a powerful campaigner for Home Rule in India. Blavatsky's motto, "there is no religion higher than truth," formed the basis of this semimystical society which incorporated the Hindu concepts of karma and reincarnation into a philosophy designed to stimulate each follower's personal search for the true nature of the universe. Theosophy, from the Greek words *theos* (god) and *sophia* (wisdom) is alive and well today with societies throughout Europe and the United States.

211

SHOPPING
Parrys Corner in Georgetown and the entire length of Anna Salai offer the main concentration of shopping centers and emporia for fabrics, crafts, and jewelry. The India Silk House, 846 Anna Salai, and Handloom House, 7 Rattan Bazar, George Town, have a wide selection of silks and cottons. Gem Palace, in Hotel Adyar Park, is great for traditional South Indian jewelry. Poompuhar, 818 Anna Salai, is the place if you're after good-quality bronze items.

The South

TOURIST OFFICES

Government of India, Communidade Building, Church Square, Panaji (*Open* Mon–Fri 10–5, Sat 10–1; tel: 0832 223412). GTDC, Trionora Apartments, Dr Alvares Costa Rd, Panaji (*Open* Mon–Fri 10–5; tel: 0832 226615/ 728, fax: 0832 223926, email: gtdc@goa.goa.nic.in). Also information desks by the Tourist Home on Patto and at the Kadamba bus station and Dabolim airport.

▶▶ Goa   202B5

Goa is a package-vacation paradise, squeezed between the sea and the lush forested hills. It offers a classic tropical cocktail of glistening sands, swaying coconut palms, and ultra-fresh seafood. Luxury hotels and budget guesthouses overlook fishermen mending their nets, and beer comes cheap and chilled. Some visitors feel that Goa is overly-westernized, and even its proud, Konkani-speaking inhabitants tend to agree. "Discovered" by pioneering hippies looking for peace and love, Goa's beaches are now filled with persistent hawkers during the day and rave parties at night, and hotel prices are soaring. For those intent on discovering the "real" India, Goa is best treated as a relaxing break on the southern trail, or even as a charter-flight gateway to the subcontinent, but certainly not as an end in itself.

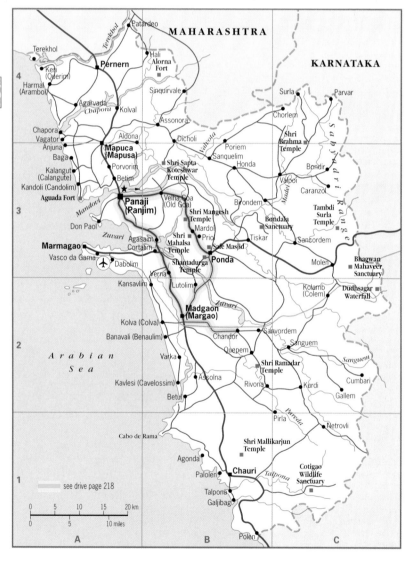

Past glory It is hardly surprising that the Portuguese who came in search of spices in the 16th century decided to put down roots in this tropical paradise. Goa's natural boundaries, the Arabian Sea and the Sahyadri mountains, had sheltered it from much of India's inland turmoil, while its strategic location on the newly discovered trade route to the East made it even more attractive. Goa had long flourished as a port, particularly under the military protection of the Vijayanagar commander Madhav Mantri, who managed to protect Goa from the acquisitive Muslim sultans. In the 1470s, however, Goa finally succumbed to the Muslims and was ruled by Adil Shah of Bijapur. Then in 1508 Alfonso de Albuquerque arrived from Portugal and captured the port, a victory that led to 450 years of Portuguese rule (see pages 214–215).

Inset: many of Goa's street sellers come from tribal families in Karnataka
Below: net repairs on Kalangut Beach

Panaji (Panjim) The capital divides the developed northern beaches from the more relaxed southern Goa. It has ramshackle old buildings with picturesquely pitted walls, tiled roofs and overhanging balconies, standing beside modern concrete structures, and shady bars. Gloomy Portuguese stores still have their late-19th-century wooden fittings. Crowning the central plaza on a small hill is the whitewashed **Church of Immaculate Conception▶▶**, dating from 1541. The cobbled back streets bordering Ourem Creek in the quarters of Fontainahas and Sao Tomé are particularly atmospheric.

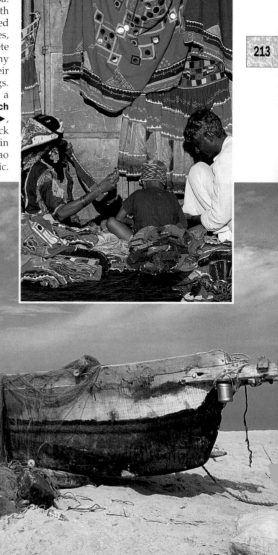

In Goa, Latin influences fuse with Indian color to produce an enchanting hybrid. Goa's traditions of language, religion, food, music, and dance have remained firmly entrenched despite the end of Portuguese rule in 1961. Goans may be Indian, but they are Goan first.

FESTIVALS

Fireworks, floats, parades, and dancing regularly fill the streets of Goa, as both Hindu and Christian festivals are celebrated with enthusiastic abandon. Carnival in February or March is a major festival; Easter and Christmas are welcomed with religious reverence and family gatherings. The annual festival of St. Francis, Goa's patron saint, is marked by numerous processions around his tomb at the Bom Jesus Basilica; in August, at the Novidades harvest festival; sheaves of paddy rice are blessed at churches.

Goa, originally founded to dominate the lucrative spice trade, was Portugal's first foothold in Asia and came to rival Lisbon in its magnificent churches and thriving port. It was from their Goan base that Portuguese merchants headed farther east in the 16th century, founding major trading ports at Malacca (Malaysia), in Indonesia's Spice Islands and East Timor, and building up important trading networks. This was their golden century before other European powers caught up with them.

Settling in After naming the tropical paradise Dourada ("golden"), soon corrupted to Goa, the Portuguese appropriated other territories along the Malabar coast. Daman, Diu, Salcete, Bassein, and, not least, Bom Bahia ("beautiful bay"), better known as Bombay (now Mumbai) all fell to their flag. The Portuguese were initially on good terms with local Hindus and the nearby Vijayanagar kingdom, with whom they set up trading links, and they appointed local officials, built forts and employed Indian troops. A notable new law prohibited *sati*, where widows threw themselves

on their husband's funeral pyre. Other laws relating to property gave a woman the right to half the estate of her husband, unlike the rest of India. This has no doubt contributed to the easy confidence of Goan women. Above all, uniquely among all the colonizing nations, Portugal encouraged intermarriage, a policy designed to preserve the unity and multiply the offspring of settlers. As a result, Portuguese names such as Pereira, Alvares and Braganza are still prominent and Goans have Latin features. Portuguese is spoken by the older genera-tion and a few landowners, but Konkani (Goa's own language) and Marathi (from Maharashtra) are more general.

Catholicism The most visible legacy of the Portuguese is their churches, not only the imposing monuments of Old Goa but also the more typical whitewashed facades nestling among palm trees elsewhere. Christians form a third of the population, but the introduction of Christianity was not painless. Franciscans, Dominicans, and Jesuits arrived in the 1540s, all intent on converting the "heathens".

Portuguese influences pervade all aspects of life in Goa, from church architecture and religious festivities (left) to its cuisine

Despite the more compassionate influence of Francis Xavier (see panel page 216), persecution and violence were used by the Portuguese Inquisition. Permission was obtained from the Portuguese Viceroy to criminalize Hinduism and raze temples. These actions resulted in thousands fleeing from their homes to more tolerant Muslim areas inland, and building temples near Ponda, just outside Portuguese jurisdiction.

Pork and plantains A happier meeting of cultures produced Goan cuisine. Alongside tandoori, rice, and dal, Goan restaurants offer *chourisso* (a spicy pork sausage), *sarpotel* (pickled pig's liver cooked in vinegar with tamarind), and *vindalho* (spicy pork or beef marinated in garlic, chilis and vinegar). Chilis and cashew nuts were introduced by the Portuguese, as were plantains brought from their African colonies; Goans also use coconut sauces. *Pomfret* (a local flat fish) and *bangra* (mackerel) abound, while lobsters, clams, prawns, or kingfish may be smothered in *balchao*, a hot curry and onion sauce. Bread is usually excellent; sweets are made with coconut, rice, nuts, and jaggery (palm sugar). You will also find India's best choice of beers and local wines (port being the most palatable), local rum and *feni* or toddy (made either from fermented cashew apples or from the sap of palm trees).

RHYTHMS
Music flows in the Goan blood and most Goans can pluck at a guitar or pick out a tune on the piano. Old-time taverns in Panaji will invariably have back-ground music, traditional or otherwise. Much Goan music is derived from haunting and lyrical Portuguese love songs, but young musicians have also taken to hard rock and many work the nightclub circuit of India's big cities.

ST. FRANCIS XAVIER

The "Apostle of the East" is largely the reason why there are millions of Christians throughout India and Southeast Asia. He was born in 1506 in Spain, studied in Paris, was ordained in Venice and joined the fledgling Jesuit order. In 1541 the Portuguese king sent him to bring some morality to the newly founded diocese in the East, and he was soon building churches, healing and converting. From Goa he traveled on to Sri Lanka, Malacca, Ambon in the Spice Islands, China, and Japan, proselytizing and founding churches. After dying prematurely at sea, he was buried on an island off China. Malaccan Christians brought his body back to bury in their church, from where it was dug up again and removed to Goa.

GETTING AROUND

Kadamba Transport runs buses throughout the state from the main bus stands at Panaji, Mapuca and Madgaon (also called Margao). Auto-rickshaws are easily available, as are normal taxis, though rates are well above the average for India. Goa's unique motor-cycle taxis take pillion passengers, and are recognizable by their yellow mudguards and white number plates. Better still is another Goan speciality—motor-cycle rental, with models ranging from a standard 50cc machine to a 350cc Enfield Bullet, suitable for Easy Rider clones breezing up into the Ghats. An international driver's license is required, though not always demanded.

Velha Goa (Old Goa)

"Velha Goa", about 5 miles east of Panaji (Panjim), was the original walled town built as the bastion of Portuguese Catholicism in Asia, and at the time dubbed the Rome of the Orient. Abandoned in the 17th century due to repeated cholera outbreaks, this town of grandiose churches, wide avenues, gardens, and stately mansions is now populated only by busloads of tourists and pilgrims. Towering in splendor beside the main road is the **Basilica of Bom Jesus▶▶** (*Open* Mon–Sat 9–6:30, Sun 10–6:30. *Admission free*), a red laterite edifice completed in 1605 that houses the tomb of the Jesuit missionary, St. Francis Xavier. This is located to the right of the heavily gilded, baroque altar with its figures of Jesus and Ignatius Loyola, the founder of the Jesuit order. The ornate chapel and tomb made of marble and jasper were donated by the Medici ruler, Cosimo III, in 1696, and come to life every decade when the severely decaying corpse is ceremonially carried over to the Se Cathedral opposite.

Se Cathedral▶▶▶ The cathedral was the fruit of lengthy construction, 1562–1640, in a purist Tuscan style, and is staggering in proportions (*Open* all day. *Admission free*). Only one of the twin towers remains; the other was struck by lightning in 1776. Within the flaky, whitewashed walls, massive pillars divide the nave from side aisles and numerous chapels where the main decoration is concentrated. In one chapel is kept the Cross of Miracles, which said to grow in size and have healing properties. The heavily gilded central altar depicts the martyrdom of St. Catherine, to whom the cathedral is dedicated.

More crosses At the back is the **Church of St. Francis of Assisi▶▶**. Its convent section is now the Archaeological Museum (*Open* Sat–Thu 10–5. *Admission: free*), housing a rich collection of Goan antiquities. The beautiful church (1521), now under restoration, displays superb decorative paintwork and woodcarving, and the floor is inlaid with elaborately engraved tombstones. Of Velha Goa's many other monuments, the most interesting are opposite the cathedral: the domed Church of St. Cajetan (1651), modeled on St. Peter's in Rome and, nearer the ferry landing, the Viceroys' Arch, which commemorates Vasco da Gama (1597, rebuilt in 1954). A rare relic of pre-Portuguese Goa, the Adil Shah Gate, stands on the site of the Bijapur Sultans' fortress. The now ruined palace was later occupied by the Portuguese Viceroys.

North Goa

This is Goa's most developed coast, increasingly spoiled by uncontrolled hotel and villa developments, characterless

The magnificent altar in Se Cathedral, Velha Goa

restaurants, and endless souvenir stands. The 5-mile stretch of golden sand between Aguada Fort and Baga includes Kalangut (Calangute), a rapidly built package-tour destination. This said, for those looking for lively nightlife combined with a quick dip beside the fishing boats, it fits the bill. Baga itself is popular with budget travelers both for techno music bars and for safe swimming. Beyond the cliffs to the north are the beaches at Anjuna and Vagator. At Anjuna the "alternative" lifestyle of the 1970s continues, complete with beach parties and drugs; Vagator is more sedate and popular with day-trippers.

Rave time Despite witnessing years of rave-parties and hosting a Wednesday "hippie" market, **Anjuna▶** beach retains its natural beauty thanks to its classic palm-lined curve. Little Vagator cove, just a short walk south of the main beach, is more secluded and less populated than both Vagator and Anjuna beaches. It is a favorite with youthful sybarites. Both resorts can be reached from Mapuca (Mapusa), a dilapidated inland town which comes to life only for its colorful Friday market. For a really untouched setting, head north of the Chapora River to the fishing village of **Harmol (Arambol)▶▶**. Here, two beaches offer low-key café bars and, behind the smaller beach, a sulphurous lake with therapeutic mud baths.

Last of the northern beaches at 27 miles from Panaji is **Terekhol▶**, reached by an antiquated car ferry from the village of Keri after a circuitous but scenic drive through paddy fields and palm groves. Tiracol Fort, now a hotel with superb river views, dominates this last tip of Goa.

BEACH ETIQUETTE
There is a long-running battle over nudism in Goa, and sadly many tourists hot off the plane blatantly flout local sensibilities. Despite years of hippie freedom tolerated by some Portuguese Goans, nudism is still distinctly offensive to the Hindu population. Signs on the main beaches clearly state "No nudism" and there are sporadic police efforts to enforce this. Apart from anything else, a nude sunbather soon attracts a crowd of oglers, which somehow lessens the pleasure. Otherwise, the main drawback to beach life is the steady flow of vendors and masseurs: you cannot escape them, but be polite about your refusals.

Drive

Goa

This full day's drive takes in Goa's Christian, Hindu and Muslim past, visiting historic temples, a mosque and a 17th-century church, The route takes you through stunningly beautiful, lush hills, plantations and paddy fields.

From Panaji, drive east to Velha Goa and its wonderful churches, then follow the NH4 southeast through Priol towards Mardol. It is worth stopping

A stately Portuguese mansion

here to visit the popular and ornate 18th-century Shri Mangesh temple, Goa's main Sivaite shrine. The Sri Mahalsa temple, 3 miles south of here, is where carvings depict the incarnations of Vishnu. A few miles farther are the peaceful gardens of the Safe Masjid, a modest whitewashed mosque built in 1560 by the Bijapuri sultan. This is one of only two Goan mosques to have survived the ferocious Portuguese Inquisition.

Continue to the chaotic, unattractive administrative town of Ponda with its ruined fort. A cluster of Hindu temples was built here because Ponda was outside Portuguese territory. Outstanding is the Shantadurga temple (1738) that rises out of the forest about 2 miles west of town at Kavalem.

Drive southwest past plantations of cinnamon, turmeric, and lemongrass, cross the Zuvari River and reach Lutolim, a pretty, typically Portuguese town just off the main road. Lush gardens surround grand old mansions, some of which can be visited by appointment; contact the Madgaon (Margao) tourist office at the Tourist Hotel in advance (*Open* Mon–Fri 10–5; tel: 0834 721966/720470). Continue south, stopping to see the baroque Church of the Holy Spirit (1675) on the main square. Nearby are the sumptuous De Joao Figueiredo House and Da Silva House and the labyrinthine covered market. Lutolim is also home to Ancestral Goa, a model village depicting traditional Goan life.

If you still have energy, strike out 8 miles east to Chandor to visit the star of Goa's mansions, the magnificent Menezes-Braganza house (*Open* daily 9–6, but check. *Admission free*; but moderate donations expected). It is stuffed with antique furnishings and Chinese porcelain, and exudes an air of faded grandeur. Return to Panaji via Madgaon and the fast NH17.

South Goa

From Panaji a highway runs due south, crossing the wide Zuvari estuary to reach **Madgaon (Margao)▶**, a market town with a beautiful baroque church and some fine Portuguese mansions. This is the main stop for all trains from Mumbai (Bombay) or Mangalore before Vasco da Gama, so many people stay overnight here—without staying long enough to spoil the relaxed atmosphere.

To the west is a string of beaches whose powdery white sand and undeveloped hinterland offer a much more rewarding experience of Goa than the beaches in the north. Traffic goes slower and back roads meander through paddy fields, passing hamlets with proud churches and pretty Portuguese houses.

Relax Due west of Madgaon is Kolva (Colva), which has more facilities than any other beach along this stretch and is the most popular with domestic tourists. Far more peaceful is **Benavali (Benaulim)▶▶**, a tiny, relaxed resort a few miles south. This has several budget hotels, excellent seafood restaurants and a verdant village inland. Next south is Goa's expensive paradise, Varka, continuing into **Kavlesi (Cavelossim)▶▶**, also known as Leela Beach. The international hotels here are self-sufficient luxury havens, but less expensive options do exist.

Paradise Beyond the idyllic fishing village of **Betul▶** and Cabo de Rama, the landscape changes dramatically. Roads twist through the jungle-clad slopes of the Sahyadri Hills past stark black laterite headlands and secluded coves. This is where Goa becomes the stuff of dreams, and **Palolen▶▶▶** is there to fulfil them. Its crescent shaped beach offers safe swimming, while village life merges harmoniously with growing tourism. Weekends can be crowded. Farther south still are magnificent, pristine beaches. The **Cotigao Wildlife Sanctuary▶** lies 16 miles east of Chauri. This remote tract of forest harbors gazelles, panthers, and hyenas, but visitors are more likely to spot the usual monkeys or wild boar.

219

Sunset at Palolen beach, South Goa

The South

VERY BEAUTIFUL
Hampi reached its zenith during the reign of Krishna Deva Raya, when it was described by the Portuguese traveler, Domingo Paes, in 1520 as being as large as Rome with a king's palace that was more spacious than the castles of Lisbon. Chariot Street was "... a very beautiful street full of very beautiful houses with balconies and arcades in which are sheltered pilgrims... there are also houses for the upper classes and the king has a palace in the same street where he resides when he visits the temple."

By the Tungabhadra River at Hampi, where huge granite boulders characterize the landscape

►►► Hampi   202C5

This star of the Deccan spreads its drama over 10 square miles of low hills, wild vegetation and sculptural granite boulders, integrating nature with ruins to captivating effect. When choosing the site for their 14th-century capital, the Vijayanagar kings (see page 43) were drawn by Hampi's legendary significance as much as by its strategic qualities as it was thought to have been the site of the monkey kingdom in the *Ramayana* (whose descendants still leap around the ruins). The Vijayanagar founders were two brothers, officers of the declining Hoysala kingdom, who broke away to set up a new political order on the banks of the Tungabhadra river. As the Vijayanagar dynasty grew in strength so did the Hampi's splendor (then known as Vijayanagar), but in 1565 it succumbed to a combined onslaught by Muslim rulers, who sacked the city and massacred over 100,000 inhabitants.

Practicalities Hampi is one of India's greatest sights, but its isolation has so far saved it from excessive tourist invasion. Other than by road, the only access is by overnight train from Bangalore to Hospet, where accommodations remain pleasantly low key. The village of Hampi itself offers a few guesthouses, which are much in favor with backpackers taking a break from Goa. Unfortunately, though, the open sewers draw malarial mosquitoes. From Hospet there are regular buses covering the 9 miles to Hampi Bazar or to Kamalapuram, a village on the south side of the site where the **Archaeological Museum** (*Open*

Sat–Thu 10–5. *Admission free*) and one hotel are located. Bicycle-rickshaws and auto-rickshaws are also readily available.

Spiritual center Along the south bank of the leisurely Tungabhadra River, starting from Hampi Bazar, is the sacred center, announced by the *mandapas* of Hemakuta Hill. In the village itself looms the 164-foot *gopuram* of the **Virupaksha Temple**▶ ▶ (*Open* daily dawn–dusk. *Admission: free*); which dates from the 9th century and is still in use. The highlight of the courtyards is the ceiling outside the main shrine, which is richly decorated with frescoes depicting mythological scenes. Running east from here is a broad, 800-yard avenue that was once the Chariot Street of the Vijayanagar kings, but is now lined with tourist cafés, booths and village houses.

Just before the avenue ends at Matanga Hill, a turn-off to the left, thronged with pilgrims, follows a circuitous riverside path. This passes many temples, including a small and much visited Siva shrine at a beautiful bend of the river where locals gather to wash and fish. Giant boulders and idyllic rural landscapes continue to the **Vithala Temple**▶ ▶ ▶ (*Open* daily dawn–dusk. *Admission: inexpensive*). This well-preserved complex displays remarkable sculptural skill in a variety of styles, not least in the 56 pillars of the main pavilion, each of which was carved out of a single block of granite to depict mythical animals and figures. In the courtyard stands an intricately carved stone chariot, the vehicle for Garuda, Vishnu's steed. Green parrots and frangipani trees add to the atmosphere, while outside stands the King's Balance. On this, the story goes, rulers would weigh themselves against gold and jewels which were then distributed to the population.

Palatial relics Another generous half-day can be spent exploring the royal urban site, that lies just over a mile south of Hampi Bazar and ends at Kamalapuram. The main **palace buildings**▶ ▶ here betray a gradual influx of Islamic styles. They include the graceful domed two-story pavilion called the **Lotus Mahal**, inside the walled *zenana*, and the striking **Elephant Stables**. South of here is the small but superbly carved **Hazara Rama temple**, with its rare depictions of Vishnu as Buddha inside the sanctum and prolific friezes outside. Grouped with it are the **Mahanavami Dibba**, a high platform used for watching festivities and faced in bas-reliefs of animals, and the **Pushkarini**, a stepped *tank*. Last on the road to Kamalapuram is the **Queen's Bath**, a large square bath area surrounded by a delicately decorated arched corridor and projecting balconies. Hampi is now a designated World Heritage site.

Carved stone chariot at the Vithala Temple in Hampi

HOSPET
When the night train from Bangalore creaks into Hospet bringing a flurry of new travelers, a rickshaw race for accommodations follows. Hospet's hotels are limited in number and many visitors end up staying longer than they intended, so demand is intense. The small, friendly town has a reasonable choice of restaurants, the best being attached to hotels, and a lively market area at its southern end. Halfway along the main street, Station Road, is the bus station which provides connections (albeit circuitous) with Bangalore, Hubli (for Goa), Badami, Mysore, Bijapur and Hassan. Money can be changed at the State Bank of India.

Varadarajaperumal temple and temple tank at Kanchipuram

▶▶ Kanchipuram · · · · · · · · · · · · · · · · 203D3

This major pilgrimage center, one of India's seven sacred cities, lies in the hot, dusty interior of Tamil Nadu, 43 miles southwest of Chennai (Madras). It is renowned for its wealth of sculptural styles reflecting the maturity of Pallava art (see page 38) but its importance stretches back to the pre-Christian era when it was a great center of Buddhist learning. Ashoka built *stupas* here and over 100 Buddhist monasteries existed. After the Pallavas (4th to 9th century AD) came the Cholas, who retained Kanchipuram as their capital, and then Chalukyan and Vijayanagar rulers. Decline came in the 18th century when Madras emerged under the British as the foremost city in the region and Kanchipuram became a backwater. It remains a fairly small town, little touched by the 20th century. There are three main areas, each devoted to a particular belief (Siva, Vishnu, or Jain), and altogether over 100 temples are still used by the faithful. Remember that non-Hindus cannot enter the main sanctuaries. The easiest way to get around is by rickshaw, alternatively you can rent bicycles near the bus station.

The greats The earliest surviving temple, and one of the most impressive, is **Kailasanatha▶▶▶** (*Open* daily dawn–noon, 4 PM–dusk. *Admission: inexpensive*), west of the center. This relatively small 7th- to early-8th-century structure is laid out according to canonical texts with eight small shrines aligned from the entrance, ending at a beau-tiful courtyard overlooked by a pyramidal tower. Images of Siva and Parvati abound, as do traces of frescoes. The largest and most important of the Sivaite temples, the **Ekambaresvara▶▶** (*Open* daily dawn–noon, 4 PM–dusk.

Admission: inexpensive) lies less than a mile northeast. Most of it dates from the 16th–17th centuries. Five granite *prakarams* are introduced by a towering *gopuram* and lead to the "hall of a thousand pillars" (in fact, numbering about half that). Behind the sanctum, inaccessible to non-Hindus, that contains an earth *lingam,* and through gloomy hallways lies another open courtyard dominated by a very ancient mango tree (estimated to be over 2,000 years old).

Back towards the center, the **Kamakshi Aman temple▶** (*Open* daily 6–noon, 4–8:30 PM. *Admission: inexpensive*) displays a variety of styles covering a span of about eight centuries. The riotously colored *gopurams* are the most recent addition. The temple is dedicated to Siva's wife Parvati in her form as Shakti, representing cosmic energy. In Kanchipuram she becomes Kamakshi, the ruling deity of the town. Closest to the railroad is the **Vaikuntha Perumal temple▶▶**, an 8th-century Pallava structure that has three vertically rising sanctums dedicated to Vishnu and crowned by a superb carved *vimana*. Bas-reliefs narrate the history of the Pallava dynasty, including their battles against the Chalukyas, and the main entrance hall contains pillars sculpted with lions, a Vijayanagar addition.

▶ Kanniyakumari   *202C1*

Also known as Cape Comorin, this is the extreme tip of India and a pilgrimage town, now irredeemably devoted to commercial concerns. The island **Vivekananda temple▶** (*Open* daily 7:45–11 AM, 2–4 PM. *Admission: inexpensive*), just offshore, honors a 19th-century Bengali theologist and monk who once meditated on the rocks. He preached religious tolerance and later founded the Ramakrishna Mission in Chennai (*Ferries* Wed–Mon every half-hour 7–11, 2–5). The rocks also attract hundreds of pilgrims to see the "footprint" of the Devi Kanya, an incarnation of Parvati as an eternal virgin, and the protector of India's coast. She is also worshipped on the mainland opposite, at the Kumari Amman temple.

Close by stands the **Gandhi Mandapam** (*Open* daily 7–12:30, 3–7. *Admission free*), where the Mahatma's ashes were displayed before being immersed in the sea.

SEA, SUN, MOON, AND WIND
Kanniyakumari is the point where the Bay of Bengal meets the Arabian Sea, and both mingle in the great sweep of the Indian Ocean. During the April full moon, the horizon offers the spectacle of the sun setting and the moon rising simultaneously—for a brief moment that invariably draws crowds. A few miles north is a vast field of wind turbines—a striking experiment in new sources of energy. The winds of the cape create the perfect natural motor.

223

ASHRAMS
Ashrams are places for renewing the spirit, with the help of a guru (or his followers). South India's most traditional *ashram* is probably the Sankaracharya *math* (monastery) at Kanchipuram. Since Adi Sankara (7th–8th century) founded it, there has been an unbroken line of *sanyasins* (ascetics nearing spiritual perfection) serving at its head.

Vivekananda temple lies on an island just off Kanniyakumari

It is easy to lose all sense of time on the Keralan backwaters as you drift through silent lagoons, watching swooping kingfishers and flying fish. People have been using this vast network of rivers and canals in the same ways for centuries, and even today, they act as the only link between more remote villages and the town.

224

CHRISTIANITY
Pretty little whitewashed churches are a common sight in the backwaters. This reflects the fact that the south, and Kerala in particular, is home to a large proportion of India's 23 million or so Christians. The first Christian converts in the Keralan region may have been those who followed the teachings of the apostle Thomas Didymus (Doubting Thomas), martyred in Madras in the 1st century. From the 5th to the 6th centuries, Syrian Christians came from the Middle East to the Keralan coast, full of missionary zeal.

SNAKE BOAT RACES
January, July, August, and September are the months of Alappuzha's snake boat races, with 130-foot long boats manned by crews of over 100 men flying through the backwaters at breakneck speed. The most famous is the Nehru Trophy Race in August, when some 40 highly decorated boats compete in front of enthusiastic crowds. They are joined by naval helicopters showing off their prowess.

Above: transportation boat in the backwaters. Right: coconut cutter

From north to south the dreamlike, watery expanse known as Kuttanad extends 47 miles, from Kochi (Cochin) through Allapuzha (Allepey) to Kollam (Quilon), and inland to Kottayam. This "Venice of the East" boasts 932 miles of waterways, once used by merchant ships laden with ivory, gold, silver, rubber, and spices heading for the port of Cochin, and by maharajas with their royal court in tow. Meandering channels edged by lush vegetation, groves of coconut or banana, palms and rice fields connect with wide open rivers and lagoons in an endless succession of idyllic images. Life moves slowly—a pace matched by local transportation, as it takes up to 12 hours from Allaphuzha to Kollam using the motorized public ferry.

Daily life Apart from their undeniable tropical beauty, the backwaters offer a fascinating insight into the rural lifestyle of their inhabitants. Colorful thatched or tiled houses (*nalukettu*) pop up between the palms or cluster together in communities complete with whitewashed Portuguese church, Hindu temple, mosque, bank, and the occasional hospital (with ambulances that go by water). Most houses are built close to the banks to make use of the unending water supply, and some inhabitants, despite living on a narrow spit of land, manage to pack in cows, pigs, chickens, and ducks alongside vegetable plots.

Children with satchels trot over log bridges on their way to school or are paddled in canoes. Utensils and clothes are washed from the banks and huge loads of coconuts or bananas are moved in precarious dugouts. Larger boats made of seasoned wood bound with coir rope transport heavier cargoes, sometimes shaded with woven bamboo roofs, while fishermen and nets pile into longboats with sides that swoop into curved prows.

Tourist cruises There are numerous choices for visitors. The budget options are the boats operated by DTPC (District Tourism Promotion Council) between Kollam and Alappuzha, with daily departures in both directions at 10:30 AM, to arrive at 6:30 PM—meal stops en route. The full-day trip can be monotonous, so it's worth considering an overnight break at Coir Village Lake Resorts (where you can watch the coir being processed), or leaving the boat halfway and continuing by bus.

To check schedules and book, contact DTPC, Government Guest House, Kollam (*Open* Mon–Sat 10–5; tel: 0474 742558, email: dtpcqln@md3.vsnl.net.in). In Alappuzha contact either ATDC, Komala Road (tel/fax: 0477 243462, email: info@atdcalleppey.com), or KTDC, Motel Araam (tel: 0477 251796/253308).

Local transportation The frequent local ferries are less expensive and bring you closer to the locals. Many have flat roofs, which give more space and wider views—but take a hat, plenty of water, and a supply of local cashew nuts. Recommended is the route from Alappuzha to Kottayam, taking under three hours, time enough to capture the atmosphere.

Luxury specials For more expansive budgets, Kumarakom is a lagoon about 31 miles south of Kochi and can be reached by speedboat in just over an hour. Here on a private island stands the Coconut Lagoon, a sumptuous heritage resort displaying the best of traditional Keralan architecture. Nearby, in a grand old colonial house that once belonged to a British estate owner, is the Taj Garden Retreat. Both establishments offer comfortable accommodations and organize sunset cruises in kettuvallom (converted cargo boats) or overnight trips in houseboats, by far the best way to experience the backwaters from dawn to dusk.

The South

TOURIST OFFICES
Government of India
Tourist Office, Willingdon
Island, next to Malabar
Hotel (*Open* Mon–Sat
9–5:30; tel: 0484
668352). Helpful with
information and guides.
KTDC Reception Centre,
Shanmugham Road;
Ernakulam (*Open*
Mon–Sat 8 AM–7 PM; tel:
0484 353234, email:
ktdc@vsnl.net). KTDC
hotel-booking, tours.
Tourist Desk, Main Boat
Jetty, Ernakulam (*Open*
Mon–Sat variable hours;
tel: 0484 371761). This
enthusiastic private opera-
tion offers good informa-
tion on buses, ferries, and
backwater trips.

*Below: Chinese-style fish-
ing nets at the mouth of
Kochi harbor.
Right: Kathakali
performer*

▶▶ Kochi (Cochin)   202C2

With a history stretching back to the time of King
Solomon, when it was known as the "Queen of the
Arabian Sea", Kochi has long been the most cosmopolitan
of India's cities. Arab, Phoenician, and Chinese traders all
stopped here in search of the precious pepper, cardamom,
and coriander that still grow profusely in the nearby
Nilgiri Hills. Ivory, silks, and fragrant sandalwood were
further enticements. Marco Polo and Vasco da Gama
followed, as did the Dutch East India Company and later
the British. Today, Christians, Jews, Muslims, and Hindus
still live side by side, and Chinese fishing nets, introduced
by merchants from the court of Kublai Khan, continue to
haul in fish. The adjoining backwaters make a popular
tourist destination (see pages 224–225).

Layout Curling around the water, Kochi is made up of
several islands and two main centers: Ernakulam, the
modern town, and Fort Cochin/Mattancherry, the historical settlement on the peninsula. In between lies
Willingdon Island, created by the British to improve deep-
water harbor facilities. To the north is Bolgatty Island.
Bridges and ferries connect the various parts of this waterbound city. At the same time as promoting its rich cultural
past, Kochi continues to function as a major port, giving it
a rough edge that is not always enjoyable. Services and
hotels are situated in Ernakulam, the airport and railroad
terminus is on Willingdon Island, and the sights are all
concentrated in Mattancherry and Fort Cochin. Ferries run
very frequently and there are plenty of auto-rickshaws to
take you around each area.

Fort Cochin This sleepy enclave is the original Portuguese
settlement on the tip of the peninsula, but its architecture
came to be dominated by Dutch and British styles. India's

oldest European church, **St. Francis►►** (*Open* Mon–Sat 9:30–5:30, Sun afternoon. Sunday service in English at 8 AM), was built here in 1503 by Portuguese Franciscans, originally in wood, later in stone. It was subsequently taken over and modified by both Dutch Protestants and British Anglicans. Vasco da Gama, the Portuguese explorer and the first to sail around Africa to reach Asia, was buried here in 1524 but his body was later transferred to Lisbon. It is a charming, simple structure with a vaulted wooden ceiling, *punkah* fans and a tropical facade. Just south is the rather more kitsch, 20th-century Santa Cruz Cathedral. A short walk to the north reveals one of Kochi's picture-postcard images, the cantilevered **Chinese fishing-nets►►**. At high tide, levers and weights are operated by teams of fishermen to lift piles of silvery fish from water. Identical structures line the backwaters farther inland. Fish are also caught using trawlers, and there is a fish market on the beach on the west of the peninsula, teeming with porters bearing head baskets.

Painted palace Due east of Santa Cruz is the **Mattancherry Palace Museum►►►** (*Open* Sat–Thu 10–5. *Admission free,* but donations expected), entered from Moulana Azad Road. he palace was origi-

nally built in 1557 by the Portuguese to placate the Raja of Kochi. It was later extensively renovated by the Dutch, who gave it a massive square tiled roof, and it is often referred to as the "Dutch Palace," In traditional Keralan style, two white-washed stories surround a central court-yard and temple. The outstanding feature of the palace is the wealth of fres-coes that decorate the walls of the royal bedrooms and private chambers, depict-ing lively scenes from the *Ramayana* and the *Mahabharata*. They were painted in a Keralan technique using vegetable and mineral pigments finished with a coat of oil and pine resin. Similar painting techniques can also to be seen at Padmanabhapuram (see page 248) and at the Siva temple in Ettumanur. The oldest frescoes, dating from the late 16th century, face the royal bedroom next to the Coronation Hall, and 19th-century versions cover the walls of the women's bedrooms. The palace also houses some wonderful regal relics and old Dutch maps of Kochi.

KATHAKALI
Kochi has four major venues for Kathakali, but Art Kerala gives preference to groups. Dancer-actors enact stories from the Hindu epics, preceded by a public make up period, when you can watch the symbolic make up being applied. At Kochi Cultural Centre, Souhardham, Manikath Road, Ravipuram (tel: 0484 367866), make up is at 5:30 PM, the performance at 7 PM. Kerala Kathakali Center, Cochin Aquatic Club, River Road, Fort Kochi (tel: 0484 809810), starts with make up at 5 and performance at 6:30. The city's oldest show is at the See India Foundation, Devan Gurukalam, Kalathiparambil Lane, near Ernakulam Junction station (tel: 0484 369471). Make up at 6, performance at 6:45.

*The tropical
climate ensures an abun-
dance of fruit*

Jew Town South of the palace lies the neat quarter locally known as Jew Town, a community dating back to the 2nd century AD when Palestinian Jews fled persecution by Romans. Long before, "black" Jews had come from Babylon and Persia, then in 1492 another wave arrived after being expelled from Spain. Today, only a handful of families remain and their traditional spice stores and trading agencies have given way to stores targeting the luxury tourist trade, mainly dealing in antiques—some genuine, some reproductions, and worth investigating. At the heart of Jew Town stands the **Pardesi Synagogue**▶▶ (*Open* Sun–Fri 10–noon, 3–5. *Admission: inexpensive*), built in 1568 for the "white" Jew community. It was completely rebuilt in the 1660s after Portuguese–Dutch battles had destroyed it. Of particular and curious interest are the floor tiles: 18th-century Cantonese hand-painted ceramics depicting a love story between a Chinese princess and a commoner (evidence of the vast and flourishing trade network of the time). Crowning the synagogue is a clock-tower erected by Ezekiel Rahabi, who was also responsible for importing the tiles (see panel).

CHANGING PICTURES

"No two are identical. The tiles from Canton, 12" x 12" approx., imported by Ezekiel Rahabi in the year 1100ce, covered the floors, walls and ceilings of the little synagogue. Legends had begun to stick to them. Some said that if you explored for long enough you'd find your own story in one of the blue-and-white squares, because the pictures on the tiles could change, were changing, generation by generation, to tell the story of the Cochin Jews. Still others were convinced that the tiles were prophecies, the keys to whose meanings had been lost with the passing years."
Salman Rushdie, *The Moor's Last Sigh*, 1995

Ernakulam Apart from the atmospheric palace hotels of Willingdon Island (the Taj Malabar Hotel) and Bolgatty Island (Bolghatty Palace), the rest of Kochi's interest is centered on Ernakulam. Stores and banks are concentrated along MG Road. It is worth taking a taxi or bus 8 miles southeast to the **Hill Palace Museum**▶▶, Chottanikkara Road, Thripunitra (*Open* Tue–Sun 9–12:30, 2–4:30. *Admission: inexpensive*), a Keralan-style palace in beautiful, grounds. As well as some exceptional Hindu ritual artifacts, bronzes, and paintings, it now contains the royal memorabilia that was in Kochi's Parishath Thamburan Museum.

Lakshadweep Islands Kochi is the base for flying to these idyllic islands, scattered some 124 miles away over the coral reefs. Apart from local fishing communities, who also make coir products from coconut, Lakshadweep remains an ultra-exclusive haven. Only one island, Bangaram, is open to foreign visitors with expensive twice-weekly flights operated by NEPC. The tiny airport is on the island of Agatti and from there a boat or helicopter (during the monsoon) connects with **Bangaram**▶▶▶, where stunning beaches and mesmerizing coral reefs are well served by the Island Resort hotel. Kadmat island's beach resort is also open.

Groups can get permits in advance through recognized travel agents. Individuals should contact Casino Hotel, Willingdon Island, Kochi (tel: 0484 668421/221, fax: 0484 668001, email: casino@giasmd01.vsnl.net.in), or Sports, Lakshadweep Office, Indira Gandhi Road, Willingdon Island, Kochi (tel: 0484 668387, fax: 668647).

▶ Kodaikanal   202C2

Kodaikanal lies at over 7,546 feet on the southern ridge of the Palani Hills, about 68 miles northwest of Madurai from where it is a four-hour bus ride. It was founded in the mid-19th century by the British. Although very popular with Indians from April through June, this hill station is not of major interest to foreigners except for walks. Nights can be very cold and damp October through December, while in summer it suffers from sweltering heat.

Flower-power There are some beautiful forest walks and waterfalls in the surrounding hills and the town itself has several parks. At its center is a large octopus-shaped lake. Bicycles, boats, and horses can all be rented here. The main services, including a tourist office, are along Anna Salai. Immediately south is Bryant's Park and the scenic **Coaker's Walk▶** which, on a clear day, offers stunning views. At the northern tip of the lake is Observatory Road, leading up to the Observatory (*Museum open* Apr–Jun, Sep–Oct daily 10–12:30, 7–9; at other times it opens only Fri 10–noon, 3–5. *Admission free*). Several miles south are the **Pillar Rocks▶**, rising dramatically above the hillside. North of the town is **Chettiar Park▶**, home to the curious Kurinji flower that blossoms once every 12 years.

KOCHI FERRIES
Much faster, less expensive and more scenic than buses, ferries are the ideal form of transportion for this waterbound city. The most popular route runs from Ernakulam's main jetty to Fort Kochi Customs (the stop for all Fort Kochi's sights), then continues to Mattancherry Jetty. The first runs at 7 AM the last around 9:30 PM. Frequent ferries connect Ernakulam main jetty with Willingdon Island's Embarkation Jetty (close to the tourist office) and others between Fort Kochi's Customs Jetty and Willingdon's Terminus Jetty (close to the train station). Ferry timetables are posted at ticket offices beside every jetty.

An idyllic, palm-fringed beach in the Lakshadweep Islands

Gopurams of the Sri Meenakshi, the vast temple complex that lies at the heart of Madurai

TOURIST OFFICE
The very helpful Tamil Nadu Tourist office is in the Hotel Tamil Nadu, West Veli Street, near the Periyar bus stand (*Open* Mon–Fri 10–5:45; tel: 0452 34757, www. tamilnadutourism.com). Also tourist information counters at the train station and the airport.

ELEPHANT CITY
Elephants crop up everywhere in Madurai, but one place where you are certain to meet one is at the temple. Alongside dozens of priests working full-time to keep the cogs of Hinduism turning, there is an elephant "blessing" visitors. No marriage, political function, or religious feast takes place in Madurai without an elephant, and banks are known to give loans for their purchase. Feeding them or giving them money is considered a religious action.

▶▶▶ Madurai   203D2

This extremely sacred city, Tamil Nadu's oldest, was originally designed in a lotus motif but has since expanded into a cacophonous labyrinth of temples, bazaars and narrow streets packed with stalls, squatting vendors, rickshaws, cows, buffaloes, and the odd ambling elephant. It is a perfect size, small enough for easy orientation and large enough for interest to spread over several days. Garlands of scented jasmine, graceful Tamil women, vegetarian specialities, and friendly people make it a quintessential southern town, not to be missed.

Heart of the matter The vast walled complex of the **Sri Meenakshi temple▶▶▶** (*Open* daily 5 AM–12:30, 4–9:30. *Admission: inexpensive*) with its shadowy chambers, *tank*, carved columns, shrines, and courtyards built between twelve towering *gopurams*, is considered south India's finest example of Dravidian architecture, and is Madurai's spiritual and geographical heart. Certainly it has one of the most powerful and revealing atmospheres of any Hindu temple. Most of the structure dates from the Nayak dynasty (16th–18th centuries) but certain individual shrines date back earlier, to the Pandiyas (see page 39). The inner sanctums containing the stone images of the goddess Meenakshi (a form of Parvati) and that of Siva (Sundareswarar) are closed to non-Hindus but there is plenty to see outside.

The main entrance is through the East Gate, leading to a corridor lined with temple-souvenir stands. In the northeast corner is the Temple Museum in the Ayirrakal Mandapa ("Hall of 1,000 Pillars", in fact 985). The magnificent hall is flanked by prancing lions and other creatures superbly sculpted round the columns. Stone carvings mingle with curious drawings of "thought forms" as perceived by yogis, but display panels detract from the structural splendor and scale. In a courtyard outside stands a *nandi*, symbolically guarding the Siva shrine.

Closer to the south entrance is the magical pool of the Golden Lotus Tank, always crowded with worshippers, some bathing before *puja* to remove guilt, others just sitting and chatting. West of here is the Meenakshi shrine where, every evening at 9 PM, Siva's statue is ceremonially brought "to sleep", accompanied by the elephant, priests, musicians, and devotees. North of this area a maze of dark corridors contains countless statues splattered with *ghee* and pigment, both being traditional offerings. It is well worth hiring a guide to explore the highlights, but the temple is also fascinating just for the sight of worshippers hurling *ghee*, circling statues, or applying *tikkas* (the dots painted on the forehead by Hindus).

Palatial sights The streets surrounding the temple are a hive of tailors' premises, jewelers, and general souvenir stores. The Pudu Mandapa is an extraordinary tailors' market inside a crumbling palace that opens onto East Chitrai Street. On the northern side, hustlers spirit visitors to rooftops for sweeping views over the temple and especially the gold-topped *gopuram* that is above the central sanctuary. A short walk or rickshaw-ride southeast takes you to the **Thirumalai Nayaka Palace▶▶** (*Open daily 9–1, 2–5. Admission: inexpensive*), built in 1636 and partially renovated. Intricately stuccoed domes rise above an open quadrangle edged by lofty arcades, all that remains of the original palace. An excellent museum recounts the history of the palace and various entertainments are staged in the courtyard.

Educational tour A few miles northeast of the center, beyond the Vaigai River on the Tammukam Road, is a landscaped complex that includes the **Gandhi Museum▶▶** (*Open daily 10–1, 2–5:30. Admission free*), in a lovely 17th-century palace. It gives a fascinating photographic account of the freedom struggle and Gandhi's role. The *dhoti* that he was wearing when he was assassinated is preserved in a dark room, still bloodstained, like a religious relic.

The Teppam Festival is held at full moon in late January–February, to commemorate the birth of King Thirumalai Nayak. The normally empty pool of the Teppakulam *tank*, about 3 miles southeast of the center of Madurai, is filled for the occasion. Statues of Siva and Meenakshi are brought to the central island temple, from where they circle round the vast *tank* on floats. Thousands of pilgrims line the banks watching the progress of their gods, while the full moon hangs above.

231

Golden Gopuram, Sri Meenakshi temple

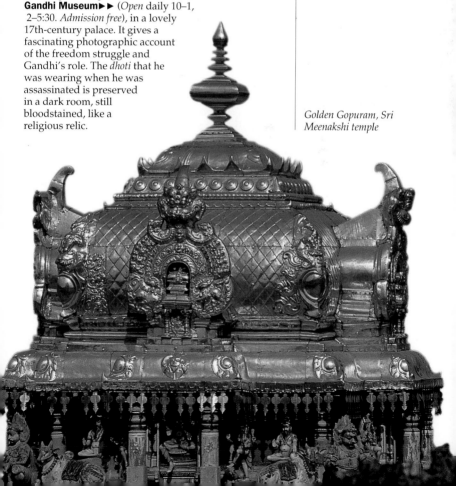

Ayurvedic medicine has been practiced in India for over 2,000 years. Its complex principles are based on the use of natural ingredients to restore the balance of mind and body. Medication can be purely herbal or use minerals and metals, while treatments involve specially prescribed diets, elixirs, yoga, steam baths, and massage.

Ayurvedic cures for sale in the Kodaikanal bazaar

PULSE-READING

A major diagnostic tool for Ayurvedic practitioners is pulse reading. They claim that by placing three fingers on the pulse and pressing it, they can tell within seconds what is wrong. The problem might be constipation or cancer, or a psychological condition such as anxiety or depression. They also say they can tell if you live on junk food (your pulse will be muted) or take the contraceptive pill. Above all, they claim to predict the onset of diseases, as these have six definable stages.

No visitor to India's south can escape mention of Ayurveda, usually applied to bogus massages that are offered at every tourist center, but also associated more seriously with certain health resorts. Ayurveda is Sanskrit for "laws of health" and is one of the four *Vedas*, or Hindu sacred texts. Over the centuries, this traditional Indian medicine became modified by contact with foreign systems but is now enjoying a resurgence in popularity. Ayurvedic products include toothpaste and shampoo, and the system has been adopted and extensively researched in Russia and China.

Air, water, fire Many of Ayurveda's more extraordinary practices, such as vaccination, anaesthesia by inhalation and dietetics, have been adopted in the West in the last century or so, but the system is in principle holistic as it aims to treat people's physical, psychological and spiritual attributes together. At its basis is *Tridosha*, the theory that there are three elements: fire, water, and air. All human functions are located in one of these three *doshas* (cosmic forces) that, in turn, are divided into two aspects: the matter and the essence. Further complex sub-divisions identify specific organs, and take into consideration temperature, emotions, physical alertness, and personality. All are examined in the context of the patient's age and family circumstances and all these interconnected factors form the basis of the doctor's diagnosis and treatment.

Ayurvedic therapy Body functions are divided according to the three characteristics of the doshas. *Vayu* (wind or air) incorporates respiratory and sound-producing apparatus, the digestive tract, bladder, and substance-retaining organs, as well as wind and flatus. *Pitta* (sun or fire) is related to the liver, spleen, heart, and eyes. *Kaph* (moon or water) controls the flow of moisture in the body from the brain to salivary and gastric juices, cardiac fluids, and those in joints. The physician's formidable task is to maintain the balance of these three forces and, since the same three classifications are identifiable in foods, choose the appropriate remedy. Asthma, for example, is thought to indicate that the air element is over-dominant. A diet is prescribed to exclude any *vayu* foods such as rice and spices, and therapies are practiced to stimulate the other two elements. Surgery was a highly developed science in the early days of Ayurveda but an organ was removed only if it was considered a threat to the proper functioning of the rest of the body.

Positive relationship Unlike Western medicine, Ayurveda is based on a positive interaction between doctor and patient that extends to the latter's spiritual welfare. Even in times of good health, an Ayurvedic doctor advises on diet, the regulation of personal habits, the choice of marital partner, and sexual behaviour. Seeing the patient as more than a passive biological system, Ayurveda emphasizes the patient's own responsibility in developing physical and spiritual well-being.

Treatments Ayurvedic health resorts offer a variety of treatments, best experienced on a daily basis for two weeks. These include massages with herbal oils, good for rheumatic problems and stress; *njavarakizhy*, a treatment that induces perspiration by the application of medicated rice compresses, good for joint pains, arthritis, and some skin diseases; *dhara*, a mental relaxant of herbal oils and buttermilk poured on then massaged into the forehead and upper body to help insomnia, mental tension, and skin problems; *pathrasweda*, a massage with bunches of boiled medicinal herbs, used to improve circulation and tone muscles; and *udvarthanam*, a massage with herbal powders designed to help obesity, paralysis, and rheumatism. Medicated steam baths are another favorite treatment for eliminating toxins, reducing fat tissues and helping skin disorders.

AYURVEDIC STRESS-BREAKERS
- Eat at regular times.
- Sip hot water thoughout the day, or lukewarm water in summer.
- Use a stainless-steel tongue scraper or the back of a spoon to remove impurities every morning.
- Make lunch your biggest meal.
- Eat dinner by 8 PM.
- Get to bed by 10 PM.
- Never use an alarm clock.
- Practice meditation.

Ayurvedic potions (above) and massage (below)

TOURIST OFFICE

Tamil Nadu Government Tourist Office, Covelong Road, at entrance to town on Chennai road (*Open* Mon–Fri 9:45–5:45; tel: 04114 42232). You can hire guides, useful for understanding temple intricacies, bicycles, essential for getting around the scattered sights, and cars. Bicycles can also be rented in the center.

BEACH LIFE

The waters of the Bay of Bengal are relatively safe to swim in but female swimmers in particular will find they attract appreciative crowds of spectators. The best bet is to use the beaches north of the village in front of the more expensive hotels. These can be reached either by the inland road or by walking along the sand.

Sculptor in Mamallapuram

▶▶▶ Mamallapuram (Mahabalipuram)   203E3

The sculptural extravaganza of Mamallapuram is yet another highlight of south India and has been designated a World Heritage site by UNESCO. Under the Pallava dynasty (4th–9th centuries) this flourishing port became the place where the art of temple construction was redefined. Although only one of the seven shore temples remains, the rock-cut temples nearby incorporate superb bas-reliefs. Mamallapuram still thrives as a major stone-carving center—the dawn call here is the rhythmical sound of chisel chipping stone. All this, along with local fishing activities, an unspoiled palm-lined beach and a wide selection of accommodations, provide the ingredients for deserved popularity.

Continuing enigma Before the reign of Narasimha Varman I (AD 630–668), Indian shrines had been built of wood or carved into existing caves. Narasimha Varman and his architects used the boulders and rocky outcrops of the local landscape to carve scale replicas of temples or *rathas* (chariots of the gods), but their purpose is still a mystery as they were never used for worship and many remained unfinished. It is possible that they were purely to show off the talents of local sculptors, and their influence certainly spread, from Ellora to Java.

Tumultuous tale The Pallavas' greatest work is an immense relief depicting the **Descent of the Ganga▶▶▶**, or "Arjuna's Penance". The name depends on whether the central figure is Siva's ancestor, Bhaghiratha, the holy ascetic responsible for persuading the gods to release the heavenly Ganga (Ganges) onto earth or Arjuna, the warrior from the *Mahabharatha*. Measuring about 89 feet long and 29 feet high, it is a work of art as tumultuous as Indian life itself. A wealth of animals and gods interact with the protagonist. In the central cleft where water once flowed from a cistern above, sculpted *nagas* swim upstream watched by two huge elephants to the right.

To the lighthouse West, north and south are several notable *rathas* and *mandapas* (pillared halls). Carved into the boulders and fronted by pillars with squatting lions are bas-reliefs illustrating Hindu mythology. They include Vishnu as Varaha (the cosmic boar), Vishnu asleep on the giant serpent experiencing the cosmic nightmare (Vishnu Anantasayin), and Krishna lifting Mount Govardhana. Furthest

north (about 1,640 feet) are the **Trimurti cave-temples▶**; before this looms **Krishna's Butterball▶▶**, a gigantic boulder that sits poised on a sloping rock face, apparently ready to roll. From here a path winds southward and uphill towards the Old Lighthouse that once doubled as a Siva temple. It now stands beside the New Lighthouse, and both have panoramic views. Just below is the mid 7th-century **Mahhasura Mardini temple▶▶**, which shows the buffalo demon being slain by a masterfully sculpted, eight-armed Durga, a feminine aspect of Siva, sitting astride her lion in supremely confident and regal style.

Five rathas About 2 miles south of the village is an outstanding group of *rathas* from the 7th–8th centuries known as the **Pancha Pandava▶▶▶**. Four of them are carved from one long granite boulder running north to south, while the fifth stands just out of line. There are also a gigantic elephant, lion, and bull. The architectural styles show a marked Buddhist influence. Every wall and level is profusely sculpted (some are more complete than others).

On the shore Whipped by the wind and eroded by the thundering waves, the stunning **Shore Temple▶▶▶** is majestic and somewhat melancholy, standing in isolation on the beach. It is thought to be India's oldest freestanding temple, and was built in the early 8th century. The approach is through an enclosure surmounted by small *nandis*, behind which rises the main *vimana* on six richly carved levels beside a smaller one. There are two shrines dedicated to Siva, one each side of another devoted to Vishnu, entered from the south.

The Descent of the Ganga, or "Arjuna's Penance", carved in stone

DESCENT OF THE GANGA
The great relief at Mamallapuram (Mahabalipuram) probably depicts the descent of the the goddess Ganga to earth, one of Hinduism's greatest tales. For a thousand years (a mere drop in time for Hindu myths), Siva's ancestor Bhagiratha performed great acts of austerity and penance in order to persuade the gods to release the heavenly Ganga (Ganges). When he finally succeeded, the next challenge was to prevent the impact of the falling water from destroying the earth. In stepped Siva himself, who stoically agreed to receive the river on his head where it meandered for further aeons through his tangled hair before flowing gently onto the earth from the Himalayas.

The Maharaja's Palace illuminated by thousands of light bulbs

ROYAL TRAINS
Mysore's regal sights continue at the train station, where the royal retiring rooms were favorites with the former Maharani. A long colonnaded veranda leads to the Rani's room with its floor-length curtains and regal bed, and the public waiting room has a fountain. Beside the station is the Rail Museum (*Open* Tue–Sun 10–1, 3–5. *Admission: inexpensive*); where old locomotives and special cars for the royal family are displayed.

▶▶▶ Mysore 202C3

Few Indian cities can rival the stately charm and easygoing atmosphere of Mysore, a former princely capital 87 miles southwest of Bangalore. With a population of around three quarters of million, it remains a manageable size, with tree-lined streets and well-maintained historic buildings, and makes an excellent base for this region's numerous cultural relics and wildlife sanctuaries. Often dubbed the "city of palaces,", it in fact has five, and several mansions, too, some of which have been converted into attractive, atmospheric hotels. Jasmine, incense, silk, carved sandalwood, and rosewood are the main local products, bringing fragrance to the Devaraja market. *Mallige* is Mysore's jasmine speciality and its heady scent permeates the air when it blossoms in spring. Mysore is fairly westernized, though. You will not see many people in loincloths, and auto-rickshaw drivers ruthlessly raise their fares for visitors.

Palaces and more palaces Hard to miss at the heart of town is the massive **Maharaja's Palace▶▶▶**, standing within walled gardens (*Open* daily 10:30–5:30. *Admission: inexpensive*. No cameras or shoes inside but free lockers available at northern entrance). Built in 1897–1912 to replace a palace that burned down, it was designed by the prolific Henry Irwin in typical Indo-Saracenic style, sprouting turrets, arches and columns at every opportunity. Every Sunday night and during festivals the palace is lit by 50,000 bulbs—a dazzling sight.

Inside, flashy decoration takes over. Though it borders on kitsch it is still remarkable for its state of conservation and incredible craftsmanship. The central octagonal Peacock Pavilion in particular is a riot of colorful art nouveau tiles and stained glass, with walls lined with paintings of Mysore festivities. Doors of fabulously carved Myanmar teak lead to a portrait gallery before you reach the second floor eye stopper, the public Durbar Hall. This vast colonnaded turquoise and gold hall, open to the front, incongruously combines paintings of Hindu divinities with royalty; while chandeliers and a "Durbar lift" add a western touch. From here solid silver doors inlaid with ivory lead to the private Durbar Hall, harboring more stained glass, chandeliers, and a carved wooden ceiling. Visitors shuffle through the palace along a clearly marked route; palace guards throughout are always willing to give out information.

On the western flank of the palace, beyond a small temple and camel rides, is the **Maharaja's Residential Museum▶▶** (*Open* daily 10:30–6:30. *Admission: inexpensive*). This idiosyncratic collection is well worth the visit, giving a far more human picture of Mysore's royalty than the grandiose palace. Broken chairs, toy cars, paintings protected with plastic sheets, palanquins, sepia photos, brocade costumes, and even a daybed with crystal legs are all jumbled together, and the guardroom contains a collection of weapons.

Sensuous sights West of the Maharaja's Palace stands another palatial abode, the Jaganmohan Palace now used as the **Jayachamarajendra Art Gallery▶▶** (*Open* daily 8–5. *Admission: inexpensive*), with more regal relics, including portraits of the royal family, miniatures, furniture, glass, porcelain, musical instruments, and Western and Indian *objets d'art*. A short stroll north to KR Circle, with its ornate clock tower (not to be confused with another one near Gandhi Square) leads to the hectic activity and noise of the **Devaraja market▶**. This maze of narrow medieval alleys is lined with booths selling neat piles of brilliantly colored textile dyes, sandalwood incense, piles of jasmine and marigolds, antiquated tools and utensils, and much more besides, altogether creating a very magical atmosphere at nightfall . The avenue running north from KR Circle, Sayyaji Rao Road, is the main shopping street of the city and includes the Cauvery Arts and Crafts Emporium. To see Mysore specialties being made, take a rickshaw three miles southwest to the Government Silk Factory, Manathandy Road (*Open* Mon–Sat 8–11, 12:30–5. *Admission: inexpensive*; tel: 0821 521803).

TOURIST OFFICE
Regional Tourist Office, Old Exhibition Buildings, Irwin Road, Mysore (*Open* Mon–Sat 10–5:30; tel: 0821 422096, fax: 0821 441833). Also counters at the train station and bus stand.
Information also available at the Chamundi Guest House, Jhansi Lakshmibai Road (tel: 0821 521152/520653), and Hotel Mayura Hoysala, 2 JLB Road (tel: 0821 425349).

Marigolds are sold in Devaraja market—the demand for them is such that they are sold by weight

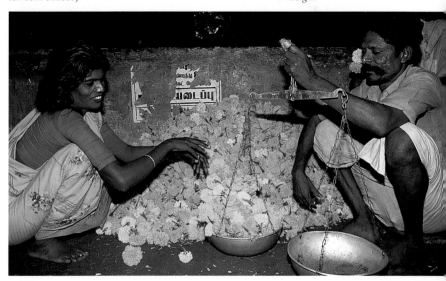

Statue of Gommata at Shravanabelgola

THE WORLD COLOSSUS?
The monolithic Gommata is the largest statue carved from a single block of stone in India, but is it the biggest in the world? The Buddha images at Bamiyan in Afghanistan are at least twice as high but are not carved out of a single block as is Gommata. Egypt's image of Ramses II is bigger, but is not freestanding. Memnon's two colossi are at least 10 feet taller than Gommata and about two millenniums older, but they are not monolithic.

Excursions

Chamundi Hill▶ An 8 mile drive south of Mysore leads to this symbolic hill crowned by the 12th-century Chamundeshwari temple (*Open* daily 7–1, 4–7:30. *Admission free*; or pay to avoid the line). The temple is dedicated to Mysore's ruling goddess, Chamundi, better known as Durga. There are special worship days on Tuesdays and Fridays, when it is nearly impossible to see the goddess's solid gold statue. True pilgrims reach the temple by climbing 1,000 or so steps from the base, passing the superb 16-foot tall black granite **nandi▶▶** (made in 1659) about two-thirds of the way up. Sweeping views show the Lalitha Mahal Palace (1931), with a dome copied from St. Paul's cathedral in London, and the Rajendra Vilas Palace (1939), both now converted into luxury hotels.

Shrirangapattana▶▶ This island town is inextricably linked to the history of Mysore and its rulers. It sits in the Kaveri (Cauvery) River 10 miles to the north, and was once the headquarters of Hyder Ali and his son, Tipu Sultan, the Muslim conquerors of Mysore's Wodeyar family. "Better to live one day as a tiger than a thousand years as a sheep" said Tipu (*ca*1750–1799) who, after allying himself with the French to defeat the British invaders, died in a bloody battle against Arthur Wellesley, later the Duke of Wellington. Tipu's summer palace, the Daria Daulat Bagh (*Open* Sat–Thu 9–5. *Admission: inexpensive*), is an exquisitely decorated 1784 teak structure that was occupied after his death by his English conqueror. Superb frescoes in naive style illustrate various battles, and upstairs a collection of paintings and memorabilia overlooks the lovely Mughal gardens. At the eastern end of the island town stands the Gumbaz, a mausoleum with doors of ebony inlaid with ivory, where father and son are buried.

Long before the arrival of its Muslim conquerors, Shrirangapattana was famous for the Sri Ranganatha Temple, an imposing 10th-century Vishnuite edifice that still attracts throngs of pilgrims. This stands near a mosque within the walled fort that dates from the Vijayanagar dynasty in 1454; when Vijayanagar power waned in the early 1600s they gave way to the Wodeyars.

Shravanabelgola▶▶▶ 58 miles north of Mysore, this extraordinary Jain pilgrimage site spreads over two hills, several *tanks* and a village. Its highlight is the main temple (*Open* daily 6–6. *Admission free*) crowning Indragiri Hill. Inside its precincts stands a 56-foot monolithic statue of Gommata. With long arms and legs entwined with creepers, he is wonderfully serene and oblivious to the crowds of prostrate pilgrims below. This fantastic feat of engineering dates from around AD 980 and makes a fitting climax to the long climb up the granite hill that goes up nearly 700 steps, passing numerous rock inscriptions and intermediary *basadis* (shrines). Take water and socks to protect your feet—no shoes allowed. Every 12 years a major anointing ceremony takes place to honor Gommata: devotees pour holy water, *ghee*, coconut milk, turmeric, and honey liquids over the head from specially erected platforms while crowds watch in complete, devotional silence. The next ceremony will be in 2005. Sculptures of Jain *tirthankaras* (prophets) and *yaksas* (demigods), as well as 9th to 19th-century reliefs carved into boulders, continue on Ghandragiri, the small hill to the north.

Wildlife sanctuaries (*Admission: expensive* to both parks) There are panthers, elephants, chital, sambhar and barking deer, together with numerous bird and reptile species at **Nagarhole (Rajiv Gandhi) National Park►►**, 60 miles southwest of Mysore. The state-run Kabini River Lodge has excellent amenities and guides, and is the best place from which to explore the park. Otherwise the Forest Department at Kutta organizes tours. Due south of Mysore is the **Bandipur National Park►►**, set up by the Maharaja of Mysore in 1931 and one of 23 national parks in India selected to participate in Project Tiger in 1973 (see page 100). You may not see a tiger, but wild elephants, other mammals and birds are plentiful among the teak, rosewood, and bamboo that borders the Mudumalai Wildlife Sanctuary.

DASARA FESTIVAL
This 10-day event takes place every September–October, transforming Mysore into a center of nonstop pomp and pageantry as the city celebrates the victory of the goddess Chamundeswari over the demon. The jewel-encrusted gold throne is brought out of the Maharaja's Palace, and the palace facade is illuminated nightly as a backdrop to countless cultural events. The climax comes on the 10th day, when an elephant carrying a statue of the goddess in the maharaja's golden *howdah* leads a procession from the palace to Bannimantap on the outskirts, accompanied by soldiers and royal chariots.

239

National parks like Nagarhole employ working elephants

The Hoysala dynasty built three quite magnificent temples within easy striking distance of Mysore, at Somnathpur, Halebid, and Belur. Each one has its own remarkable features, but all three temples have outstandingly ornate filigree stonework that is a tribute to the prowess of the sculptors and stonemasons.

JAIN EXTENSIONS
The Parsvanatha Jain temple (12th century) stands 1.6 miles south of Halebid's main temple. It consists of three *bastis* (sanctuaries). In the first stands an impressive monolithic statue of the 23rd *Tirthankara* (prophet), the last manifestation before Mahavir, surrounded by lathe-turned pillars. The second, smaller temple is of little interest, but the third reveals a superbly worked interior dome and a statue of the 16th *Tirthankara*, Santinatha. Outside stands a Jain dovecot raised high on a pillar, and said to enclose a statue of Brahma as protector.

Kesava temple at Somnathpur

For about two centuries the Hoysalas remained within the feudal domain of the Chalukyas, who ruled from successive capitals around Badami. By the mid-13th century, the Hoysalas had attained power and at their zenith they controlled most of Karnataka and parts of Tamil Nadu. By then they had already built over 100 temples, making prolific use of the local soapstone (chloritic schist). When first quarried, this is soft enough to allow intricate carving before slowly hardening and darkening in color on exposure to the air. The Hoysala dynasty supported Siva, Vishnu and also Jain beliefs; their fall came in the mid-14th century with the rise of the Vijayanagar dynasty at Hampi.

To the temples The three main examples of Hoysala art are the well preserved temples at Somnathpur (22 miles east of Mysore) and at Belur and Halebid, both near Hassan, 98 miles northwest of Mysore. The latter two are best visited on a day-trip that can also take in Shravanabelgola (see page 238). Somnathpur can be included on a half-day trip to Shrirangapattana (see page 238). The tourist office in Mysore organizes a day tour to Belur and Halebid.

Style The compact sanctuaries of all three temples share a unique star-shaped form raised on a layered platform—originally within a colonnaded cloister (most evident at Somnathpur). These platforms allow for walking around the temple (always in the sacred, clockwise direction), and show off bands of finely carved gods, goddesses, warriors, musicians, animals, birds, and foliage, alongside brackets carved as supple feminine figures.

Somnathpur The temple here is often considered the highlight of the three. It was constructed in 1268 by a Hoysala general with three shrines devoted to Vishnu in different forms: Kesava, Janardana and Venugopal. The façade sculptures are raised on a platform flanked by crouching elephants. From the base upwards they show elephants, galloping horses ridden by soldiers and, at eye level, heavily bejeweled deities in flowing garments. Scrollwork above works its way around the jutting angles of the star-shape before culminating in three profusely carved tapered towers. Inside are lathe-

Ornate sculpture, typical of Hoysala structures, at Belur temple

turned pillars, another hallmark of the Hoysala style. These horizontally ridged columns reappear at the Hassan temples, as do the spectacular domed ceilings carved with banana buds and lotus flowers. The shrine figure of Venugopal is particularly lively, showing Vishnu with inclined head and flute (unfortunately broken) raised to lips. Unusually for Indian temples, these bear the sculptors' signatures.

Belur The Chennakesava temple (1117) stands within a huge compound and contains a single shrine. This is filled with lathe-turned pillars and columns with a jagged-edged symmetry, all barely visible in a gloom penetrated only by shafts of light through the jali walls. The Narasimha pillar is profusely carved on the capital, shaft, and base with niches containing images. Outside, as well as friezes of animals and deities, the Hoysala sculptors created 42 bracket figures of voluptuous women. Everything is carved with incredible detail, including a fly on a lizard.

Halebid More complex and fluid in style than Belur, the Hoysaleswara temple (started in 1121) at Halebid stands in open gardens next to a small museum (*Open* Sat–Thu 10–5. *Admission: free*). The two shrines, probably for Siva and his consort, now contain *lingams*. The elaborate carvings over the porches show makaras (mythical creatures symbolizing the Ganges) with a few erotic couples. Inside, the colossal statues include an image of Ganesa, the legendary ancestor of the Hoysalas.

MORE HOYSALA
The Hoysaleswara temple was not the only one at Halebid. Over a dozen temples are mentioned in records and others still exist, less well preserved but obviously carved by the same team of artists. Among these are the Manikeswara temple (1136) and the Kedareswara temple on the western bank of the Dvarasamudra Tank. The latter had a tower as recently as the 19th century, but rampant vegetation and general neglect eventually destroyed it.

**BLUE MOUNTAIN
RAILROAD**
The twisting narrow-gauge
track of the Nilgiri "toy
train" climbs up through
magnificent dense forest
and tea plantations,
crossing 250 bridges and
crawling through 16
tunnels over a total
distance of 28 miles.
This short distance can
take over four hours, but
the train is comfortable
and views are superb. If
you miss the train, there
are frequent buses cover-
ing the Coimbatore–
Mettuppalaiyam–Coonoor–
Ooty route.

▶▶ **Nilgiri Hills** 202C3

Tamil Nadu's Nilgiris (meaning "blue mountains")
occupy the junction of the Eastern and Western ghats and
are an obvious destination for cooling off from the heat of
the plains. The highest peak, Doda Betta, rises to 8,648 feet,
while Udagamandalam lies at 7,349 feet and Coonoor at
6,102 feet. Temperatures rarely rise above 77°F in summer,
and during winter nights descend to freezing point. As a
result, landscapes are spectacularly green, carpeted in the
tea estates that brought local prosperity, or in spices such
as cinnamon, cardamom and cloves. On the northern
flanks, the road descends through the **Mudumalai Wildlife
Sanctuary**▶▶ with its popular Elephant Camp before
entering Karnataka through the Bandipur National Park to
Mysore. To the south access is from Coimbatore, an uninspiring textile town. From here trains connect with the
Nilgiri Blue Mountain Railway, a scenic narrow-gauge "toy
train" service that twists slowly through the hills from
Mettuppalaiyam through Coonoor to Ooty (see panel).

Coonoor▶ Smaller, less popular
and less commercialized than Ooty,
Coonoor (divided into Lower and
Upper) has managed to preserve an
old-fashioned, peaceful flavor.
There is little to do here except
indulge in long walks, taking in the
tea plantations, Sim's Park (*Open
daily 8–6:30. Admission: inexpensive*)
and its well-tended botanical
garden with hundreds of rose varieties, or Lamb's Rock, a sheer
precipice commanding wonderful
views of the plains, about 5 miles
from town. A good area for seeing
wildlife is around Dolphin's Nose,
which is 7.5 miles away and about 4
miles south of Coonoor, Law's Falls
is worth the trip to see it thunder
down some 197 feet through the

forest. **Kothagiri▶** The oldest of the Nilgiris' three hill stations lies at 6,496 feet, 15 miles northeast of Coonoor, and is shielded from the monsoons by the Doda Betta range. From here it is about 12 miles to Kodanad View Point, along a precipitous road with fabulous views of the tea estates and the Moyar River. Accommodations in Kothagiri remain limited and fairly basic, so it is best visited just for the day.

Udagamandalam (Ooty)▶ Most visitors are disappointed by this once fashionable hill station, now a characterless concrete sprawl with endless souvenir stores and hotels aimed at the flocks of domestic tourists escaping the heat. At the base of the town is a large racetrack (the season is in March–April), with the bus station and artificial lake (boating available daily 8–6) to the west and the market flanking it to the north. Hotels and guesthouses are gradually filling the slopes to the south, while the very British colonial relics lie uphill and north of the bazaar, beyond the intersection of Charing Cross.

Local interest It is easy to explore the commercial center on foot, stopping to sample local confectionery, countless natural oils (eucalyptus, geranium, lemongrass), honey, tea, or coffee, all products of the Nilgiris. Other sights of interest are fairly scattered but auto-rickshaws are always plentiful. At the **Botanical Gardens** (*Open* daily 8–6. *Admission: inexpensive*), laid out in 1847 by the Marquis of Tweeddale, over 1,000 exotic and ornamental plants and flowers blanket the beautiful grounds, and there is an ancient fossilised tree trunk. Next door stands the elegant Raj Bhavan, built in 1877 by the Governor of Madras to resemble his family seat at Stowe in England. Only the well-tended grounds are open to the public. The neo-Gothic St. Stephen's Church (1820s), with an evocative interior and graveyard, is thought to have been built using timber from Tipu Sultan's palace at Shrirangapattana, hauled up to Ooty by elephants. West and uphill again from here is the once snooty Ooty Club (1830), which is still functioning as a club. Farther along the Mysore Road is the Government Museum (*Open* Mon–Thu 9–1, 2–5. *Admission: inexpensive*) with fascinating displays on the indigenous Toda people and their crafts. There are also some lovely walks in the area, to the Elk Hills (3 miles), Wenlock Downs (5 miles), and around the Avalanche Lake (17 miles) and the Mukurthi National Park (25 miles).

243

Opposite: Nilgiri steam train at Coonoor (top) and a Toda village hut Below: tribal woman

TOURIST OFFICES
Pondicherry TDC, 40
on Goubert Salai (*Open*
Mon–Fri 10–1, 2–5; tel:
0413 34574, email:
tourism@pondy.pon.nic.in)
Auroville Information
Centre/La Boutique
d'Auroville, Ambur Salai,
12 Jawarhalal Nehru
Street. *Open* Mon–Fri
9:30–5:30; tel: 0413
339497/333855).

▶▶ Periyar National Park   *202C2*

At the southern end of the Western Ghats on the Kerala–Tamil Nadu border lies a 280 square foot stretch of water whose thickly forested banks are reputed to be among the best in India for wildlife. Elephants, langurs, wild boar, bison, sloth bear, sambar deer, porcupines, flying squirrels, leopards and the increasingly elusive tiger all inhabit the depths of this 297 square mile sanctuary, and herons, egrets, darters, kingfishers, and the great Malabar grey hornbill are among the 260 or so bird species sighted. Apart from this, the sanctuary is stunningly beautiful and its best accommodations (former royal hunting lodges) occupy prime lakeside spots with lovely misty early morning views.

Periyar National Park is one of India's most popular national parks

PERIYAR
There are three major sources for accommodations and activities in the Park (which include boat excursions, elephant rides and treks). These are: the Wildlife Warden, Thekkadi (tel: 0486 322027), the Forest Department (tel: 0486 322028) and Kerala Tourist Development (tel: 0486 322023). Tours of the local spice and tribal villages are run by the District Tourism Office at Kumily (tel: 0486 322620).

Timing Periyar's high season is December through March, but accommodations fill up at any weekend or public holiday, making reservations essential. It is not worth visiting during and just after the monsoon, when lakeside sightings become rare as the wildlife has no need of water from the lake, and the high humidity also encourages leeches.

On the trail The nearest access town is Kumily, which has good bus connections with Kottayam, in the Keralan backwaters, and Madurai. Between Kumily and Thekkadi, where budget and mid-range accommodations are concentrated, seemingly endless plantations of cardamom, pepper, coffee, bananas, and tapioca eventually give way to evergreen and semi-deciduous forest, typical of this altitude (between 2,460 and 4,921 feet). The best way to observe wildlife is from a boat in the early morning or late afternoon, when animals and birds are most active and wild elephants come to the lake. Unfortunately Periyar's growing popularity has led to a parallel growth in boats, some large and noisy enough to scare away even the most fearless of mammals. A better bet is to hire a guide and trek through the surrounding forest or, better still, stay overnight in one of the viewing towers run by the Forest Department in Thekkadi.

► Puduchcheri (Pondicherry) 203D3

The most famous of France's four trading posts in India was, until recently, a sleepy backwater with little evidence of its former status. The opening of a new coastal highway has now reduced the bus journey from Chennai (Madras) to less than 4 hours and, inevitably, the number of visitors is growing.

Established in the early 18th century and with short interludes of Dutch and British control, it finally entered independent India in 1954. It still has some ornate Catholic churches (including the neo-Gothic Sacred Heart). It has a grid layout, split north–south by a canal that once divided the French quarter (edging the sea), from the Indian quarter inland.

Breezy stroll Goubert Salai is the main beach promenade, dominated at its northern end by a gigantic statue of Gandhi. The Hôtel de Ville is also here. The Raj Nivas, an elegant 18th-century building, was built for the French governor and fronts the shady Government Park. Immediately south is the **Pondicherry Museum►** (*Open Tue–Sun 10–1, 2–5. Admission: inexpensive*), with artifacts from Pondicherry's original prehistoric settlement and Pallava, Chola and Vijayanagar sculptures, alongside French bourgeois furniture and other items. Far livelier than these relics is the large, colorful **central bazaar►►** that lies inland on MG Road, just north of the Cathedral.

Aurobindo For the mystically inclined the **Aurobindo Ashram** (*Open daily 8–noon, 2–6. Admission: free,* but donations are requested), in rue de la Marine, is more of a crowd puller than Pondicherry's Gallic past. It includes educational facilities, countless commercial outlets for *ashram* products, and several over-priced guesthouses. Though the principal concern may be spiritual welfare, it is also one of India's wealthiest *ashrams* (see page 223). The tombs of Aurobindo and his faithful follower, Mirra Alfassa, are here. Alfassa founded the splinter-group experiment in international utopia at **Auroville►►**, 6 miles away, a fascinating, half-hippy, half-New Age community, whose inhabitants seem far more fulfilled than the poker-faced ashramites in town. There were bitter disputes at the *ashram* and Auroville when Alfassa died in 1973, which were resolved only when the government stepped in. Despite this, Auroville has over 1,200 inhabitants occupying over 80 settlements. Followers are international, with a high proportion of Indians, as well as Americans, Europeans, Russians, and Japanese. Auroville products, such as fine paper and silk, are sold all over India.

Market-trader in Puduchcheri

SRI AUROBINDO
Aurobindo (1872–1950), a Bengali philosopher, originally came to Pondicherry in 1910 to escape persecution by the British authorities, who had already imprisoned him for supporting the independence movement. The *ashram* that he set up combined his own yogic systems with modern science and ideals of community living. Among its disciples was Mirra Alfassa, a Parisian of Arab origin, who came to be known as *la Mère* (mother). On Aurobindo's death, this much revered woman took over.

Faded splendor at the Royal Palace, Thanjavur

The architectural star of the Chola dynasty (late 9th to mid-12th century), the **Brihadeshwara temple▶▶▶** (*Open daily 6–12, 4–8:30. Admission free*), rises above the small town of Thanjavur in splendid perfection. Its audacious conception and scale, perfect symmetry and incredible sculptural finesse make it one of India's greatest temples. It has been designated a World Heritage monument. The temple was built by King Rajaraja I in around AD 1000 to honor Siva and also to project his own great power. Inscriptions record that 400 dancers were employed, as well as 200 other temple functionaries. The lofty 198 foot *vimana* is India's tallest.

Temple prowess The main entrance is from the east, leading through two successive *gopurams*, both of them lavishly carved, to the enormous central courtyard whose walls display beautiful Chola frescoes. Here, a pavilion containing the obligatory *nandi*, a 20-foot-long monolithic masterpiece, faces the main temple. A colonnaded *mandapa* leads to the sanctuary containing a massive granite platform profusely carved with god images and inscriptions. Above this rises the awesome *vimana*, with the sacred Siva-*lingam* below its dome. Theories abound as to how this 80-ton block was raised to the apex: the most probable method was a ramp similar to those used by the ancient Egyptians. Steps rise to the inner sanctum, open only to Hindus. The surrounding ambulatory passages contain huge sculptures of Siva and more impressive frescoes.

Museums The **Archaeological Museum▶** (*Open daily 9–noon, 4–8. Admission free*), in the southwest corner of the temple courtyard, illustrates restoration work and displays some sculptures. A more interesting collection is housed in the dilapidated but impressive **Royal Palace▶▶** (*Open daily 9–noon, 3–6. Admission: inexpensive*). This 16th- to 17th-century complex lies 1.25 miles northeast of the

TOURIST OFFICE (THANJAVUR)
Tamil Nadu TDC, Jawan Bhawan, opposite main post office (Open Mon–Fri 10–5:45; tel: 04362 30984). Counter at Hotel Tamil Nadu, Gandhi Road. The TTDC organizes a daily tour of Thanjavur's temples. There are over 90 Chola temples.

temple. Inside are the superbly renovated **Durbar Hall Art Gallery►** (*Open* daily 9–1, 3–6. *Admission: inexpensive*), exhibiting Chola bronzes, the Rajaraja Museum (with more Chola bronzes and stone sculptures) and the Royal Museum (*Open* daily 9–6. *Admission: inexpensive*), displaying the rulers' accessories. Visitors can climb the restored Bell Tower, for great views (*Admission: inexpensive*).

►► Thiruvananthapuram (Trivandrum) 202C1

Now that it has an international airport receiving charter flights directly from Europe, Kerala's state capital has recently awoken to the potential of tourism and some inhabitants have become very demanding. The town's undulating layout remains attractive and, as the capital of Travancore from 1750 to 1956, it offers a good introduction to Keralan culture. The leafy town center slopes uphill along MG Road, from the fort, train, bus terminals, and bazaar to the museums and luxury accommodations that dominate the northern hill.

Museum and park complex At the center of a park stands the **Arts and Crafts Museum►►** (formerly the Napier Museum), an extraordinary architectural hybrid of geometric brickwork, Keralan roofs, stained glass, and arabesque windows designed by R. F. Chisholm in the 1870s. Inside is a no less striking collection of Chola bronzes, Keralan woodcarvings, ivories, Buddhist sculptures, and Southeast Asian objects. To the east, through the frangipani trees, is the **Natural History Museum►**, with a classic display of stuffed birds and animals, including kangaroo and porcupine embryos. North of the Napier is the **Sri Chitra Gallery►** devoted to Asian art, with works by Raja Ravivarma figuring strongly, his earlier output more successful than the later. The three museums (*Open* Tue–Sun 10–5, but closed Wed AM. *Admission: inexpensive*) are covered by a single ticket, obtainable at the Natural History Museum. North of the museums are a zoo and botanical gardens, attractively laid out along shady paths.

Fort At the bustling southern end of town, a large walled fort contains the Padmanabha Swami temple, open only to Hindus, whose *gopuram* rises behind a large *tank*. Built in 1733 by a Tranvancore raja, the temple contains a large statue of Vishnu reclining on the serpent, Anantha, after whom the town is named ("the abode of the sacred serpent"). Flanking the west side of the *tank* is the **Kuthiramalika Palace Museum►►** (*Open* Tue–Sun 8:30–12:30, 3:30–5:30. *Admission: moderate*). This has been the Travancore royal family's main palace since the late 18th century and is a fine example of Keralan wood architecture, with verandas, screens, shutters, and superbly carved pillars surrounding a motley collection of regal paraphernalia.

TOURIST OFFICES
Tourist Information Center, Park View, Thiruvananthapuram, opposite park. Helpful. (*Open* Mon–Sat 10–5; tel: 0471 321132/322279, email: deptour@vsnl. com).
Government of India tourist office at airport is also very helpful.
KTDC, Mascot Square (*Open* Mon–Sat 10–5; tel: 0471 318976/314406, email:ktdc@giasmd01.vsnl .net.in). Also at train and Thampanor bus station. KTDC tours include a marathon bus ride to Kanniyakumari.

A participant in Thiruvananthapuram's Elephant March

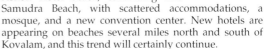

Excursions

Kovalam►► Although its popularity overstretches the facilities of this low-key beach resort, Kovalam offers an idyllic sweep of palm-lined beaches, a hedonistic atmosphere and a beautiful hinterland of lagoons, coconut groves, and paddy fields. The main concentration of budget guesthouses, bars, and restaurants is squeezed into the southern Lighthouse Beach, with some better accommodations on the headland dominated by the lighthouse. Adjoining it to the north is Eve's Beach (or Hawah Beach). For the moment, this remains relatively unspoiled, as most of the hotels are on the verdant slopes and main road behind the coconut palms. Beyond the headland is the private Ashok Hotel beach, continuing into Samudra Beach, with scattered accommodations, a mosque, and a new convention center. New hotels are appearing on beaches several miles north and south of Kovalam, and this trend will certainly continue.

Lighthouse on the head-land at Kovalam

248

Colorful temple, Varkala

Marking time Swimming is dangerous due to riptides, and drownings occur frequently despite the presence of numerous lifeguards. Oblivious to the dangers and the prostrate bodies of Western sun worshippers, fishermen sing as they haul in their nets. Other locals offer Ayurvedic massages (see pages 232–233), make inexpensive clothes on clacking sewing machines, or harass tourists with endless piles of sarongs and fruit. Beachside restaurants offer excellent fresh seafood, with dazzling sunsets thrown in. There are some pleasant walks through the paddy fields behind the beach or south of the lighthouse to Vizhinjam, a busy fishing village dominated by a large mosque.

Padmanabhapuram►► (*Open* Tue–Sun 9–4.30. *Admission: inexpensive*; includes tour, but tip expected); situated 34 miles southeast of Thiruvananthapuram on the road to Kanniyakumari, is the former palace of the Rajas of Travancore. It was the raja's seat of government from around 1550 to the 1750s. The palace typifies traditional Keralan architecture, with tiled, gabled roofs, carved wooden screens, slatted windows, trapdoors, and stone pillars surrounding verdant courtyards, all exceptionally well maintained. A small museum at the entrance displays sculptures and copies of the beautiful murals in the upstairs rooms now closed to the public.

Throughout the palace tropical hardwoods are used to stunning effect: superbly crafted items include the four-poster bed carved out of Ayurvedic woods in the raja's bedroom, elaborate Belgian mirrors, Thanjavur miniatures, and suspended beds in the women's bedrooms. There are shrines to the goddesses Durga and Saraswati, but best of all is the bedroom designed for Vishnu, the official Travancore deity, where brass lamps and superb frescoes honor his name (*Padmanabha* refers to the lotus in Vishnu's navel).

Varkala▶▶ When Kovalam was discovered by the charter-flight operators, backpackers moved on to this idyllic village. It lies about 34 miles northwest of Thiruvananthapuram, is easily reached by train and is rather like Bali with its magical combination of temples, palms, rice paddies and beach. From the temple intersection a lower access road (Beach Road) connects a handful of hotels with the beach while, immediately north, a clifftop road leads to the main cluster of budget accommodations. On the way it passes a Taj Hotel that blocks the view of a former Travancore palace, now a government guesthouse. Mineral springs gush out of the dramatic red laterite cliff-face at the northern end of the beach, an added bonus for thirsty beach bums. The springs were also inspiration for the clifftop Nature Cure Hospital where patients are treated with natural therapies.

Spiritual concerns Thought to be about 500 years old, the hilltop Janardhana Swami temple overlooks the temple lake. Behind the Keralan gable-roofed entrance gates is a fervent world of worshippers (although the temple is dedicated to Vishnu, there is a major Siva shrine by a massive banyan tree). The worshippers circle round the various shrines, throwing *ghee* for *puja*. Down at the crossroads are a Hanuman temple and a colorful Anyappan temple. The low wooden building beside the *tank* is sometimes used for Kathakali performances (see panel page 227) and hotels often stage their own. Pilgrims also flock to the *ashram* and shrine of Sri Narayana, a guru whose egalitarian teachings brought Mahatma Gandhi to Varkala.

Fishermen at the resort of Kovalam

TOURIST SERVICES (KOVALAM)
Several hotels organize boat excursions around the local lagoons. The Western Travel Service (*Open* 8 AM–midnight; tel: 0471 481334) opposite the bus stand (up the slip-road from Eve's Beach) organizes tours to Kollam's backwaters, Periyar, Kanniyakumari, and Ponmudi. A tourist information office (tel: 0471 480085. Erratic opening times), is located on the road leading to the Ashok Beach Resort.

CULTURE AND CRAFTS
Thiruvananthapuram is a lively center for the performing arts, including the Keralan martial art of Kalaripay, and Kuttiyattam (9th-century Sanskrit drama). Enquire at the tourist office about locations and dates.
The town also sells local crafts, best seen at the government emporium SMSM (Kairali) Handicrafts, behind the Secretariat, and at numerous stores along MG Road.

▶▶ Tiruchchirappalli 203D2

More easily known as "Trichy", this sprawling town is a stopover between Chennai (Madras) and Madurai, whether traveling by air or by road. It also serves as a base for visiting Thanjavur, 34 miles to the east. Ruled successively by the Pallavas, the Cholas, Vijayanagar, and the Nayaks of Madurai, Trichy is now a thriving commercial town, known particularly for its *bidis* (Indian cigarettes) and artificial gemstones.

Trichy's main showstopper is a few miles north at the temple town of Srirangam, on an island in the Kaveri River. Here looms the **Sri Ranganatha Swami temple**▶▶▶ (*Open daily 6:15–1, 3:15–8:45. Admission free*), a labyrinthine Vishnuite monument that encloses courtyards, homes, stores, and shrines. Founded in the 5th century, the temple has continued to expand over the centuries, gradually acquiring seven concentric enclosures and 21 *gopurams*, the most recent of which, the garishly painted southern gatehouse, is late 20th century.

The oldest and most beautiful buildings start at the fourth *prakaram* (enclosure) where shoes must be removed before you enter the superb Kalyan Mandapa (thousand-pillar hall). The Sheshagiriraya Mandapa (horse court), is a Vijayanagar creation of rearing horses and hunters formed as massive and elaborate pillars. Opposite is the earlier, 13th-century shrine to Krishna as Venugopala, displaying more superb stone-carving and brightly painted frescoes. The last section open to non-Hindus is the fifth *prakaram*, but you can get a ticket (*inexpensive*) to climb to the top of the wall for an overall view of the bristling *gopurams* and gilded *vimana*

Tiruchchirappalli, a thriving commercial town

Painted rock sculpture in Tiruchchirappalli

topping Vishnu's inner sanctum. Before leaving Srirangam, it is worth walking through to the riverbanks to the north, where the daily business of body- or sari-washing continues in exactly the same way that it has done through the centuries.

▶▶ Tirupati 203D4

Beautifully located at the foot of forested hills studded with red-ocher rocks, Tirupati is renowned for its Vishnuite **Sri Venkateswara temple▶▶** (*Open* daily dawn–midnight. *Admission free*) 9 miles away up the Tirumalai hill (identified as the mythical Mount Meru). Thousands of pilgrims climb the wooded slopes daily to see the fearsome image of Vishnu at the heart of the complex; alternative access is by hair-raising taxis and buses from Tirupati. To escape waiting for hours in long lines, it is worth paying extra for a special viewing—in fact an official form of avoiding the line. Avoid visiting the temple on any festival day, when the flood of humanity is overwhelming. It is nevertheless a highly organized place that copes admirably with pilgrim control, and its astute hair-cutting industry (see panel) is a lucrative sideline.

The temple dates from the Pallavas and later Cholas but it was the Vijayanagar kings who poured in their wealth and craftsmen, as well as arranging the details of festivals and worship that continue to this day. Three *prakarams* lead to the inner sanctuary with its gilded *vimana* and gates surrounding the striking 6-foot, black-faced and jewel-studded statue of Vishnu. Outside the sanctum is a small museum (*Open* daily 8–6. *Admission: inexpensive*) displaying the various temple sculptures.

▶▶ Tiruvannamalai 203D3

Arunachala Hill, which rises above Tiruvannamalai, has an almost mythical status in Indian culture, as it is reputed to be the place where Siva appeared to Brahma and Vishnu as a fiery column (see page 17). Inspired by this, Tiruvannamalai's most important temple, the **Arunachaleswara temple▶▶** (*Open* daily 6–1, 5:30–10. *Admission free*), is dedicated to Siva in the form of Agni, the god of fire. The fire festival which is in November or December attracts thousands of devotees who watch ritual flames on the hilltop and worship at the *agni-lingam* inside the temple.

Dating back to the 11th-century Chola dynasty, this enormous temple complex was much extended by later Vijayanagar rulers. Four *prakarams* surmounted by lofty *gopurams* surround the central sanctum (open to non-Hindus) containing the sacred *lingam*, which is ceremonially bathed six times a day in a special ceremony. Access is through the eastern gateway and a long, incongruous covered bazaar specializing in metalware. In the first, highly populated courtyard a large *tank* stands opposite the thousand-pillar hall, and in the next stands the shrine to Parvati, Siva's consort, faced by his steed, Nandi. The final courtyard is rimmed by superbly carved pillars and images of numerous gods, and encloses the central Siva sanctum.

The town itself is a peaceful little place, and site of the Ramanashram, founded by a local sage who died a few decades ago. The *ashram* is open to day visitors.

TRICHY'S ROCK FORT
Dominating the northern end of Trichy by the train station and lively China Bazar, the Rock Fort is a sandstone hill ascended by a steep flight of steps which passes numerous Pallava rock-cut temples before emerging beneath the summit, crowned by a Ganesh temple. The shrines are open only to Hindus but panoramic views over Trichy and Srirangam justify the climb.

251

LUSTROUS LOCKS
In 1996 the Sri Venkateswara temple raised over U.S.$1.7 million to finance its charitable institutions (schools, hospitals, and orphanages) and maintain the temple. This enormous sum was amassed by the efforts of the temple's 600 resident barbers, who each year shave the heads of 6.5 million pilgrims, exporting the hair to the United States, Japan, and Europe for wig making. The temple is undoubtedly one of India's richest, with an annual turnover said to be in excess of one billion rupees.

Lurking behind the male-dominated Hindu pantheon is the Mother Goddess (Devi), an archetype imprinted on the Indian psyche. This is the most powerful and complex of the goddesses, a multiple personality who is as closely linked to nurturing as to destruction.

CELLULOID DEVI
Indian moviemakers find Devi a rich source of metaphors and symbols. Satyajit Ray's *Devi* (1960) shows an image of the goddess taking shape in clay and straw, before entering a narrative about myth and religious belief. Mainstream Hindi cinema is full of references to the maternal rather than wifely aspects of Devi, representing her as outside sexuality and therefore not threatening to man.

252

Devi, or Mahadevi (Great Goddess) owes her strength to her ancestry in the great mother goddess of pre-Aryan times and to her role as Siva's consort, when she embodies *shakti*, or female energy, and reflects the multiple natures of her husband. Her identities range from the mild-mannered, self-sacrificial Sati, through seductive Parvati and destructive Durga, to the homicidal Kali.

Sweetness and light The ultra-feminine Sati married Siva against her father's wishes and later burned herself to death in defence of Siva's honor. While Siva was giving her his last embrace, creating the cosmic dance of destruction, Sati's body was dismembered by Vishnu, its 50 pieces creating 50 sacred sites. This is the origin of the Tantric worship of the *yoni*, the female organ that balances the male *lingam*. Sati's self-immolation was the example for widows who threw themselves on their husband's funeral pyres. Parvati, the voluptuous reincarnation of Sati, was the daughter of the Himalayas and sister of Ganga, the goddess of the River Ganga (Ganges). In order to seduce Siva, who had turned to asceticism, she underwent severe penance. Their subsequent marriage was far from harmonious, despite Parvati's ability to calm the volatile temper of her husband.

A 16th-century bronze of Kali armed with hammer, trident, knife and bowl

Destruction and death At the other extreme, the mother goddess rides into battle. Swinging her ten arms astride her tiger, Devi was born to kill demons, above all the buffalo demon and later Durga, whose name she adopted. To conquer this demon, Devi grew one thousand arms and produced nine million beings from her body to form an invincible army. More terrifying still is Kali ("conqueror of time"), the black-faced earth mother who is associated with demonic rites and even human sacrifice.

Travel Facts

Arriving

By air The majority of visitors arrive at India's international airports of Delhi or Mumbai (Bombay), and less commonly at Chennai (Madras) and Kolkata (Calcutta). Goa and Thiruvananthapuram (Trivandrum) are for charter flights. European flights generally land and depart in the dead of the night. Arrival in the nocturnal streets of the big cities is quite an experience, but airports are well prepared, with exchange facilities, hotel-reservations and prepaid taxi-counters as well as official tourist offices; all open to cater for incoming international flights. Theoretically, it is possible to find accommodations when you arrive, but for peace of mind and particularly in Delhi, which fills up with business travelers, it is worth reserving a room in advance through your travel agent. Immigration procedures can be long, sometimes lasting over an hour, so be prepared for the additional waiting time at the airport (but that's the beauty of Indian bureaucracy…).

In Delhi, the Indira Gandhi International Airport (tel: 011 565 2021) is about 15 miles southwest of the center, a distance rapidly covered by taxis at night but taking much longer in daytime traffic. Terminal One (tel: 011 565 2011) handles domestic flights and is linked to Indira Gandhi by frequent shuttles.

The busy Sahar International Airport in Mumbai (Bombay) is 19 miles north of the center, with the Santa Cruz domestic terminal slightly closer. Free shuttles ply between the two.

In total and surprising contrast, the airports at Kolkata (Calcutta) and Chennai (Madras) are well organized, modern and clean, although Kolkata's little-used Dum Dum international and domestic terminal, 12 miles northeast of the center, is a modest affair. Prepaid taxis are bargains here, with the alternatives of an airport bus or Kolkata's state-of-the-art metro. Chennai (Madras) has its international and national terminals in the same building at Meenambakkan airport, 10 miles southwest of the center, and organizes prepaid taxis and express buses.

By sea The only sea routes into India are on-off services from Sri Lanka and between Penang and Madras. Cruise-ships dock at certain Indian ports: enquire at your local travel agent.

By land Road access to India is from Nepal by bus (through four border-points), from Lahore (Pakistan) to Amritsar by bus (the actual border-crossing being on foot) or by train (it takes hours to clear customs), from Bangladesh via the Jessore–Kolkata (Calcutta) highway or from Bhutan by road to Darjiling or Gangtok (this requires a special permit). Make sure your visa is multiple entry if you are considering an excursion out of India and want to return. For all these crossings, check on requirements and political developments in advance at the relevant embassies.

Customs regulations
Duty-free allowances of 35 fluid ounces of spirits and 200 cigarettes (or 50 cigars) apply. Anyone bringing over U.S.$10,000 in cash or travelers' checks should theoretically complete a currency declaration form. Small items such as perfume, binoculars, a camera, and five rolls of film are allowed, but more valuable items such as special camera or video equipment and laptops should be declared on a Tourist Baggage Re-export (TBRE) form that is submitted to customs on departure.

Travel insurance
It is essential to take out a good travel insurance that covers you for repatriation if necessary. Make sure your policy has a 24-hour emergency number in the region. If paying for your ticket by a credit card that includes travel insurance, check to see exactly what this covers.

Visas and permits
Visas are necessary for all nationalities to visit India. Tourist visas are valid for 90 or 180 days from the date of issue and are either single entry or multiple entry. Business visas are available for up to five years. Two photos, a completed application form and a valid passport are needed, together with a reasonable fee.

Visa-processing has speeded up; in some places, such as the Indian Consulate in New York, tourist visa applications take only a few hours. Postal visas take considerably longer. Special permits for restricted areas such as Sikkim, certain northeast states and the Lakshadweep islands are best applied for at the same time; allow two weeks. Otherwise they are issued at Foreigners' Regional Registration Offices in Delhi, Mumbai (Bombay), Kolkata (Calcutta), and by the Chief

Taxi outside the magnificent City Palace, in Jaipur

Immigration Officer in Chennai (Madras).

Departing

Remember to reconfirm your international flight at least 72 hours before departure. India's international departure tax should be included in your ticket—but do check this with your travel agent.

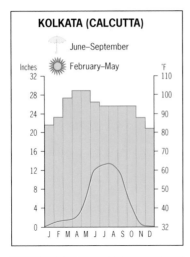

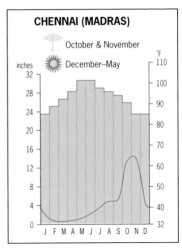

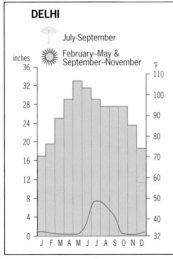

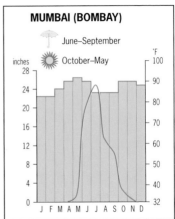

Essential facts

Climate

India's climate varies enormously, from the parched northwest to the lush, subtropical south and snow-capped Himalayas. Above all, it is determined by the monsoon. One arm of the monsoon generally hits the southwest coast in early June, spreading up the Western Ghats to reach the northwest about two weeks later, by which time rainfall is much lighter. In the last few years, it has even been nonexistent in parts of Gujarat and the desert of Rajasthan. The other arm swoops across the Bay of Bengal to unleash its torrents on Kolkata (Calcutta) and the northeast, before moving westward toward Delhi. During this period, June through September, landslides and floods can be disruptive, even fatal. The southeast sees a dry summer and a rainy season with cyclones, from mid-October through December.

The build up to the monsoon in mid-April through May produces stifling, humid heat, rising to well over 104 °F in the plains: visitors should head for the Himalayan hill stations or Western Ghats. When the monsoon madness ends in October, the clear skies of Indian winter set in. By January–February temperatures are quite low in the northern plains, but the south remains warm.

When to go
For deserts and beaches, the high season in Rajasthan, Kerala, and Goa is December through February. Hill resorts have a huge influx of visitors in April and May, sending prices up. The Himalayan region is extremely cold in winter, and Ladakh is only accessible from June through September. Most national parks are closed in the monsoon season. The best times for most regions are March and April, and October and November.

National holidays
Strictly speaking there are only four national holidays: January 26 (Republic Day); August 15 (Independence Day); October 2 (Mahatma Gandhi's birthday); and December 25 (Christmas). However each region and each religion celebrates a string of festivals: on one official list they amount to 87. Muslim holidays vary according to the Islamic calendar, while Hindu, Jain, and Buddhist festivities follow the lunar calendar. See pages 24–25.

Time differences
India is 8½ hours ahead of EST. The extra half hour was invented at Independence to differentiate from Pakistan's 5 hours. As India is a tropical region, dawn and dusk hardly vary throughout the year.

Opening times
Banks generally open Mon–Fri 10:30–2:30, Sat 10:30–12:30; post offices Mon–Fri 10–5, Sat 10–12; and government offices Mon–Fri 9:30–5, Sat 9:30–1. Stores open Mon–Sat 9:30–6 or sometimes later. Even in the big cities and bazaars, Sunday is very much a day of rest. Closing days for museums vary according to regions, but most close on Mondays.

Money matters
Indian currency is the rupee, with notes ranging from Rs2 to Rs500. (those under 10 are being phased out). There are 100 paise to a rupee, although only 50 paise coins still circulate. Always keep low-denomi-nation notes handy for beggars, tips, and small purchases.

Your main supply of money should preferably be a balance of travelers' checks and cash. Most major currencies are changed in larger city banks, with U.S.$ and £ sterling the most popular. You may be surprised by banks closing on unexpected public holidays, but there is always a store that will change cash at a reasonable rate. Hotels generally cash travelers' checks only for guests and at poorer rates. Airport exchange counters offer good rates and also efficient service.

Credit cards including Visa, Diners, Mastercard, and Amex are widely accepted at more expensive establishments, airlines, and in tourist areas, but not in remote areas. When you make purchases by credit card, the vendor will raise the price to cover the bank's percentage. Cash against cards can be obtained at a growing number of banks.

257

Tipping
Be liberal, and bear in mind that the price of a box of matches in the West is regarded as a very reasonable tip in India. It is a good idea to keep a stash of Rs10 notes handy. In hotels tip anyone from the porter to the *dhobi wallah*, and add 5–10 percent to your bill if service is not already included. In restaurants, it is always appreciated if you round up the bill. As rickshaws and taxis usually require advance negotiation, tips are not necessary, but tip if you feel it is merited. Drivers and guides appreciate tips of up to Rs100 a day.

Getting around

By air
There is an extensive network of reasonably priced domestic flights. The monthly publication *Excel*, available at major airports and central bookstalls in Delhi, lists the routes, times and prices for the three major airlines. There are several smaller airlines but these are mainly regional.

The state-run Indian Airlines serves the majority of routes (linking 59 Indian cities and 16 cities in neighboring countries). It can be reserved through travel agents worldwide, but has an appalling record of delays and cancellations. A better service is Jet Airways, covering 25 domestic destinations which can be pre-arranged in many countries (U.S.A., tel: 212/286 0667; U.K., tel: 020-8970 1555).

Both these airlines offer two passes: "Discover India" provides 15 or 21 days unlimited travel throughout the country; "Wonder Fare" offers seven days unlimited travel within a given area (North, South, East or West). They can be worthwhile if time is limited but are not always a saving, as you are likely to spend several days in one spot and use trains or buses for less accessible places.

Sahara India Airlines is the other major airline, but as it prides itself on cheap fares, it offers no air passes.

Always use a hard currency (in cash, travelers' checks or credit cards) when buying passes/tickets. It not only exempts you from domestic airport tax (currently 10 percent of basic fare), but also means no charges for either cancellations or reservation changes, subject to availability.

Overbooking is a perennial problem. If you are a victim, ask to see the manager and try gentle persuasion. If all else fails, a healthy tip might help to solve the problem.

By car and motorcycle
Driving yourself It is very rare for Westerners to rent cars in India, although it is possible through international companies such as Hertz, Europcar or Budget, (lower rates if you reserve in India and you will need an international driver's license.

Driving yourself is not advisable: it means confronting the chaos of Indian traffic with cows, bullock carts, bicycles, rickshaws, trucks, and buses. Driving is on the horn and the bigger vehicle always wins. Accident rates are high, road signs are rare, roads in general are in bad condition, and night driving is particularly dangerous.

Motorcycles The main places for renting motorcycles are Goa and Kovalam. Insurance is compulsory but helmets are not obligatory in India, so bring one from home or buy one locally. Again, avoid night driving and if you have the misfortune to have an accident, go straight to the local police; mechanics are not always easy to find, except for puncture-repair experts.

Chauffeur driven Although this has connotations of extreme luxury in the West, in India it is quite usual and by far the best option. Drivers generally know their region, and if hired through a reputable agency (local tourist offices will advise), can also be excellent guides. Daily rates vary considerably but expect $25–50 per day, depending on distance. There is a mileage charge above a basic allowance, and overnight journeys cost more. Drivers usually sleep in the car, but passengers pay for meals, a minimal cost. The most common vehicle is the wonderful Ambassador (a trumped up version of the British Morris Oxford, *c*1950), although Japanese Marutis are slowly encroaching in more affluent areas.

By Jeep Jeeps come into their own in the Himalayan region, offering fast transportation. Save money by using share jeeps where available, such as around Darjiling and Sikkim.

By train
The mysteries of train travel in India leave many first-time visitors bemused, but it is the most sociable, economical, and illuminating way of getting around the country. Some 12 million passengers are transported daily over a vast network of "up" and "down" trains. These were once proudly run by the Anglo-Indian community, and most of the Raj-era

habits survive, from Ladies' Retiring-rooms to red-jacketed porters. Many meter-gauge tracks have been converted to faster broad gauge, notably around Goa, but this does not mean your locomotive will be speeding along. Train journeys are slow affairs, allowing plenty of time to take in the landscape, get to know your fellow-travelers and buy endless cups of *chai*. Food vendors are omnipresent but official railroad meals are safest (and they can be ordered in advance), or carry your own.

Steam trains, known as "toy-trains", still run on the stupendous Darjiling and Nilgiri Hills narrow-gauge tracks.

For night trains, take your own mineral water, reading-material, toilet paper, and a padlock and chain to attach your bag to the bunk. This is common practice and an effective though not infallible deterrent to thieves. Keep your money and all

Porters at Mumbai Chhatrapati Shivaji (Victoria Terminus), Mumbai (Bombay)

documents on your body.

Rail cars, in descending order of cost and ascending order of crowded-ness, are: AC first class (air-conditioned, two- or four-berth cabins with lockable doors); standard first class (non-air-conditioned, two- or four-berth curtained cubicles—being phased out); ACII tier (air-conditioned carriage, with two- or four-berth curtained cubicles); AC chaircar (air-conditioned carriage with reclining seats—great for day travel) and second class (non-air-conditioned seats/berths, some wooden). Not all routes have first class or air-conditioned carriages. Some luxury air-conditioned trains, such as the Shatabdi Express (daytime journeys) and the Rajdhani Express (overnight journeys), link the major cities and impose surcharges, but meals, mineral water, and hot beverages are included in the cost. Air-conditioned chair cars with reclining seats or Executive Class are the ultimate for day travel.

Reservations on night-trains should be made as far in advance as possible. Reserving through tourist counters at the train stations of large cities gives you access to special tourist quotas (berths reserved for foreigners and non-resident Indians). Otherwise you join the general lines for Indian travelers and are allocated berths according to availability through an efficient computerized system. For both, you need to complete a form with the train identification number, date of departure, your name, age, nationality, and sex.

When you finally board the train, passenger lists will be on each carriage and you will be grouped with other foreigners, or if female, with other women or families. Reservations made abroad must be reconfirmed, in person, at the official office/counter of a major terminal. Deal only with people at the designated counter. Anyone else, however respectable or plausible, is a tout. Railroad employees are not issued with identity cards, so any you are shown are fakes and the office is always within the station itself.

Bedding can be ordered in advance for second-class travel—it's included for the other classes. Indrail passes are available for periods from a half day to 90 days. There are three types: a) AC first class, b) second class, and c) valid for all the in-between categories. Passes give booking priority, allow easy cancellations, and waive reservation fees, sleeper charges and supplements. They do not necessarily offer savings on the already low fares and can be purchased at major railroad offices or through appointed agents abroad, and paid for in dollars or sterling. Luxury tourist trains in

Latecomers on a public bus

Rajasthan and Gujarat are booked through separate offices (see page 74). If you are traveling extensively by train, buy a copy of *Travel Links* or *Trains at a Glance*, for train timetables.

By bus
Long-distance bus travel is sometimes unavoidable, particularly in mountainous areas or regions where railroad tracks are still narrow gauge and therefore extremely slow. There are numerous private "luxury" buses that operate along much-visited routes (as popular with domestic tourists as foreigners) and offer marginally more comfort than the state-run equivalent. Local tourist offices will advise on the best option. Private buses generally require advance reservations for their numbered seats, as do some state-run express routes, but many public buses are first in, first served—often chaos, with the last ones hanging out the door or on the roof.

By taxi/rickshaw
Taxis are easy to find; negotiating the fare is harder as few drivers use

On-street repairs being made to an auto-rickshaw or "auto"

meters—except in Kolkata (Calcutta). Mumbai (Bombay) taxis in particular require hard bargaining.

Motorized three-wheeler taxis are called auto-rickshaws (shortened to "autos") as opposed to bicycle-rickshaws, the human-propelled variety. Kolkata is the only big city that still has human-pulled rickshaws; in other cities they are being phased out. Autos are an excellent way to buzz through heavy traffic, if you can bear the pollution. You can negotiate a price for several hours if you plan intensive sightseeing. Meters are used in smaller towns, but rarely in tourist areas and cities. You will inevitably be overcharged at first, but will soon get a clear idea of average fares. Avoid the haggling syndrome: the foreigner's compulsion to barter over prices that are negligible at home.

Student and youth travel
There is a 25 percent discount on standard fares for those aged 12–30 years and on some late-night flights.

An STD/ISD phone-booth, Delhi

Communications

Media

India has a thriving press, a result of its many regional languages and identities. National newspapers and weekly newsmagazines in English are also widely read and readily available, making it easy to keep abreast of internal and external affairs, though the accent is usually on the former. *The Hindu* and *The Asian Age* are probably the best, closely followed by the *Statesman, Times of India, Indian Express, Independent, Economic Times,* and the Calcutta-based *Telegraph*. Like their British role models, many have special Sunday editions with extra supplements. Of the weekly magazines, *Outlook* gives good in-depth reporting; next best is the more sensationalist *India Today*. *Business India* concentrates on financial news. Each state also has its own English-language daily, as well as newspapers in the local language.

Television was transformed in the 1990s, with over 50 satellite and cable TV channels reaching India. Indians now watch BBC World, CNN, sports and entertainment channels, and tend to give the government-run Doordarshan the cold shoulder.

They have, however, remained ultra-faithful to their own cinema.

Post offices

The mail service functions far more efficiently for international than for internal mail. Postcards and letters abroad take 7–10 days, while air-mail parcels may surprise you by their speed (one week to Europe is common) and surface mail by its slowness (six months on average). Parcels should be wrapped by professionals, who can usually be found outside large post offices and are artists in the use of cloth and sealing-wax. Stores will also send your purchases home but in all cases make sure they are sent by registered post (costing a minimal extra) and use your own judgement as to whether the storekeeper is honest or not. When possible obtain the registered-post receipt. Speedpost and other air-courier services are also available.

Poste Restante facilities exist at all main post offices. Have mail sent with your surname in capitals and underlined to GPO, followed by the town name and state name.

Telephone and fax

STD/ISD phone booths are found everywhere in India and operate long opening hours. Call charges are calculated by the second, shown on an automatic screen as you speak, and rates vary little between rival booths. Trunk calls become cheaper after 8 PM, when you can expect crowds, but international rates are the same whatever the hour.

In larger towns, some phone booths double up as fax offices, and internet offices are now appearing. Several million new telephone lines are being installed in India. Unfortunately numbers have become a complicated puzzle, with which the usually busy Directory Enquiries (Information) offers little help.

- **International code** 00 + country code
- **Directory enquiries (Information)** 197
- **Dialling code for India** 91

Language

Over 550 million people speak Hindi, which is India's official language, though in some areas, particularly the south, English can prove to be more useful. When using the latter, roll the "r" in exaggerated fashion. The "a" in Hindi is long, the "i" as in "me".

Hello/goodbye	**Namaste** (to a Hindu: while saying this, hold your palms together at chest level)
	Aslam alequm (to a Muslim)
Yes/no	**Ji han/ji nahin**
That's all right	**Koi bat nahin/ Thik hai**
What's your name?	**Apka nam kya hai?**
My name is …	**Mera nam … hai**
Do you speak English?	**Ap ko angrezi ati hai?**
I don't understand	**Samaj nahin aya**
What is this?	**Yeh kya hai?**
How much is this?	**Iska kya dam hai?**
Where is … ?	**… kahan hai?**
How far?	**Kitna dur?**
Which is the Jaipur bus/train?	**Jaipur ka bas/train kahan hai?**
When does the Jaipur bus leave?	**Jaipur bas kab jaegi?**

Morning/afternoon	**Suba/dopahar**
Evening/night	**Sham/Rat**
Straight on	**Sidha**
Wait	**Thero**
Stop	**Ruko**
A room/bathroom	**kamra/bathroom**
Fan/air-conditioning	**pankha/air-conditioning**
Clean sheets/blanket	**saf chadaren/kambal**
Laundry man	**dhobi-wallah**
The menu please	**Menu dikhaiye**
The check please	**Bill dijiye**

1	**ek**
2	**do**
3	**tin**
4	**char**
5	**panch**
6	**chhai**
7	**sat**
8	**ath**
9	**nau**
10	**das**
11	**gyara**
12	**barah**
13	**terah**
14	**chaudah**
15	**pandrah**
16	**solah**
17	**satrah**
18	**atharah**
19	**unnis**
20	**bis**
100/200	**sau/do sau**
1,000/2,000	**hazar/do hazar**
100,000	**lakh**

tea	**chai**
chicken	**murg**
shrimp/fish	**jhinga/macchli**
mutton	**gosht**
diced curd	**panir**
potato	**aloo**
boiled rice	**bhat/sada chawal**
seasoned fried rice	**pulau**
lentils/with garlic	**dal/tarka dal**
unleavened bread	**roti/chapati**
leavened bread	**nan**
deep-fried bread puff	**puri**
curd/yogurt	**dahi**
scrambled eggs	**keema**
cauliflower	**gobi**
chickpeas	**chana/chana dal**
spinach	**sag**
okra/ladies' fingers	**bhindi**
onions	**piaz**

263

Emergencies

Crime, safety, and police

Apart from banditry in the state of Bihar, India is generally a safe destination. Use your common sense: keep passport, travelers' checks, credit cards and money in a money-belt or on your body, particularly when using public transportation, and don't flourish wads of large-denomination notes. If using mid-range to expensive accommodations, lock valuables in your bag in your room or, better still, leave them in a safe-deposit box. Budget travelers should be extra careful, particularly if sleeping in dormitories. Buy a padlock and chain to secure your bag on night trains and don't put any valuable items into your checked-in luggage on flights: X-ray machines reveal all, and bags can be slit open.

Goa is the black spot for muggings but police are cracking down on this. The most common crime in India is confidence trickery: touts flourish in tourist areas and are adept at deceiving visitors. Beware of anyone approaching you in large train stations such as Delhi or Mumbai (Bombay) and be extra careful in surrounding streets. Unofficial money changers are not to be trusted. When using a credit card, do not let it out of your sight: duplicate forms can easily be made and signed.

If you are the victim of a crime, report it to the police immediately. They are unlikely to resolve anything, but for insurance claims you will need a copy of the police report. Travelers' checks take time to replace (keep serial numbers separate), as do passports. For the former, contact the issuing bank and for the latter, your embassy or consulate.

Embassies and consulates

Australia 1/50G Shantipath, Diplomatic Enclave, New Delhi (tel: 011 688 8223, fax: 011 687 4126)
Canada 7–8 Shantipath, Diplomatic Enclave, New Delhi (tel: 011 687 6500, fax: 011 687 6579, email: delhi@delhi01.x400.gc.ca)
New Zealand 50–N Nyaya Marg, Diplomatic Enclave, New Delhi (tel: 011 688 3170, fax: 011 687 3165)

U.K .50 Shantipath, Diplomatic Enclave, New Delhi (tel: 011 687 2161, fax: 011 687 2282)
U.S.A. Shantipath, Diplomatic Enclave, New Delhi (tel: 011 688 9033/611 3033, fax: 011 687 2391)

Health, vaccinations, and pharmacies

There are no vaccination requirements for entering India unless you have been in an area infected with yellow fever. It is strongly advisable to check your tetanus, polio, and typhoid shots are up to date (boosters are needed every few years). Inoculations against meningitis and Hepatitis A (contracted from contaminated food and water) are also strongly recommended. Consult your doctor several months before your trip as some courses of action need to be started well in advance of your departure. Cholera epidemics occur periodically, but the vaccine is not effective.

Malaria is widespread during the rainy season, except at higher altitudes. Preventative treatment needs to be started at least one week before departure and continued several weeks after leaving. The side effects of the pills can be strong, so avoid taking them for very long periods (several months). Use mosquito repellent liberally, above all at nightfall, and burn mosquito coils at night. These can be purchased locally.

India's worst health hazard is bacteria-ridden water, which also affects uncooked fruit and vegetables. Do not eat the latter and only ever drink mineral water (widely available). Some travelers to India brush their teeth with it. Avoid ice and cold or reheated food (be wary of buffets). It is almost inevitable that you will get some form of "Delhi-belly" (upset stomach, diarrhea): if you do, drink lots of fluids (not coffee or fruit-juices, although Coca Cola is beneficial), and take water mixed with oral rehydration salts to replenish your body. Avoid eating until you feel hungry, then start with dry toast, boiled rice, yogurt or bananas. Anti-diarrhea medication can relieve stomach cramps in an emergency but do not cure the problem. If symptoms persist for several days, consult a doctor as you may have dysentery.

Dehydration and sunburn can be seriously debilitating. Always drink lots of water, use sunscreen liberally, wear a hat if trekking or visiting large temple sites, and keep up your salt intake. Another illness that is easy to pick up and hard to get rid of is the common cold, usually caused by air conditioning or rapid changes in altitude. Always dress in layers that you can add to or take off easily.

While it is advisable to have a small first aid kit with you (including antiseptic ointment, antihistamine cream for insect bites, anti-diarrhea tablets, aspirin or other pain reliever, a general antibiotic and a roll of plaster for cuts), pharmacies stock all basic medication. Sunscreen and tampons are rarities, so bring them with you. Premoistened towelettes and antibacterial hand lotion can also be indispensable. Emergency treatment and consultations are offered at Indian clinics and hospitals, where doctors are usually very competent and speak good English.

Simple precautions with food and drink can help to prevent illness

Other information

Alcohol

Prohibition is now in force only in Gujarat, Manipur, and Mizoram. Some other states operate "dry days" or impose high taxes on alcohol, or apply both measures. In Goa, on the other hand, beer and spirits (Indian-made whisky, rum, or gin) flow like water and are extremely inexpensive.

Begging

Beggars are everywhere in India and visitors have to learn to deal with them at their own discretion. Alms-giving at temples or to mutilated beggars is common practice, but many so-called *sadhus* are quite simply conmen. Kolkata (Calcutta) presents the most difficult situations, but the pleading women and babies pursuing tourists in Sudder Street are actually part of an organized syndicate. Keep a stock of rupee coins handy, but don't let yourself be pressurized if a crowd of beggars suddenly materializes. Children are adept at asking for rupees or pens and many visitors are a soft touch, but it is not a good idea to encourage them. It is far better to give money or items such as pens to their parents.

Camping

As budget accommodations are already extremely inexpensive, camping is not common in India, except in certain hotel grounds and on organized treks (by camel or on foot) when all facilities will be provided. Some states are developing campgrounds with youth-groups in mind, and tourist offices will advise on these. The Indian YMCA has information on their own camping facilities: contact the YMCA Tourist Hotel, Sansad Marg, New Delhi.

Clothing

The mainly tropical climate of India demands loose cotton, linen or silk clothing, with a sweater and/or windjacket for higher altitudes and for northern India during the winter months. Women especially should dress modestly: avoid cropped tops, shorts, above-the-knee skirts, and tight clothing. Local clothing is the

CONVERSION CHART

FROM	TO	MULTIPLY BY
Inches	Centimeters	2.54
Centimeters	Inches	0.3937
Feet	Meters	0.3048
Meters	Feet	3.2810
Yards	Meters	0.9144
Meters	Yards	1.0940
Miles	Kilometers	1.6090
Kilometers	Miles	0.6214
Acres	Hectares	0.4047
Hectares	Acres	2.4710
Gallons	Liters	4.5460
Liters	Gallons	0.2200
Ounces	Grams	28.35
Grams	Ounces	0.0353
Pounds	Grams	453.6
Grams	Pounds	0.0022
Pounds	Kilograms	0.4536
Kilograms	Pounds	2.205
Tons	Tonnes	1.0160
Tonnes	Tons	0.9842

MEN'S SUITS

U.K.	36	38	40	42	44	46	48
Rest of Europe	46	48	50	52	54	56	58
U.S.	36	38	40	42	44	46	48

DRESS SIZES

U.K.	8	10	12	14	16	18
France	36	38	40	42	44	46
Italy	38	40	42	44	46	48
Rest of Europe	34	36	38	40	42	44
U.S.	6	8	10	12	14	16

MEN'S SHIRTS

U.K.	14	14.5	15	15.5	16	16.5	17
Rest of Europe	36	37	38	39/40	41	42	43
U.S.	14	14.5	15	15.5	16	16.5	17

MEN'S SHOES

U.K.	7	7.5	8.5	9.5	10.5	11
Rest of Europe	41	42	43	44	45	46
U.S.	8	8.5	9.5	10.5	11.5	12

WOMEN'S SHOES

U.K.	4.5	5	5.5	6	6.5	7
Rest of Europe	38	38	39	39	40	41
U.S.	6	6.5	7	7.5	8	8.5

best, from *kurta-pajamas* (cotton tunics and pants) to *salwar kameez* (long-sleeved dress and pants for women), or heavy wool sweaters, scarves, and shawls in the Himalayas. Beach resorts such as Goa and Kovalam offer endless "travelers' clothing" at rock-bottom prices. Bring as little with you as possible, and supplement as necessary on the way. If you are traveling during the rainy season, an umbrella is a vital accessory and easily bought locally. The main item to choose carefully before departure is footwear: bring good, comfortable walking shoes, and leather sandals. Although the latter are available in some areas, quality is variable. Multiple changes of clothing are not necessary. *Dhobi wallahs* will pick up your laundry in the morning and return it, impeccably washed, in the evening, at an absurdly low cost.

Electricity
220–240V. Socket sizes vary, so take a universal adaptor with you. Power-cuts are common in many areas, as are fluctuations in current. Make sure you have a good flashlight.

Etiquette and local customs
Indians, whether Hindu, Muslim or Buddhist, have a strong code of conduct and are also polite when addressing strangers. Long train and bus journeys are often punctuated with inquisitive grillings by fellow travelers. Some diplomacy is needed: for example if traveling as a hetero-sexual couple, it is safer to say that you are married.

Hindus and Muslims traditionally use the left hand for performing ablutions, so it is never used for eating or even touching other people. If eating with your fingers (common with *thalis* and in the south), use only your right hand. Body contact in public is not accepted except in very Westernized places where hand shaking may be practised. Very often the most you will see is men holding hands, which is a common sign of comradeship. Feet should be kept on the ground (not stretched out on tables or over car seats), as they too are perceived as "unclean". When entering any home, temple, or

mosque, always remove your footwear. If necessary try to carry a clean pair of socks with you to put on to protect your feet from hot stones or dirt.

Remember above all to respect worshippers (in some inner sanctuaries non-Hindus are forbidden entry; the same applies to mosques for non-Muslims). Jain temples post strict rules outside (banning menstruating women, any items made of leather, and very often cameras). Give donations when appropriate. If a temple guardian or priest takes time to explain the history or significance of a site, he will appreciate a small tip.

Women should not indulge in topless sunbathing as this is highly offensive to Indians.

Photography and video
Color print and slide film is inexpensive and readily available in large tourist towns, but check expiration dates and avoid buying from street hawkers—their film sits for hours in the sun. Have a reasonable supply

Photography and video fees at some monuments can mount up

with you as well as spare batteries when visiting more obscure places. Many monuments and wildlife sanctuaries charge photographic and video fees which can mount up exorbitantly, particularly in Rajasthan. Photography is prohibited, or limited, in some Jain temples and this should be respected.

Places of worship
As well as Hindu temples, Muslim mosques and Sikh gurudwaras, India is well provided with Christian churches, above all in the big cities, the south, the once Portuguese areas, and former colonial hill stations.

Restrooms
Airports, large museums and decent restaurants have reasonable public restrooms but standards plunge lamentably at roadside bus rest stops and railroad stations. Keep a supply of toilet paper with you, and expect to use squatters often.

Visitors with disabilities
India's potholed sidewalks, high curbs and teeming crowds do not

Hall of Victory in Amer Palace, Rajasthan

make life easy for visitors with disabilities. It is not a suitable destination for people in wheelchairs except for certain well-appointed hotels in Goa, Delhi, and Mumbai (Bombay). It is best to make enquiries at an organization for disabled people in your home country, or ask your local Indian tourist office for names of specialist tour operators.

Women travelers
India is an ideal country for women travelers, although they will experience a lot of curiosity and sometimes unwelcome attention. This can become annoying, but sexual attacks are very rare. Use common sense: avoid dark streets at night, ignore any persistent attention, and keep to mid-range hotels whenever possible. Indian women have a great sense of solidarity, so stick with other women while traveling. Curiosity about marital status and number of offspring can be dealt with by inventing an absent or imminently arriving husband.

Tourist services
Indian tourist offices overseas

- **Australia** Level 2, 210 Pitt Street, Sydney, NSW 2000 (tel: 02 9264 4855, fax: 02 9264 4860, email: indtour@ozmail.com.au)
- **Canada** 60 Bloor Street West, Suite 1003, Toronto, Ont. M4 W3 B8 (tel: 416 962 3787, fax: 416 962 6279, email: india@istar.ca)
- **U.K.** 7 Cork Street, London W1X 2LN (tel: 020 7437 3677, fax: 020 7494 1048, email: info@india-touristoffice. org)
- **U.S.A.** 3550 Wilshire Boulevard, Room 204, Los Angeles, CA 90010 (tel: 213/380 8855, fax: 213/380 6111, email: la@tourismindia.com); 1270 Avenue of the Americas, Suite 1808, New York, NY 10020/1700 (tel: 212/586 4901, fax: 212/592 3274, email: bala@tourindia.com)

State tourist offices in New Delhi
Not always reliable. Alternatively the Government of India Tourist Office (88 Janpath) is well staffed and covers the country.

Andaman and Nicobar Islands 12 Chanakyapuri (tel: 011 687 1443)
Andhra Pradesh AP Bhawan, 1 Ashok Road (tel: 011 338 1293, www. aptourism.com)
Assam B-1 State Emporia Complex, Baba Kharak Singh Marg (tel: 011 334 5897)
Bihar 216–217 Kanishka Shopping Plaza, 19 Ashok Road (tel: 011 336 8371)
Goa Goa Sadan, 18 Amrita Shergil Marg (tel: 011 462 9968, fax: 011 462 9954, www.goacom. com)
Gujarat A-6 State Emporia Complex, Baba Kharak Singh Marg (tel: 011 336 4724, tel/fax: 011 373 4015, email: cgi.del@rmt. sprintrpg.ems.vsnl.net.in, www.gujarattourism.com)
Himachal Pradesh Chandralok Building, 36 Janpath (tel: 011 332 4764/5320, fax: 011 373 1072, email: hpturism @del2. vsnl.net.in, www. himachal-tourism.com)
Jammu & Kashmir 201–203, Kanishka Shopping Plaza, 19 Ashok Road (tel: 011 334 5373, fax: 011 336 7881, email: jaktour@ndf.vsnl.net.in)

Karnataka C-4 State Emporia Complex, Baba Kharak Singh Marg (tel/fax: 011 336 3862, www.karnatakatourism.com)
Kerala 219 Kanishka Plaza, 19 Ashok Road (tel/fax: 011 336 8541, www.ktdc.com)
Madhya Pradesh 204–205 Kanishka Shopping Plaza, 19 Ashok Road (tel: 011 334 1187, fax: 011 334 7264, email: mpstdc@del6.vsnl.net.in, www. mptourism.com)
Orissa B-4 State Emporia Complex, Baba Kharak Singh Marg (tel/fax: 011 336 4580, www.orissa-tourism.com)
Punjab 214 Kanishka Shopping Plaza, 19 Ashok Road (tel: 011 334 3055)
Rajasthan Bikaner House, Pandara Road (tel: 011 338 1884/6069, fax: 011 338 2823, www.rajasthan-tourism.com)
Sikkim 14 Panchsheel Marg (tel: 011 611 5346, www.nic.in/sikkim)
Tamil Nadu C-1 State Emporia Complex, Baba Kharak Singh Marg (tel: 011 373 5427, www.tamilnadu-tourism.com)
Uttar Pradesh Chandralok Building, 36 Janpath (tel: 011 332 2251/371 1296, fax: 011 371 1296, email: upstdc@lwl.vsnl.net.in, www. uptourism.com)
West Bengal A-2 State Emporia Complex, Baba Kharak Singh Marg (tel: 011 373 2840/ 336 3775, fax: 011 336 5430, www.westbengal.com/ travel/)

269

Glossary

apsara	temple dancer: often depicted in sculpture
ashram	hermitage
avatar	incarnation
bandhani	tie-dying
bastis	sanctuaries
Bhagavad Gita	philosophical text from the epic poem *Mahabharata*
Bodhisattva	person on the path to Buddhahood
Brahma	one of the Hindu trinity; the creator
chai	tea
chaitya	Buddhist worship hall that was originally rock cut
char-bagh	Islamic-style quartered garden
chhatri	domed, open-sided pavilion
dacoits	bandits
dalits	lower castes
darsha	mystic ecstasy (Buddhist)
deul	ribbed, bell-shaped structure
dharma	abiding by natural law and religious teachings
dhobi	laundry
dhooli	carried chair
dhoti	white loincloth
dhurri	rug
durbar	public audience hall
Ganesh	Hindu god; son of Siva and Parvati. The bringer of prosperity; depicted with an elephant's head
Garuda	bird-man (steed of the Hindu god Vishnu)
ghat	steps leading down to a river; mountains
gopuram	gatehouse
gurudwara	Sikh place of worship
hammam	steam bath
Hanuman	Hindu monkey god
haveli	multistory courtyard house
howdah	seat for riding on an elephant or camel
huqqa	water pipe
jaggery	palm sugar
jali	carved latticework
jyotirlinga	twelve sacred sites associated with the Hindu god Siva
lingam	phallic symbol of Siva
lunghi	colored loincloth
Mahabharata	ancient, highly revered Hindu text. An epic poem that recounts a battle between good and evil

Mahavir	founder of Jainism; meaning great leader
Makaras	mythical creatures symbolizing the River Ganga (Ganges)
maidan	open grassy space
mandapa	pillared hall
mihrab	prayer niche
minar	tower of a mosque
muezzin	Muslim crier
naga	snake; frequently depicted in sculpture
Nandi	bull; Siva's steed
nirvana	state of total peace
Parvati	Siva's consort
prakram/prakaram	enclosure
puja	religious offering or prayer
Ramayana	ancient Hindu epic poem
ratha	chariot of a deity
Rig Veda	oldest and most sacred of the ancient Hindu texts, the Vedas
sadhu	ascetic
sati	Hindu rite, where a widow throws herself on her husband's funeral pyre (banned by the British in 1829)
shakti	female creative force
shikhara	tapered tower
Siva	Supreme Lord of the Hindu trinity; the destroyer
stupa	dome; domed building containing Buddhist relics
Sufism	Muslim mysticism
tank	artificial lake
thali	small servings of several dishes
thangka	Buddhist scroll
Tirthankar	Jain prophet
tongas	pony carts
torana	gateway
Upanishads	ancient texts establishing the philosophical basis of Hinduism
Vedanta	early Hindu doctrine meaning "end of Vedas"
Vedas	sacred Hindu texts
vihara	Buddhist monastery, usually simple and austere
vimana	sanctuary tower
vinaya	rules of monastic conduct (Buddhism)
Vishnu	One of the Hindu trinity; embodiment of mercy and goodness; the preserver
zenana	women's quarters

Accommodations and Restaurants

Accommodations price ratings:

- **budget** ($) up to 1,500 Rs per night

- **moderate** ($$) 1,500–3,000 Rs per night

- **expensive** ($$$) over 3,000 Rs per night
Budget accommodations have at least some rooms with showers and air-conditioning (the others have fans). Rooms in mid-range accommodations generally offer satellite/cable TV and direct-dial phones. The luxury hotels are of international standard and include business facilities, air-conditioning/central heating, room service (often 24-hour), laundry, currency exchange (for residents), a bar and at least one restaurant. Some of the budget and mid-range hotels give off-season discounts (May–September). A variety of taxes is applied to all accommodations and can increase the bill by about 25 percent, particularly when the basic rate is high enough (currently 1,500 Rs a night) to attract an extra 10 percent luxury tax.

272

Restaurant price ratings (excluding drinks):

- **budget** ($) up to 350 Rs

- **moderate** ($$) 350–700 Rs

- **expensive** ($$$) over 700 Rs
Bills are increased by the addition of various local taxes, but these are usually detailed on menus. In the listings below, entries preceded by an asterisk (*) are recommended as places to eat. They include both independent restaurants and the better hotel restaurants. The latter are usually the best places for food in smaller towns.

DELHI
(STD code 011)
*Ambassador ($$$)
Sujan Singh Park
tel: 463 2600 fax: 463 2252/8219
email: ambassadorhotel@vsnl.com
Taj hotel with 88 comfortable rooms and 12 suites. Pleasant garden, but no pool. Restaurants offer Indian, Chinese and Continental cuisine. Reservations required for the excellent **Dasaprakash** (South Indian) restaurant ($$).
*Broadway ($/$$)
4/15A Asaf Ali Road tel: 327 3821–5
fax: 326 9966 email: owhpl@nda.vsnl.net.in
Renovated 1950s hotel well placed near Delhi Gate, with 32 clean rooms (spacious doubles, small airless singles), some with balconies, all with TV. Service quick and friendly. Excellent bar and Kashmiri/Tandoori restaurant, the aptly-named **Chor Bizarre** ($$$). Walks organized through Old Delhi.
*Claridges ($$$)
12 Aurangzeb Road
tel: 301 0211 fax: 301 0625
email: claridge@del2.vsnl.net.in
162 rooms and suites. Beginning to show signs of age, but still reigning supreme over elegant residential area close to center. Old-fashioned atmosphere,

with amenities including pool, health club, beauty salon, travel agent and four good restaurants covering the gastronomical gamut, including **The Corbett** ($$), a jungle mock up offering authentic North Indian cuisine, and **Pickwicks** ($/$$) for Continental in 19th-century decor.
*Grand Hyatt ($$$)
Vasant Kunj (phase II), Nelson Mandela Road
tel: 612 1234 fax: 689 5891 www.hyatt.com
State-of-the-art 390-room hotel (opened 2000), set in 10 acres of landscaped gardens and handy for the airport. Decor incorporates works by Indian artists and sculptors. Spacious rooms, interactive TV and internet ports. Gym, spa, outdoor pool, tennis, beauty salon. Choice of cuisine.
*Hyatt Regency ($$$)
Bhikaji Cama Place, Ring Road
tel: 679 1234/1150 fax: 679 1122
email: hyatt@del2.vsnl.net.in
The decor and facilities are superb, but it is rather impersonal, with over 500 medium-size rooms and suites. Good restaurants offer a range of cuisine and prices: **Delhi Ka Angan** ($$) is the world's first restaurant specializing in the cuisine of Delhi, while **La Piazza** ($$) has excellent Italian, including wine. Disco, night club, health club, tennis, pool in garden, beauty parlor.
*Imperial ($$$)
Janpath tel: 334 1234/5678
fax: 334 2255 email: hotel@imperialindia.com
Nearly 300 rooms and suites. An old colonial-style favorite uplifted to luxury category while maintaining traditional atmosphere. Relaxing gardens with coffee shop and three restaurants serving Indian and Continental cuisine. The **Spice Route** ($$$) offers an interesting mixture of Thai and other Asian styles. Good pool, travel agency, beauty parlor, gymnasium, health club, tennis.
La Sagrita Tourist Home ($$)
14 Sunder Nagar, near Nizamuddin station
tel: 460 1249/464 3973/469 4541/8572
fax: 463 6956 email: lasagrit@del3.vsnl.net.in
The 25 rooms are of variable quality. A bit run-down and air-conditioning can be unreliable, but there are plans to upgrade and it is a pleasant place, on a quiet side street, with friendly staff and a small garden. No restaurant, but 24-hour room service (Indian and Continental). Good value.
Maharani Guest Lodge ($$)
3 Sunder Nagar tel: 469 9521–4/3128–9/3134/2403
fax: 462 4562 email: mgh@vsnl.com
24-room hotel at entrance to Sunder Nagar enclave. Simple, but clean, comfortable and friendly, with central air-conditioning. Spacious rooms with carpets and good bathrooms. Roof terrace, exchange, laundry, 24-hour room service. A little noise from the road, but very good value. Reserve at least a week in advance.
*The Manor ($$$)
77 Friends Colony (West)
tel: 692 5151 fax: 692 2299
email: manordel@ndf.vsnl.net.in
An oasis in the hectic city, this was an exclusive residential area well away from the center. The city has now spread around it, but this tastefully custom-designed hotel retains an air of exclusivity. 18 bedrooms and suites, with large beds and modem connections. Restaurant (modern European),

exchange (at bank rates), health club—but no pool. A peaceful place, with more personal service than at big accommodations in the same price bracket.

Marina ($$/$$$)
G-59 Connaught Place tel: 332 4658
fax: 332 8609 email: marina@nde.vsnl.net.in
Very central, but pleasant. Some of the 94 rooms are very small, but all have been refurbished. Reasonable value, with coffee shop, cozy bar, multi-cuisine restaurant and snacks. Live Indian music in evening.

*Maurya Sheraton Hotel and Towers ($$$)
Sardal Patel Marg, Chanakyapuri
tel: 611 2233 fax: 611 3333
email: maurya@welcomgroup.com
The huge flagship of the Welcomgroup is 10.5 miles from the center, with a lobby overlooking ornamental pools. All creature comforts, but get a room well away from the disco. Excellent service. Outdoor pool. Noted for superb food: restaurants (some with dance floors) include **Dum Phukt** ($$/$$$) for melt-in-the-mouth Nawabi dishes, slowly cooked in traditional Chinese sealed *deghs*, **Bukhara** ($$$), one of the best eating places in Delhi with many Central Asian specialties. 1920s-style Jazz Bar with live music and expensive drinks.

*Nirula's ($$)
L-Block Connaught Circus tel: 332 2419
fax: 332 4669 email: nirulas@nirula.com
Popular, established restaurants, including **Potpourri** ($$) for good Indian/Continental food, the **Chinese Room** ($$) for Szechuan-style, an English-style pub called **Pegasus**, and (takeout) ice cream and pastry shops.

*Oberoi Maidens ($$$)
7 Sham Nath Marg, Old Delhi
tel: 291 4841/252 5464 fax: 398 0771
www.oberoihotels.com
Old colonial building with great atmosphere and 54 well-equipped rooms and suites. Less luxurious than other accommodations in this upscale chain and prices reflect this. Still very comfortable, with coffee shop overlooking gardens, tennis courts and excellent pool. The **Curzon** ($$/$$$) restaurant, in British Raj style, offers Indian and Continental cuisine and there are good barbecue nights.

*Park Balluchi ($$/$$$)
Inside the Deer Park, Hauz Khas
tel: 685 9369/696 9829
Frequent winner of restaurant awards, in peaceful sylvan surroundings. The concentration is on Mughlai specialties and special gourmet requests are possible—with a little notice.

*Rodeo ($/$$)
12-A Connaught Place tel: 371 3780-1
Restaurant with a cowboy theme and a lively atmosphere for excellent Mexican, Tex-Mex, Italian and Continental dishes, with fast service. Bar area heats up as the tequila hits home and the karaoke or live music gets going.

Sunstar Heritage ($$)
8A/43 WEA Channa Market, Karol Bagh
tel: 571 9790/577 2486/2602
fax: 584 1367
email: hsunstar@ndb.vsnl.net.in
Fairly new hotel (opened 1998), with 16 air-conditioned, clean and comfortable rooms, each with different decor. All have refrigerator and tea/coffee-making facilities. No restaurant, but there's 24-hour

room service—from the restaurant at **Sunstar Residency** ($$), just down the road at 8A/50 Channa Market (tel: 574 718 6/585 3687–9). This opened in 2000 and has 19 rooms and suites, all with facilities as above, plus a small but comfortable restaurant ($/$$) for Indian, Chinese and European food, travel desk and net access. Both hotels have elevators, reliable electricity and helpful service.

*Taj Mahal Hotel ($$$)
1 Mansingh Road
tel: 302 6162 fax: 302 6070
email: tajmahal@giasdel01.vsnl.net.in
Large (300 rooms and suites), but manages to retain a personal feel. Attractive decor includes a lobby that emulates a Buddhist hall of worship, marble and chandeliers. Predictably good (and friendly) service. Well located. Delicious food includes Mughal and Peshwari cuisine in the **Haveli** restaurant ($$$), seafood in nautical surroundings in the **Captain's Cabin** ($$$), superb French food in **Longchamp** ($$$) and multi-style Chinese in the award-winning **House of Ming** ($$). Live evening entertainment. Large outdoor pool surrounded by sundeck and trees.

*Taj Palace ($$$)
2 Sardar Patel Marg, Chanakyapuri
tel: 611 0202 fax: 611 0808
email: bctpd@tajgroup.sprintrpg.ems.vsnl.net.in
Over 400 rooms designed for business travelers, with excellent facilities. **Orient Express** ($$$) restaurant offers superb French *nouvelle cuisine* (and matching service), in one of the train's original cars. Other specialty restaurants with themed decor provide Chinese and Indian cuisine. Large outdoor pool, beautiful gardens, tennis, golf, dancing.

*United Coffee House ($/$$)
E-15 Connaught Place
tel: 332 2075/373 1697
One of Delhi's old favorites, open all day and still going strong under the chandeliers. Old fashioned but relaxed and stylish setting, very lively and popular for power lunches. Friendly and efficient service. Mezzanine area for (good) snacks and nonsmoking customers. Continental, Chinese and North Indian food—all with a reasonable choice, including dishes aimed at the calorie conscious.

*Village Bistro ($/$$)
12 Hauz Khas Village tel: 685 2227/3857
This is a complex of half a dozen restaurants, providing Continental, Indian and Chinese cuisine. Weekend brunches are particularly good value. A variety of live entertainment is offered.

YMCA Tourist Hotel ($)
Jai Singh Road tel: 374 6031 fax: 374 6032
This is where to get general information about the YMCA. 120 rooms. Restaurant offers Indian and Western food. Good pool (extra charge). Travel desk and baggage storage. Neither helpful nor very clean, but good value—so reserve ahead.

YWCA International Guest House ($)
Sansad Marg
tel: 336 1561/1662/1970/1740
fax: 334 1763
email: ywcaind@del3.vsnl.net.in
Basic, but good value and central. 24 air-conditioned rooms, with shower and (reasonable cost) phone. Western breakfast included and 24-hour room service available until new restaurant is installed. Good, inexpensive laundry service and travel office.

Accommodations and Restaurants

THE NORTHWEST

GUJARAT
Ahmadabad
(STD code 079)
*Holiday Inn ($$$)
Khanpur Road, near Nehru Bridge, Khanpur
tel: 550 5505 fax: 550 5501
email: holiday.ahd@sml.sprintrpg.ems.vsnl.net.in
Palatial style for a reasonably priced high-class hotel
with 63 well-appointed rooms. Good multi-cuisine
restaurants. Indoor pool, dance floor, disco, travel
desk, health club. Very helpful staff.
*Inder Residency ($$$)
Opposite Gujarat College, Ellisbridge
tel: 656 5222 fax: 656 0407
email: inder@adl.vsnl.net.in
A modern, comfortable hotel with 79 rooms.
Facilities include a pool, tennis, health club, travel
desk, coffee shop and multi-cuisine restaurants.
Rivera ($/$$)
Khanpur Road tel: 550 4201/5220
fax: 550 2327 email: rivera@satyam.net.in
River views in some of the 69 rooms;tea/coffee-
making facilities, refrigerator and room service. Quiet
and comfortable. Restaurant, travel desk, car rental,
free airport transfer, exchange, lawn. Good value.
Stay-Inn ($)
Khanpur Gate tel: 550 3993 fax: 550 4053
14 excellent value clean and colorful rooms with
decent bathrooms, though traffic noise can be annoying. TV, phone, room service. Friendly staff. Centrally
located a few steps from Holiday Inn.
*Vishalla ($)
Vasana, on southern edge of city
tel: 403 4357
Eating here is an experience of Gujarati village life.
Sit on the floor and eat all you can of the set vegetarian meal—live entertainment in the evenings.

Bhuj
(STD code 02832)
*Hotel Anam ($)
Station Road tel/fax: 53397
Friendly, clean, well maintained, central and modern
hotel with 27 spacious rooms and rapid room service.
TV, phone. Good *thali* restaurant.
*Hotel Prince ($/$$)
Station Road
tel: 02832 20370–1 fax: 50373
Stylish and central modern hotel with 41 rooms (a
few de luxe). Good restaurants, and snacks are avail-
able in garden. Exchange service offered. Tours and
free airport transfer can be arranged. However, the
hotel can be noisy.

Diu
*Samrat ($)
Bunder Road tel: 02875 52354
Small, simple establishment offering 12 clean rooms,
with TV and balconies. The restaurant serves good
food, there's a bar and helpful staff.
Tourist Cottages ($)
Jallandhar Beach tel: 02875 52654
Consists of a row of spacious cottages about ten min-
utes' walk from a good swimming beach. Main
attraction is the relaxed atmosphere. All rooms with
TV and porch.

Palitana
*Sumeru ($)
Station Road, near bus station
tel: 02848 2327
16 comfortable rooms and five dormitories. TCGL
tourist information. Restaurant has limited menu, but
it's inexpensive and does English breakfast.

Sasan Gir National Park
(STD code 02877)
Gir Lodge ($$$)
Sasan Gir, Junagadh tel: 85521 fax: 85528
This Taj-group lodge offers a variety of comfortable
rooms, the upstairs ones with balconies. Dining (at
fixed times) can be a slow process. Pool, gardens,
library, travel desk, jeep rental, airport/rail pick ups
on demand. Reservations required.
*Maneland Jungle Lodge ($$/$$$)
On the edge of the sanctuary tel: 85555
email: ssibal@adl.vsnl.net.in
Isolated location a few miles north of main village.
Small complex of bungalows and cottages, affording
suites and rooms. Well organized, with excellent
restaurant and guides. Reservations required.
*Sinh Sadan Forest Lodge ($)
Sasan Gir, Wildlife Division
tel: 02877 85540–1
A large complex with facilities ranging from air-condi-
tioned rooms with bath (in bungalows) to 30-bed
dormitories and two-bed tents. Reserve in advance.
Food (excellent) must be reserved.

RAJASTHAN
Ajmer
(STD code 0145)
*Mansingh Palace ($$/$$$)
Ana Sagar Circular Road, Vaishali Nagar
tel: 425855–7/702 fax: 425858 email: mansingha-
jmer@mailcity.com
Situated in beautiful grounds northwest of the cen-
ter, this is the best in town, though somewhat
overpriced. A well-appointed, modern, 57-room hotel.
Excellent multi-cuisine restaurant and bar.
Regency ($)
Outside Delhi Gate tel: 620296/622439
fax: 420747 www.fhrai.com
24 well-maintained rooms. Lively, central location.
TV, phone. Reasonable vegetarian restaurant and
bar. One of the town's better options.

Alwar
(STD code 0144)
*Arawali Hotel ($)
Near railway station tel: 332011
Run by helpful family and offering a range of accom-
modations, from dormitory to air-conditioned doubles.
Can be noisy, so ask for a quiet room. Decent bar and
restaurant. Pool in summer.
Sariska Palace ($$/$$$)
Jaipur Road, near park entrance
tel: 41322–4/41460 fax: 41323
email: sariska@del2.vsnl.net.in
Large, converted and refurbished royal hunting lodge,
now a Heritage hotel in extensive grounds. Main
lodge has atmospheric interior full of memorabilia.
Newer facilities include gymnasium, pool, library,
restaurant, Ayurvedic and yoga center. The Forest
Reception Center is across the road.

Bharatpur/Keoladeo
(STD code 05644)
Bharatpur Forest Lodge ($$)
Keoladeo National Park tel: 22760/22
fax: 22864 www.fhrai.com
ITDC lodge fabulously located inside park, offering 17 comfortable rooms, all doubles with balconies. Restaurant ($) with Indian and Continental food, room service, exchange, friendly staff. Facilities (including boats) for touring sanctuary, though birds come to your window and animals enter the compound. Reservations required.
*Laxmi Vilas Palace ($$/$$$)
Kakaji-ki-Kothi, Raghunath Nivas, Agra Road tel: 23523 fax: 25259 www.laxmivilas.com
Haveli-style 19th-century lodge which retains some period atmosphere, with 22 comfortable rooms and suites. Good Indian and Continental food, pool, travel desk and friendly service.

Bikaner
*Bhanwar Niwas ($$)
Rampuria Street, 500m from Kote Gate
tel: 0151 529323/201043
fax: 0151 200880
Intriguing 20th-century *haveli* (courtyard house) tucked away in backstreets of Bikaner's old city (if lost, ask for the Rampuria *haveli* hotel, rather than the Bhanwar Niwas). 14 large rooms with decorative Indian flourishes; best on upper floor. The vegetarian food is very good and there's a bar.
*Gajner Palace Hotel ($$/$$$)
Gajner, Teh tel: 01534 55063–5
fax: 01534 55060/522408
email: resv@hrhindia.com
Beautiful lakeside palace with bags of atmosphere: an oasis in the desert about 12 miles west of Bikaner. Great birdwatching, boating, camel and jeep safaris, with antelopes and wild boar in surrounding sanctuary (and game on menu!). Endless maharaja memorabilia, friendly staff. Barbecues, buffets and cultural programs. Really top-notch.
Harasar Haveli ($)
Opposite stadium tel: 0151 527318/209891
fax: 0151 525150
18 clean rooms, with room service. Veranda and garden. Use of pool across the road. Multi-cuisine restaurant. Good value and service.
Lalgarh Palace ($$$)
Ganga Avenue Road tel: 0151 540201
fax: 0151 522253 email:
gm.bikaner@welcomemail.wiprobt.ems.vsnl.ent.in
4 miles north of train station on outskirts of town. 38 lavishly-furnished rooms in an attractive, palatial, red sandstone Heritage hotel/museum, built 1902–12 by Sir Swinton Jacob. Lawns, restaurant, billiards, indoor pool.

Jaipur
(STD code 0141)
*Alsisar Haveli ($$)
Sansar Chandra Road tel: 368290/36485
fax: 364652 www.haveli.com
This is an exceptionally well converted 1890s house which is attractive and full of ethnic character. 30 comfortable rooms, some featuring four-poster beds and frescoes. Inviting outdoor pool and courtyards. Good food, Indian and Continental. Quiet and with

superb service. Exchange. Frequent puppet shows and dance evenings in the bird-filled gardens.
Bissau Palace ($/$$$)
Outside Chandpol Gate
tel: 304371/391 fax: 304628
email: sanjai@jp1.vsnl.net.in
A stately 1920s Heritage palace-cum-museum packed with antiques, art and books. A welcome oasis in Jaipur with pool, tennis, travel desk, laundry, large grounds, pleasant staff, excellent atmosphere and 45 rooms. Two multi-cuisine restaurants, one rooftop with good views of the lively area (northwest of city walls). Folk dance and sitar recital on request. Tours arranged, including camel safaris. Exchange. Bookshop.
*Diggi Palace ($)
Diggi House, Shivaji Marg, SMS Hospital Road tel: 373091/366120 tel: 379359
email: diggintl@datainfosys.net
Beautiful gardens and wide range of rooms, travel desk, good multi-cuisine restaurant, puppet shows and folk dancing on request. Good value and very popular. Reservations required.
*Jai Mahal Palace ($$$)
Jacob Road, Civil Lines tel: 371616
fax: 365237 www.fhrai.com
102 rooms and suites only 1½ miles from train station. Very attractive old palace in Taj group, with lovely gardens, multi-cuisine restaurant.
Maharani Palace ($$/$$$)
Station Road, opposite Polo Victory
tel: 204702–6/378–82 fax: 202112
email: maharani@jp1.dot.net.in
Central, with 60 spacious, double-glazed rooms, Basement bar and multi-cuisine restaurants ($$). Small pool on rooftop terrace where outdoor meals are served in summer. Travel desk, exchange. Live Indian music.
*Niros ($)
MI Road tel: 374493/371874
A restaurant popular with Indians and Westerners for Chinese, Continental, tandoori and vegetarian dishes, served in an elaborate, air-conditioned interior. They also do take-outs. Open all day.
*Rambagh Palace ($$$)
Bhawani Singh Road tel: 381919
fax: 381098 email: rambagh@jp1.dot.net.in
Jaipur's showiest Taj palace hotel, dating from mid-19th century. The 113 rooms vary in size. Large grounds are superb. Outdoor pool, health club, jacuzzi, beauty parlor, travel desk, tennis, squash, badminton, birdwatching, camel riding. Eating options include barbecues (Oct–June) and the **Suvarna Mahal** restaurant ($$/$$$), with a superb Indian, Rajasthani, Continental and Chinese buffet and mouth-watering desserts. Evening Rajasthani dancers and puppet shows.
*Samode Haveli ($/$$$)
Gangapol tel: 631942–3/068/632407/370
fax: 632370/631397
email: reservations@samode.com
A 19th-century Heritage *haveli* in northeast of walled city. Secluded garden courtyard with outdoor Rajasthani buffet lunch and dinner, superbly decorated dining room, bar, pool, games. 21 tasteful rooms with antique furnishings. Good rooftop views and friendly service. It's very Indian in feel and popular with groups, so reserve well ahead.

Accommodations and Restaurants

*The Trident ($$$)
Opposite Jal Mahal, Amber Fort Road
tel: 630101 fax: 630303
email: trident@jp1.vsnl.net.in
In a superb location: all rooms have balconies with
views of the Aravalli Hills or Man Sagar Lake and the
Water Palace. Opened in 1997: custom-built 138-
room hotel with state-of-the-art facilities, including a
purifying plant which ensures that every drop of water
in the hotel is drinkable. **Jal Mahal** restaurant
($$/$$$) offers delicious Continental, Asian and
Indian food. Outdoor pool. Travel desk.

Jaisalmer
(STD code 02992)
Gorbandh Palace Hotel ($$)
*No.1 Tourist Complex, Sam Road, 15.5 miles from
town tel: 51511–3 fax: 52749*
email: resv@hrhindia.com
Traditionally-inspired grandiose Heritage hotel, set in
gardens with great swimming-pool. 67 rather worn
grand rooms and suites around a courtyard, but good
amenities. Restaurant ($$), coffee shop, bar. Travel
desk, camel rides, puppet shows and outdoor tradi-
tional song and dance by a campfire.
Hotel Paradise ($)
Jaisalmer Fort, opposite Royal Palace
tel: 52674
23-room *haveli* hotel with fabulous rampart and
desert views. Most rooms with balconies, room ser-
vice. Range of budget options, including camping on
the roof. Camel safaris.
*The Trio ($)
Gandhi Chowk, Mandir Palace tel: 52733
Jaisalmer's original rooftop restaurant, partly tented
and with great evening views of fort. Elegant setting
and presentation. Lamb, tandoori and Rajasthani
specialties. Live entertainment, pleasant service and
very popular.

Jodhpur
(STD code 0291)
*Hotel Adarsh Niwas ($/$$)
Near train station
tel: 624066/615871/627338–11
fax: 627314
www.fhraindia.com/hotel/jodhpur/adarshniwas
Comfortable, with 34 clean spacious rooms, all with
TV and refrigerator. 24-hour check out. Stylish multi-
cuisine restaurant, the **Kalinga** ($) is open all day.
Elevator, exchange, travel desk.
*Ajit Bhawan ($$/$$$)
Opposite Circuit House, Airport Road
*tel: 510410/610/511410 fax: 510674 email:
abhawan@del3.vsnl.net.in*
Lovely old Heritage palace built in rambling style
around well-tended gardens (with cows) and great
pool. 50 varied rooms have traditional features.
Barbecued Indian food at **On the Rocks** ($); delicious
bakery items. Jeep safaris.
*Davi Bhavan ($)
1 Ratanada Road tel/fax: 434215
Undoubtedly a great-value place, but only eight
rooms (with bath, but not air-conditioned), so reserve
ahead. Family-run and friendly, providing an excellent
Indian dinner ($). Lovely garden. Tours.
*Taj Hari Mahal ($$$)
5 Residency Road tel: 0291 437900/438985

fax: 614451 email: thmbc.jodh@tajhotels.com
Set in landscaped gardens, this 93-room luxury hotel
is a tasteful blend of traditional and modern.
Restaurants offer Indian, Continental and Asian cui-
sine. Pool, sports facilities and travel desk.
*Umaid Bhawan Palace ($$$)
3 miles from center tel: 510101–4
fax: 510100 email: ubp@ndf.vsnl.net.in
Luxurious Welcomgroup accommodations in art-deco
palace of Maharaja (still partly a royal residence). 96
palatial rooms and suites, luxury tents in peak season. Marble-lined indoor pool, health club, beauty
parlor, sports, library, formal gardens, travel desk and
theater showing nightly Hollywood films. Four restau-
rants, including informal **Pillars** ($$) providing all-day
snacks, and **Marwar Hall** ($$$), for sumptuous multi-
cuisine buffets. Non-residents may visit on payment
of a charge (deducted from food/drink they
consume).

Mount Abu
(STD code 02974)
Connaught House ($/$$)
Rajendra Marg, opposite bus stand
tel: 38560/43439 fax: 542240
email: marwar@del3.vsnl.net.in
Once the summer residence of the Maharaja of
Jodhpur, this atmospheric old Heritage bungalow lies
in quiet gardens. 14 rooms, all with quaint furnish-
ings, some with porches. Multi-cuisine restaurant.
Reservations required for both rooms and meals.
*Hilltone Hotel ($/$$)
Near bus stand, PO Box 18 tel: 38391–4
fax: 38395 email: hilltone@ad1.vsnl.net.in
Good location on edge of town. Modern 68-room
hotel with extensive facilities (restaurant, bar, pool,
sauna, exchange). Also cottages in grounds.

Pushkar
(STD code 0145)
Payal Guest House ($)
Main Bazar tel: 72163
Cheap but with pleasant rooms. Meals available. A
shady courtyard and laid-back atmosphere add to its
deserved popularity with budget travelers.
*Pushkar Palace ($)
Near the lake tel: 72001/72401–3
fax: 72226
Atmospheric Heritage hotel in renovated palace on
eastern shore of lake, wide selection of rooms, some
with lake views. Laundry, travel desk. Pretty gardens,
vegetarian restaurant ($), jeeps, camel and horse-
back safaris, birdwatching. Reserve in advance.

Ranakpur
*Ghanerao Castle Hotel ($/$$)
Ranakpur Road tel: 02934 84035
20-room hotel 11 miles from Ranakpur. The royal
family still inhabit part of the castle. Large colorful
rooms, lawn, pool, good inexpensive restaurant.
*Maharani Bagh ($$)
Orchard Retreat, Ranakpur Road
*tel: 02934 85105/51 (or book in Jodhpur
tel: 0291 433316 fax: 0291 635373)*
The best accommodations are 2.5 miles from the
center of town. In the lovely former summer garden of
Jodhpur's rulers are 18 traditionally-furnished
thatched bungalows with verandas. Bougainvillea.

Ranthambhor

(STD code 07462)
***Sawai Madhopur Lodge** ($$/$$$)*
*Ranthambhor Road tel: 20541/20247
fax: 20718 email: smlodge@jp1.dot.net.in*
With 25 rooms, two suites and six tents (Oct–Mar), this Heritage palace, very close to the station, retains something of a colonial feel, with animal heads on the walls and cricket/croquet on the lawn. Other features include a small outdoor pool, table tennis, good multi-cuisine food and lots of langur monkeys in the gardens.

Shekhawati

***Castle Mandawa** ($$/$$$)*
*Mandawa tel: 01592 23124
fax: 01592 23171*
Wonderfully renovated Heritage castle, marble floors, arches, 70 beautiful bedrooms and bathrooms. Imaginative dining area with frescoes, but a bit run down. Linked with the less expensive and better-maintained **Desert Resort** ($$) just outside town (tel/fax: 01592 23151/23245), which is superbly designed in mud-hut style, with all necessary comforts and a pool. Camel rides.

Dera Dundlod Kila ($/$$)
*Dundlod Fort tel: 01594 52580
fax: 01594 52519*
Heritage hotel with 48 rooms of widely differing quality and some suites. Pool, tennis, entertainment and library. Atmospheric, with murals and very pleasant staff. Rambling corridors link rooms with traditional features, tucked into bastions. Cheap restaurant. Camel, jeep and horseback safaris ranging from one hour to several days.

Mukundgarh Fort ($$)
*Mukundgarh tel: 01594 52396–8
fax: 01594 52395*
Well-run Heritage hotel converted from 18th-century fort. Superb setting with lawns and ramparts. Nearly 50 reasonably-priced and attractively-furnished rooms and four suites. Frescoed corridors. Restaurant, bar, pool, travel desk, exchange.

Samode Palace ($$/$$$)
*Samode, c/o Samode House, Jaipur
tel: 01423 44123/44 fax: 01423 44123
email: jagdish@jpl.vsnl.net.in*
Stunning palace converted into 42-room Heritage hotel, 25 miles from Jaipur. Superlative interior and beautiful hill setting. Restaurant ($/$$).

Udaipur

(STD code 0294)
***Fateh Prakash Palace Hotel** ($$$)*
*City Palace tel: 528016–9
fax: 528006 email: resv@hrhindia.com*
Sumptuous Heritage accommodations with stunning lake and island views. Seven suites and ten de luxe rooms, decorated with Maharaja's antiques. Personalized service, pool, holistic fitness center, riding, travel desk, boats, squash, billiards.
Two restaurants: **Gallery Restaurant** ($$$), serving Continental set meals, including English cream teas; and **Sunset View Terrace** ($), with great snacks and live Indian music in the afternoon.

Jheel Guest House ($)
56 Gangaur Ghat tel: 421352
This consists of two family-run guest houses, one in an old *haveli* and the other (better quality) in a new annex, offering Udaipur's best lakeside budget accommodations. Some rooms with balconies over lake. Good rooftop restaurant with predictable Indo-World menu.

Kankarwa Haveli ($)
*26 Lalghat, 3 minutes from bazaar
tel: 411457/103 fax: 521403*
Renovated, family-run, 18th-century lakeside *haveli* offering 15 clean, quiet rooms, some with lake view. Roof terrace with great views provides snacks and breakfast—other meals are on request. Friendly. Car rental, travel help, excursions. Reserve well ahead.

***Lake Palace Hotel** ($$$)*
*PO Box No.5, Lake Pichola
tel: 527961/528800 fax: 528700
email: lakepalace.udaipur@tajhotels.com*
In a fabulous location, with spectacular views of Lake Pichola, this unique Taj hotel has 84 rooms and suites, most of which have a lake view, excellent facilities and service and extravagant decor. Excellent but expensive Indian and Continental food. Outdoor pool, travel desk, car rental. Reserve in advance. Restaurant open to non-residents only when hotel is not full—advance reservations essential.

***Sai Niwas** ($)*
*75 Narghat Marg, near City Palace gate
(telefax: 524909*
Varying room prices and sizes in this extraordinary family-run hotel, decorated in brilliant colors. Some traditional raised beds with eye-level windows and lake views, baths and some balconies. Good service and freshly-cooked food.

***Shiv Niwas Palace** ($$$)*
*City Palace tel: 528016–9 fax: 528006–12
email: 1phm.hrh@axcess.net.in*
Legendary Heritage palatial residence transformed into 34 rooms and suites at southern end of City Palace complex. Upper floors, added in 1980s, are deluxe rooms with private terraces and panoramic views. Many have antique fixtures from Mawar royal households. Tennis, squash, badminton, riding, billiards, boats, holistic massage, marble pool, travel desk. There's also a multi-cuisine restaurant. Reservations are essential.

THE NORTH

Agra

(STD code 0562)
***Chakraview** ($)*
Vibhav Nagar tel: 332609
Small and friendly, but efficient hotel with 11 decent rooms. There is also an excellent restaurant, but allow plenty of time there because everything is prepared to order.

***Clarks Shiraz Restaurant** ($$$)*
54 Taj Road tel: 361 421–7
Fabulous rooftop restaurant specializing in Mughlai dishes and with live Indian music at night. Reservations essential.

Grand Hotel ($)
*137 Station Road tel: 364014/320
fax: 364271 email: grand@nde.vsnl.net.in*
Large, old-fashioned bungalow. Rooms with TV, camping in garden. Lawns, exchange, indifferent restaurant, bar. Very popular.

Accommodations and Restaurants

*Mughal Sheraton ($$$)
Taj Ganj, Fatehabad Road
tel: 331701 fax: 331730
email: fom.mughal@itchotels.co.in
Spectacularly-designed large modern hotel in Mughal tradition, with hammocks in the gardens and court-yards. Very well-appointed rooms and suites, excellent service. Rooftop views of the Taj Mahal. Mughlai cuisine and live Indian music at **Nauratna** restaurant ($$). Other restaurants include **Tajbano** ($$), for superb multi-cuisine buffet, and a Continental restaurant with a live dance band in the evening. A variety of sports, library, car rental, guides, sauna, beauty salon, movie room.

Corbett National Park
A variety of very low-grade accommodations ($) are available within the park, but must be reserved in advance. Cabins (these have bathrooms), log huts and tourist huts can be arranged by the Tourist Reception Center at Ramnagar (tel: 05946 85489, fax: 05946 85376). Forest rest houses can be arranged by the Chief Wildlife Warden, 17 Rana Pratap Marg, Lucknow tel: 0522 283903).

Claridges Corbett Hideaway ($$$)
Zero Garjia, Dhikala tel: 05946 85959
Luxury in the wilds in the form of "tribal" cottages in an orchard. Well-appointed rooms, full board, pool and good service. Tours arranged; bicycle rental.

Tiger Tops Corbett Lodge ($$$)
8 miles north of Ramnagar tel: 05946 85279
Luxurious with old-world atmosphere, 24 rooms and high-quality full board. Friendly service. Facilities include a pool, elephant rides, jeep safaris and evening wildlife slide shows.

Gwalior
(STD code 0751)
*Usha Kiran Palace ($$/$$$)
Jayendraganj, Lashkar
tel: 0751 323993–4/213–4 fax: 321103
www.fhrai.com
Heritage hotel in converted maharaja's guest house, set in lovely gardens beside Jai Vilas Palace. Slow service compensated for by character and peaceful ambience. 28 large and well-appointed rooms and suites. Good multi-cuisine restaurant ($$$). Beauty parlor, croquet, billiards, badminton, table tennis, jogging, travel desk.

Khajuraho
(STD code 07686)
*Chandela ($$/$$$)
Jhansi Road tel: 42355–66/86–7
fax: 42366/85
email: chandgm.khj@tajgroup.sprintrpg
Taj hotel, reasonably priced for comfort and service. Well-designed; 95 rooms in large grounds, two excellent restaurants, pool, tennis, archery, croquet, badminton, table tennis, miniature golf, yoga, health center, bookstore, puppet shows.

*Clarks Bundela ($$/$$$)
Jhansi Road tel: 42386 fax: 42385
email: clarksvaranasi@deartmaildarnet.com
Two-story hotel with well-appointed rooms opening on to lawns, garden and pool. Sober, classical style. There is also excellent Indian food at **Bhuj Bundela** restaurant ($$).

Khajuraho Ashok ($/$$)
500m north of the Western Group
tel: 44024/42/44336/61
fax: 42239 www.fhrai.com
37 rooms, all with phone. Uninspired decoration but reasonable comfort, good pool, restaurant (Continental, Indian, poolside and barbecue), coffee room, bar, exchange, garden.

Hotel Marble Palace ($)
Opposite Gole Market tel: 44353 fax: 44131
Outstanding budget address, 200 yards from Western group. Surprising marble floors throughout, spacious front rooms, smaller budget ones at back. All with good bathrooms, insect screens and unexpected comforts. Also a dormitory.

Leh
Bijoo ($$)
Library Road tel: 01982 52131
Atmospheric old Ladakhi house close to bazaar. Comfortable rooms, good restaurant (full board), gardens, terrace. Treks and tours, helpful staff.

*Kokonor Tibetan Restaurant ($$)
On second floor in alley off Main Bazaar Road.
Despite the name, good Chinese and Western food is available at fair price, as well as Tibetan.

Manali
(STD code 01902)
Ambassador Resort ($$$)
Sunny Side, Chadiyan tel: 52235–8/52110
fax: 52173 www.fhrai.com
Perched on hillside with lovely views over rooftops of old town. Strikingly designed, 42 comfortable rooms and suites. Restaurants with multi-cuisine. Gym, jacuzzi, sauna, beauty parlor, watersports, disco, skating rink, squash, travel desk.

*John Banons ($/$$)
Manali Orchards, Old Manali Road
tel: 52335/88 fax: 52392 www.fhrai.com
A long-standing Manali classic. 13 well-maintained, pleasant rooms and a suite. TV, multi-cuisine restaurant, garden, views. A peaceful and personable establishment, situated in an apple orchard.

Sunshine Hotel ($)
The Mall tel: 52320
Lovely old colonial building full of original furnishings, good views, some rooms with balconies. Pleasant garden and restaurant. Good value.

Rishikesh
(STD code 0135)
*Ganga Kinare ($/$$)
16 Virbhadra Road tel: 0135 431658
tel/fax: 435243 email: hotelgangakinare@hot-mail.com
Quiet location south of main temples, by river with its own private *ghat*. 38 carpeted rooms, most overlooking the Ganga, two decent restaurants ($$), travel desk which arranges activities as well as tours, exchange. Watersports and free boating.

Sanchi
*Travellers' Lodge ($)
On the road to Bhopal tel: 07482 62723
MP Tourism hotel in good location near main *stupa* and train station. Relaxing garden. Only eight rooms. Indian and Chinese restaurant. Reserve in advance.

Shimla

(STD code 0177)

Chapslee House ($$$)
Lakkad Bazar tel: 202542 fax: 258663
email: chapslee@nde.vsnl.net.in
Full board (first-class food) in this beautiful old colonial mansion on outskirts of town. Only six suites. Reservations required.

Himland Hotel East ($)
Circular Road tel: 222901–4 fax: 224241
email: himland@nde.vsnl.net.in
16-room modern hotel, clean, some rooms with balconies and views, exchange. Next door is slightly more classy **Himland West** ($/$$) (tel: 224596/312), with a multi-cuisine restaurant.

*Oberoi Clarkes ($$$)
The Mall tel: 251010–5 fax: 211321
email: clarkes@nde.vsnl.net.in
This was Mohan Singh Oberoi's first hotel, and one of the earliest in Shimla, and is not air-conditioned. Lots of character, very comfortable, good service, and a restaurant.

*The Cecil ($$$)
Chaura Maidan, Ambedkar Chowk
tel: 204848 fax: 211024
email: reservations@thececil.com
Classy establishment, providing indoor pool, golf, billiards, steam room, health club, gymnasium, tea room, library, travel desk, multi-cuisine restaurant ($$$). Great views of the Himalayas.

*Woodville Palace ($$/$$$)
Raj Bhawan Road, The Mall
tel: 223919/224038 fax: 223098
www.fhrai.com
Another of Shimla's royal jewels, set in grounds at western end of town. 14 vast 1930s rooms and suites full of antiques. Excellent multi-cuisine restaurant ($$), worth visiting for decor alone. Billiards, table tennis, badminton. Reservations required.

Varanasi (Benares)

(STD code 0542)

*Alka Hotel ($)
D 3/23 Meerghat tel/fax: 328445
email: hotelalka@hotmail.com
Semi-modern hotel that opened in 1997. Very basic, but some rooms have balconies. In superb position, with terraces overlooking *ghats*. Wide price range, good terrace restaurant. Reservations required.

*Clarks Varanasi ($$$)
The Mall tel: 348501–10 fax: 348186
email: clarks.varanasi@dartmail/dartnet.com
Raj-era establishment with pleasantly designed modern extension, in well-tended gardens with good pool. Three excellent restaurants (multi-cuisine), travel desk, tennis, golf, yoga, meditation on banks, Indian dance and music on request and 135 well-appointed rooms. Efficient service.

Hotel de Paris ($/$$)
15 The Mall, Varanasi Cantonment
tel: 346601–8 fax: 348520 www.fhrai.com
1900s British officers' club designed by French architect. Large grounds. Good service. Cavernous rooms. Two multi-cuisine restaurants, pool, health club, golf, disco, watersports, tennis, laundry, exchange. One of Varanasi's best deals.

*Ideal Tops ($/$$)
The Mall tel: 348091–2/250 fax: 348685

www.fhrai.com
Modern hotel with 40 comfortable rooms, two good multi-cuisine restaurants (especially the Indian), bar, laundry, travel desk, exchange and helpful staff. No pool, but splendid value.

Surya ($)
A-5 The Mall, Varuna Bridge
tel: 343014/511012 fax: 348330
In Cantonment near station and tourist office. Decent rooms, most overlooking relaxing garden. Camping on lawn. Steam room, massage, multi-cuisine garden restaurant (average food), laundry, exchange, travel counter.

*Temple Restaurant ($)
Hotel Ganges, Dasaswamedh Road, Godowlia
tel: 321097
Good views over bazaar. Restaurant opens at 6:30am and is popular for Western breakfast after early morning boat trips on the Ganges. At other times good Indian and Chinese food are offered. Live classical Indian music in the evenings.

THE NORTHEAST

Bhubaneshwar

(STD code 0674)

*Oberoi Bhubaneshwar ($$$)
Naya Palli tel: 440890 fax: 440898
email: reservation@oberoibh.com
Near Botanical Gardens, 3 miles from town, with own garden, jogging track and pool. Tasteful decor reflects Orissan culture. Restaurant with good à la carte menu, health club, tennis, travel desk.

*Sahara ($)
76 Budhanagar tel: 417331
Roughly half of the (25) rooms are air-conditioned, with hot-water baths. From all angles, this is a good-value place and delicious food is an added attraction.

Calcutta see Kolkata

Darjiling

(STD code 0354)

Bellevue Hotel 1 ($)
1 Nehru Road tel: 54178/54075 fax: 54330
A charming old-fashioned ten-room hotel in untouched 1930s house. Superb views, lovely garden, spacious and generously-furnished rooms with fireplaces, basic bathrooms (hot water). Eccentric. WBTDC office in same building.

Bellevue Hotel 2 ($)
The Mall, Chowrasta tel: 54075 fax: 54330
Good standard in 1940s building. Large, functional, friendly, clean rooms with views and good bathrooms. Restaurant. Rooftop terrace. Not to be confused with main Bellevue (above).

*Windamere Hotel ($$$)
Observatory Hill tel: 54041–2
fax: 54211/54043
email: windmere@cal.vsnl.net.in
Darjiling's best, a Heritage hotel dating from 1939, with the chintzy charm of an English cottage. Timber construction, old photos, comforts (no TV), terrace views on both sides, gardens, tennis, library, travel service. Efficient, friendly staff. Full board only, which includes traditional afternoon tea—non-residents can make reservations for main meals. Absolutely no smoking allowed.

279

Accommodations and Restaurants

Gangtok
(STD code 03592)

Mintokling Guest House ($)
Tashiling Road tel: 24226/26368
email: mintokling@hotmail.com
Small family-run establishment, which offers eight carpeted rooms, all with bath, phone and TV. It has a garden, but no air-conditioning.

Shambala ($/$$)
Mountain Resort, Rumtek tel: 52240/43
email: sikkim@ahmedindia.com
Family run. The main building has 25 rooms and there are three cottages in verdant surroundings. All rooms with bath, TV and phone, but not air-conditioning. Multi-cuisine restaurant and bar.

Kalimpong
(STD code 03552)

*Himalayan Hotel ($$)
Upper Cart Road tel: 55248/55122
fax: 55122
Atmospheric 1920s colonial house converted by the MacDonald family and now a Heritage hotel. 11 delightful rooms with fireplaces and large suites in new "cottages". Good restaurant, gardens and views, car rental. Reserve in advance in season.

*Kalimpong Park Hotel ($/$$)
Ringkingpong Road tel: 55304 fax: 55982
Once a royal weekend retreat, still redolent of the 1920s. Comfortable rooms and suites with dressing rooms and water closets. Friendly staff, garden, good restaurant, bar and good local information.

Kolkata (Calcutta)
(STD code 033)

*Fairlawn Hotel ($$)
13A Sudder Street tel: 245 1510
fax: 244 1835 email: fairlawn@cal.vsnl.net.in
Old-fashioned, eccentric and overpriced relic of the Raj. Verdant front garden (bar) and chintzy, green interior. Run by the memorable Violet Smith and her husband, a retired English Army officer. Cheaper rooms are airless and badly maintained. Full board, but multi-cuisine restaurant not restricted to residents and does marvelous English breakfasts.

Lytton Hotel ($$)
14 Sudder Street
tel: 249 1872/217 1383–5 fax: 249 1747
email: lytton@giasd01.vsnl.net.in
77 clean rooms and four suites in modern hotel at heart of Kolkata. Geared towards businessmen. Chinese and Indian restaurants, and a bar. Good value.

*Oberoi Grand ($$$)
15 J Nehru Road tel: 249 2323
fax: 249 1217/245 3229
email: grand@giasd01.vsnl.net.in
This is the cream; a sumptuous luxury hotel dating from 1870s, though much extended since. 250 rooms surround an attractive pool and garden with lofty palms. Superbly appointed rooms and personalized service. Excellent Thai, French and Indian restaurants ($$$). Tea room, two bars, health club, beauty salon, travel desk, car rental.

*Zaranj ($$)
26 J Nehru Road tel: 249 0369/5572
Air-conditioned restaurant, next to Indian Museum. Very good Punjabi and Bengali dishes.

*Zurich Restaurant ($)
3 Sudder Street
An extremely popular, good, budget restaurant. Delicious Indian and Western snacks.

THE CENTER

Aurangabad
(STD code 0240)

*Ambassador Ajanta ($$/$$$)
Airport Road, Chikalthana tel: 485211–4
fax: 484367 email: amau@vsnl.com
Large (96 rooms and suites) but quiet hotel, with pool in garden, sauna, health club, sports complex, beauty parlor, barber shop, travel desk and car rental. Good service and excellent food ($$$).

*Printravel Hotel ($)
Dr Ambedhar Marg tel: 29707
An old Aurangabad favorite that's seen better days, but is well run. Rock-bottom rates for clean and spacious fan-cooled rooms with showers and nets. Friendly, helpful staff. Good vegetarian restaurant and terrace.

Vedant ($$)
Station Road tel: 350701 fax: 350700
Smart, modern Quality Inn hotel with 100 rooms, good bathrooms. Breakfast included in rates. Pool, health club, two restaurants, bar.

Bandhavgarh National Park

Bandhavgarh Jungle Lodge ($$$)
c/o Tiger Resorts, Delhi tel: 07653 65317 bookings: 011 685 3760 fax: 011 686 5212 email: T.Resorts@indiantiger.com
Close to the river, off Umaria Road. An attractive complex of well-equipped pseudo-mud huts. Expensive, but the cost covers full board, park fees and safaris with good naturalist guides.

White Tiger Forest Lodge ($)
Umaria Road, Tala tel: 07653 65308
Excellent value and well-organized by MP Tourism. Some bungalows by the river (elephants bathe in the river) and 26 rooms (few are air-conditioned), good restaurant, bar, jeep rentals. Advance reservations are advisable.

Bombay see Mumbai

Hyderabasd/Secubderabad
(STD code 040)

*Grand Kakatiya Hotel & Towers ($$$)
Begumpet tel: 331 0132 fax: 331 1045
email:ga.kakatiya@welcomemail.wiprobt.ems.vsnl.net.in
Luxury hotel, part of Welcomgroup. Pool, health club, travel desk. 24-hour multi-cuisine food.

Taj Mahal Hotel ($)
Abids Road, corner King Kothi Road
tel: 237998
Popular 70-room hotel in central location. Large rooms, with TV and room service. Vegetarian restaurant ($$) and coffee shop, roof garden.

Kanha National Park

Kanha Safari Lodge ($)
Mukki; bookings through MP Tourism, Bhopal, tel: 0755 553006/066/5774407
tel/fax: 0755 553076

Located at southern end of park, with easy access to more isolated area. 22 rooms (a few air-conditioned) and multi-cuisine restaurant. Guides and vehicle rental. Good value. Reserve in advance.

Kipling Camp ($$$)
2.5 miles from Khatia tel/fax: 07636 77219; bookings through Tollygunge Club, Kolkata, tel: 033 473 4539 fax: 033 473 1903
This is the best option, a cottage complex in rustic safari style. Beautiful setting. Rates include full board, guides and jeep tours. Resident elephant. Reserve well in advance in peak season.

Mumbai (Bombay)
(STD code 022)
Garden Hotel ($$/$$$)
*42 Garden Road, Colaba
tel: 284 1476/1700/283 4823 fax: 204 4290
email: gardenht@bom5.vsnl.net.in*
Good, modernized hotel in quiet leafy street one block from sea. Air-conditioned rooms. Multi-cuisine restaurant, exchange, travel desk.

*Jewel of India ($$)
*Nehru Centre, Dr Annie Besant Road
tel: 494 9435*
Elegant, spacious restaurant serving Mughlai and Kashmiri specialties in the evening. The lunch-time buffet branches out, with Continental, Chinese, Italian and Parsi offerings.

*Leela Kempinski ($$$)
*Sahar, Andheri tel: 836 3636/835 3535
fax: 836 0606
email: leela.bom@leela.sprintrpg.ems.vsnl.net.in*
Luxurious (over 400 rooms) airport hotel. Palatial Mughal-style design, with pool, health club, beauty parlor, golf, disco. Five multi-cuisine restaurants ($$$). One of the most luxurious accommodations in Mumbai. Good for a civilized drink or excellent meal if you have a wait between flights.

*Oberoi ($$$)
Nariman Point tel: 202 5757 fax: 204 3282
Is connected to **Oberoi Towers** ($$$)
(tel: 202 4343/5757, fax: 204 3282/1505, email: reservations@oberoi-mumbai.com)
Guests at either can use all the facilities of both, including superb views, two pools and several top-notch restaurants, some with live entertainment. The choice of cuisine includes Mediterranean, Mexican, French and seafood. The scale is vast (getting on for a thousand rooms and incredible suites), but the service is excellent.

*Taj Mahal Hotel ($$$)
*Apollo Bunder, Colaba tel: 202 3366
fax: 287 2711 email: business.centre@vsnl.com*
The Taj Group's flagship hotel (in unassailable position opposite Gateway of India) has expanded: a new skyscraper joining the original structure to provide a total of 600 rooms, many with sea views. Deluxe prices for wide-ranging amenities including five multi-cuisine restaurants and three bars, pool, gymnasium, disco and travel desk. The performance does not always live up to the reputation.

*Trishna ($$)
7 Rope Walk Lane, Fort tel: 267 2176/0117
Lively seafood restaurant, bringing ultra-fresh lobsters and crabs to the table; also Chinese, Mughlai and South Indian. Extremely popular with the locals, so reservations are advisable.

THE SOUTH

Badami
(STD code 08357)
Badami Court Hotel ($$/$$$)
*Station Road tel: 65230–3 fax: 65207
www.fhrai.com*
On main road northeast of town, a well-run modern hotel with 25 clean, comfortable rooms and two suites. Garden, exchange, travel desk, two multi-cuisine restaurants.

*Mookambika Deluxe Lodge ($)
*Station Road, opposite bus-stand
tel: 65067 fax: 65106*
Reasonable budget hotel, clean, but unreliable plumbing. Small fan-cooled rooms with TV. Efficient travel desk offers excellent day tours by car to Aihole, Pattadakal. The attached **Kanchana Restaurant** ($) offers a good range of food, vegetarian and otherwise with Western breakfasts.

Bangalore
(STD code 080)
Bombay Anand Bhavan ($)
*68 Vittal Mallya tel: 221 4581–3
fax: 227 7705
email: gupta.babh@axcess.net.in*
Well-maintained colonial-style mansion in lush gardens not far from MG Road. Plenty of character. No air-conditioning, but rooms have phone and TV. Room service, business center, 24-hour check out.

*Ivory Tower ($$)
*12th Floor, Barton Centre, 84 MG Road
tel: 558 9333 fax: 558 8697
email: ivorytower@vsnl.com*
Good value, but strictly for the non-vertiginous, with splendid views over the city. 22 large, very clean rooms, with refrigerator, tea/coffee-making facilities and good room service. Exchange, bar. The **Ebony** multi-cuisine terrace restaurant ($$) is a favorite rendezvous for business people.

*Nahar's Heritage ($$)
*14 St Mark's Road tel: 227 8731–6
fax: 227 8737 www.fhrai.com*
A friendly 48-room, good-value hotel, with a very good multi-cuisine restaurant.

*The Rice Bowl ($$)
215 Brigade Road tel: 558 7417
A popular Tibetan Chinese restaurant, noteworthy for being run by the Dalai Lama's sister.

Chennai (Madras)
(STD code 044)
*Annalakshmi ($/$$)
804 Anna Salai (opposite LIC) tel: 852 5109
A volunteer-run restaurant which donates the profits to charity. Renowned for delicious vegetarian food, sometimes with unusual dishes of South-east Asian origin. Reservations are essential.

*Connemara ($$$)
*2 Binny Road tel: 852 0123 fax: 852 3361
email: tajcon@giasmd01.vsnl.net.in*
Huge, central, art deco Taj hotel near Anna Salai, set in large grounds. Very comfortable. Pool, health club, beauty parlor, bookstore, palmist, travel desk. Restaurants include Chinese, French and the outdoor **Rain Tree** ($$), serving local cuisine, often with live Indian entertainment. Reserve in advance.

281

Accommodations and Restaurants

*New Woodlands Hotel ($)
72–5 Radha Krishnan Road, Mylapore
tel: 827 3111 fax: 826 0460
email: murali@newwoodlands.com
Pleasant large hotel in good location. Clean, spacious rooms and suites, some in bungalows. Two Indian vegetarian restaurants ($), good *thalis*; small pool, efficient service. Reserve in advance.

Goa
*Leela Palace ($$$)
Mobor, Cavelossim, Salcete
tel: 0834 746363/373/424–5
fax: 0834 746352 email: leela@goa1.dot.net.in
Newly refurbished and upgraded resort around artificial lake, offering rooms and villas, with a range of prices.

*The Mandovi ($/$$$)
DB Bandodkar Marg, Panaji
tel: 0832 426270–3/224405–9 fax: 0832 225451 email: mandovi@goa1.dot.net.in
Established 1940s favorite on banks of Mandovi river. 66 spacious rooms with balconies. Good multi-cuisine restaurant, bar, helpful GTDC staff.

*Palm Grove Cottages ($)
1678 Vasvaddo, Benaulim tel: 0834 722533
Lush garden setting with chalets and a bar. Range of rooms. Garden. Outdoor restaurant.

*Tamarind Hotel ($)
Kumar Vaddo, Anjuna
tel: 0832 274319/273363 email: kamron@bom2.vsnl.net.in
Set in a secluded location about 5 miles inland from Anjuna. Air-conditioned stone cottages in lush gardens with pool. Outstanding restaurant and bar.

*Tansy Cottages ($)
Vasvaddo, Benaulim Beach Road, Benaulim
tel: 0834 734595
Good location halfway between main road and beach. Large, clean rooms in old house, garden annex. Basic, but adequate, and budget prices. Good outdoor restaurant/bar: wide-ranging menu.

*Tiracol Fort ($/$$)
Fort Heritage, Tiracol tel: 02366 68248
fax: 0834 782326
Fort conversion, on border with Maharashtra. Isolated position with lovely views from rooms and suites. Menu limited, but good seafood restaurant in old moat. Bar, room service. Cycle rentals.

Hospet
*Malligi Tourist Home ($)
6/143 Jambunatha Road tel: 08394 28101
fax: 08394 27083
Large, dilapidated hotel with popular garden restaurant **Waves** ($) by the pool. Better to eat here than to stay overnight.

*Priyadarshini Hotel ($)
45A Station Road tel: 08394 28036/28838
Modern hotel between train and bus station. Clean, spacious rooms with balconies and rural views. Garden restaurant/bar ($) and interior restaurant.

Kochi
(STD code 0484)
*Bolgatty Palace ($$/$$$)
Mulavukadu, Bolgatty Island
tel: 355003/354059/353985/998
fax: 354879 www.fhrai.com

Lovely Dutch palace (1744) with rambling verandas, 26 vast rooms and suites. Landscaped grounds, totally refurbished by KTDC in 1999. Atmospheric location and two good multi-cuisine restaurants. Bar, health club, pool, exchange.

*Casino Hotel ($$$)
Willingdon Island tel: 668421/221 fax: 668001
email: casino@giasmd01.vsnl.net.in
Comfortable 68-room hotel with range of facilities. Very convenient for visiting Lakshadweep Islands; it is the center for information, permits and reservations. Multi-cuisine restaurant ($/$$) specializes in seafood. Gardens with pool; poolside snacks.

*Metropolitan ($/$$)
Chavara Road, near train station
tel: 369931/352412/361285/382008
fax: 382227 email: metropol@md3.vsnl.net.in
With 39 clean, modern rooms, this hotel is good value. Two very good multi-cuisine restaurants, bar, exchange, travel desk and friendly service.

*Taj Malabar ($$$)
Willingdon Island tel: 666811/668010 fax: 668297 email: malabar.cochin@tajhotels.com
Superb Taj hotel in fabulous bay-side location. 100 stylish rooms and suites; good views. Restaurants include the **Waterfront Café** ($$) with Keralan and Western buffets. Extensive gardens, good pool.

Kottayam (Keralan Backwaters)
(STD code 0481)
Coconut Lagoon ($$$)
Kumarakom or c/o Casino Hotel, Kochi
tel: 525834–6 fax: 524495
email: casino@giasmd01.vsnl.net.in
Heritage resort combining traditional architecture with Ayurvedic facilities. Spacious Keralan houses in lush gardens, restaurant in converted temple, good pool, health center, watersports, fishing, canoeing, birdwatching, travel desk. Friendly.

*Taj Garden Retreat ($$$)
1/404 Kumarakom
tel: 524377/525711-7 fax 524371
email: tgrgm.kmr@tajgroup.sprintrpg.ems.vsnl.net.in
Lakeside resort in renovated colonial mansion. 22 rooms and suites. Adjacent bird sanctuary. Pool and watersports. Houseboats available. Good multi-cuisine food, including Keralan specialties.

Kovalam
(STD code 0471)
Blue Sea Hotel ($)
Beach Road, near telegraph office
tel: 481401 fax: 480401
Traditional Keralan house set back from road leading to Ashok Hotel and beach. Tasteful rooms and quaint family cottages, but basic bathrooms. Luxuriant garden, large pool. Breakfast included.

*Hotel Rockholm ($)
Lighthouse Road tel: 480306/406
fax: 480607 www.fhrai.com
Friendly hotel in dramatic position on rocks beside lighthouse. Good restaurant. Comfortable rooms, some with balconies and sea views. Exchange, Ayurvedic massage, travel desk, library, airport and railroad pick-ups. Reservations required.

Hotel Samudra ($$/$$$)
GV Road, Samudra Beach Garden
tel: 480089–94 fax: 480242
email: samudra@gmd3.vsnl.net.in

Modern hotel geared towards tour groups. Decent accommodations on quiet beach north of Kovalam, refurbished in 1995. KTDC-run, so provides tours and travel help. Rooms with balconies and sea views. Pool, travel desk, Ayurvedic health center, garden restaurant, bar, beer parlor, exchange.

Surya Samudra ($$$)
Chowara tel: 480413 fax: 481124
Beautifully designed cliff-top resort in gardens overlooking sea, about 5 miles south of Kovalam. Traditional Keralan houses reconstructed and tastefully furnished. Ayurvedic treatment, pool, excellent restaurant.

Madras see Chennai

Madurai
(STD code 0452)
*Hotel Supreme ($/$$)
110 West Perumal Maistry Street
tel: 743151–60 fax: 742637
email: supreme@md3.vsnl.net.in
Modern hotel with 69 suites and rooms. The **Surya** ($) is an excellent Indian vegetarian rooftop restaurant. Also Indian, Continental and Chinese restaurant. Bar, exchange, 24-hour travel desk, room service, business center. Reservations required.

Tamil Nadu I ($)
West Veli Street, opposite TTC bus-stand
tel: 547470/737471–8 fax: 731945
In central location, with varying room standards and rates. Breezy verandas, good restaurant, bar, exchange. Good value. Tourist information. Can be noisy. Another, pricier, Tamil Nadu Tourism hotel is located several miles north across the river.

Mamallapuram (Mahabalipuram)
(STD code 04114)
*Fisherman's Cove ($$/$$$)
Covelong Beach tel: 44304 fax: 44303
Luxury in splendid isolation. A Taj-group complex on the beach 20 minutes north of Mamallapuram. Multi-cuisine restaurant and barbecue on the beach. Watersports, pool, travel desk.
*Mamalla Bhavan Annexe ($)
105 East Raja Street
tel: 42260/42360/42060 fax: 42160
email: mamatta@md3.vsnl.net.in
An old favorite. Clean and friendly, with reasonably well maintained rooms, 24-hour room service, TV. Vegetarian restaurant. Exchange, travel desk.
Tamil Nadu Beach Resort ($/$$)
Covelong Road tel: 42235/42361–5
fax: 42268
Government-run hotel overlooking beach. Spacious two-story cottages, balconies with sea views. Pool in leafy garden, restaurants, bar, exchange.

Mysore
(STD code 0821)
Hotel Mayura Hoysala ($)
2 Jhansi Lakshmibai Road tel: 425349
Charming hotel run by KTDC. 21 rooms. Garden, bamboo-style restaurant, bar, travel desk.
*Ritz Hotel ($)
Nilgiri Road tel: 422668
Four sought-after rooms with four-poster beds, in atmospheric colonial mansion in city center. Book

well ahead. Very popular courtyard restaurant ($) serving South Indian and Western cuisine, bar.

Nilgiri Hills
*Taj Garden Retreat ($$$)
Hampton Manor, Church Road, Upper Coonoor
tel: 04264 30021/20021/42
fax: 04264 32775/22775
Lovely old colonial mansion with cottages and garden. Well-maintained. Excellent multi-cuisine restaurant, sports (no pool), trekking, helpful staff.
Tamil Nadu ($)
Charing Cross Road
tel: 0423 44370–8/43977 fax: 0423 44369
Spacious Tamil Nadu Tourism hotel in center of Udagamandalam. Cottages in garden. Restaurant, coffee shop and bar. Exchange.

Periyar National Park
(STD code 0486)
Periyar House ($)
Sanctuary, Thekkadi tel: 322026
fax: 322282/322526
KTDC's budget hotel, halfway between park entrance and boat jetty. Best rooms face lake, most are simple but clean and comfortable and there's a dormitory. Restaurant (buffet), bar, boats, exchange, massage, car and bicycle rental.
*Spice Village ($$$)
Thekkadi Road tel: 322314–5 fax: 322317
email: casino@giasmd01.vsnl.net.in
Cottage complex with lovely gardens, including a spice garden. Pool, travel desk, international cuisine and service to match. A peaceful place.

Thiruvananthapuram (Trivandrum)
(STD code 0471)
*Jas ($/$$)
Thycaud/Aristo Junction
tel: 324881/163–72 fax: 321477/324443
email: jas@md2.vsnl.net.in
Pleasant tranquil 43-room hotel towards station area. Good multi-cuisine roof-garden restaurant, bar, travel desk, exchange.
*Mascot Hotel ($/$$)
Mascot Junction, MG Road
tel: 318990/438990 fax: 317745/437745
email: ktdc@giasmd01.vsnl.net.in
Convenient for museums and tourist office, run by KTDC (who can arrange tours). Decent rooms. Excellent open-air restaurant, 24-hour coffee shop for good snacks, bar, ice cream parlor, pool, health club, travel desk, exchange.

Tiruchchirappalli
(STD code 0431)
Sangam ($$/$$$)
Collector's Office Road tel: 414700/480
fax: 461779 email: hotelsangam@vsnl.com
Near central bus-stand. Garden, multicuisine restaurant, 24-hour coffee shop, bar, exchange, health club, travel desk, 24-hour room service.
Tamil Nadu ($)
McDonald's Road, opposite bus-stand,
Cantonment tel: 414346–8/414471–2 fax: 460725
Simple accommodations in good central location. Small garden, good restaurant, bar.

Index

Index

285

Index

287

Acknowledgments

Picture credits

The Automobile Association wishes to thank the following photographers and libraries for their assistance in the preparation of this book:
FREDRIK ARVIDSSON 3, 5a, 6b, 9b, 10/11, 12a, 13c, 14b, 15a, 16b, 16c, 18a, 18c, 19b, 20a, 22b, 25a, 25b, 26/7, 27, 29b, 35a, 35b, 36b, 38b, 40b, 41a, 41b, 44b, 46a, 46b, 76, 77, 78, 79, 80, 81, 82, 82/3, 84/5, 86/7, 87, 88, 94, 99a, 99b, 101, 102, 103, 106, 107, 109a, 117, 119, 120, 124, 124/5, 125, 131, 144/5, 147, 148/9, 155, 158a, 158b, 159, 165, 166, 166/7, 175, 176, 177, 178a, 178b, 181, 182a, 184a, 184b, 185, 186/7, 187, 197, 200/1, 204, 205a, 205b, 207, 209, 210, 213a, 213b, 214a, 214b, 214c, 215, 216/7, 219, 220, 222, 223, 224a, 224b, 225, 226, 227, 228, 230, 231, 232b, 233b, 234, 234/5, 236, 237, 238, 239, 240b, 243, 244, 246, 247, 248a, 248/9, 250a, 250b, 253a, 261, 268; LAWRENCE ARVIDSSON-PUJOL 21b, 43; J BALDWIN 8b THE BRIDGEMAN ART LIBRARY 31b Lord Hastings, Govenor of India by Thomas Gainsborough (1727–1788) (Museo de Arte, Sao Paulo/Giraudon), 32a & 33b Conch & faience bangles and ear studs, Harappa, 2300–1750 BC (National Museum of India, New Delhi), 32b Copper vase, Harappa, 2300–1750 BC (National Museum of India, New Delhi), 34a & 34b Alexander the Great addressing his men in the hope of persuading them to continue into India, late 15th century, Quinte Curse Ruffe des Fais du Grant Alexandre (British Library, London), 36a Vairochana Buddha (wall painting), Balawaste, 7th–8th century (National Museum of India, New Delhi), 37b Buddha, bronze, Gupta, Phopnar, 6th century (National Museum of India, New Delhi), 38a Nataraja (King of Dancing, one of the representations of Siva), bronze, late Chola, 12th century, Tamil Nadu, (National Museum of India, New Delhi), 39 Somaskanda, bronze, Chola, 10th century, Tamil Nadu, (National Museum of India, New Delhi), 45a Red Fort at Agra during construction, from the 'Akbarnama', Mughal, 1565, (illustrated text), (Victoria & Albert Museum, London), 45b Shah Jahan (1628–1657) and Qudsia Begum: the Begum pours away the wine, Kalam Delhi School, late–19th century, (gouache on paper) Delhi, (Cheltenham Art Gallery & Museums, Gloucester), 48/9 A Hunting Party in India by William Daniell (1769–1837), (Maidstone Museum & Art Gallery, Kent), 48 Storming of Delhi in 1857, from 'The Campaign in India, 1857-8', engraved by George McCulloch (fl.1859–1901) 1859 (litho) by George Franklin Atkinson (1822–59) (after) (British Library, London), 58/9 Red sandstone frieze with animals from the Sultan Ghari's tomb near Delhi, Gupta, 6th century (National Museum of India, New Delhi), 64a Portrait of Sir Edward Lutyens (1869–1944) as Master of the Art Workers' Guild, 1933 by Meredith Frampton (1894–1984) (The Artworkers' Guild Trustees Limited, London), 64b Front View of the Viceroy's House, New Delhi, designed by Sir Edward Lutyens (1869–1944), 104 Radha & Krishna, from the "Gita Govinda", inscribed in Devanagari, Mewar Rajput School, 1550 (National Museum of India, New Delhi), 113a Raja Sarupsingh (1842–61) of Udaipur, on a boar hunt, by Tara Chand, Rajasthan, 1855, (Victoria & Albert Museum, London); BRUCE COLEMAN COLLECTION 26, 84, 100a, 100b; FIONA DUNLOP 17, 123, 148, 150b, 194, 198b, 206, 218, 240a, 241, 245, 248b, 253b; E.T. ARCHIVE 31a, 33a, 37a; MARY EVANS PICTURE LIBRARY 42a, 42c, 44a, 46/7, 47; ROBERT HARDING PICTURE LIBRARY 50a; HULTON GETTY PICTURE COLLECTION 12b, 50b, 51b, 151b; ILLUSTRATED LONDON NEWS 183; IMPACT PHOTOS 196 (Ben Edwards); MAGNUM PHOTOS 13a (Eve-Arnold), 13b (Raghu Rai), 51a (Henri-Cartier Bresson), 137a, 137b, 139a (Raghu Rai); OTTO PFISTER 180; PICTURES COLOUR LIBRARY 4, 6a, 7, 11, 118/9, 141, 170/1, 192, 229; SPECTRUM COLOUR LIBRARY 61, 142a, 221, 242/3, 242; TONY STONE IMAGES F/Cover TRIP/DINODIA 168a, 168b, 169a, 169b, 182b; ROBERT VAN DEN BERGE 143; WERNER FORMAN ARCHIVE LTD 40a, 252a, 252b.

All remaining pictures are held in the Association's own library (AA PHOTO LIBRARY) and were taken by Douglas Corrance, with the exception of:
FREDRIK ARVIDSSON 2, 5b, 8a, 10, 14a, 15b, 16a, 18b, 24b, 28a, 30a, 49, 67, 86b, 114/5, 116, 118, 126a, 126b, 127a, 127b, 127c, 128, 129, 132, 133, 134, 135, 136, 138/8, 139b, 140, 142b, 149, 150a, 151a, 152/3, 153, 156, 157, 160/1, 161, 162, 163, 174, 188, 189, 190, 191, 195, 233a, 259, 262, 267; JIM HOLMES 232a.

Author's Acknowledgments

The author would like to thank the following for all their help: Nicola and Ramesh Durvasula; Nazir Butt at Magic Travel in Delhi; Yasin at Indus Travel in London; GS Sachdev, Government of India Tourist Office in London; Shankar Dandapani of SD Enterprises in Wembley; Maggi Niton of Oberoi Hotels in London; Government of India Tourist Offices in Varanasi, Aurangabad and Bhubaneshwar; Rajasthan Tourist Development Corporation; Mr Jethi at the Maharao of Kutch tourist office; Yuvraj Digvijay Singh.

Contributors

Copy editor: Antonia Hebbert   Designer: Barfoot Design
Verifier and additional research and text: Carol Sykes   Captions: Chris Caldicott
Indexer: Marie Lorimer